CARSWELL

Canadians Resident Abroad 2017

by

Garry R. Duncan
B.Comm., FCPA, FCA, CFP

THOMSON REUTERS®

Dedication

This book is dedicated to the late R.W. McRae, whose vision of assisting Canadian expatriates inspired the author to create CANADIANS RESIDENT ABROAD.

Preface

Canadians are on the move, seeking employment, adventure, a sunny retirement, a lower cost of living and, yes, freedom from Canadian taxes.

If you are a Canadian planning for a future beyond our borders, you will likely investigate many aspects of life overseas — climate, working conditions, cultural differences, compensation and health care to name but a few. You may, however, neglect an essential financial consideration.

Most Canadians going to live abroad wish to become non-residents of Canada for tax purposes. As a non-resident, you would be freed from Canadian income tax obligations (although some Canadian taxes may still apply). You may or may not be taxed in your new country of residence, but even if you are the burden is likely to be less onerous.

If you do not take care in arranging your affairs you may get a nasty surprise when, while toiling, let us say, in a faraway oil field, you find that the Canada Revenue Agency (CRA) still considers you a resident of Canada and liable for Canadian taxation on income you earn anywhere in the world. How can this be? The answer is based on two alarmingly simple facts:

1) The Canadian income tax system is based on residency, not citizenship.
2) Residents of Canada are liable for income tax on their world income.

This is where things became much less simple. Not only is "residency" not defined anywhere in Canadian law, but becoming non-resident does not depend on adherence to a limited and unchangeable set of criteria. Rather, residency is considered a "question of fact" and the tax authorities reserve the right to examine the particular facts in every individual case before passing judgment.

That is why any Canadian who is now or may want to become a non-resident of Canada needs this book. The contents combine tax law (dreadfully boring) and real life situations (stranger than fiction), all written (I hope) in understandable language.

CANADIANS RESIDENT ABROAD considers all those factors which conspire to make you a resident or non-resident of Canada for income tax purposes, and provides an overview of current tax law and Canada Revenue Agency administrative practice.

I look at your life as a non-resident. Even if you have achieved non-resident status, you may still have Canadian tax responsibilities. This will depend on how well you cut your ties and what you left behind — such as investments, business income, employment income, pensions, retirement payments.

If you settle in a country that has concluded a tax treaty with Canada, that document can have a major impact on your tax situation. I review treaties in general and point out some of their more important features. (Those of you who settle in non-treaty countries can skip this chapter.)

I also have information for those Canadians who continue to be residents of Canada while working abroad. Continuing resident status may result from a factual circumstance or simply be deemed to exist. While this is not an ideal tax position, there are a number of provisions which grant tax relief.

Some day you may want to return to Canada. Like departure, coming home requires careful planning to minimize potential tax burdens.

CAVEAT

I have relied on Canadian tax law, the Canada Revenue Agency's forms and administrative positions at the time of writing. Like most things in life, these change. As well, I have prepared this material so that it is general in nature. This book should not be relied upon to replace specific professional advice.

About the Author

Garry R. Duncan

Garry R. Duncan, B.Comm., FCPA, FCA, CFP, was a senior tax partner with BDO Dunwoody LLP where he specialized in tax and financial planning. Garry retired from BDO in 2005, but continues to consult on retirement, estate and expatriate planning.

Garry was a Director and past Chairman of the Financial Planners Standards Council and a frequent speaker on estate and expatriate planning.

Garry has also authored *Migration to Canada* and *When I Die: Financial Planning for Life and Death.*

Table of Contents

1

Canadian Resident

GENERAL COMMENTS

The Canadian tax system is based on residency and not citizenship. There are basically two types of residents: factual residents and deemed residents. The Canada Revenue Agency's (CRA) Income Tax Folio S5-F1-C1 (see in Appendix) explains Canada's position regarding the determination of an individual's residence status.

- *Factual residence* is a question of fact and is determined by weighing various factors. The principal ones are the location of your permanent home and of your economic, social and family ties.
- *Deemed residence* is determined by statute and most commonly comes into effect when an individual who is normally resident elsewhere remains in Canada for 183 days or more during any calendar year, or when a member of certain defined groups — such as the Canadian Armed Forces — takes a posting outside of Canada.

Residents of Canada (whether factual or deemed) are taxable on their world income. If all or part of their world income comes from foreign sources subject to foreign income taxes, Canada will usually allow a foreign tax credit or a deduction to reduce the incidence of double taxation.

FACTUAL RESIDENCE

If you are a Canadian resident contemplating employment or retirement opportunities abroad and nothing in your circumstances will cause you to be a deemed resident of Canada (see below), then you will need to determine whether you will remain a factual resident of Canada while abroad or whether you will be able to establish non-resident status for tax purposes.

It comes as a surprise to many prospective non-residents that there is no mandatory application process by which an individual requests and is granted non-resident status. Rather, as stated above, the Canada Revenue Agency has the right to examine the facts in every individual case in order to determine residency status.

The rule that residency is determined by examination of the facts in each situation is well established in Canadian case law. In *Thomson v. M.N.R.* (1946), a decision of the Supreme Court of Canada which has been used as a precedent many times, one of the learned judges stated:

> . . . one is "*ordinarily resident*" in the place where in the settled routine of his life he regularly, normally or customarily lives. One "*sojourns*" at a place where he unusually, casually or intermittently visits or stays. In the former the element of permanence; in the latter that of the temporary predominates. The difference cannot be stated in precise and definite terms, but each case must be determined after all of the relevant factors are taken into consideration, but the foregoing indicates in a general way the essential differences. It is not the length of the visit or stay that determines the question. . . . (emphasis added)[1]

Another judge in the same case (yes, there was more than one judge) expressed the following:

> The graduation of degrees of time, object, intention, continuity and other relevant circumstances, shows, I think, that in common parlance "residing" is not a term of invariable elements, all of which must be satisfied in each instance. It is quite impossible to give it a precise and inclusive definition. It is highly flexible, and its many shades of meaning vary not only in the contexts of different matters, but also in different aspects of the same matter. In one case it is satisfied by certain elements, in another by others, some common, some new.....

> For the purposes of income tax legislation, it must be assumed that every person has at all times a residence. It is not necessary to this that he should have a home or a particular place of abode or even a shelter. He may sleep in the open. It is important only to ascertain the spatial bounds within which he spends his life or to which his ordered or customary living is related. Ordinary residence can best be appreciated by considering its antithesis, occasional or casual or deviatory residence. The latter would seem clearly to be not only temporary in time and exceptional in circumstance, but also accompanied by a sense of transitoriness and of return.[2]

Establishing Non-Resident Status

If you wish to establish non-resident status for tax purposes, it is your responsibility to ensure that any examination of the facts of your *status quo* would support the contention that you have ceased to be a resident of Canada and have become resident elsewhere.

---

[1]   [1946] C.T.C. 51 at 70 (S.C.C.).
[2]   [1946] C.T.C. 51 at 63-64 (S.C.C.).

INCOME TAX FOLIO S5-F1-C1: Determining an Individual's Residence Status

INCOME TAX FOLIOS (ITF) - A NEW INCOME TAX TECHNICAL PUBLICATION

The Canada Revenue Agency (CRA) recognizes the value that income tax interpretation bulletins had for taxpayers and for tax professionals.

They have undertaken an initiative to introduce a new technical publication product to update the information currently found in the income tax interpretation bulletins and to introduce improved web functionality.

The new publications are known as the income tax folios (ITF). The folios are organized by broad categories into seven series. Each folio within a series will be subdivided into topic-specific chapters to better enable users to locate the information they need.

PHASE-OUT OF INCOME TAX INTERPRETATION BULLETINS AND ITTNS

A chapter of an income tax folio will be an updated version of the technical content in one or more income tax interpretation bulletins. The folios will also incorporate material currently contained in the income tax technical news (ITTNs). Chapters will be published as the content has been updated. At that time, the interpretation bulletin or bulletins and any ITTN updated by a folio chapter will be cancelled. It is expected that the update process will occur over a number of years.

Author's Note: As a result of the above, you will see references to both Interpretation Bulletins (ITs) and Income Tax Folios (ITF) until such time as CRA replaces a particular IT. Various tax forms still contain a reference to an IT rather than the new folio. So, if you cannot find a particular IT Bulletin, check under folios on the CRA web site.

PERMANENCE OF STAY ABROAD

According to the Canada Revenue Agency, in order to become a non-resident there must be some permanence to your stay abroad. A former version of IT-221 (IT-221R2) indicated that where you were absent from Canada, for whatever reason, for less than two years, you would be presumed to have retained your resident status while abroad unless you could clearly establish that you had severed all residential ties when leaving Canada. If there was evidence that your return to Canada was foreseen at the time of your departure (for example, a contract for employment upon return to Canada), the Canada Revenue Agency presumed that you did not sever all your residential ties.

The last version of IT-221 (IT-221R3) eliminated the reference to the two-year period. ITF S5-F1-C1, which replaced IT-221R3, continues to confirm that the length of stay abroad is one factor to be considered but points out that there is no particular length of stay outside Canada that causes an individual to become a non-resident of Canada. Each case will be judged on its facts.

Even if you are leaving Canada for a number of years, the Canada Revenue Agency will also insist that you satisfy various other requirements for non-resident status.

ITF S5-F1-C1 does not refer to the purpose of your departure. In absence of any official guidelines, I feel that the purpose of your stay abroad will have a significant influence on your residency status. For example, if you go on an extended world tour, you will be considered to have retained your Canadian residency. This and other examples are noted below under "Listed Factual Residents".

On the other hand, if you leave Canada to work or retire in another country, sever your Canadian ties and intend to remain outside of Canada for a number of years, you will be considered to be a non-resident unless you are a listed factual resident. Even then you may not be taxable in Canada if Canada has a tax treaty with the other country.

RESIDENTIAL TIES WITH CANADA

In order to become non-resident for tax purposes you must sever your residential ties with Canada. Primary residential ties would include your dwelling place and the location of your spouse and dependents. Secondary ties would include your personal property and social ties.

Author's Note: The following indicators of residency may cause you to retain your resident status with Canada unless you emigrate to a country that has a tax treaty with Canada. Canada has a rule that deems you to be a non-resident of Canada if the tax treaty deems you to be a resident of the tax treaty country that you emigrated to. (Please see Chapter 4, Tax Treaties).

Primary Ties with Canada

DWELLING

If you leave Canada but maintain a dwelling place in Canada that is available to you year-round, the Canada Revenue Agency will *not* consider you to have severed your residential ties with Canada. Your Canadian dwelling could remain "available" by virtue of being left vacant, being leased to a non-arm's length party or by being leased at arm's length with the right to terminate the lease on short notice (generally less than three months).

SPOUSE AND DEPENDENTS

If you leave your spouse (spouse includes a common-law partner[3]) and dependents in Canada, the Canada Revenue Agency will consider you to remain a resident of Canada during your absence. However, an exception is made where you and your spouse are legally separated and you have permanently severed all other residential ties with Canada.

The primary residential ties of a single person are more difficult to judge. If you were a single person who was supporting someone in a dwelling maintained or occupied by you in Canada and, after your departure, you continue to support that person in the dwelling, the Canada Revenue Agency considers you to have retained a significant residential tie and may view you as a resident of Canada.

Secondary Residential Ties

ITF S5-F1-C1 provides a list of types of personal property and social ties which "an individual who leaves Canada and becomes a non-resident would likely not retain". These include furniture, clothing, automobiles, bank accounts, credit cards and social ties within Canada. Where you retain these ties in Canada, the Canada Revenue Agency (CRA) will examine the reasons for their retention and determine if they are significant enough to conclude that you have continued to be a resident of Canada while absent. Other obvious ties that may be relevant are provincial hospitalization and medical insurance coverage, a seasonal residence in Canada, professional and other memberships in Canada.

Canada Revenue Agency created a form NR73 – *Determination of Residency Status* (Leaving Canada). Anyone who was leaving Canada to become a non-resident could complete Form NR73 and file it with Canada Revenue Agency. It lists a number of ties to Canada. An earlier version of the NR73 had listed the ownership of a Canadian passport and your intention to renew it as two secondary ties. Fortunately, sanity prevailed when CRA issued its next update. The reference to the renewal was eliminated. See NR73 – *Determination of Residency Status* for more details (Appendix).

CRA's introduction of possessing a Canadian passport as a secondary tie raised concerns that the Government of Canada, through the administration of the *Income Tax Act* and CRA assessing practice planned to tax Canadians on a

---

[3]   The term spouse used throughout this book applies to a legally married spouse and a common-law partner.

basis of citizenship. At this time, there does not appear to be any change in the law and/or assessing practice.

While the courts will look at a person's citizenship in residency cases, it is still not part of income tax legislation in Canada.

Regardless, cut as many ties as possible to secure your non-resident status. While secondary ties are less of a problem if you live in a treaty country, severing as many ties as possible remains critical to achieve non-resident status.

While the residential ties outlined in ITF S5-F1-C1 will give you some guidance, this folio does not attempt to list all the minor details of day-to-day living that could contribute to a determination of residency. In fact, no such list could be exhaustive as the facts of every individual's life are unique.

Nonetheless, if you wish to find a more comprehensive treatment of the subject, you can turn once again to the courts. A case (*Lee v. M.N.R.*, 1990)[4] was noteworthy in that the decision included a list of some of the criteria relevant in determining whether an individual was resident of Canada for Canadian income tax purposes.

In studying the list, you should be aware that no one or any group of up to four of these items will in themselves establish that an individual is resident in Canada. However, a number of additional factors considered together could cause that individual to continue to be a resident of Canada for Canadian income tax purposes.

- memberships with Canadian churches or synagogues, recreational and social clubs, unions and professional organizations;
- registration and maintenance of automobiles, boats and airplanes in Canada;
- holding credit cards issued by Canadian financial institutions and other commercial entities including stores, car rental agencies, etc.;
- local newspaper subscriptions sent to a Canadian address;
- rental of Canadian safe deposit box or post office box;
- subscriptions for life or general insurance including health insurance through a Canadian insurance company;
- mailing address in Canada;
- telephone listing in Canada;
- stationery including business cards showing a Canadian address;
- magazine and other periodical subscriptions sent to a Canadian address;
- Canadian bank accounts other than a non-resident bank account;
- active securities accounts with Canadian brokers;
- Canadian driver's licence;
- membership in a Canadian pension plan;
- holding directorships of Canadian corporations;
- membership in Canadian partnerships;
- frequent visits to Canada for social or business purposes;

---

[4]   [1990] 1 C.T.C. 2082 (T.C.C.).

- burial plot in Canada;
- will prepared in Canada;
- legal documentation indicating Canadian residence;
- filing a Canadian income tax return as a Canadian resident;
- ownership of a Canadian vacation property;
- active involvement in business activities in Canada;
- employment in Canada;
- maintenance or storage in Canada of personal belongings including clothing, furniture, family pets, etc.;
- obtaining landed immigrant status or appropriate work permits in Canada.[5]

Establishing Ties in Your New Country

The foregoing deals with residential ties within Canada. The Canada Revenue Agency also looks at the ties you establish elsewhere. ITF S5-F1-C1 indicates that if you go abroad and do not establish a permanent residence elsewhere, there is a presumption that you remain a resident of Canada. In general, the types of residential ties which support the contention that you have established residence elsewhere will parallel those you needed to sever in Canada. However, the fact that you establish a permanent residence abroad does not in and by itself mean that you have become a non-resident of Canada.

Visits to Canada

Fortunately, the Canada Revenue Agency concedes that when you leave Canada and become a non-resident, your tax status as a non-resident will generally not be affected by occasional returns to Canada, whether for personal or business reasons. However, ITF S5-F1-C1 states that when such visits are regular, these factors together with other residential ties that may exist would be examined to determine whether they are significant enough in total to conclude that you are continuing to be a resident in Canada. Remember, if these occasional visits exceed 183 days in any calendar year, you will be deemed to be a resident of Canada for that year. See "Deemed Residence", below, for more details on this rule.

When Does Non-Residency Begin?

The date you cease to be a resident of Canada and become a non-resident is generally the latest of (1) the day you leave Canada, (2) the date your spouse

---

[5]   [1990] 1 C.T.C. 2082 at 2085-86 (T.C.C.).

and/or dependents leave Canada (where applicable) or (3) the date you become a resident of the country to which you are emigrating. An exception is made where you are resident of another country prior to entering Canada and you are leaving to re-establish your residence in that country. In this case, you will generally be considered a non-resident on the date you leave Canada even if, for example, your spouse remains temporarily behind to dispose of your dwelling place in Canada.

Tax Avoidance

Finally, the Canada Revenue Agency states that where one of the main purposes of your absence from Canada is to avoid Canadian taxes that would otherwise be payable, they may consider this to be tax avoidance. If this is the case, the Canada Revenue Agency would consider you to be a resident of Canada and tax you accordingly.

NR73, Determination of Residency Status

The Canada Revenue Agency Form NR73 (see in Appendix) may be used if you plan to leave or have left Canada, either permanently or temporarily and you need to know your residency status for Canadian tax purposes. This situation will arise when you are paid by Canadian employers who want to be assured that you are considered to be a non-resident of Canada. It may also be required by institutions that make pension, annuity, registered retirement savings plan or registered retirement income fund payments.

If you compare the list of queries posed on the NR73 with those listed in the court case quoted above (*Lee v. M.N.R.*), you will note a striking similarity. While the NR73 may be submitted by anyone wishing assistance in determining residency status, this form is not mandatory unless it is requested to confirm you are a non-resident. As a result, I do not recommend its use unless it is requested.

I have encountered a number of situations where a potential emigrant on the advice of CRA or some well meaning friend completed and filed an NR73. CRA reviewed the contents of the NR73 and ruled that the applicant retained too many secondary ties and continued to be a resident of Canada for Canadian tax purposes. As a result, the emigrant continued to be taxed as a Canadian taxpayer even though they had left Canada for good.

In one particular case, a subsequent review of the facts dictated an appeal of the assessment as a resident. After a failed appeal at CRA, the case went to the Tax Court. It was resolved in favour of the emigrant, resulting in taxation of only 6 months as a Canadian taxpayer rather than 4 years.

While this case was successful, the emigrant suffered financial loss (my fees) and many anxious moments. The lesson learned was never file an NR73 unless it is formerly requested. And, have someone review it before it is filed with CRA.

Regardless of the warnings above, I do recommend that prospective emigrants obtain a current version of the NR73 (www.cra-arc.gc.ca) and review the questions. If you tick more than five boxes, you may have a problem. Seek professional help.

Listed Factual Residents

The Canada Revenue Agency has been good enough to provide a list of certain individuals whom it considers to be factual residents of Canada while living abroad, generally because of ties they retain with Canada while absent. If you fit one of the following categories, the Canada Revenue Agency will treat you as a resident, unless you can argue that you are a non-resident.

However, if you also establish residential ties in a country with which Canada has a tax treaty, and you are considered to be a resident of that country for the purposes of the tax treaty, you may be considered a deemed non-resident of Canada for tax purposes. (See Chapter 4 and Dual Resident Status for more discussion on the issue.)

STUDENTS

When you attend school in another country and you keep your residential ties with Canada, you have to pay tax on your world income. World income can consist of:

- the taxable portion of Canadian and foreign-source scholarships, fellowships, bursaries and prizes;
- net research grants and similar payments;
- amounts you received from a registered education savings plan; and
- all Canadian and foreign source income you received.

TEACHERS

When you teach outside Canada, and retain your residential ties with Canada, you have to pay Canadian tax on your world income. If your income is being taxed by both Canada and the country in which you are teaching, you may only have to pay tax to one country if Canada has a tax treaty with that country.

When the terms of a tax treaty do not apply, you may be able to claim a credit on your Canadian tax return for the foreign taxes you paid.

MISSIONARIES

As a missionary in another country, you may be considered a factual resident of Canada if you:

- file a Canadian tax return and report your world income for each year you are absent from Canada;
- are a Canadian citizen or a permanent resident of Canada;
- are in the service of a religious organization that has its national ministry office in Canada; *and*
- are sent out of Canada for five years or less.

If you paid tax to a foreign country, you may be able to claim a foreign tax credit on your Canadian tax return. Alternatively, you may be exempt from Canadian tax if a tax treaty exists and its provisions deem you to be a resident of the foreign jurisdiction.

VACATIONERS

If you are on vacation outside Canada, you are a factual resident of Canada as long as you keep your Canadian residential ties and your stay outside Canada is not permanent. If you earn income in the country in which you are vacationing, you have to report it on your Canadian tax return and pay tax on it.

COMMUTERS

If you live in Canada and commute to work locations outside Canada, you are a factual resident of Canada, and you have to pay tax on your world income. You may be taxed by both Canada and the country in which you are working. In this case, you may claim the tax you paid to the other country as a credit against your Canadian taxes.

OTHER EMPLOYEES

If you leave Canada to work in another country knowing that you will be out of Canada for a short period of time, the Canada Revenue Agency will consider you to be a factual resident of Canada. For example, if you have a one-year employment contract and there is evidence that you intend to return to Canada, the Canada Revenue Agency will consider you to be a resident of Canada. For instance, this could arise if you failed to completely sever residential ties in Canada or you have some type of commitment for future activities that requires you to be a resident in Canada.

This does not include a situation where you emigrate with the intent of remaining outside Canada for a number of years but return to Canada for reasons beyond your control. The Tax Courts have concluded that unexpected changes to your plans will not jeopardize your non-resident status even where the period outside of Canada has been cut short.

If you are one of the foregoing individuals, you may be considered to be a resident of both Canada and where you work. As a result, you could be taxable in both countries.

If a tax treaty exists between the two countries, you can look to the tie-breaker rules to determine where you should pay tax (See Chapter 4, "Tax Treaties" — "Dual Residence Status"). If no treaty exists, you can look to Canadian tax law and recent amendments to determine if you can receive relief from double taxation. This may range from a complete exemption from Canadian tax to the application of foreign taxes paid to reduce Canadian tax on the same income (See Chapter 6, "Miscellaneous Tax Relief, Residents of Canada" — "Foreign Tax Credit").

TAX RELIEF?

There may be situations when you are a resident of Canada but your country of employment (foreign) requires you to remit tax and even have you file a tax return.

Depending on your circumstances, your Canadian employer who sent you to this foreign land may be required to remit tax on your behalf in Canada. Later on you would file a Canadian tax return, report your world income, claim a foreign tax credit for the tax you paid in the foreign jurisdiction and get a refund of tax. This can be avoided by filing a form with the CRA to request permission for your Canadian employer to reduce the amount of Canadian tax at source. You, the employee must file this form and do so prior to the year in question. The form is T1213-Request to Reduce Tax Deductions at Source for Year(s)____(see Appendix). CRA will reply to you within four to six weeks and confirm whether or not it agrees with your request. If they agree, you give the response to your employer and it will reduce the amount deducted and remitted from your pay.

Your request will state that you pay tax in a foreign jurisdiction on the income you receive from your Canadian employer. You must file this form every year before the year in question begins.

DEEMED RESIDENCE

Canadian tax law contains provisions that deem certain individuals to be residents of Canada. These provisions are summarized in ITF S5-F1-C1. If you fall into one of these categories, you will be subject to Canadian tax on your world income.

Sojourners

Where a resident of another country sojourns (is temporarily present) in Canada for 183 days or more in a calendar year, he or she is deemed to be a resident of Canada for the entire year. While this provision commonly affects foreign visitors, it would apply if you are a Canadian who has established non-resident status and you return often enough to have sojourned in Canada for a total of 183 days or more during a calendar year. The provision will not, however, deem you to be resident of Canada for the full year if you leave Canada to reside elsewhere in the second half of the year. When you enter Canada with the intention of living here and establish residential ties within Canada, you will generally be considered to have become resident of Canada for tax purposes on the date you enter Canada. Please refer to Chapter 2, "Emigration" and Chapter 5, "Immigration" for details on the taxation of part-time residents.

Other Deemed Residents

The deeming provision will also cause any person who is included in any of the following categories to be a resident of Canada:
- persons who are members of the Canadian Forces at any time during the year;
- persons who are officers or servants of Canada or a province/territory, at any time during the year, who receive representation allowances or who are resident or deemed resident in Canada (members of the Canadian Forces who are not factual residents of Canada and have been serving abroad) immediately prior to their appointment or employment by Canada or a province;
- individuals who perform services, at any time in the year, outside Canada under an International Development Assistance Program of the Canadian International Development Agency (CIDA) described in the regulations of the Income Tax Act provided they were resident in Canada at any time in the three-month period prior to the date the services commenced;
- persons who were, at any time in the year, members of the Overseas Canadian Forces school who have filed their returns for the year on the basis that they were resident in Canada throughout the period during which they were such members; and
- any dependent child of a person described above who was under 18 years of age at any time during the year or 18 years of age or over throughout the year and dependent by reason of either physical or mental infirmity.

In the past, spouses and children of the foregoing deemed residents were also deemed to be residents of Canada. This status arose because of their relationship to the employed spouse even though the family had severed all the ties that would make any other Canadian a non-resident. This provision caused inequities where the spouse worked in the foreign jurisdiction yet continued to be taxed in Canada.

The rule that deemed a spouse to be a resident was repealed by the February 24, 1998 Federal Budget. Now you will be deemed to be a resident of Canada only if you are entitled to claim exemption from an income tax payable in your new country of residence because of the relationship to your spouse who was a deemed resident of Canada at the time. As a result, if there is no agreement or convention with a country, you will not be deemed to be a resident of Canada. If an agreement or convention exists with Canada, you will only be deemed resident in Canada if the convention or agreement exempts you from tax because of your relationship with your spouse.

It is important to note that if one spouse is *not* deemed to be a resident because of the forgoing rules, he/she will be taxed like any other emigrant — deemed disposition of assets, non-resident withholding tax on various types of Canadian income, filing a departure tax return, etc. Ensure you check your tax status to avoid any unwanted surprises in the future.

RESIDENCY — QUESTIONS AND ANSWERS

Question — Date of Departure
I left for Saudi Arabia on June 30, 2016. My spouse and children remained in Canada until November 1, 2016. Will I be considered to be a resident of Canada up until June 30, 2016 or November 1, 2016?

Answer
Based on the fact that your spouse and children remained in Canada until November 1, 2016, you will be considered to be a resident of Canada up until November 1, 2016. You must report the income you earned in Saudi Arabia for the period ending November 1, 2016.

Question — Child in Boarding School
I left Canada in June 2016. I severed all ties except I left my child in a boarding school. Will I be considered a resident of Canada?

Answer
The fact that you severed all your ties but left a child in a boarding school will not cause you to be considered a resident of Canada.

I queried the Canada Revenue Agency regarding this issue. The Agency responded stating, that each determination of residency is done so [sic] on an individual basis and that one factor alone, such as a fee structure at a Canadian boarding school, is not sufficient in itself to make a correct determination. The fee structures at boarding schools vary from school to school, and the type of fee charged would in and by itself not be a deciding factor when making a determination of residency.

When reviewing a request for a determination of residency, the Department (the Canada Revenue Agency) must establish whether or not an individual does in fact have significant residential ties in Canada. When a child is attending a Canadian boarding school additional factors are taken into consideration. For example, would a bank account and credit cards be maintained in Canada, would there be a provincial medical plan for the child, would visits to Canada be frequent and would there be an apartment or home and vehicle available for the parents' use while visiting their child? These and other questions must be answered before residence status can be determined.

Question — Recreational Property
I left Canada on January 31, 2016, sold my principal residence but maintained a recreational property suitable for year-round use and available at any time. Will this jeopardize my non-resident status?

Answer
The Canada Revenue Agency would consider the retention of this recreational property as a significant tie and likely rule that you are still a resident of Canada.

Question — Child Living with a Relative
I left Canada in September 2016. I severed all my ties and have been a non-resident ever since. My oldest child has reached an age where there is no school in Saudi Arabia. I propose to send my child, who is 16, back to Canada to live with his grandparents and attend school. Will this jeopardize my non-resident status?

Answer
Based on the Canada Revenue Agency's current position on this matter, the fact that your child is living with his grandparents would not cause you to be a resident of Canada.

Question — CIDA
I left Canada to work on a CIDA-sponsored project in a non-treaty country. Will I be considered to be a resident of Canada?

Answer
You will be deemed to be a resident of Canada unless you were a non-resident of Canada during the three months prior to accepting CIDA employment.

Question — Rental of Principal Residence
I left Canada on June 1, 2016. I could not sell my principal residence so I leased it to my brother on a month-to-month lease. Will I be considered a resident of Canada?

Answer
Based on the fact you leased your house to a relative, the Canada Revenue Agency would likely rule that you are still a resident of Canada. In order to correct this situation, you should lease your principal residence to an unrelated person and have a long-term lease with a termination clause of at least three months.

Question — Leased Condo Available
I left Canada on September 25, 2016. I cut most of my ties except I retained possession of a condo that I leased from a non-related individual. I kept the rental unit so that I have someplace to stay when I visit Canada. Will this arrangement cause a problem for me to establish and maintain my non-resident status?

Answer
The short answer is yes. The leased condo will be considered a primary tie and could cause CRA to consider you to still be a resident of Canada. The only factor that could change CRA's position would occur if your new country of residence has a tax treaty with Canada.

Question — 183 Day Rule
I spent half of a day in Toronto while I was a non-resident. Is this considered one day for the purposes of the 183 day rule?

Answer
The Canada Revenue Agency states that any portion of a day counts as one entire day for purposes of the 183 day rule.

Question — NR73
I filed Form NR73 and received a confirmation from the Canada Revenue Agency that, based on the facts provided, I was a non-resident. Several facts have changed since I received the Agency's response. Will this response still be relevant?

Answer
The Canada Revenue Agency based their response on the facts given. If these facts have changed, the Canada Revenue Agency's original response is invalid and cannot be used to support your non-resident status if it is challenged. You may resubmit the new facts and have them rule again or wait until they challenge your claim and then submit the new information.

Question — Visits to Canada
I ceased to be a resident of Canada on December 20, 2016. I wish to return to Canada for two months in 2017 and every year thereafter for the next three years. Will this jeopardize my non-residency status?

Answer
If you have severed all your ties with Canada and only return for periods of two months each year, your non-resident status should not be jeopardized. However, I recommend that you keep your visits to a minimum in the first year to ensure that you have established non-resident status.

Question — Canadian Employer
I severed all my ties and emigrated from Canada on January 5, 2016. I shall be employed by a wholly-owned foreign corporation of my former Canadian employer. Will I be considered to be a non-resident of Canada?

Answer
Assuming you severed all your ties with Canada and intend to be out of Canada for a number of years, you will be considered a non-resident for Canadian tax purposes.

Question — Sale of House
A friend told me I cannot become a non-resident unless I sell my house in Canada. Is this true?

Answer
The retention of a house is a significant tie in Canada. If you are able to move into it at any time, the Canada Revenue Agency will consider you to have remained a resident of Canada. You may rectify this situation by leasing it out to an arm's-length party on a long-term lease with a three-month termination clause.

Question — Payment of Canadian Tax

If I have to have lived outside Canada for a number of years in order to establish non-resident status, does that mean that I have to continue to pay Canadian taxes for that period?

Answer

If you intend to remain outside Canada for a number years and have severed all your Canadian ties, you do not have to pay Canadian tax during the first initial years.

Question — Retention of Cottage

I want to establish non-resident status but I am very reluctant to give up my family cottage. The cottage is unheated and can only be used in the summer months. Will this jeopardize my non-resident status?

Answer

The retention of a cottage is considered a residential tie with Canada. However, if this is the only tie you retained with Canada and it cannot be used throughout the year, its retention should not cause you to be a resident of Canada.

Question — Rental of House to a Daughter

My 18-year-old daughter will be staying in Canada to attend university. Can I rent our family home to her and some of her friends as long as they sign a proper lease?

Answer

The Canada Revenue Agency states that the leasing of a family home to a relative is not sufficient to sever this tie. The fact that her friends are arm's-length may help but a long-term lease with a termination clause of at least three months would be necessary.

Question — Canadian Employer
I am being transferred overseas by my Canadian employer for a length of time which is undetermined but expected to last at least two years. At some time in the future, I will no doubt return to Canada and remain employed by the same firm. Does this arrangement make it difficult for me to establish non-resident status?

Answer
Indicating your intention to return to Canada and the fact that you will be employed by the same Canadian firm will cause the Canada Revenue Agency to consider you to continue to be a resident. Even if you can prove that you are a non-resident, you may still be taxable in Canada. See Chapter 3, "Taxation of a Non-Resident" — "Persons Deemed to be Employed in Canada".

Question — World Cruise
I have always wanted to sail around the world. I plan to be away from Canada for at least two years. Will I be able to establish non-resident status for tax purposes?

Answer
The Canada Revenue Agency maintains that you must be resident someplace. If you are unable to establish that you are resident elsewhere, the Agency will consider you to have retained Canadian residency.

Question — Return to Canada
My wife and I have been non-residents of Canada for 5 years. My wife plans to return to Canada to finish her education. I shall remain in our present home in the Bahamas and continue to work at my present job. I will be supporting my wife while she is going to school. Will the fact that my wife returns to Canada while I remain to live and work in the Bahamas cause me to be a resident of Canada for tax purposes?

Answer
The Canada Revenue Agency will consider you to have established ties in Canada upon the return of your spouse. However, all the facts must be reviewed to determine if the return of your wife to complete her education would in and by itself, make you a resident of Canada.

Question — Sojourning

If my husband is in Canada for more than 183 days in a calendar year and is deemed to be a resident of Canada, as his wife, am I also deemed to be a resident of Canada? I never visited Canada during the year.

Answer

The fact that your husband is deemed to be a resident of Canada does not deem you to be a resident as well.

Question — School in Canada

I am a single student from Grand Cayman. I go to a Canadian university for 7 months and return to and work in Grand Cayman for the remaining 5 months. Where am I resident for income tax purposes?

Answer

Based on your information, you have been in Canada more than 183 days during the calendar year. Our tax laws deem anyone who has resided in Canada for 183 days or more during a calendar to be a resident of Canada for income tax purposes. The only thing that could alter this status comes from the existence of a tax treaty between Grand Cayman and Canada. Since there is no tax treaty between Grand Cayman and Canada, you will be a resident of Canada and subject to Canadian tax on your world income.

Question — Common-law

I have been living common-law for the past 3 years in Canada. I plan to go to Nassau, Bahamas to work for 4 years. My common-law partner will remain in Canada to finish school. If I sever all my ties except my common-law partner, have I ceased to be a resident of Canada?

Answer

A common-law partner is the same as a spouse. As a result, you continue to have a primary tie in Canada and will be considered to continue to be a resident of Canada.

Question — Departure Return
I left Canada several years ago but did not file a final tax return (very little income) to indicate that I left. Should I file a late tax return for the year of departure?

Answer
You may want to review your filing requirements for the year of departure to determine if there was any requirement for you to file that return. For example, you may have a number of assets that should have been disclosed on Form T-1161, *List of Properties by an Emigrant of Canada* or gains arising from deemed dispositions of property to name two.

Question — Non-resident?
I have been away from Canada for a number of years. I still file a Canadian tax return. Recently, someone advised me that I may be a non-resident of Canada. What should I do to become a non-resident of Canada?

Answer
First step is to determine if in fact you are a non-resident of Canada for tax purposes. This can be done by reviewing your situation with someone who deals in this area. Second, you should determine when you became a non-resident. The results of this exercise may give rise to taxes owing in the year of departure. Once you have established that you are in fact a non-resident you can file amended tax returns claiming that you are a non-resident of Canada. A word of caution: this will be an uphill battle with Canada Revenue Agency. Remember, you have already filed as a resident.

Question — Employed by a Canadian NGO

I have been a non-resident of Canada for a number of years. I recently became employed by a Canadian NGO in Haiti. My pay comes from Canada but I perform my services and reside in Haiti. Do I have to pay tax in Canada?

Answer

The fact that you have been a non-resident of Canada for a number of years and now work for a Canadian NGO in Haiti does not cause you to be taxable on that income in Canada. If for whatever reason you perform some of your duties in Canada, the income related to that service could be subject to Canadian tax. However, you would be taxed as a non-resident of Canada and only on the income received for duties performed in Canada.

Author's Note: Most of the foregoing responses are based on situations that did not involve residing in a country that has a tax treaty with Canada. If a treaty exists and your income is taxed in both Canada and the foreign jurisdiction, the treaty should be reviewed to see if it will cause you to be taxed only in the foreign jurisdiction.

Please note that regardless of what Canada Revenue Agency may assert, the existence of a tax treaty between Canada and your new country of residency may prove helpful to support your claim that you are a non-resident of Canada. This involves the application of a provision of the treaty called the tie-breaker rules. These rules come into play when you are considered to be resident in two countries for tax purposes at the same time. If you meet the conditions to in effect be more resident in the other country rather than Canada, the tie-breaker rules will deem you to be a resident of your new country rather than Canada. Canadian tax law will also kick in to deem you to be a non-resident of Canada.

Chapter 4 – Tax Treaties, outlines an actual case that I dealt with several years ago. It involved a husband who lived and worked in Indonesia while his wife and children lived in Canada. Canada Revenue Agency considered him to be a resident of Canada for tax purposes. Indonesia also taxed him as a resident. Fortunately, Canada and Indonesia had a tax agreement that had tie-breaker rules that dealt with this problem. After several meetings, Canada Revenue Agency agreed that under the tie-breaker rules, the individual was more resident in Indonesia than Canada, even though his wife and children lived in Canada. Please see a more detailed discussion of this in Chapter 4 — Tax Treaties — Tie-Breaker Rules Application.

Emigration

When, after faithfully following the guidelines set out in Chapter 1, you leave Canada to become a non-resident for tax purposes, you may still have any one of a number of tax commitments to Canada entailing both current and future filing requirements.

FINAL TAX RETURN

Since you will no doubt leave Canada part way through a calendar year (unless you are incredibly well-organized and leave on December 31), *you will be required to file a "final tax return"*. By completing the area entitled "date of departure" on page 1, you officially inform our tax authorities that you have left Canada. This return must be filed on or before April 30 (June 15 if self-employed) of the year following your year of departure.

Regardless of whether you can file on April 30th or June 15th, the tax is payable on or before April 30th.

Your final tax return will include your world income up to your date of departure from Canada, along with any capital gains or losses on deemed dispositions of property which may occur on your departure (see below, Deemed Dispositions).

For the portion of the year after you cease to be a Canadian resident, you must continue to report certain types of Canadian-sourced income. These may include employment income such as sick leave or vacation pay paid to you by a Canadian employer after you became non-resident, income from any business carried on in Canada, the taxable portion of scholarships, bursaries, research grants and fellowships you received from Canadian sources and gains arising from the disposition of taxable Canadian properties. Certain other types of Canadian-sourced income will be subject to a non-resident withholding tax while others will not be taxable at all.

Question — Final Return on Departure
I left Canada on September 30, 2016. I earned employment income up to September 30, 2016 and received a bonus on or about October 16, 2016. In addition, I continued to operate a business in Canada and realized capital gains from the disposition of real estate in December 2016. Do I include all these incomes in my final return or do I prepare one tax return for the income earned up to the date of departure and a second non-resident tax return for the income earned in Canada after my departure?

Answer
You will prepare one tax return and report the various types of income noted above in that return.

Deemed Dispositions

The government of Canada wishes to ensure that all capital gains which arose during the time when an individual was a resident of Canada are taxed by Canada. For this reason, Canadian tax law requires that individuals realize a deemed disposition of many types of property on departure. Since the inception of this book, a vast array of new investment vehicles have been created. Some of the more common ones include income trusts (now history, except for real estate income trusts (REITs)), exchange traded funds (ETF), tax-free savings accounts (TFSA), Registered Disability Savings Plans (RDSP), etc. I have attempted to cover the tax implications arising from some of these, but nothing surpasses a sit down with a tax professional who knows the tax consequences that can arise on emigration.

All property owned by an emigrant will be deemed to be disposed of and reacquired at its fair market value with the exception of the following assets:
- Canadian real or immovable property;
- Canadian resource property or timber resource property;
- capital property, eligible capital property or inventory that is used in a business carried on by the person through a permanent establishment in Canada;
- stock options and certain pensions and similar rights;
- RRSPs, RRIFs, LIRAs, LIFs, RDSP, RESP, TFSA, DPSP; and
- life insurance (other than segrated fund policies).

The list of items that are exempt from the deemed disposition on emigration include many others not noted above. One that was exempt was an interest in a non-resident testamentary trust. After 2015, this exclusion from the disposition rule will only apply to an estate that has been in existence for less than 36 months. This will be applicable for emigrations occurring after 2015.

These assets will remain excluded from the deemed disposition rules on emigration because Canada maintains the right to tax gains on these assets or income whether or not the individual is a resident of Canada.

The deemed disposition rules apply to all other types of property. This means that tax will have to be paid on accrued capital gains on these assets at the time of emigration. In particular, the tax on accrued gains on shares of private Canadian companies must be paid or deferred by election and provision of acceptable security, when an individual shareholder leaves Canada. This will occur on his/her departure income tax return.

March 4, 2010 Budget Change — TCP

There are two categories of capital property — Taxable Canadian Property (TCP) and Non-taxable Canadian Property (Non-TCP). The important aspect of having these two separate categories relates to how each is taxed by Canada once you become a non-resident of Canada for tax purposes.

TCP (with certain exceptions) will be deemed to be disposed of when you cease to be a resident of Canada for tax purposes. Also, TCP gains will be subject of Canadian tax after you cease to be a resident of Canada unless you live in a country that has a tax treaty with Canada that provides an exemption from Canadian tax on that gain.

Non-TCP will be deemed to be disposed of when you emigrate. However, if you have an actual disposition after you cease to be a resident of Canada, any gain arising over and above the deemed gain on departure, is not taxable in Canada.

Our taxing authorities found that in many cases, the gains on certain TCPs arising after you became a non-resident were exempt from Canadian tax by virtue of a tax treaty. This result gave rise to amendments in the definition of Taxable Canadian Property (TCP) on March 4, 2010.

Prior to March 5, 2010, TCP included the following assets:
- Canadian real estate and shares of private Canadian companies;
- property used in carrying on a business in Canada;
- shares of public Canadian companies (where you, together with persons with whom you do not deal at arm's length, own 25% or more of any class of shares);
- shares of non-resident corporations where more than 50% of the corporation's assets consist of TCP at any time in the 5-year period prior to disposition;
- interests in non-resident trusts or partnerships whose assets are primarily composed of TCP;
- non-resident trust and partnership interests, the value of which arose from holding various assets including TCP which represented more than

50% of the value of all its assets at any time in the preceding 5 years; and

- any capital stock which is not listed on a prescribed stock exchange (i.e. over-the-counter or unlisted stock).

Effective after March 4, 2010, TCP includes the following assets:
- real or immovable property situated in Canada;
- property including goodwill, inventory used by you in a business carried on in Canada;
- shares of capital stock of a corporation (other than a mutual fund corporation) that is not listed on a designated stock exchange, an interest in a partnership or an interest in a trust (other than a mutual fund trust or an income interest in a trust resident in Canada), if at any time during the past 60 months, more than 50% of the value of the corporation's shares or interest in a partnership or trust is derived from one or any combination of
  - i.   real or immovable property situated in Canada,
  - ii. Canadian resource property,
  - iii. timber resource property, and
  - iv. options or interests in any of the properties listed in i, ii and iii.
- shares of a corporation that is listed on a designated stock exchange, shares of a mutual fund corporation or units of a mutual fund trust, where you together with related persons own 25% or more of the issued shares of any class of capital stock or issued units of the trust and, at any time in the past 60 months, more than 50% of the value of those shares or units was derived from the items listed in i, ii, iii and iv above;
- an option in respect of, or an interest in any of the properties listed above, whether or not the property exists;
- Canadian resource property;
- timber resource property;
- income interest in a trust resident in Canada;
- retired partner's right to share income or losses from his/her former partnership, and
- a life insurance policy in Canada.

The new provisions are law. If you left Canada before March 5, 2010 with what was TCP under the former definition, it may not be TCP now. What impact if any does this have on you? First the bad news: the shares were deemed to be disposed off at the time you ceased to be a resident for tax purposes. The good news is that any appreciation arising after your departure will not be taxable in Canada.

Providing Security in Lieu of Tax

It is possible to elect to defer paying tax (See Appendix — Form T1244, Election, Under Subsection 220(4.5) of the Income Tax Act, to Defer the Payment of Tax on Income Relating to the Deemed Disposition of Property) on your accrued gains from TCP if you provide acceptable security to the Canada Revenue Agency. The tax can then be paid when the asset is ultimately sold, with no interest charges on any tax that was owing on the date you left Canada. Acceptable forms of security include bank letters of guarantee, bank letters of credit and government bonds. Other types of security that may be acceptable include shares of private or publicly traded corporations, certificates of precious metals, various other marketable securities or a mortgage on real property. Note that because these assets are TCP, the taxable portion of the gain (attributable to when you were a resident and after you left) on these assets will be subject to tax when they are ultimately sold unless the gain which accrues after you leave Canada is exempt by virtue of a tax treaty.

If you plan to elect to defer the payment of tax and provide security, you should contact CRA ahead of your departure and obtain their approval.

It is worth repeating that what was TCP prior to March 5, 2010 may not be TCP after March 4, 2010. For example, shares of many private corporations may now qualify as non-TCPs after March 4. They will still have to be valued and tax paid or deferred on any gain arising from the deemed disposition when you cease to be a resident of Canada. But now the gains accruing while you are a non-resident will not be taxable by Canada if you sell the shares while you are a non-resident. However, your new country of residence may tax you.

Valuations — TCP

The deemed disposition rules require many Canadians to incur the cost of valuations even though no real sale (i.e. no consideration) occurs. For example, if Canadians own shares of a Canadian private corporation, they must value the shares at the time of departure, report the deemed disposition in their final tax return and either pay the tax or post acceptable security. This requirement can cause emigrants additional cost and aggravation.

Non-TCP

If you own property that is not TCP, such as shares of certain private Canadian corporations, most Canadian public corporations, shares in foreign corporations, interests in mutual funds or foreign real estate, you will be deemed to have sold this property at fair market value on the date of your departure. Any capital gain or loss arising from this disposition must be included in your final tax return.

Unlike TCPs, gains on non-TCPs which accrue while you are a non-resident, for example, capital gains on investments in the Canadian stock market or in a Canadian mutual fund, will not be subject to tax in Canada.

Non-TCP — Deferral of Payment of Tax

You may also elect to defer the payment of tax (Appendix: Form T1244) arising from the deemed disposition of non-TCP. Upon ultimate sale, only the tax on the gain which arose at the time of departure is payable. Any gain accruing after the date of departure is not subject to Canadian tax.

Losses arising from the actual sale of non-TCP after the time of departure cannot be applied to reduce gains arising on departure.

If you elect to defer the tax arising from the deemed disposition on departure and acceptable security was provided to the Canada Revenue Agency, the tax must be paid when the non-TCP is sold. This requirement will apply when the particular property is sold, gifted or deemed disposed on death.

On the other hand, if you don't realize a disposition and you return to Canada, you may elect to undo the deemed disposition arising on departure and get your security (or tax if paid) back. See Chapter 5, "Immigration" — "Returning Former Residents" for more details.

Security — TCP and Non-TCP

If the total gain arising from the deemed disposition of both TCP and non-TCP is less than $100,000, no security is required. However, you must elect (Form T1244) in your departure tax return to defer the tax on deemed dispositions.

Acceptable Security

Canada Revenue Agency will accept bank letters of guarantee, bank letters of credit, and bonds from the Government of Canada or a province or territory of Canada.

Other types of security may also be acceptable such as shares in a private corporation (very doubtful) or publicly traded corporations, certificates in precious metals, various other marketable securities, a charge or mortgage on real property or valuable personal property.

If in doubt about the acceptability of your security, you should contact the Canada Revenue Agency tax service office in the region that the property is located to confirm that they will in fact accept the security you plan to provide.

As noted above, Form T1244 must be filed (along with the security if necessary) to make the election to defer the payment of tax arising from the deemed dispositions on departure.

Question — Partnership Interest
I own a partnership interest which will have a negative tax cost when I leave Canada. Will I realize a gain from a deemed disposition of this property?

Answer
Since you have a negative tax cost at the time you emigrate from Canada, you will be required to include the negative amount plus an amount equal to the fair market value in your final return as proceeds. You may wish to take steps to eliminate or reduce the negative tax cost prior to your departure.

Keep in mind, the income you receive from the partnership will likely continue to be taxable even though you are a non-resident. As a result, if you can delay your departure until after the partnership's fiscal period, all or a portion of the negative tax cost may be eliminated by the income.

Question — Life Insurance Policy
I own a life insurance policy. Is it deemed to be disposed of when I leave Canada?

Answer
So far, life insurance policies (other than segregated fund policies) have been excluded from the deemed disposition rules. They continue to be taxable or non-taxable in the same manner had you remained a resident of Canada.

Question — Foreign Exchange
I plan to leave Canada next month. I have a foreign bank account in a foreign currency. It has unrealized foreign exchange gains which will be realized when I emigrate from Canada. How do I go about calculating the gain from the deemed disposition of the foreign exchange account?

Answer
The current value in Canadian dollars will be your deemed proceeds. The tax cost is much more difficult and will require you to go back to your records to determine the foreign exchange rates each time you deposited money into the account. If you left interest to accumulate, look at the values you used in reporting this income on your Canadian tax return. The converted Canadian dollar deposits plus any reinvested interest will give you your tax cost.

Question — Non-TCP Losses
I left Canada in January 2011. I realized a large capital gain from the deemed disposition of my investment portfolio (Non-TCP). It is now August 2017 and my investment portfolio is only worth one-half of what it was worth when I left Canada in January 2011. Is there any way I can reduce the tax on the gains arising from the deemed disposition of my investment portfolio when I left in January 2011?

Answer
If you sell any of your investment portfolio while non-resident of Canada, the losses cannot be used to reduce the gains that arose from the deemed disposition of non-TCP on departure.

The only way you can reduce the tax that arose when you departed, occurs if you return to Canada. If you have all or some of the investment portfolio on hand when you return to Canada, you can elect to undo the deemed disposition that occurred when you left Canada. This relief is only allowed for the same non-TCP that were deemed disposition on your departure.

Question — Business Assets
I own business assets which will not be deemed to be disposed of when I leave Canada. What happens if a year after I leave Canada, I cease to use these assets to carry on a business in Canada?

Answer
These assets will be deemed to be disposed of and reacquired at their fair market value at the time you cease to carry on that business in Canada. Tax must be paid unless you elect to defer payment until the asset is actually sold.

Question — Virtual Currency
I have an asset which is in the form of what is referred to as a virtual currency. Mine is better known as Bitcoin. I acquired this currency a couple of years ago for a total cost of $1,000. It is now worth $2,500. Is it deemed to be disposed of when I leave Canada?

Answer
Yes. It is not included in the exemptions.

Election to Dispose of Taxable Canadian Property

You may also elect to cause any or all the rest of your Taxable Canadian Property to be disposed of on your departure. This may be accomplished by filing Form T2061A — Election by an Emigrant to Report Deemed Dispositions of Property and any Resulting Capital Gain or Loss (see in Appendix). You may do this to realize gains, utilize capital losses or create losses to offset capital gains realized on other dispositions. However, you may only elect to cause dispositions that will create losses in order to offset gains realized on deemed dispositions arising on departure.

This election to have any or all of the rest of your Taxable Canadian Property disposed of on your departure will be filed as part of your tax return for the year of your departure from Canada. There are provisions to accommodate late filing and also to amend these elections.

Exception

There is an exception to the deemed disposition rules for short-term residents. If you have been a resident of Canada for less than 60 months in the ten years immediately preceding your emigration, property owned when you last became a resident and property inherited since you established residency will be excluded from the deemed disposition rules. Only property you acquired while resident will be subject to the deemed disposition rules.

Tax Relief — Deemed Dispositions

A number of relief provisions exist including reduction of Canadian tax by foreign taxes paid, application of losses arising from TCP, reduction of double taxation and the ability to elect to undo the deemed disposition if you return to Canada. The following is a review and analysis of the impact these provisions will have on an individual leaving Canada. Like most relief provisions, they have been worded so that you can't have your cake and eat it too. Read on, dear emigrant.

Reduction of Canadian Tax

If you leave Canada, you will be deemed to have disposed of most of your assets. The tax may be paid or deferred. Later, if you sell these assets, you may also have to pay tax in your new country of residence on the same gain you already paid tax on when you left Canada. Since the deemed disposition in Canada occurred in a year prior to the actual disposition, your new country of residence will likely not give you credit for Canadian taxes already paid or payable (if you elected to defer). The result: double taxation.

Our legislators recognize that double taxation is inappropriate and have promised to amend all tax treaties to eliminate this problem. In the meantime, you may apply any tax paid in your new country against Canadian tax paid (or payable) when you left Canada. There are a number of complex restrictions to take into account. First of all, this provision will only apply (except for real estate) when you live in a country that has a tax treaty with Canada. Also, you will only get a credit up to the amount of the foreign tax that relates to the tax on the deemed gains arising on departure.

Fortunately, our government has been hard at work amending tax agreements with other countries to provide relief from double taxation.

If you migrate to a country that has a tax agreement with Canada, go to the Article that deals with Capital Gains or Alienation of Property. This is usually Article 13.

The wording of this relief provision may vary from treaty to treaty but the intended result occurs. In general, one can elect to have the provision apply to have your new homeland recognize that the tax cost of all those assets that Canadian tax law deemed you to have disposed when you emigrated from Canada, to be equal to the fair market value on the day you ceased to be a resident of Canada.

Please note that not all treaties have been amended to contain this provision. Also, this is an elective provision. You will note that the provision is silent regarding specific procedures or forms to use to make this election. As well, is it an asset by asset election or is it an all or nothing election? These questions will be the administrative headache of the taxing authority of your new homeland. As noted elsewhere in this book, seek professional tax assistance in your new homeland.

And, you can always ignore the treaty relief and use the existing Canadian tax provisions noted above to eliminate the double taxation.

Application of Losses from TCP

As we all know, what goes up may also come down. Imagine what would happen if you had a gain on a deemed sale on departure, but realized a loss equal to all or part of that deemed gain when you actually sold the property. Under normal rules, if the loss occurred within four years of the deemed disposition, the loss could be applied against the gain and the tax reduced accordingly. But what about a loss that occurs beyond this time frame? The rules now permit the application of this loss to reduce gains arising from TCP only with no time limit.

This rule does contain limits and ensures that you do not create a loss by some creative scheme to reduce or eliminate the tax arising from the deemed disposition on departure.

For example, assume you had shares of a private Canadian company, which were deemed disposed of at $500,000 on your date of departure. You later wound-up the company and realized a deemed dividend of $500,000, subject to Canadian non-resident tax of 25% or lower if reduced by a tax treaty. So far, this appears to be lousy tax planning — a taxable gain of $500,000 on departure and a $500,000 deemed dividend subject to Canadian non-resident withholding tax. The magic relates to the creation of a capital loss of $500,000 which could have been (prior to the restriction outlined hereinafter) applied against the gain on departure.

The restriction, which is effective for dispositions after December 23, 1998, will cause any capital loss realized on the sale of shares which are TCP to be reduced dollar for dollar by any taxable dividends received on those shares. The result of this restriction will eliminate the capital loss of $500,000 mentioned above ($500,000 loss minus $500,000 taxable dividend). Under this restriction, you appear to be worse off — $500,000 capital gain and now a $500,000 taxable dividend — double taxation. Some plan! It's bad, but not as bad as it seems. As you will see in "Reduction of Double Taxation" below, you will be able to use the non-resident withholding tax paid on the dividend to reduce the tax paid or payable on the deemed disposition.

If you don't receive any dividends and do suffer a capital loss on the actual disposition of TCP, this loss may be applied to reduce the gain arising on the deemed disposition of TCP at date of departure. As for non-TCP, no loss may be applied to reduce the departure gain.

Due to the complexity of these rules, I recommend you seek professional help to minimize your tax burden relating primarily to private company shares.

March 4, 2010 — Amendment TCP

It is worth mentioning that the March 4 amendment to the meaning of TCP may impact the application of losses and foreign taxes paid. You should review this area with a tax professional to determine what the final outcome of a sale of Canadian property will be.

Reduction of Double Taxation

The original version of the deemed disposition rules caused not only the wary taxpayer but our government to realize that the same gain could be taxed twice and in some cases, three times. For example, you own $500,000 worth of shares in a private Canadian corporation; you realize tax on the deemed gain of $500,000. You pay tax on the taxable dividend of $500,000 and may even pay tax in your new country. Fortunately, the rules will permit you to apply the Canadian non-resident withholding tax paid on the taxable dividend and the tax paid in the treaty country to reduce the tax on the deemed gain on departure. The bottom line is that if you sell the TCP before you return to Canada, you will pay the tax realized on the gain arising on departure, as well as any gain that arose after your departure. The only way you can eliminate the tax on the subsequent gain occurs when a tax treaty exempts that gain from Canadian tax.

As noted previously under Reduction of Canadian Tax, your new country of residence may tax capital gains. As a rule, their domestic tax rules likely do not recognize your new tax cost caused by the deemed disposition rules that applied when you left Canada. But, if the country has an up-to-date tax agreement with Canada, you can avoid double taxation on gains already taxed by Canada when you left.

Elect to Undo Deemed Disposition

If you return to Canada at any time in the future and you still own the properties (TCP and non-TCP) that you were deemed to have sold on departure, you may elect to reverse the deemed disposition. I refer you to Chapter 5, "Immigration" — "Returning Former Residents" for more details.

Employment Stock Option — TCP

If you receive stock options from a Canadian controlled private corporation (CCPC), specific rules apply which defer the taxation of the benefit realized on exercising the option until you sell the shares. However, emigration and the expanded deemed disposition rules caused that benefit to be realized prematurely. The tax legislators realized (or were told) of the inequities that could arise and created an amendment to defer the taxation of the benefit component until the shares are actually sold. Only actual appreciation arising on the shares from the time you exercised the option to the date of departure will be realized when you leave. If you sell your shares while you are a non-resident, the benefit will be realized as Canadian employment income. You may reduce your Canadian income by an amount equal to 50% of the benefit.

In addition, you may have realized a gain from the date of departure, which will be taxable, if the shares are TCP. This sale will require a number of tax filings — a Request for Clearance (T2062) and a personal tax return. In addition, if you elected to defer the payment of tax that arose on the deemed disposition of the shares on your departure, you will be required to pay up.

If the shares are not TCP as a result of the March 4, 2010 amended definition, the gain realized from the date of departure to the date of sale will no longer be taxable by Canada. In addition, there will be no need to request a clearance certificate.

The foregoing only applies to shares of a CCPC that a Canadian resident received through an employee stock option plan.

Unexercised employee stock options are excluded from the deemed disposition rules regardless of whether the employer is a private or public company. The benefit on the private shares will be realized when the shares are actually sold. The benefit on non-private or public shares will be recognized as Canadian employment income when the option is exercised. New rules which allow non-CCPC employees to defer the taxation of the benefit do not apply to non-residents.

Declared Unpaid Dividend

After the introduction of the expanded deemed disposition rules in 1993, most properties and rights were deemed to be disposed when you emigrated. What was not fully appreciated was the impact of these rules on things such as declared but unpaid dividends, accrued bonus or accrued unpaid interest. These are rights that you had when you left that do not qualify for the various exceptions. As a result, these rights will be deemed to be disposed of at fair market value. Then when the dividend or interest is paid, Canada will levy a non-resident withholding tax of up to 25%. A careful review of the rules indicates that double taxation will not apply. It is strongly recommended that you take advantage of the relief provided to ensure that there is no double taxation.

A WORD OF CAUTION

Correct filing of deemed dispositions on departure can be a complex matter, depending on the nature of your assets. As well, ascertaining whether or not a property is TCP will be critical to determining if you will be taxed on any gains accruing after you become non-resident of Canada. If you own property which may fall under the deemed disposition rules, I suggest that you seek professional taxation advice.

Principal Residence — Change of Use

If you owned a home in Canada prior to becoming non-resident and decided to lease it to someone, in taxation terms you will realize a *change of use*. This change of use will cause a deemed disposition of your house (unless you elect *not* to have a change of use — see below).

The property will be deemed to have been sold and reacquired at its fair market value at the time the change of use occurs. As long as the house can be designated as your principal residence for the entire period you owned it, no tax liability will arise from the deemed disposition.

Any gain or loss from a future sale will be calculated on the fair market value of the property used for the deemed disposition. If the future sale price is higher, you will have a capital gain and if it is lower, you will have a capital loss on the land and a terminal loss on the building. Remember a capital loss may only be applied against capital gains while a loss (terminal loss) arising from depreciable property (building) can be applied against both capital gains and other income unless you are a non-resident.

You may elect *not* to have a change of use. This election may be made in the tax return for the year the change of use occurred or later subject to certain penalties. *As a non-resident you cannot designate a property to be your principal residence for those years that you are a non-resident of Canada* (see in Appendix: T2091(IND)).

Change of Use — Deemed Disposition

Should you make this election not to have a change of use or not? This decision requires considerable foresight and may be made on a late-filed basis. For example, if you purchased a house in 2000 for $250,000 and it was worth $300,000 in 2014, the year of emigration, and you leased it on an arm's length, long-term lease, you could realize and shelter a gain of $50,000 by having the change of use cause a deemed disposition to occur.

Fair Market Value — Change of Use	$ 300,000
Tax Cost (purchase price)	250,000
Capital Gain	50,000
Less Principal Residence Exemption*	50,000
Taxable Gain	$ 0.00

Change of Use Election

Let us assume that the property does not go up in value and you sell it in 2016 for $300,000. Since you had a deemed disposition in 2014 from the change of use (leasing), no gain arises on sale in 2016. If you had elected not to have a change of use, you would have paid tax on about $1,500 (50% of $3,000) of the $50,000 gain.

Options	No Election change of use	Election no change of use
Fair Market Value	$ 300,000	$ 300,000
Tax Cost	300,000	250,000
Gain	—	50,000
Principal Residence Exemption (rounded)*	—	47,000
Capital Gain	$ —	$ 3,000
Taxable portion	—	1,500

---

* See Chapter 3, "Taxation of a Non-Resident" — Question — Sale of a former principal residence for the calculation of the principal residence.

However, what if the value of the house goes up to $400,000 in 2016? Then you would have a gain of $100,000 on which you would be required to pay Canadian tax. But if you had elected not to have a change of use, you would have paid tax on only a $4,500 (50% of $9,000) gain rather than $100,000.

Options	No Election change of use		Election no change of use	
Fair Market Value	$	400,000	$	400,000
Tax Cost		300,000		250,000
Gain		100,000		150,000
Principal Residence Exemption (rounded)*		—		141,000
Capital Gain	$	100,000	$	9,000
Taxable portion		—		4,500

These results illustrate the tax consequences you can encounter if you elect not to have a change of use in a stable real estate market compared to the tax relief you can enjoy if you elect in a rising market. As noted earlier, it may be prudent to wait and elect at a later date. Remember, you will be subject to a penalty if you file this election late. While the Canada Revenue Agency is not obliged to accept the late-filed election even if you pay the penalty, I have not encountered any refusals to date.

If you are still a resident of Canada, either deemed or factual, then this election makes sense because it will extend the number of years (up to four) you may claim it as your principal residence even though it is leased out.

Question — Deemed Disposition, Principal Residence
I am moving to the U.S. I understand that the U.S. tax rules will tax the entire gain since they do not recognize the principal residence exemption.

Answer
The Canada/U.S. rules deem you to have sold your principal residence at its fair market value when you enter the U.S. Only the gain arising after that date will be taxable in the U.S. This appears to indicate that you should elect to have a disposition or if leasing, to permit a change of use to occur. If only life were so simple. Due to the various Canadian implications, you should review all possible results.

Question — Election not to have a Change of Use
I propose to lease my principal residence when I emigrate from Canada. I wish to elect not to have a change of use. How should I do this?

Answer
The Canada Revenue Agency does not have an election form. As a result, you should write a note in your tax return for the year of departure stating that you elect not to have a change of use occur on your principal residence. You should identify the property you are electing on.

Question — Election not to have a Change of Use
If I make an election not to have a change of use and later decide that I should not have done so, can I rescind the election?

Answer
You may rescind the election at any time. However, the cancellation will not be effective until the year it is made. As a result, the deemed disposition will occur in that subsequent year and Canadian tax may arise.

> **Question — Late File Election "not to have a Change of Use"**
> *I purchased a home in 1995. I left Canada in 2012. At that time, I leased my home and reported a deemed disposition caused by the change of use (personal to rental). I recently sold the property and realized that I should have elected not to have a change of use in 2012. Can I now file a late election not to have a change in use in 2012?*
>
> **Answer**
> You may submit a late filed election not to have a change of use in 2012. Details regarding how to do this are contained in Information Circular IC07-1, *Taxpayer Relief Provisions* (www.cra-arc.gc.ca). A penalty of $100 per month after the due date (April 30, 2013) to a maximum of $8,000 will be levied unless you have a good reason for not filing the election on time. The penalty must accompany the request to file the late election.

Deferred Capital Gains

The tax rules permit Canadians to defer the taxation of capital gains if all the proceeds of consideration have not been received. The taxation may be spread over 5 years (10 years for shares of small business corporations, farm property and farm corporations). Unfortunately, this deferral is denied for a taxation year if you cease to be a resident of Canada during that year or in the immediate following year.

Deductions: RRSP

Whether or not you contribute to your RRSP in your year of departure will depend on your previous year's income and your current year's income. The amount of your present year's income that you can shelter from tax (your "deduction limit") is based on 18% of your prior year's earned income minus any pension adjustment (up to $26,010 (2017)). You don't need to calculate this amount because the Canada Revenue Agency provides you with the appropriate figures on your assessment notice for the previous year.

Your deduction limit for your emigration year will not be affected by the fact that you were a non-resident for part of the year. However, if you leave Canada early in the year, your taxable income for the year of emigration may not be high enough to utilize your full deduction limit.

What you do will depend on your individual circumstances. If you do not contribute up to your full deduction limit, you have until the end of the calendar year in which you turn the age of 71 to use the deduction limit if you earn taxable income in Canada. You may use your deduction limit to shelter business or employment income you still receive from Canada (on which you pay

Canadian tax). If you elect to treat rental income on a net basis (see below) you may also be able to deduct the RRSP contributions from the net rental income.

If you have (accidentally or intentionally) made RRSP contributions which exceed the amount you are able to deduct from any of these types of income in your year of departure, you may request a refund of the over-contribution by filing Form T3012A, Tax Deduction Waiver on the Refund of Your Unused RRSP Contributions Made in _____. As long as this filing is made within certain time limits, you will not be charged non-resident withholding tax, which is usually 25%.

Prior to 1996, the Canadian government actually allowed you to maintain RRSP balances of up to $8,000 in excess of the deduction limit in any year. After 1995, the $8,000 excess allowance is reduced to $2,000. Any amount over the excess allowance is subject to a tax of 1% per month until the excess is removed. Transitional rules were introduced to allow you to reduce excess contributions and avoid this penalty tax.

Even though a number of Canadians have used this scheme, I do not recommend it for non-residents, since a refund of this excess will be subject to a 25% non-resident withholding tax.

And last but not least, what happens if you contribute not only your deduction limit and $2,000, but additional funds? These additional funds will cause you to pay a 1% per month tax until the excess is removed. If the excess arose from a deliberate act on your part, the refund of the excess will be subject to non-resident withholding tax of 25%.

In conclusion, you may contribute to your RRSP in the year of departure or even while you are a non-resident. However, you must analyze the perceived benefits and determine if it really makes sense. It is important to consider the tax laws of your new home and native land. These may not recognize the tax shelter feature of the RRSP and tax the annual income as earned.

RRSP: Home Buyers' Plan

If you took advantage of the RRSP Home Buyers' Plan while you were a resident of Canada, certain tax consequences arise when you emigrate.

If you had withdrawn from your RRSP under the Home Buyers' Plan and became a non-resident before acquiring your Canadian home, your withdrawal will be disqualified and added to your income in the year of withdrawal. You may avoid this disqualification by refunding the withdrawal and cancelling your participation in the plan.

You have withdrawn the funds and emigrated after acquiring your Canadian home, you must repay the entire unpaid balance of the withdrawal amount within 60 days of becoming a non-resident. If you have not made repayment within the 60 days, the unpaid balance will be included as income in the tax return you file for the year you departed from Canada.

RRSP Withdrawal for Education

After 1998, you may borrow up to $20,000 from your RRSP to finance your education. This must be repaid in equal instalments over a period of 10 years. However, if you emigrate, the unpaid balance must be repaid within 60 days of departure or the outstanding balance will be included in your return for the year of departure.

TFSA Tax-Free Savings Account

Effective for 2009 and subsequent years, a TFSA will permit a Canadian resident to earn tax-free investment income. However, upon becoming a non-resident you will not be able to contribute to your TFSA and no contribution room will accrue to it. The annual limit is $5,500 (2014).

The April 2015 Federal Budget proposed to increase the $5,500 per annum limit to $10,000 per annum, effective for 2015 and future years.

However, starting January 1, 2016, the annual TFSA dollar limit will decrease from $10,000 to $5,500.00. The future TFSA annual room limit will be indexed to inflation and rounded to the nearest $500.

As a non-resident, you can keep your TFSA and continue to benefit from the exemption of Canadian tax on both investment income and withdrawals. In other words, no non-resident withholding tax on payments to you as a non-resident. However, there is always a however, your country of residence may tax you on earned/accrued income, capital gains and payments.

The TFSA is a Canadian creation and will be viewed as an ordinary investment account in many taxing jurisdictions.

There is no deemed disposition on either emigration or immigration. To the extent you withdraw funds while you are non-resident, you must wait until you become a resident before you can recontribute these funds. As usual, contributions over the yearly limit and/or while you are a non-resident will be viewed as excess contributions subject to a penalty tax.

Deductions: Moving Expenses

Get serious! The only time you will be able to deduct moving expenses occurs when you leave Canada to attend a post-secondary educational institution as a full-time student *and* you receive a Canadian scholarship, bursary, fellowship or research grant to attend that educational institution.

Capital Gains Deduction

The rules dealing with this area were changed significantly on February 22, 1994. The $100,000 deduction was eliminated for any gains realized after February 22, 1994.

This deduction will have no relevance in 1995 and subsequent years, except for capital properties which are qualified small business corporation shares, qualified fishing property, qualified farm properties and shares of qualified farm corporations. But like all other so called incentives, these too will likely find their way to the not so great previous government idea recycling area. It is wise to utilize this capital gain exemption sooner than later. This may occur before you leave or on departure because of the deemed dispostion rules. It is important that the shares qualify for this exemption at the time of the disposition. This may require careful planning prior to the disposition to ensure that they do qualify.

The lifetime capital gain exemption for 2015 is $813,600. However, the April 2015 Federal Budget raised this amount to $1,000,000 for qualified farm and fishing property. This amount will apply for sales that occurred after April 20, 2015.

Tax Credits

And what about tax credits in the year you emigrate? Well, you get to claim the following non-refundable tax credits to the extent that they apply to the part of the year you were resident in Canada:
- Canada Pension Plan or Quebec Pension Plan contributions;
- Social Security Arrangement;
- Provincial Parental Insurance plan premiums paid;
- Employment Insurance premiums;
- Volunteer firefighters' amount;
- search and rescue volunteers' amount;
- Canada employment amount;
- public transit amount;
- children's arts amount;
- home buyers' amount;
- adoption expenses;
- pension income amount (for yourself);
- interest paid on loans for post-secondary education made to you under the *Canada Student Loans Act*, the *Canada Student Financial Assistance Act*, or similar provincial or territorial government laws;
- tuition, education, and textbook amounts (for yourself);
- medical expenses; and
- donations and gifts.

In other words, if you had any income amount or outlay related to the foregoing while you were a resident, you may claim the resulting credit.

The remaining credits, which are also non-refundable, may be claimed *pro-rata* based on the number of days you are resident in Canada. These include the:

- basic amount;
- age amount (now restricted if income too high);
- spousal amount (don't forget spouse includes common-law spouse);
- equivalent to spouse amount;
- disability amount transferred from someone other than a spouse;
- tuition fees and education amount transferred from a child;
- amount for children 17 or younger during the year;
- amount for infirm dependants age 18 or older;
- caregiver amount;
- disability amount for yourself; and
- amounts transferred from your spouse.

Under certain circumstances, you may be able to claim these credits for the entire taxation year. For the first set of credits, you need only be reporting Canadian employment or business income for the rest of the year of departure. For the second batch of credits to be used for the entire year, your Canadian return must contain at least 90% of your world income.

Tax Rate

The Canada Revenue Agency will require you to pay the federal tax rate and the provincial or territorial tax where you lived just before you left Canada. You may pay different provincial/territorial rates if you have a business in several provinces/territories.

OTHER TYPES OF INCOME

As a non-resident you may receive certain types of Canadian source income that will be subject to non-resident withholding tax. The most common examples are dividend income from investments, pension income and rental income. *Before you leave Canada you should make appropriate arrangements to ensure that the payment of your non-resident withholding tax will be handled smoothly.*

In general, the institution (bank, trust company, mutual fund, pension, RRSP, insurance company) which pays you is responsible for withholding the correct amount of tax, forwarding it to the Canada Revenue Agency and sending the balance on to you. It is your responsibility, however, to ensure that all such entities know that you are non-resident and use your non-resident address as the address of record for your account. If you intend to use a

Canadian agent, the payer may be given the agent's address but will still need to know your country of residence.

Rental Income

Where rental income is involved, it is the responsibility of your tenants to withhold 25% of their gross rental payments, remit it to our government on your behalf and issue to you a non-resident information slip (NR4) each year giving details of the rent paid and the tax remitted on your behalf.

If tax has been paid on the gross rent, as a non-resident landlord you have two years after the year the rent was paid to elect to file a Canadian tax return (T1159-Income Tax Return for electing under Section 216 see Appendix) recalculating your tax bill so that you pay tax only on the net rent (the amount which was left over after your expenses).

Alternatively, arrangements can be made in advance to pay non-resident withholding tax on the net rental income. You and your Canadian agent (who usually ends up being a brother or a sister) may file an undertaking (Form NR6 — see in Appendix) before the rental payments commence promising to file a tax return within six months of the end of the year in question reporting the rental income on a net basis. If you have filed an NR6, your agent need only withhold and remit 25% of the net monthly rent. If your rental expenses exceed your rental income you may even end up with a net rental loss and owe no tax. Even in a loss position, however, you must file a tax return reporting your calculations. The NR6 itself is an annual filing and must be submitted prior to January 1 of each rental year.

Sounds good, but there is one catch. If you read the fine print, the Canadian agent is responsible to remit 25% of the gross rent if the tax return is not filed on time. This can place an enormous burden on the agent particularly if he or she is unable to file the tax return on time. Please ensure that you give your agent total control over this area. Otherwise, he or she may refuse to be your agent. Recent encounters with the Canada Revenue Agency have disclosed that it intends to apply the six-month rule by the book. Agents beware!

Question — NR6
I am a non-resident with a rental property in Canada. Can I take advantage of the benefits arising from filing an NR6 without a Canadian agent?

Answer
The Canada Revenue Agency stipulates that the agent must be a Canadian resident.

Question — Tax on Gross Rent
I plan to lease my house when I emigrate from Canada. Who is responsible for withholding and remitting the non-resident tax?

Answer
Technically, the tenant is responsible. However, both you and your tenant are jointly liable for both the tax and interest, that may be levied for not withholding and remitting the non-resident tax.

Question — No Tax Withheld
What happens if you are unaware that you should be remitting tax on rent payments? Is there any way to correct this situation?

Answer
I have approached the Canada Revenue Agency on several occasions and requested that it consider accepting late-filed tax returns to correct this oversight. I am pleased to report that the Canada Revenue Agency usually takes a sympathetic approach to our requests and treats them as voluntary disclosures. When late filed tax returns are accepted, you will pay tax on the net rent and interest and penalties based on the gross rent. Requests may be made to waive the latter if the circumstances warrant.

The voluntary disclosure approach appears to be somewhat costly and may cause you to ponder whether it is really worth the effort. From experience, I feel it is worth the effort. If you do nothing and the Canada Revenue Agency assesses, you will pay the 25% tax plus interest and penalties with no opportunity to file on the net basis. Your oversight may be discovered by way of audit or when you sell your property. When you sell your property, the buyer will want confirmation that all taxes have been taken care of which requires you to file Form T2062 (see in Appendix), and remit 25% of the gain. The form contains a number of questions, one of which asks if the property has been rented. Need I say more.

Question — No Tax Withheld but Filed Tax Return

I rented my house to an arms-length party when I became a non-resident. Neither my tenant nor I withheld and remitted the required non-resident withholding tax. I did however file a tax return on or before April 30th of the following year and reported the rental income and paid Canadian tax when required to do so. Do I have a problem?

Answer

As noted, neither you nor your tenant withheld the required 25% non-resident withholding tax from the rent payments. However, you filed a non-resident tax return to report the rental income and paid any tax that might be owing. Interest may still be charged by the tax authorities but only for the time that the non-resident tax should have been remitted until the date you filed your tax return to report the rental income. This position is supported by a court case, PECHET Vs MNR, 2009 FCA 341.

Question — Mortgage Interest

I own a house with a mortgage. Effective November 30, 2013, I shall be a non-resident of Canada. I plan to rent my house to an arm's length party on a long-term lease with a three-month termination clause. I have an agent in Canada and will elect to pay tax on my net rental income. Can I deduct the interest expense incurred on my mortgage on my house to determine my net income?

Answer

If the mortgage was obtained when you acquired the house, the interest expense may be deducted to determine your net rental income for purposes of calculating your Canadian tax.

Question — Mortgage Interest

I am a non-resident of Canada and own a rental property there. If I obtain a mortgage on the property, can I deduct the interest expense against my rental income? The money received on the mortgage was used to obtain a five-year term deposit.

Answer

This interest may not be used to reduce your rental income because the interest expense was not incurred to purchase property to realize rental income. The only time you would be allowed to deduct this interest arises when you use the money obtained from the mortgage to acquire another rental property in Canada and you elect to report the rental income on a net basis.

Question — Net Rent — Capital Cost Allowance
Can I claim capital cost allowance for purposes of determining NR-6 net rent for withholding tax and remittance purposes?

Answer
No. Capital cost allowance may only be used when you file your tax return (T1159) for the year in question.

Question — Rental Income, Year of Departure
If I leave in June and earn rental income after that date, do I include the rental income in my departure return or do I file a separate tax return for the rental income?

Answer
First of all, you have a change of use and must decide whether to accept that reality or elect not to have a change of use. Your tenants should remit 25% of the gross rent to the tax authorities, on your behalf. You may file a separate rental return (T1159) for the rental income earned after you emigrated from Canada. Do not report the rental income you receive as a non-resident on your departure tax return.

Question — Filing on a Net Basis
I have had tax withheld and remitted on the gross rent. Can I recover this tax by filing a net basis?

Answer
You have two years from the particular year to file a Canadian tax return, report the rental income (T1159) on a net basis and recover the previously withheld tax. This time is reduced to six months if an NR6 has been filed.

Other Income

Finally, there are certain types of income from which non-resident tax is withheld which you may elect (yes, yet another election) to include in your final tax return to receive a refund of non-resident tax withheld. These payments include:

- old age security;
- Canada/Quebec Pension Plan benefits;
- certain pension benefits;
- certain pooled registered pension plan payments;

- death benefits;
- employment insurance benefits;
- certain retiring allowances;
- payments under a registered supplementary unemployment plan;
- registered retirement savings plan payments;
- deferred profit sharing plan payments;
- registered retirement income fund payments;
- life income funds (LIFs);
- amounts received from a retirement compensation arrangement;
- prescribed benefits under a government assistance program; and
- Auto Pact benefits.

This election which is made under s. 217 of the Income Tax Act of Canada must be filed within six months of the particular year.

Question — Section 217
I feel that I may benefit by making the election to have s. 217 apply to my pension income. Is there an election form?

Answer
There is no election form. You only need to file a regular Canadian tax return within six months of the year in which you received the pension income, report the income therein and request that s. 217 apply to the income.

Question — Section 217, Year of Departure
I left Canada on June 15, 2015. I received a retiring allowance after I departed which was subject to 25% non-resident withholding tax. Based on my income both from Canada and outside Canada, I feel that I can benefit from a s. 217 election. Do I file a separate tax return for the s. 217 election or do I include the retirement allowance in my regular final return?

Answer
If you elect to use s. 217, the retirement allowance is included in your final Canadian tax return filed for the year of departure.

This particular election (s. 217) is by far the most complex a non-resident must face. Unfortunately, it does not yield significant benefits even when it is applicable. I feel it is really much ado about nothing. I refer you to Chapter 3, "Taxation of a Non-Resident" — "Other Canadian Source Income" for more information regarding how this election works and when it may be useful.

As noted, these payments are subject to non-resident withholding tax at a rate of 25% unless reduced by a tax treaty. The reduced tax rate may depend on the nature and the size of the payment. For example, lump sum payments from an RRSP will remain subject to the 25% withholding tax except for certain treaties (see Chapter 4, "Tax Treaties"). Tax on other payments such as amounts from RRIFs and LIFs will depend on both the amount paid and the treaty. Generally speaking, the Canada Revenue Agency treats payments from these as periodic payments except for the portion of the payment in excess of two times the minimum amount. The excess is considered a lump sum payment and subject to a 25% tax rate unless a treaty states otherwise.

Reporting Requirement — T1161

The government introduced a reporting requirement for individuals who emigrate from Canada. If you leave Canada to reside elsewhere, you may be required to file Form T1161 — List of Properties by an Emigrant of Canada (see in Appendix) containing information about some of your assets when the total value of these assets exceeds $25,000. You can exclude any asset that you use primarily for personal purposes, such as a car, but only if that asset has a value of less than $10,000. This return will be due with your Canadian tax return for the year in which you leave and must be completed even if there is no deemed disposition of any assets when you leave.

These assets could include:
- an automobile;
- a house;
- a cottage;
- boat;
- an airplane;
- GICs, term deposits;
- shares of public corporations;
- shares of private corporations;
- interest in trusts;
- bonds, debentures, promissory notes;
- offshore assets;
- antiques;
- jewelry; or
- partnership interest.

The reporting rules do not indicate whether mortgages or other indebtedness will be taken into account to determine whether a property should be listed. One can only imagine what the Canada Revenue Agency will do with this information.

There is some redundancy with CRA's emigration reporting requirements. An emigrant must file a Form T1161, and also complete Form T1243, Deemed Disposition of Property by an Emigrant of Canada! This begs the question whether someone who purchased a '56 Chevy Corvette for $5,000 and it had a value of $9,500 at the date of departure would feel obligated to report a deemed disposition (?)

For what it's worth, there is a penalty for not filing the redundant form (T1161) on time. And even though the '56 Chevy is not reported on the T1161 (less than $10,000), he should report a deemed disposition of the '56 Chevy Corvette on the T1243.

Question — Virtual currency
I own about $5,000 worth of Bitcoin. It cost me $3,000. Do I record this on the T1161?

Answer
While these are a form of cash, I would err on the side of caution and include it on the T1161. You will have to declare it on the T1243 and realize a deemed disposition in the year of departure.

PLANNING

I have spent a great deal of paper and ink explaining the finer points of Canadian residency and non-residency. I know that your primary objective is to become a non-resident. With that in mind and a firm conviction that you will achieve non-resident status, you must also plan for your arrival in your new home and not so native land.

It may well be worth your while to talk to a local tax specialist who should be up on the latest ways to legitimately structure your foreign source income so as to minimize both Canadian (if any) and domestic tax. If your new home is a treaty country, you should review both the domestic tax laws and the treaty benefits (if any) or restrictions.

If you can control your departure date, you may either reduce or defer tax. For example, if you leave in December, your income on your final return will include your world income up to the date of departure, plus any gains arising from the deemed disposition of your various properties. The latter will be taxed at the highest marginal tax rate and be payable when you file your tax return on or before April 30 (June 15 for individuals who report business income) of the following year. If you are able to delay departure until January of the following year, you may pay less tax and defer the payment of that tax (unless you have to make instalments) for up to 16 months.

Please note that tax is payable on April 30th regardless of the fact that they carry on business and do not have to file the tax return until June 15th.

New rules relating to business or professional taxation years may have caused you to claim a reserve of untaxed income which will be taxable when you leave Canada and cease carrying on that business or profession in Canada. By delaying your departure until January, you may reduce the tax and defer the payment of tax on that reserve.

If you plan to continue to carry on business through a permanent establishment in Canada after you cease to be a resident, you may be able to continue to claim the reserve permitted by law. This status will require you to continue to file a Canadian return, albeit as a non-resident and report this business income.

You may have claimed other types of reserves during the prior year. In particular, if you sold land inventory and claimed the three-year reserve, this reserve may not be permitted in either the year preceding departure or the year of departure. Once again, careful planning must occur to reduce or defer tax.

Caution must be exercised to ensure that this planning does not cause detrimental tax consequences in your new homeland.

The receipt of certain payments may be more tax effective as a non-resident than a resident. For example, a retiring allowance will be fully taxed unless you are able to roll some of it to an RRSP. If you cannot roll the entire amount to an RRSP, Canada will only tax it at 25% if you receive it as a non-resident.

RRSP/RRIF/TFSA Planning — Emigration

From a Canadian point of view, contributions to an RRSP are tax deductible and income earned is tax sheltered until it is paid out. While nothing happens to your RRSP when you leave Canada, you may find that your new homeland does not recognize its tax-sheltered feature. As a result, any income earned in your RRSP may be taxable, not in Canada, but by your new homeland. In order to minimize the problem, I recommend you crystallize all unrealized gains in your RRSP before you become a non-resident of Canada.

RRIFs, LIFs, TFSAs and other deferred tax plans have similar issues. They are tax sheltered from Canadian tax but not recognized as such by other countries. As a result, you should review the investments held by these plans and crystallize any large gains prior to leaving Canada.

Don't worry about the unrealized losses, but do review each investment to ensure that a crystallization of the gain does not create undo charges and penalties—deferred service charges.

If you are going to a country that has a tax treaty with Canada, check both the new country's domestic tax rules and the tax treaty.

Lastly, don't forget the expanded rules relating to deemed dispositions and reporting assets on hand. The listing should be done prior to departure and presented to your tax preparer to facilitate the preparation of your final tax return in an orderly manner.

3

Taxation of a Non-Resident

As a non-resident of Canada, you remain liable for Canadian tax on most types of income earned in Canada. This may include income from employment in Canada, income from carrying on a business in Canada, gains from the disposition of taxable Canadian property and certain other types of Canadian source income. You may also be liable for Canadian tax on employment income earned outside of Canada (fortunately in very limited circumstances). Income from these sources will be reported on a Canadian tax return similar to the one you completed while a resident. The amount of federal tax payable will be determined according to the same marginal tax rate paid by Canadian residents. Provincial/territorial tax may apply or be replaced by an additional federal tax which may be greater or less than provincial/territorial rates, depending on the province/territory.

Other types of Canadian income such as dividends, pensions withdrawals from RRSPs, RRIFs and LIFs will be subject to a uniform level of non-resident withholding tax. This will be deducted and remitted to the Canada Revenue Agency by the financial institution which administers your account. The standard rate of non-resident withholding tax is 25%; this may be reduced if you live in a country which has a tax treaty with Canada. In certain situations, you may elect to file a separate return to reduce the overall tax.

This chapter looks at these filing requirements and your responsibility as a non-resident. For more information see Interpretation Bulletin IT-420R3SR — Non-Residents — Income Earned in Canada, which may be obtained from the Canada Revenue Agency's web site: www.cra-arc.gc.ca.

INCOME TAX — NON-RESIDENT TAX RETURN

Income from Employment

If you earn income from duties performed in Canada, you will be required to include these amounts in your Canadian income. Such income may include employment benefits, living and personal allowances and director's fees, as well as salaries and commissions. This income may be reduced by various expenses such as travelling, to the extent such expenses are reasonable and applicable to the income.

If you perform part of your duties inside Canada and part outside Canada, you are permitted to make a reasonable allocation of the resulting income and pay Canadian tax only on the portion which relates to Canada.

Our tax law contains rules that determine a non-resident person's taxable income earned in Canada, which is subject to tax in Canada. This determination is generally a question of fact.

Non-resident Employed as an Aircraft Pilot

It was particularly difficult in the context of a non-resident aircraft pilot who was employed by a Canadian airline and who flew international flights.

The tax law did not contain specific rules for determining what portion of a non-resident pilot's income was attributable to duties performed in Canada (and was, therefore, part of the non-resident's taxable income earned in Canada). There have been judicial decisions on the determination of income attributable to duties performed in Canada by a non-resident aircraft pilot (see *Sutcliffe v. The Queen*, 2006 TCC 812 and *Price v. The Queen*, 2011 TCC 449) and the methods used in those decisions for income attribution to Canada were very complex. This complexity was criticized by the Tax Court of Canada.

In order to simplify the determination of taxable income earned in Canada and to provide greater certainty to taxpayers, new rules were introduced for determining the Canadian source income of a non-resident aircraft pilot who is employed by a Canadian airline. For the purposes of Canadian tax law, the following income of a non-resident employed as a pilot, if it is paid directly or indirectly by a person resident in Canada, will be considered to be income from the duties of an office or employment performed in Canada:

- all of the non-resident pilot's income attributable to a flight that departs from a location in Canada and arrives at a location in Canada;
- half of the non-resident pilot's income attributable to a flight that departs from a location in Canada and arrives at a location outside Canada;
- half of the non-resident pilot's income attributable to a flight that departs from a location outside Canada and arrives at a location in Canada; and
- none of the non-resident pilot's income attributable to a flight that departs from a location outside Canada and arrives at a location outside Canada.

For these purposes, a flight will include any portion of a flight that involves a take-off and landing (i.e. each leg of a flight is considered a flight). Income that is not attributable to any specific flight will continue to be considered Canadian source if the income is received for services performed in Canada.

This new tax rule applies to the 2013 and subsequent taxation years.

Question — Non-Resident Employee
I am currently a non-resident of Canada. However, my employment requires that 15% of my time be spent in Canada while the balance is outside Canada. Since I am a non-resident of Canada, do I have to pay Canadian tax?

Answer
Canadian tax law requires non-residents to pay tax on income from employment performed in Canada. As a result, you would be required to file a Canadian tax return and report that portion of employment income earned in Canada.

If you reside in a country that has a treaty with Canada, you may find that the income is exempt from Canadian tax. This result does not preclude the necessity to file a Canadian tax return. You must still prepare a Canadian tax return, report the Canadian employment income and claim an exemption to the extent that one is available under the treaty.

Income from Business

If you earn income from a business that you carry on in Canada, you are required to include this amount in your income earned in Canada unless the income is exempt by virtue of a tax treaty. Canadian tax laws will deem you to be "carrying on a business in Canada" if:

a) you solicit orders or offer anything for sale in Canada through an agent or servant;

b) you or an agent acting on your behalf produce, grow, create, manufacture, fabricate, improve, pack, preserve or construct, in whole or part, anything in Canada; or

c) you dispose of real property other than capital property.

If you carry on your business both inside and outside Canada, you are permitted to make a reasonable allocation of the income since only income earned in Canada is subject to Canadian tax. Expenses relating to the business will be allocated on the same basis.

If you carry on business in a partnership, you will report your share of the partnership income which relates to Canada.

It is noteworthy that income from business does not include income from property, such as rent, interest or dividends. These amounts, with the exception of interest paid to arm's length non-resident payees, are usually subject to non-resident withholding tax unless reduced or eliminated by a treaty. Where these amounts may be attributed to your Canadian business, they may escape the fixed non-resident withholding tax and be included in your business income. Whether this is beneficial will depend on the level of withholding tax which would otherwise have been applicable compared to the rate of Canadian tax applied to your business income. The latter is usually higher.

Question — *Non-Resident, Consulting Income*
I currently provide consulting services to a Canadian client. I do all my work outside of Canada. Do I have to pay Canadian tax on this income?

Answer
Canadian tax law requires you to pay tax on income earned from businesses carried on in Canada. Since you do not carry on this business in Canada, you do not have to pay Canadian tax.

Disposition of Taxable Canadian Property (TCP)

As noted in Chapter 2 — March 4, 2010 Budget change — TCP, the definition of taxable Canadian property (TCP) has changed. In other words what may have been TCP when you left Canada, may not be TCP to you as a non-resident.

Effective after March 4, 2010, TCP includes the following assets:

- real or immovable property situated in Canada;
- property including goodwill, inventory used by you in a business carried on in Canada;
- shares of capital stock of a corporation (other than a mutual fund corporation) that is not listed on a designated stock exchange, an interest in a partnership or an interest in a trust (other than a mutual fund trust or an income interest in a trust resident in Canada), if at any time during the past 60 months, more than 50% of the value of the corporation's shares or interest in a partnership or trust is derived from one or any combination of
  i.   real or immovable property situated in Canada,
  ii. Canadian resource property,
  iii. timber resource property, and
  iv. options or interests in any of the properties listed in i, ii and iii.
- shares of a corporation that is listed on a designated stock exchange, shares of a mutual fund corporation or units of a mutual fund trust, where you together with related persons own 25% or more of the issued shares of any class of capital stock or issued units of the trust and, at any time in the past 60 months, more than 50% of the value of those shares or units was derived from the items listed in i, ii, iii and iv above;
- an option in respect of, or an interest in any of the properties listed above, whether or not the property exists;

- Canadian resource property;
- timber resource property;
- income interest in a trust resident in Canada;
- retired partner's right to share income or losses from his/her former partnership, and
- a life insurance policy in Canada.

For example, shares of a Canadian Controlled Private Corporation were TCP when you ceased to be a resident of Canada in say, 2009. Now you wish to sell your shares. After a review of the new definition of TCP, you may find that the shares are not TCP and therefore any gain arising from the time your left Canada to date of sale should not be subject of Canadian tax or any filing procedures.

Keep in mind that you may be subject to tax on that gain in your new homeland.

If you gift, transfer or sell TCP as a non-resident, regardless of whether or not the property was deemed to be disposed of on your departure from Canada, you have certain filing requirements and will be required to pay Canadian tax if a capital gain arises. In order to assure the transferee or the purchaser that all Canadian income tax has been paid, you must file Form T2062 or T2062A (see in Appendix) and remit 25% of the gain to the Canada Revenue Agency. If you do not comply with these requirements, the transferee or purchaser will be required to remit 25% of the total purchase price to the Canada Revenue Agency. Upon receipt of the required form and remittance, the Agency will issue a clearance certificate which will be given to the transferee or purchaser to assure them that you have complied with these requirements. For more detail on this area refer to Information Circular IC 72-17R6 (see in Appendix).

The provisions (see Chapter 2) which caused you to have a deemed disposition on departure from Canada of certain types of TCP do not eliminate the requirements listed above with regard to obtaining a clearance certificate. I advise that appropriate inquiries be made at the time of any such sale or transfer to ensure that there are no delays for you to obtain your clearance certificate and proceeds from the sale of the property.

If you realized a gain (loss) on the transfer of TCP as a non-resident and remitted the required tax, you must file a Canadian tax return and report the gain (loss). Normally, a refund will arise because various selling costs are not taken into consideration when filing the request for clearance, Form T2062. As well, your overall Canadian tax rate will usually be less than 25% of the gain.

This income tax return is not to be confused with the tax return (T1159) filed to comply with an undertaking to file a rental return pursuant to Form NR6. This tax return will include the capital gain arising from the sale of your property along with other items of income subject to Canadian tax — e.g. Canadian employment and business income mentioned above. It must be filed on or before April 30 (June 15) of the following year if tax is owing.

A gain arising from any property other than TCP will not be subject to Canadian tax regardless of whether you paid the tax or elected to defer the payment of tax when you left Canada. These types of property will include shares of public companies, investments in mutual funds and interests in partnerships where less than 50% of their value is attributable to taxable Canadian properties.

Please note, if you elected to defer the payment of tax on departure, that tax will be payable when you sell the particular property that caused the deferred departure tax.

The March 4, 2010 amendment to the definition of TCP, will eliminate a number of properties which were TCPs before March 5, 2010.

Question — Sale of Taxable Canadian Property

I propose to sell my former home. Due to market conditions, I will suffer a loss on this sale. Is it necessary to file Form T2062, "Notice by a Non-Resident of Canada Concerning the Disposition or Proposed Disposition of Taxable Canadian Property"?

Answer

Yes. Regardless of whether you realize a capital gain or loss, you must file Form T2062.

Question — Form T2062

I propose to sell a rental property. Do I file Form T2062 or Form T2062A?

Answer

If you have both a capital gain or loss and a recapture of depreciation previously claimed, you have to file both T2062 and a T2062A. The former is for capital property such as land and shares, while the latter is required for property that may be written off such as depreciable property and resource property. If you have to file both, they are filed together. The confusing part of this sale arises when you file your Canadian tax return to report the gain. You file one tax return to report the capital gain and a second tax return under s. 216 to report the net rental income up to the date of sale and the recapture of depreciation.

Question — Sale of Taxable Canadian Property
I filed Form T2062 relating to the sale of capital property in Canada. I remitted 25% of the gain. Do I have to file a Canadian tax return and do you foresee any benefit for doing so?

Answer
You must file a Canadian tax return and report the gain. This will likely create a refund of tax. Remember, you remitted tax equal to 25% of the capital gain, which was not reduced by selling costs and lower marginal tax rates.

TRANSFER OF TAXABLE CANADIAN PROPERTY

If you transfer a taxable Canadian property to anyone, even your spouse (don't forget this includes a common-law partner), you will have a disposition at fair market value and Canadian tax may be owing.

As well, if you die (perish the thought) and you leave your taxable Canadian property to your spouse, what would be a tax deferred event for a Canadian resident becomes a taxable event for your estate.

Question — Non-Resident Transfer of Property
I plan to gift Canadian real estate to my adult children. The property has a significant unrealized capital gain. Do I have to file Form T2062 and will I be subject to Canadian tax?

Answer
Transfers of property by any means will occur at fair market value. As a result you should file Form T2062, remit 25% of the gain and file a Canadian tax return.

Question — Non-Resident, Transfer to Spouse
I plan to gift my spouse a half interest in a Canadian cottage that has a large unrealized capital gain. Do I have to file Form T2062 and will I be taxable since it is a transfer to my spouse?

Answer
The tax deferred transfer between spouses only occurs while you are residents of Canada. Since you are a non-resident, one-half of the property will be deemed to be sold at its fair market value and a taxable gain will arise. You should file Form T2062, remit the required 25% tax and file a Canadian tax return.

Question — Death of a Joint Tenant
Both my spouse and I are non-residents of Canada. We hold a Canadian real estate property as joint tenants. What happens if one of us should die?

Answer
The death of a joint tenant will cause the deceased's estate to have a disposition of the joint tenant's interest in the property at its fair market value at the date of death. The Canadian tax rule that allows a tax-deferred transfer of property to a spouse does not apply to non-residents.

Question — Sale of Taxable Canadian Property
I left Canada on December 30, 2007. I reported and paid tax on a deemed position of shares of a private corporation. I plan to sell these shares in October 2016 for a value greater than at the date of departure. What filing requirements do I have? Can I claim foreign tax credit treatment against tax in my new homeland?

Answer
You were deemed to have sold and reacquired your property in 2007. Before you sell the shares determine if they are TCP under the new definition. If they are not TCP, no Canadian tax consequences

If the shares meet the new definition, you will be required to file Form T2062 and remit 25% of the gain that arose since the date of departure. You will file a tax return for 2016 and declare that gain.

You should be able to claim the tax paid in 2016 as a foreign tax in your new homeland. However, it is doubtful that you can use the tax paid on departure. This would be the case even if you had elected to defer the payment thereof. A portion of the foreign tax may reduce the tax you paid on departure.

Question — Sale of Taxable Canadian Property

I left Canada on October 3 (darn!) 1996 and was caught by the new rules. I reported the gain from shares of a private corporation in my departure tax return and elected to defer the payment of the tax. It is now May 2016 and I wish to gift these shares to my spouse. Will this action cause me to have to pay the deferred tax in 2016?

Answer

First determine if the shares are TCP under the March 4, 2010 amendments. If the shares are TCP the following will occur.

You were permitted to defer the payment of the tax from the deemed disposition until you actually dispose of the shares. A gift to your spouse is considered to be such a disposition. As well, since you are both non-residents, any gain that has accrued since October 3, 1996 will also be taxable. You should file Form T2062 before the transfer and remit the required 25% of the gain and file a tax return for 2016.

If the shares are no longer TCP, the deferred tax arising on your departure will be payable. There will be no Canadian tax on the gain that arose after you left Canada.

At time of revision, there were no instructions regarding how to pay the deferred tax. As a result, I suggest you write CRA a letter and send them a cheque for the deferred amount.

Question — Sale of Taxable Canadian Property, Loss

I left Canada on November 1, 2011. Since I left Canada, the value of my shares of a Canadian private company have declined in value. Do I have to sell my shares in 2017 so I can carry the loss back? Does the fact that I have received dividends after departure affect my loss?

Answer

The normal three-year carryback for capital losses is extended for shares caught by the emigration rules. Consequently, you won't have to sell the shares this year. However, the dividends you received will reduce the amount of the loss available for a carryback to 2011. The good news is that withholding tax on the dividends can be used to offset the 2011 tax on the deemed disposition (after reducing the gain for the loss carryback). As noted earlier, the change to the definition of TCP may alter the response to this question.

Question — Death and TCP
I am a non-resident of Canada. I currently own shares of a Canadian private corporation that meet the conditions for classification as TCP. What occurs if I die? Does the result change if I leave the shares to my non-resident spouse?

Answer
Since the shares are TCP, your death will cause the shares to be disposed at the fair market value immediately before your death. The same result will occur if you leave the shares to your spouse.

Question — Non-TCP Loss
When I left Canada, the deemed disposition of my non-TCP created a large capital gain. I now wish to sell this non-TCP property. Due to the world economic crisis, the sale will create a capital loss. What can I do to recover the Canadian tax I incurred when I left Canada?

Answer
If you sell the non-TCP at a loss while you are a non-resident, there is no Canadian tax relief. However, if you plan to return to Canada in the near future and can hold onto your non-TCP until you once again become a resident of Canada, you can elect to undo the deemed disposition that occurred when you left Canada. This will cause a refund of the tax you paid when you left Canada.

PRINCIPAL RESIDENCE

Exemption

The most common taxable Canadian property sold by expatriates is the family home. This event may give rise to a capital gain if the date of sale is several years after you cease to be a resident of Canada. As noted in Chapter 2, you cannot designate a property as your principal residence for any full year in which you are not a resident of Canada. Fortunately, you may designate it as a principal residence for those years when you were a resident (including the year of departure). The formula also gives you an extra year. For assistance in the determination of the portion of the gain eligible for the principal residence designation, refer to ITF-S1-F3-C2 and Form T2091 (see in Appendix).

The formula for calculating the portion of the capital gain arising on the sale of your former residence which will be excluded from your income is as follows:

Exempt portion Capital   X   1 + number of taxation years ending after 1971 for which the
of Capital Gain = Gain   property was your principal residence *and during which you were a resident of Canada*

                                    Number of taxation years ending after 1971 during which you owned the property.

As a result, if you sell your house after you cease to be a resident of Canada, a portion of the gain that would otherwise have been excluded from income if the house had been sold prior to departure from Canada could give rise to a Canadian tax liability under this formula, even if the value of the property did not increase after you left Canada. Accordingly, in considering the alternatives relating to your principal residence, it is necessary to take into account the increase in the value of the property up to the date of departure, the anticipated change in value while you are out of Canada, and your intentions with respect to the future use of the property.

Question — Sale of Former Principal Residence
We purchased our home in 2004 for $180,000 and became non-resident in 2013. We could not sell our home when we left Canada and leased it out. We elected not to have a change of use at that time. We plan to sell this property in June 2016 for $250,000. What will the tax consequences be?

Answer
You may designate your property as your principal residence for the years 2004 through 2013 (assuming you have not designated any other property). These years (10) plus 1 will form the numerator and the total years you have owned it will be the denominator (13).

Sales Proceeds	$ 250,000
Tax Cost	180,000
Capital Gain	70,000
Deduct: Principal residence exemption	
$\dfrac{10 + 1}{13}$ X $70,000	59,230
Capital Gain	$ 10,770
You will pay tax on a taxable capital gain of (50% of $10,770).	$ 5,385

As noted under "Transfer of Taxable Canadian Property", you must obtain a clearance certificate in respect of the disposition by advising the Canada Revenue Agency of the transaction (Form T2062) and remitting an amount equal to 25% of the gain. Failure to obtain the clearance certificate will cause the subsequent owner to be liable to pay an amount equal to 25% of the purchase price. The Canada Revenue Agency's administrative policy is not to require any amount to be remitted in respect of the portion of the gain that will be excluded from income under the formula set out above. In all cases, the purchaser will insist that a clearance certificate be obtained, in light of his or her potential liability.

Change of Use and Election Options

Should you decide to rent out the house rather than sell it, there are other rules to consider. Such an event will be considered a change of use and our tax rules will cause you to have a deemed disposition. The property is deemed to be disposed of at its fair market value. If this occurs after you leave Canada, the formula may cause you to incur a gain and a tax liability in Canada. You should file Form T2062 and a Canadian tax return to report this event. If you return to Canada and move into this property, there will be another change of use and tax may arise from any gain from a deemed disposition.

Both changes of use may be avoided by electing not to have a change of use when you commence renting the house. This election will cause the house to retain its classification as a personal use property. It does not permit you to designate it as a principal residence for these years during which you were a non-resident. If this election is made, you can move back into the property without a deemed disposition.

If no election is made when you commence renting your house, a taxable gain may arise because of the formula. Subsequently, if you cease leasing the property and move into it on your return to Canada, a change of use will occur. You may elect not to realize this change of use and defer any taxable gain until you actually sell the property. If there has been a substantial gain on the property to the date of non-residency, the expected additional increase in value while you are a non-resident will have to be considered. Under the formula, a portion of the gain accruing up to the date of non-residency which would otherwise be exempt from tax may become taxable if the annual rate of increase while you are a non-resident is less than the annual rate of increase during the years that you were resident in Canada and the property was your principal residence. Alternatively, if there has been a relatively small gain on the property up to the date of non-residency and it appears that the value of the property could increase significantly during the period of non-residence, by virtue of the election, a portion of the gain that otherwise may have been taxable will be exempt from tax.

If the sale of the house takes place while you are a non-resident, you should determine whether there are any provisions in a tax treaty between Canada and your country of residence that may help to relieve any foreign tax on the sale.

Question — Rescind Change of Use Election

When I left Canada several years ago, I rented my Canadian house to an arm's length party. I elected not to change use under s. 45(2). I now plan to sell the Canadian house and want to rescind my election not to change use. How do I accomplish this?

Answer

As noted, s. 45(2) is an election that one may make with respect to a property to not have a change of use occur when one stops living in a house and starts to rent it to someone. This election can be rescinded without penalty by filing a letter with Canada Revenue Agency (usually with your rental tax return) stating that you want to rescind the election. Once you notify the Canada Revenue Agency that you want to rescind the election, there is a deemed disposition and reacquisition of the house on the first day of the year you sent the notice to the Canada Revenue Agency. In other words, if you rescind the election in 2016, your deemed disposition and reacquisition at fair market value occurs on January 1, 2016.

A word of caution: your action may give rise to tax on a capital gain on the house. As well, it may prove more tax effective not to rescind the election. Do some "what if" scenarios before you rescind.

CAPITAL LOSSES

You may realize capital losses from the sale of taxable Canadian properties. These losses may be offset against capital gains arising from the sale of Taxable Canadian Property either in the year of the sale, the three preceding years or some future year. Capital losses may only be applied against capital gains. As well, if you realize a capital loss from the sale of an asset you use personally — such as your home — the loss will be deemed to be nil. This is just one more consideration to take into account when you change the use of a property. Remember, an election not to have a change of use may be made. For example, if you elect not to have a change of use when you commence renting out your principal residence, it will remain a personal use asset. If a loss arises on a subsequent sale, the loss will be deemed to be nil. Alternatively, if no election was made, and a subsequent loss is realized, it could be part terminal loss (100%

deductible) and a capital loss (50% deductible), and may be applied against capital gains from taxable Canadian properties.

Special provisions may apply to reduce the amount of capital loss and extend the application period for losses from TCPs you owned when you left Canada. See Chapter 2, "Emigration" — "Application of Losses from TCP".

Other Canadian Source Income

In addition to those mentioned above, a number of less common sources of Canadian income must be included in the computation of your income earned in Canada. These include:

   i)   negative amounts of Cumulative Canadian Development expenses;
   ii) recapture of capital cost allowance;
   iii) amounts pertaining to a Canadian resource property;
   iv) the gain on the disposition of an income interest in a trust resident in Canada;
   v)   the gain on the disposition of a right pertaining to a partnership; and
   vi) gains arising from the dispositions of certain life insurance policies in Canada.

Persons Deemed to be Employed in Canada

Under certain circumstances, you may be required to pay tax to Canada even though you are a non-resident earning income in another country. No, you are not misreading nor have I made a mistake. This situation can and does arise, much to the surprise of some non-residents.

You will be deemed to be employed in Canada if you are a non-resident and are one of the following:

   i)   a student in full-time attendance at a university or other educational institution in Canada that provides courses at a post-secondary level in Canada;
   ii) a student attending or a teacher teaching at a university, college or other educational institution outside Canada providing courses at a post-secondary school level, if, as either a student or a teacher, you had ceased in any previous year to be resident in Canada in the course of or after moving to attend or teach at that educational institution;
   iii) an individual who had ceased in any previous year to be resident in Canada in the course of or after moving to carry on research or any similar work under a grant received to enable you to carry on that research or work;
   iv) an individual who had ceased in any previous year to be resident in Canada and who in the current year received remuneration from an

office or employment paid directly or indirectly by a resident in Canada; or

v) a person who received an amount in the current year under a contract, if the amount was or will be deductible by a Canadian taxpayer and can reasonably be regarded as having been received as:

   a) consideration or partial consideration for entering into a contract of services to be performed in Canada (i.e. signing bonus) or for undertaking not to enter into such a contract with another party, or

   b) remuneration from the duties of an office or employment or compensation for services to be performed in Canada.

If you fit into one or more of the above categories, you will be required to include the aggregate of the following amounts in your Canadian income for the year:

1. Remuneration in the year from an office or employment paid directly or indirectly by a person resident in Canada.

Canadian tax rules allow you to exclude from this income any remuneration attributable to the duties of an office or employment performed by you anywhere outside Canada, provided that it is either:

   a) subject to an income or profits tax imposed by the government of a country other than Canada, or

   b) paid to you in connection with the selling of property, the negotiating of contracts or rendering of services for your employer or a foreign affiliate of your employer or any other person with whom your employer does not deal at arm's length, in the ordinary course of a business carried on by your employer or by the foreign affiliate or that other person.

For purposes of this exclusion, your remuneration is considered to be subject to an income or profits tax if it falls within the taxing jurisdiction of a country other than Canada. You will continue to qualify even if you pay no foreign income or profits tax by virtue of claiming personal allowances and any similar deductions to which a resident of that foreign country would normally be entitled. On the other hand, you will not qualify if you are not taxable in that country because of an exempting provision contained in a treaty between that country and Canada. Similarly, you will not qualify if you are exempted from taxation in that foreign jurisdiction under an agreement between foreign government authorities and you or your employer. Remuneration received by you for certain services will also be excluded. The services must be earned in connection with certain types of work performed in the ordinary course of a business carried on by the employer, its foreign affiliate or a person with whom the employer does not deal at arm's length. The phrase rendering of service would include the performance of work or duties in respect of an office or employment.

2. Canadian source scholarships, fellowships, bursaries and prizes net of allowable expenses.

3. The taxable portion of Canadian source research grants.
4. The taxable portion of registered educational savings plan payments that would have been taxable if you were a resident of Canada.

This rule caused problems and inequities for a number of Canadians who were otherwise non-resident but taxable because they could not meet the exempting provision. In particular, missionaries and employees of charitable or non-profit organizations were caught.

The foregoing rule was modified for 1998 and subsequent years to limit its application to situations where the individual is entitled to an exemption from tax on their income in the other country by virtue of a tax agreement or convention. This change permits those non-residents who work for non-profit or charitable organizations and others to not pay Canadian tax unless they are exempt from paying tax in the foreign country by virtue of a tax treaty.

Reduction of Canadian Tax

The reduction of overall tax in Canada is accomplished by a system of deductions from income and non-refundable tax credits. These are also available to non-residents, in some cases on a restricted basis.

Deductions

A number of the deductions permitted in arriving at your net income from Canadian sources are not related to a particular source of income. These include support payments, RRSP contributions to the extent they are otherwise deductible and Canadian exploration and development exploration expenses. You may also deduct specified portions of benefits arising from employee stock options which have been included in your income, amounts which are exempt from Canadian income because of a tax treaty or other government agreement, income from employment with a prescribed international organization and income from non-governmental organizations. Certain losses may be deductible from your Canadian income.

Support Payments

If you are a non-resident who has income which is taxable in Canada and you pay alimony or maintenance, you may deduct these payments from your Canadian income in the same manner you would have done had you been a resident in Canada. Unfortunately, all the same rules apply for these payments to be a deduction. They have to be periodic payments made pursuant to a written agreement.

In the 1996 Federal Budget, the government introduced major changes to rules determining how child support payments are calculated, the way they are taxed and the ability of custodial parents to collect amounts awarded. These changes were in response to growing pressure on the government to make reforms.

Under the new system, the amount of child support awarded to a custodial parent will be based on the income of the other parent and the number of children. Guidelines will be issued that judges and lawyers will use in setting child support awards. The government hopes that the guidelines will result in fairer and more consistent award payments. In addition, child support paid will no longer be taxable to the custodial parent or deductible for the payer. This is a major change from existing rules.

The changes are effective for all new court orders or written agreements entered into after May 1, 1997.

Existing agreements will continue under the old rules which means that child support will still be taxable to the custodial parent and deductible to the payer. Both parents can elect, if they desire, to have the new tax rules apply after May 1, 1997 to an existing order or agreement.

RRSP Contribution

Even though you are a non-resident, you may contribute to an RRSP and deduct the contributions from employment or business income and capital gains which are taxable in Canada. Keep in mind that the amount you can deduct will be governed by the income you earned in Canada in the preceding year. In other words, you will only be allowed to deduct an amount equal to the lesser of 18% of your earned income, which will include employment and business income (not capital gains) for the preceding year up to a maximum allowed (26,010 - 2017) in the current year. To the extent you do not have sufficient Canadian income to deduct the RRSP contribution, the excess may be carried forward to a subsequent year.

Earned income for RRSP purposes will be restricted to Canadian employment and business income. Income earned outside of Canada will not qualify as earned income for RRSP purposes unless it is taxed in Canada.

Question — Contribution to an RRSP
I have been a non-resident of Canada for two years and have an unused deduction limit of $9,000. Should I contribute to an RRSP?

Answer
You would only contribute to your RRSP if you anticipated earning Canadian income that could be reduced by claiming the RRSP contribution and it proves beneficial to do so.

Canadian Exploration and Development Expenses

If you invested in flow-through shares which give you Canadian Exploration Expenses and/or Canadian Development Expenses, you may deduct these from your Canadian income at rates of 100% and 30%, respectively.

Employee Stock Options

You may have exercised employee stock options received from a Canadian employer during the year. Generally speaking, you must include an amount equal to the excess of the fair market value of the share at the time you exercise the option over the option price in your income as a benefit. If you received the option at a time when the option price was equal to the fair market value of the stock, you will be permitted to deduct an amount equal to 50% of the benefit from your income.

If your employer was a Canadian Controlled Private Corporation with which you were dealing at arm's length, the benefit is only taxable when you sell the shares. If you have held the shares for more than two years, a benefit equal to the excess of the fair market value of the shares over the option price (at the time the option is exercised) will be included in your income when you sell the shares, and you may deduct 50% of that benefit from your Canadian income.

See "Employment Stock Option — TCP" in Chapter 2, "Emigration," for more details.

Amounts Exempt by Treaty or Agreement

Canada has concluded a number of tax treaties and agreements that contain provisions to exempt certain incomes from taxation in Canada. This subject will be covered in more detail in Chapter 4.

Losses

As a non-resident, you may deduct losses arising from employment, business and capital property if income realized from the same source would normally be included in your taxable income. Obviously, only losses realized in Canada will be eligible.

In order to be deductible, capital losses (which can only be applied against capital gains) must have been realized on the disposition of properties which are taxable Canadian properties. Remember, gains from capital properties which are not taxable Canadian properties (e.g. shares of a public corporation) are not taxable when realized by non-residents. As a result, losses arising from Canadian properties which are not taxable Canadian properties are not deductible when computing Canadian taxable income as a non-resident. Losses on TCPs may be used to reduce a TCP capital gain that occurred at departure. See previous discussion of this under "Disposition of Taxable Canadian Property (TCP)".

Tax Credits

The Canadian tax liability of a non-resident may be reduced by certain non-refundable tax credits. These include the charitable donation, disability, tuition fee, Canada Pension, Employment Insurance, medical and personal credits. Some of these may be claimed only if the income reported on your Canadian return represents more than 90% of your world income, a restriction I will refer to as the "90% income test".

More details are provided later on in this chapter under Tax Relief — Section 217 Election.

Donations

Non-residents can receive a tax credit for donations to Canadian charitable organizations and certain foreign charities recognized by the Canada Revenue Agency. The credit will be limited to donations equal to 75% of your net income and any excess may be carried forward for five years.

Gifts to the Canadian and provincial/territorial governments have been reduced to 75% of net income while those qualifying as cultural property are still deducted up to the full amount of your net income. Unused balances may be carried forward for up to five years. The charitable donation tax credit is not subject to the "90% income test".

Disability

You may claim the disability tax credit, which is not subject to the "90% income test". However, you must pass that test if you wish to claim the disability tax credit of a dependent.

Student Loan Interest and Tuition

You may claim the student loan interest and tuition for yourself without reference to the "90% income test".

Canada Pension and Employment Insurance

As a non-resident, you may claim Canada Pension Plan and Employment Insurance credits to the extent you made contributions during the year.

Medical

A medical expense credit may only be claimed by a non-resident if more than 90% of your world income is included in computing your Canadian taxable income.

If you meet the income test, you may claim the excess of medical expenses incurred both inside and outside Canada over the lesser of $2,208 (2015) and 3% of your net Canadian income.

Personal Non-Refundable Tax Credits

In order to claim the personal tax credit and unused personal tax credits of your spouse, you must meet the "90% income test".

NON-RESIDENT WITHHOLDING TAX

As a non-resident you will be subject to non-resident withholding tax when certain types of income are paid or credited to you. These incomes include management or administration fees or charges, non-arms length interest, estate or trust income, certain rents, royalties and similar payments, certain timber royalties, patronage dividends, certain pension payments, death benefits, retiring allowances, payments under a registered supplementary unemployment benefit plan, payments out of an RRSP, payments out of a RDSP, payments out of a DPSP, payments under an income-averaging annuity contract, annuity payments, payments out of an RRIF or LIF, payments out of a registered education savings plan and certain dividends.

The payer of the income is responsible for withholding and remitting a tax of 25% of the gross amount unless reduced by tax treaty. If the payer does not comply with these requirements, he or she is liable to pay the tax. This responsibility also extends to any agent who receives these amounts on your behalf. Penalties and interest may apply on late payments. Since the payer will not want to pay your tax, he or she will be careful to ensure that the appropriate amount of non-resident tax is withheld and remitted. If unpaid, you remain liable for the tax.

New Non-Resident Form

As always, our government is seeking ways to make everyone's task easier with respect to the appropriate rate of non-resident withholding tax if a tax treaty applies. This has been accomplished by creating three new tax forms — yes, three more. They are:

- NR301 — Declaration of Eligibility for Benefits Under a Tax Treaty for a Non-Resident Taxpayer
- NR302 — Declaration of Eligibility for Benefits Under a Tax Treaty for a Partnership with Non-Resident Partners
- NR303 — Declaration of Eligibility for Benefits Under a Tax Treaty for a Hybrid Entity

I have included NR301 in the Appendix. You can obtain copies of the other two forms by going to the CRA website. This form must be completed by you, the non-resident and sent to the payer, the person paying you dividends, pensions, etc. While your completion and sending this form is not mandatory, the instructions to the payer (on the record page of instructions) states the following:

Do not apply a reduced rate of withholding in the following circumstances:

- the non-resident taxpayer has not provided form NR301 or equivalent information and you are not sure if the reduced rate applies;
- the form is incomplete;
- a tax treaty is not in effect with the taxpayer's country of residence; or
- you have reason to believe that the information provided in this declaration is incorrect tor misleading.

It would appear that the payer may withhold 25% non-resident withholding tax and let you the non-resident payee request a refund by filing Form NR7 — Application for Refund of Part XIII Tax Withheld (See Appendix). You have two years to request a refund.

And yes, like all things in life there is an expiry date for your NR301:

Expiry date

For Part XIII tax withholding purposes, this declaration expires when there is a change in the taxpayer's eligibility for the declared treaty benefits or three years from the end of the calendar year in which the form is signed and dated, whichever is earlier. For example, if the taxpayer's mailing address has changed to a different country, the payer will ask the taxpayer for a revised form NR301.

And should you want more information regarding these forms you can go the CRA website:

For more information, see Part XIII Withholding Tax at www.cra-arc.gc.ca/tx/ nnrsdnts/pyr/prtxiii/wthhldng/menu-eng.html and select Beneficial Ownership or Rates for Part XIII Tax.

Now that's a website address. Good Luck!

Limitation of Treaty Benefits

Some tax treaties only reduce Canadian non-resident withholding tax on amounts that are remitted to the non-resident's country of residence. For example, the Canada-United Kingdom tax treaty contains such a rule.

The United Kingdom and a number of other tax jurisdictions have a tax system that if you are domicile somewhere else, you are only taxed on income earned or remitted to the United Kingdom.

So if you are not domicile in the United Kingdom and a Canadian pension is not remitted to the United Kingdom (remitted to the Channel Islands instead) you are likely not taxable on that income in the United Kingdom. If this is the case, you will be denied the low non-resident withholding tax rate on the pension and pay Canada 25%.

Management or Administration Fees or Charges

If a Canadian pays you management or administration fees, that individual should withhold and remit non-resident tax. No withholding tax is required if you are dealing at arm's length with the Canadian payer and it is your business to provide such services.

However, if your services are performed in Canada, the payer must withhold at least 15% of the fee unless you obtain an exemption from the Canadian tax authorities. This exemption may be granted pursuant to a tax treaty because you do not have a permanent establishment in Canada.

Interest

Effective January 1, 2008, interest paid to arm's length non-residents became exempt from non-resident withholding tax. This means that you can invest in Canadian mortgages, bonds, GICs, etc. for any period of time and no Canadian tax will be levied.

Interest paid to non-arm's length non-residents will still be subject to a 25% non-resident withhold unless the rate is reduced by a tax treaty.

Estate or Trust Income

An amount paid to you by a Canadian trust will be subject to non-resident withholding tax unless it represents a payment of capital or income classified as a taxable capital gain from a Canadian mutual fund trust.

> **Question — Taxation of Mutual Funds**
> *I am a non-resident of Canada. I hold several Canadian mutual funds. Please tell me if I pay any Canadian tax on income derived from these mutual funds.*
>
> **Answer**
> A Canadian mutual fund may earn income from various sources — interest, dividends and capital gains. Any allocation of dividends will be subject to a Canadian non-resident tax of 25% unless reduced by a tax treaty. Capital gains realized by the mutual fund and allocated to you or a gain realized on the redemption of your interest in the mutual fund is not subject to Canadian tax.

Rent

As mentioned previously, gross rental payments are subject to withholding tax unless you file Form NR6 and undertake to file a tax return by June 30 of the following year. Such an undertaking will permit your agent to withhold tax on the net rental (gross rent less rental expenses). The NR6 must be filed annually and before the year in question. (See Chapter 2, Rental)

Timber Royalties

Timber Royalties are similar to rent in that tax is withheld on the gross amount unless you file Form NR6.

Support Payments

These are no longer subject to non-resident withholding tax on the gross amount.

Pensions

Subject to several exceptions, pension payments are usually subject to non-resident withholding tax. For example, withholding tax does not apply to that portion of a pension that can be attributed to services rendered by you in a taxation year during which you were at no time resident in Canada and throughout which you were not employed, or only occasionally employed in Canada. Transfers between registered pension plans or to an RRSP, locked-in

RRSP, locked-in retirement accounts (LIRA), RRIF or LIF of which you are an annuitant are not subject to withholding tax.

Old Age Security and Canada Pension Plan payments along with other pension payments will be subject to withholding tax unless otherwise exempt.

Death Benefits

A death benefit is an amount paid by an employer to an employee's estate in recognition of the employee's service in an office or employment. Under Canadian tax law, death benefits up to $10,000 are tax free. As a result, only the excess over $10,000 will be subject to non-resident withholding tax.

Retiring Allowances

Retiring allowances are subject to non-resident withholding tax unless they relate to payment for services rendered in taxation years when you were not resident in Canada. As well, to the extent you can contribute a portion of the retiring allowances to an RRSP under which you are the annuitant, non-resident withholding tax will not apply. The amount of the retirement allowance you are able to transfer to your RRSP is restricted. Employment years after 1995 are not counted to determine how much you can transfer to an RRSP.

Registered Supplementary Unemployment Benefit Plan

Payments from Registered Supplementary Unemployment Benefit Plans will be subject to non-resident withholding tax.

Payments — RRSP, RRIF, RDSP, DPSP, LIF

Payments from an RRSP, RRIF, RDSP, DPSP or a LIF are subject to non-resident withholding tax unless the amounts are transferred to another plan or annuity of which you are the annuitant. Withholding tax levied on payments to you in a treaty country will vary depending on whether you receive a lump sum payment or a periodic payment. Periodic payment is a defined term and will have the meaning assigned to it by the treaty or the *Income Tax Convention Interpretation Act*. This area will be discussed more thoroughly in Chapter 4.

Locked-in RRSPs or locked-in retirement accounts (LIRAs) cannot be drawn out unless they are transferred to an LIF. The various provincial statutes regulate how much may be paid out of LIFs and when. Non-resident withholding tax is calculated on the same basis as an RRIF. Any payment equal to the greater of 10% of the fair market value of the LIF at the beginning of the year and two times the minimum annual amount is considered a periodic payment. Any payment in excess of the greater of the two amounts is considered a lump sum payment and subject to 25% unless reduced by treaty.

Question — RRSP Withdrawal
I wish to withdraw amounts from my RRSP on a visit to Canada. I understand that as long as the amount withdrawn does not exceed $5,000, the institution will only withhold 10%.

Answer
If you are a non-resident of Canada, the institution is required to withhold 25% of the payment from your RRSP regardless of how much it may be. You may apply to have a reduction of this tax by filing Form NR5. Alternatively, you may file a tax return within six months of the year in question and receive a refund if substantially all of your world income (more than 90%) is reported thereon.

You should ensure that the institution has your non-resident address so that it may withhold the appropriate non-resident withholding tax.

Registered Education Savings Plans

Contributions to an RESP are not deductible. As a result, the return of these amounts are not taxable. However, any payments which constitute income earned in the RESP will be subject to a 25% non-resident withholding tax unless reduced by a tax treaty.

TFSAs, ETFs, Income Trust, Segregated Funds et al.

As noted earlier, there are a number of investment vehicles that will have tax implications for the non-resident. The taxation of each of these will depend on Canadian tax law, country of residence tax law and treaty provisions (where applicable).

You can contact the issuer of the investment and determine what to expect. Notify each issuer with your date of departure, change address and country of residence. You may have income from these investments deposited in a bank account in Canada. This may cause you to receive a T5 income slip rather than a NR4 slip, which may move CRA to question where you are resident or assess you penalties for not paying the appropriate non-resident withholding tax.

Proper steps on departure will eliminate a lot of headaches when you are a non-resident.

TAX RELIEF

The tax laws of both Canada and your new country of residence may offer you relief from tax on various sources of income earned in Canada as a non-resident. These range from reduction in the withholding tax rate to complete exemption and may be contained in Canadian tax law, the foreign jurisdiction tax law and/ or the tax treaty between Canada and that country.

Canadian Tax Relief

As you have seen, certain types of income received from sources in Canada may be free of Canadian tax. However, for those which are not, you may benefit from elective provisions which allow you to file a Canadian tax return and file in a specific manner.

Reduction of Tax on Rental Income

As mentioned in Chapter 2, if you have rental property, your tenant must deduct and remit 25% of the gross rent to the Canadian tax authorities. However, you and your Canadian agent may file Form NR6 and undertake to file a Canadian tax return on or before June 30 of the following year and remit only 25% of the net rent (gross rent less related expenses).

If you fail to file an NR6, you have two years after the year in which the rental income was received to file a tax return on a net basis and obtain a refund of tax previously remitted on your behalf.

Section 217 Election

Section 217 of the Income Tax Act permits non-residents to pay a reduced rate of Canadian tax on certain sources of Canadian income by allowing them to claim full non-refundable personal tax credits. The sources of income include:
- old age security pension;
- Canada and Quebec pension plan benefits;
- superannuation or pension benefits;
- pooled registered pension plan payments;
- retiring allowances;
- death benefits;
- benefits under the Employment Insurance Act;
- Registered Supplementary Unemployment Plan benefits;
- RRSP payments;
- RRIF payments;

- LIF payments;
- DPSP payments;
- prescribed benefits under a government assistance plan;
- Retirement Compensation Arrangement payments; and
- Auto Pact benefits.

Only non-residents who include 90% of their world income in their Canadian return will qualify. Experience has shown that it is difficult to benefit from this provision.

If you do qualify to receive a benefit under this provision, you may file Form NR5 — "Application by a Non-resident of Canada for a Reduction in the Amount of Non-resident Tax Required to be Withheld" (see in Appendix). If this filing is accepted by the tax authorities, the individual or institution which pays you may reduce the amount of tax normally required to be withheld to that determined on the NR5. You must file a Canadian tax return by June 30 of the following year. Otherwise, the Canadian tax authorities will assess the tax that should have been remitted and advise the payer to commence withholding tax at the statutory rate.

Please note, that effective January 2011, only one Form NR5, Application by a Non-resident of Canada for a Reduction in the Amount of Non-Resident Tax Required to the Withheld, will have to be filed for every five tax years (if approved).

And if the NR5 is approved:

- It will always cover a period of five tax years;
- CRA will advise each relevant Canadian payer of the reduced rate of non-resident tax to deduct from the qualifying Canadian income for the entire approval period;
- The reduced rate of tax withholding will be maintained throughout the entire approval period, unless CRA has been informed of changes to the information provided on your most recently approved NR5 application;
- You are not required to file an amended Form NR5 to inform CRA of yearly increases to your pension payments due to a cost of living increase (indexing), because these changes are taken into account during the initial processing of your application; and
- You will have to file an income tax return under section 217 of the Income Tax Act (the Act) within six months from the end of each tax year covered by the approval period.

However, if you have a balance owing when you file your section 217 return on or before June 30th, you have to pay it **on or before April 30th**, to avoid interest charges.

Question — Section 217 Election
I understand that I can elect to reduce my Canadian tax on amounts received from my RRSP. How do I do this and when is it beneficial?

Answer
You may elect under s. 217 to file a Canadian tax return and pay tax as any other Canadian. In order for this election to be beneficial, you must be able to use your non-refundable personal tax credits. The ability to use these tax credits will depend on what portion your RRSP income is of your world income. I suggest that you do a pro-forma tax calculation to determine if s. 217 will give you a tax refund.

Question — Section 217 Election
I made a s. 217 election and ended up paying more tax than was withheld originally. Can I rescind this election?

Answer
Currently, there is no provision which will allow you to rescind this election. However, CRA is on record stating that if the election is not beneficial, they will not process it.

Question — Section 217, Tax Return
I wish to make a s. 217 election on RRSP income. I currently file a tax return for rental income. Can I include my RRSP income in this rental income return?

Answer
Section 217 requires that you file a separate Canadian tax return. While it does not include rental income, it may include Canadian employment income, business income and capital gains from the sale of taxable Canadian property.

Question — Section 217
I realized a capital gain from the sale of a taxable Canadian property and also received a payment from a Canadian RRSP. Would electing under Section 217 of the Income Tax Act be beneficial?

Answer
I suggest that you do a pro-forma tax return. Chances are it will not prove beneficial. It depends a great deal on how large your taxable capital gain and RRSP payment are.

As noted, CRA will not process a Section 217 election unless it is beneficial to you.

Tax Treaties

Canada has concluded a number of tax treaties with other countries. Various provisions may give you reduced Canadian withholding tax, complete exemption from Canadian tax, the ability to claim tax credits or some combination of these. I shall deal with these in Chapter 4.

Foreign Tax Relief

Your new home country may tax you on income received from Canada. If it does, its laws may contain provisions that will allow you to claim the Canadian tax as a foreign tax credit or deduction. In addition, if the country has a tax treaty with Canada, certain Canadian and possibly foreign taxes will be reduced or even eliminated. As a new resident of any country, you should review its tax filing requirements to ensure that you benefit from all relieving provisions contained in the domestic law and any tax treaty.

Estate Tax

Canada, believe it or not, is one of the few countries that does not levy an estate tax on death. Since this may be relevant in your new homeland, you should seek professional assistance to determine if there is any way to reduce or eliminate the incidence of this tax should you die. Estate tax usually applies to assets located in the jurisdiction or to world assets of persons domiciled in the country. It is important to understand these rules and take the appropriate steps to minimize your exposure.

Offshore Trusts

Now that you are non-resident of Canada, you may think that you need an offshore trust. You have read that offshore trusts can save you a pile of money with tax savings. That was the case in the past but no more. The Canadian Federal government finally enacted (June 26, 2013) a complex piece of legislation that deals with non-resident trusts. Even though the changes to non-resident trusts were enacted on June 26, 2013, they are effective from January 1, 2007. For more information regarding the current status a non-resident trusts please see Offshore Trusts in Chapter 5.

Non-Resident — RRSP Planning

As a non-resident, you may hear stories of other non-residents crashing their RRSPs. This action allows them to remove the RRSP funds at a relatively low rate of Canadian tax — 25% unless reduced by treaty. A significant savings compared to up to 50% if you took it out while you were resident in Canada. However, I suggest that you seriously consider the consequence of this action before collapsing your RRSP.

First of all, you will be required to pay a Canadian non-resident withholding tax of up to 25% unless reduced by a tax treaty. Currently, very few treaties have a lower non-resident tax. As a result, you have only 75 cents on the dollar left to invest.

Secondly, the funds will now be unsheltered. While this will not be relevant for most tax jurisdictions, it causes significant problems if you return to Canada. While the money was in the RRSP, any income earned was sheltered from tax. Once the funds are removed, the investment income will be subject to taxation.

A better strategy involves a longer process of removing funds. For example, if a non-resident lives in a tax treaty country, payments from a RRIF may be treated as periodic payments and be subject to a lower non-resident withholding tax — 15% to 0%. In fact, Canada permits payments up to the greater of 10% of the fair market value of the RRIF at the beginning of the year or two times the minimum annual amount to be paid out as periodic payments.

If you decide to return to Canada and do not require amounts from your RRIF and you are under 71 years of age, you may transfer the remaining funds in your RRIF back to your RRSP. This will permit you to continue to defer tax on the income until you turn 71.

In summary, give serious consideration to the consequences caused by collapsing your RRSP while a non-resident.

Non-Resident — Locked-in RRSP Planning

Generally speaking, the commutation of locked-in accounts has not been permitted in Canada. These include locked-in RRSPS, Locked-in Retirement Accounts (LIRAs) and Life Income Funds (LIFs). However, various provinces/territories have relaxed their rules that restricted commutation. If you have a locked-in RRSP, LIRA or LIF and you want to cash it in, check with the provincial/territorial authority that makes the rules. The provincial/territorial authority will commute your locked-in RRSP if you file an NR73 *Determination of Residency Status* with the Canada Revenue Agency and receive its blessing that you have in fact ceased to be a resident of Canada.

Our comments regarding commutation of your locked-in account are the same as those noted in Non-Resident — RRSP Planning.

Please consider all the results of your action before you proceed.

Non-Resident — RCA Planning

Retirement Compensation Arrangements (RCA) established in Canada provides no saving or deferral for Canadian residents. However, if a Canadian had an RCA before becoming a non-resident he may receive payments once he established his non-resident status. From a Canadian point of view, any payment to a non-resident will be subject to a 25% non-resident withholding tax, unless it is reduced by a tax treaty. As a result, payments which could be subject to tax rates of up to 50% can be received by a non-resident and only be subject to a 25% tax rate.

As with most planning of this nature, check the tax rules of your new homeland.

4

Tax Treaties

OVERVIEW

Canada has entered into a number of bilateral tax agreements. The primary purpose of these treaties is to reduce the incidence of double taxation. For example, if you are living outside Canada, you could be subject to taxation in Canada on Canadian business income and taxed again on that same income in your country of residence. In the absence of a tax treaty, you would have to rely on the tax laws of that country to relieve you from double taxation. If you reside in a country that has a tax treaty with Canada, the possibility of double taxation is reduced by various treaty provisions which either exempt the income from taxation in one of the countries or to permit you to claim a tax credit and/or tax deduction in your country of residence equal to the tax you paid in Canada.

As noted in Chapter 3, various types of income which originate in Canada are subject to a non-resident withholding tax of 25%. A treaty may either reduce or eliminate this tax. Relief may be provided by reference to a specific lower rate of tax or by allowing only one jurisdiction to tax the income.

Most treaties are based on a model treaty and thus bear a resemblance to one another. However, you should not assume they are exactly the same. You should undertake a careful review of the relevant treaty, together with a thorough examination of the tax laws in your prospective country of residence, before you emigrate. While countries with treaties have tax systems, these systems are not identical to Canada's. Individual countries may tax different sources of income in different ways or may exempt them entirely. Your review should be conducted with a tax specialist familiar with the tax system of your new country. This approach may result in beneficial tax planning prior to entering your new country or a complete reconsideration of where you want to settle. I have found a review of the various booklets prepared by international tax services to be helpful but not as thorough as dealing with a tax specialist living and working in that country. While obtaining the advice of such a tax specialist may cost you a few dollars, it may prove to be money well spent.

Certain words and phrases in a treaty may not be given sufficient description in the treaty to allow you to appreciate their full meaning. If you encounter this problem, you may refer to domestic law for its definition. As well, Canada has an *Income Tax Conventions Interpretation Act* to facilitate your task. For example, this Act outlines what Canada will consider to be a "periodic pension payment" for purposes of a reduced withholding tax rate.

Question — Periodic RRSP Payments
I plan to withdraw $10,000 each year from my RRSP. Will this be considered a periodic payment eligible for a lower rate of non-resident withholding tax under a treaty?

Answer
Whether this payment is eligible for a lower rate of non-resident withholding will depend on the treaty. In most situations, such a payment will be considered to be a lump sum payment subject to 25% non-resident withholding tax.

If the tax treaty is unclear, you should refer to the *Income Tax Conventions Interpretation Act* which states that a "periodic pension payment" does not include a payment before maturity, or a payment in full or partial commutation of the retirement income, under a registered retirement savings plan.

DUAL RESIDENCE STATUS

The current international employment market could create a situation where you may be considered a resident of both Canada and a foreign country for income tax purposes. If you find yourself in this position, determine whether Canada and the foreign country have concluded a bilateral tax treaty. If a tax treaty exists, refer to Article 4 thereof to ascertain whether any of the so called tie-breaker rules apply.

Tie-Breaker Rules

Where you are a resident of both Canada and a tax treaty country, the tax treaty will usually determine your tax status on the following basis:
1. You shall be deemed to be a resident of the country in which you have a permanent home available to you.
2. If you have a permanent home available in both Canada and the foreign country, you shall be deemed to be a resident of the country with which your personal and economic relations are closer. This is commonly referred to as your centre of vital interests.
3. If the country in which you have your centre of vital interests cannot be determined, or if you have no permanent home available to you in either

country, you shall be deemed to be a resident of the country in which you have an habitual abode.

4. If you have an habitual abode in both countries or in neither of them, you shall be deemed to be a resident of the country of which you are a national (citizen).

If you are a national of both countries or of neither of them, the competent authorities of Canada and the foreign country will usually settle the question of residency by mutual agreement.

Once you have established your status under the treaty, you can resolve the problem of double taxation by asking the relevant tax authority (Canadian or foreign) to confirm that you are exempt under the tax treaty. If necessary, you may request that the tax authority authorize your employer to cease withholding income tax from your pay cheque in accordance with your status under the treaty. For example, if you are working and residing in Malaysia but considered resident in both Canada and Malaysia, you would contact the Canadian tax authorities to rule on your exempt status. If you were working for a Canadian company, you would request the Canada Revenue Agency to authorize your employer not to withhold Canadian employee tax.

The fact that you are considered resident of a foreign jurisdiction for income tax purposes does not relieve you of your filing obligations in Canada. Technically, you must file a Canadian tax return, report your world income therein, claim a deduction thereof on the "additional deduction" line and claim that the tax treaty exempts you from Canadian tax.

If you have been paying tax in Canada and subsequently discover that you were exempt from Canadian tax by reason of a tax treaty, you may write to your district tax office and request an adjustment to reflect your exempt status. For the current year, you may file an income tax return, report your income, claim a deduction on the "additional deduction" line and claim a refund of taxes.

Tie-Breaker Rules Application

Several years ago, I assisted a client to argue that he was a deemed resident of Indonesia using the tie-breaker rules, current Canadian tax laws and a relevant 2005 tax case — Pamela Allchin.[1]

The client and his family moved to Indonesia in 1997 to work for an international company. He continued to work there until 2007. His spouse and children returned to Canada in 2003 and stayed here due to political unrest in Indonesia.

---

[1] *Allchin v. R.*, 2005 CarswellNat 6752, 2005 CarswellNat 911, 2005 D.T.C. 603, 2005 CCI 711, [2005] 2 C.T.C. 2701, 2005 TCC 711 (T.C.C. [General Procedure]).

My client filed Indonesian tax returns as a resident of Indonesia. He started to file Canadian tax returns when his spouse and children returned and claimed an exemption from Canadian tax under other deductions — treaty exemption.

CRA questioned his claim for the exemption since he had established significant ties in Canada — spouse, children and house in Canada. They argued that he was a resident of Canada and should pay tax on his world income and claim a foreign tax credit for tax paid in Indonesia.

The key issue in this case was whether one spouse could be a resident of Indonesia while the other spouse was a resident of Canada. A review of CRA's tax bulletins would fail to support this position. In fact, my initial discussion with CRA was quite one sided.

There were several tax cases which support the argument that one spouse can be a resident of one country while the other spouse is a resident of another country. The case I presented to the CRA involved a lady — Pamela Allchin who lived and worked in the U.S. while her spouse lived in Canada. While success was not realized initially, a higher court found that Pamela Allchin was a deemed resident of the U.S. under the Canada-U.S. Tax Convention tie-breakers rules regardless of the fact that her spouse lived in Canada.

The facts of her tax case were very similar to my client's situation. As a result, CRA had little recourse but to concur that my client was a deemed resident of Indonesia under the Canada-Indonesia Treaty.

In summary, tax treaties can be very useful to determine where you should be taxed. Second, the tax treaty will overrule domestic tax rules. Lastly, do not give into CRA without pursuing all the arguments and tax cases available to support your position.

Dual residency used to create some interesting results. Even though you paid tax to the foreign jurisdiction, you would still be considered a resident of Canada. Therefore, you could continue to enjoy many of the tax benefits allowed to Canadian residents.

With the incidence of deemed dispositions on emigration, a popular planning strategy was to try and retain residency in Canada while achieving residency status for tax purposes in another country. Assuming the other country had lower tax rates, the dual resident received the benefit of lower taxes without having to suffer the deemed disposition rules. As well, Canadians were able to retain all of the tax advantages of a resident while being taxed as a non-resident including tax deferred transfers between spouses and the ability to designate your home as your principal residence. Our tax authorities took exception to this status and introduced a rule which will cause you to be a non-resident of Canada if you are a dual resident and considered resident in the other country under the tie-breaker rules in the treaty. This will cause you to have a deemed disposition and you will lose all the tax benefits (?) enjoyed by Canadian residents. Yes, believe it or not, you do enjoy tax advantages as a resident of Canada.

These provisions apply to individuals who could qualify as a dual resident after February 24, 1998. If you were one of the lucky ones who achieved dual resident status prior to February 25, 1998, you can retain that status until you lose it. In other words, plan your future more carefully. You don't want to lose all those Canadian tax benefits and suffer deemed dispositions.

A word of caution. The fact that you reside in a country that has a tax treaty with Canada does not always mean you can establish dual residence status. First of all, most treaties require that you be taxable in both Canada and the other country. Depending on the nature of your employment or business, you may find that you are not taxable on that income in the foreign jurisdiction.

Some treaty provisions may not apply to certain individuals. For example, the treaty between Canada and the U.K. may not apply to income not remitted and taxed in the hands of an individual who is resident but not domiciled in the U.K. You should therefore not assume that you have either dual status or even protection under a particular treaty without a thorough review of its provisions.

A recent Tax Court of Canada case involving Conrad Black looked at whether he was taxable in Canada or the UK. He was resident in both countries at the same time and Canada-UK tax treaty deemed him to be a resident of the UK under the tie breaker rules. Unfortunately for Mr. Black, the Canadian Tax Court ruled against him and allowed CRA to tax him. The Federal Court of Appeal denied Mr. Black's appeal in late 2014. A further attempt to receive justice from the Supreme Court of Canada was denied in April 2015. The reasons for the failure of success involved the rules that were introduced to deny you dual residence status. It is all quite complicated but might make good reading if anyone cares.[2]

Question — Treaty
I have been employed by a foreign company in a country that has a tax treaty with Canada. I pay tax in the foreign country. Will I be subject to tax in Canada?

Answer
You must examine the tax treaty provisions to determine if you will be taxable in Canada. If you are considered to be resident and subject to tax in both countries, you should review Article 4 and the tie-breaker rule to determine where you are taxable.

---

[2]   *Black v. R.*, 2014 FCA 275, 2014 CarswellNat 4995, 2015 D.T.C. 5024 (F.C.A.), leave to appeal refused 2015 CarswellNat 1274, 2015 CarswellNat 1275 (S.C.C.).

Question — Treaty, Factual Residence
I have lived and worked in Brazil as a missionary for five years. The Canada Revenue Agency feels that I am a factual resident of Canada and makes me file a Canadian tax return. The Brazil tax authorities also consider me to be resident and subject to their tax rules. What can I do?

Answer
You should review the Canada-Brazil tax treaty to determine where you are considered resident for tax purposes. If you are considered to be a resident of Brazil, you may claim an exemption from Canadian tax in your Canadian tax return.

Question — Treaty, Factual Residence
I am in the process of updating my book Canadians Resident Abroad. I have a section on treaties. My review of the Kuwait and UAE treaties indicates that unless you are a national of these countries, the treaties have no application. In other words, if a Canadian was challenged on his residency status he could not use the tie breaker rules to determine his residency for tax purposes. Is this a correct interpretation?

Secondly, if the treaty does not apply, should CRA require a 25% non-resident withholding tax on various payments — RRIF, pensions, dividends, etc?

Answer
Thank you for your email inquiry regarding Canada's tax treaties with Kuwait and the UAE.

The ordinary rule in most tax treaties is that a "resident" is a person that is "liable to tax" in the Contracting State in question. This rule is found in paragraph 1 of Article 4 of the OECD Model Tax Convention, and in virtually all of Canada's tax treaties. In the case of Kuwait and the UAE, they do not impose personal income tax, thus the ordinary "liable to tax" test has no application. In addition, it was Kuwait and UAE who proposed to have nationality used in lieu of the ordinary rule. In both treaties, this alternative test only applies in the case of Kuwait and the UAE, whereas in the case of Canada, it is the regular "liable to tax" test that applies.

Regarding your first question, payments made to (or income received by) a Canadian resident from Kuwait or the UAE would benefit from the respective tax treaties. However, any payments made to (or income received by) someone living in Kuwait or the UAE would only benefit from the tax treaties if the recipient is a national of that country.

Regarding your second question, you are correct: where an amount is paid or credited from Canada to an individual residing in Kuwait or the UAE, and that individual is not a national of those States, then the relevant tax treaty does not apply to reduce the 25% withholding rate that is imposed under Canada's *Income Tax Act*.

Department of Finance Canada | Ministère des Finances Canada
March 12, 2009

TYPES OF INCOME

Business Income

Canada will tax a non-resident who earns income from carrying on a business in Canada. However, Article 7 of a tax treaty usually provides that as a non-resident you will pay tax in Canada only if you have a permanent establishment in Canada. Article 5 contains the various conditions used to determine whether you have a permanent establishment in Canada. In general terms, there must be a fixed place of business through which the business of an enterprise is wholly or partly carried on. The Article goes on to list a number of situations that will be considered to be permanent establishments:

- a place of management;
- a branch;
- an office;
- a factory;
- a workshop;
- a mine, an oil or gas well or any other place of extraction of natural resources;
- a building or construction site if it lasts more than 12 months; and
- a dependent agent with the authority to contract on your behalf in Canada.

Treaties also contain a list of situations which will not cause you to have a permanent establishment in Canada. I recommend that you review the particular treaty to determine whether or not you have a permanent establishment in Canada. If you have a permanent establishment in Canada, then you will pay tax on that portion of your business income that relates to the Canadian operation in a manner outlined in Chapter 3. Article 7 usually permits your country of residence to tax this income but allows you to claim tax credits or provides some other form of tax relief to eliminate or reduce double taxation.

Rental Income

Article 6 provides for the tax treatment of income from immovable property — real estate, farmland and forests. Under most treaties such income is subject to Canadian non-resident withholding tax of 25% on the gross amount. As noted in Chapter 3, you may reduce the total tax to 25% of the net rental income by engaging a Canadian agent who jointly agrees with you (on Form NR6) to file a Canadian income tax return within six months after the end of the year in which the income is received.

Article 6 does not preclude your country of residence from taxing this income. However, most treaties provide relief from double taxation through tax credits, deductions or exemptions in your country of residence.

Dividends

Article 10 provides that dividends paid to you by a Canadian company will be subject to Canadian non-resident withholding tax. As noted in Chapter 3, the usual non-resident tax is 25% of the gross dividend. This rate is usually reduced by treaty to 15% or 5% depending on which foreign country you live in, how you hold your investment and how much of the Canadian corporation you own. This article usually permits your country of residence to tax the dividend but provides for relief from double taxation.

Interest

Article 11 provides that interest paid to you by a Canadian may be subject to Canadian tax. As noted in Chapter 3, the usual non-resident tax is 25% of the interest. Where there is a treaty, this rate is usually reduced to 15% or 10%. This article usually permits your country of residence to tax the interest but provides relief from double taxation.

(As noted previously, effective January 1, 2008, arm's length interest paid or credited to non-residents of Canada is exempt from Canadian non-resident withholding tax.)

Royalties

Article 12 provides that royalties paid to you by a Canadian may be subject to Canadian tax. As with most other sources of Canadian income, the usual tax rate of 25% is reduced by treaty to either 15% or 10%. This Article usually permits your country of residence to tax the royalties but provides for relief from double taxation through tax credits or exemptions.

Capital Gains

Article 13 deals with the taxation of capital gains. This article varies from treaty to treaty but usually allows Canada to tax capital gains arising from real property and shares of corporations and interests in partnerships whose value is primarily due from real property. Gains arising from all other property will be left to the foreign country to tax unless the treaty gives Canada the right to tax any gains of a former resident for a period of up to five to ten years after emigration. If this right is specified, it will apply to taxable Canadian property (see Chapter 2). Article 13 usually permits the country of residence to tax the gain as well. As with other sources of income, the treaty will usually provide relief from double taxation in the form of tax credits or exemptions.

Since the taxation of capital gains varies from treaty to treaty, it is important to review the particular treaty to ascertain how it will affect you.

As noted in Chapter 2 — Emigration — Reduction of Canadian Tax, our government has amended a number of tax agreements with other countries to eliminate double taxation that may arise from capital gains. You will recall that certain properties were deemed to be disposed when you left Canada. Since this is a Canadian tax event, your new homeland may look to the original cost of your property to assess tax should you decide to sell it while living outside of Canada. The amendment to the various treaties will allow you to elect to have your new homeland recognize the deemed sale caused by Canada and allow the fair market value of the asset when you left Canada to be your tax cost in your new homeland.

Generally speaking, any treaty that has been concluded or amended since 1997 should include this relief provision. It is contained in Article 13. For example, the following is from the Canada-United States Convention.

Capital Gains
Article 13 — Alienation of Property

7. Where at any time an individual is treated for the purposes of taxation by a Contracting State as having alienated a property and is taxed in that State by reason thereof, the individual may elect to be treated for the purposes of taxation in the other Contracting State, in the year that includes that time and all subsequent years, as if the individual had, immediately before that time, sold and repurchased the property for an amount equal to its fair market value at that time.

Independent Personal Services (Self-Employed)

Article 14 has been deleted from the OECD model treaty and other treaties. It was felt that the rules contained in Articles 5 and 7 were sufficient to cover self-employed individuals.

Income From Employment

Article 15 provides the rules for the taxation of salaries, wages and similar remuneration. This provision varies from treaty to treaty but taxation in Canada may depend on the amount of money you earned in Canada, how long you remained in Canada to earn the income or who deducted the wage expense. You should review this provision closely to determine how you may be taxed in Canada on such income. The usual type of relief from double taxation will be available.

Pensions

The Article that deals with pension income varies from treaty to treaty. Some treaties permit Canada to levy a non-resident tax thereon but allow you to reduce that tax to 15% or to eliminate it completely depending on your total pension income. This Article will also cover periodic and lump sum payments from your RRSPs, LIFs and RRIFs. Of all the Articles, this may prove to be the most important one, particularly for those of you who have retired. The usual type of relief from double taxation will be available.

Question — Periodic RRIF Payments
I plan to convert my RRSP to an RRIF and draw out more than the minimum amount each year. I currently live in a treaty country. Will my RRIF payments be subject to the 25% non-resident withholding tax?

Answer
The amount of non-resident withholding tax will depend on the tax treaty and the amount paid out. If the tax treaty is silent on the tax treatment of amounts paid to you from your RRIF, the *Income Tax Conventions Interpretation Act* states that a periodic pension payment does not include a payment in excess of the greater of 10% of the fair market value of the plan at the beginning of the year and twice the amount of the minimum payment you are required to receive each year. If the payment is more than the greater of the 10% rule and twice the minimum, the excess will be subject to the 25% non-resident withholding tax (unless reduced by a tax treaty).

Question
I am a former Canadian resident and citizen. I am currently a resident of Australia but plan to return to Canada upon retirement here in Australia. My question relates to my Australian pension that I can receive tax free once I turn 60 years of age. Will the pension remain tax free if I return to Canada?

Answer
Unfortunately, I have not been able to find a provision in either the Canada-Australian tax treaty or our Canadian Tax Act (CTA) that would exempt payments received by a Canadian resident from an Australian Superannuation fund from Canadian tax. The only portion of the payment that might be tax free would be the portion that could be identified as coming from voluntary non-deductible contributions. This may be argued to be a return of capital.

The fact that the payment is taxable to recipients under age 60 but not for those 60 years of age and older appears to be a tax rule contained in the Australian tax laws. In other words, the payments are income up to the point in time that one reaches age 60 then not taxable.

You note that tax law and the convention refer to the nature of income remaining the same in the receiving state as the payor state. I accept that point but the payment is a pension in Australia and also in Canada. The only difference is that Canada taxes it. The taxation of the payment is caused by a lack of exemption in the tax convention and Canadian tax law.

> This conclusion is supported by the Tax Interpretation 2011-0409121E5E-Australian Pension Fund I forwarded to you in an earlier response:
>
> *You noted that, at the time your client made contributions to the APSF, a flat rate of tax applied to the contributions. As a result of a change in Australian tax policy, no amount of tax is currently paid in respect of payments from the APSF. However, there is no provision the Act (CTA) or the treaty which would exempt from Canadian income tax that portion of the payment that would have been exempt from Australian income tax.*
>
> Our tax authorities are the ones who will administer our tax laws. As you can see from the above, they also feel that the payments would be taxable.

Miscellaneous

All treaties contain provisions dealing with director's fees, artists, government services, students, estates, trusts and other income. The provision dealing with "other income" usually provides that if any item of income is not mentioned in any other article, it will be taxable only in the country of residence.

DOUBLE TAXATION

As noted above, all treaties contain provisions to eliminate or reduce double taxation. These include the ability to use Canadian tax paid on a particular source of income to reduce the tax levied by your country of residence or the complete exemption of that income from tax in that jurisdiction.

SPECIAL PROVISIONS

Most treaties contain a number of other provisions that deal with non-discrimination, mutual agreement procedures, exchange of information and treatment of diplomatic agents and consular officers. If you have to review a treaty, make certain that you obtain the most recent version. As well, once you have examined a particular article in the treaty, determine if any additional provisions have been added at the end. This section is generally referred to as the Protocol. The Protocol may deal with a subject in greater detail than does the Article in the original treaty. And last but not least, look to see if the treaty and/or protocol has been ratified and when the various provisions thereof apply.

It is beyond the scope of this book to provide you with a copy of every treaty. For more information, you may request copies of the following material from the International Taxation Office — Information Circular IC 75-6R2, "Required Withholding From Amounts Paid to Non-Residents Providing

Services In Canada", Information Circular IC 76-12R6, "Applicable Rate of Part XIII Tax on Amounts Paid or Credited to Persons in countries with which Canada has a tax convention and Information Circular IC 77-16R4, "Non-resident Income Tax". Please refer to our schedule of withholding tax rates for the current status of the relevant tax treaty. (The above Information Circulars are available from the Canada Revenue Agency's web site: www.cra-arc.gc.ca).

You may also go to Department of Finance Canada web site www.fin.gc.ca/treaties-conventions/treatystatus for actual copies of the treaties or conventions.

Question — Refund of Non-resident Tax
If Canadian non-resident withholding tax was withheld at 25% when it should have been 15% under the Canada-Australian tax treaty, can I receive a refund of the excess?

Answer
You may file Form NR7-R, "Application For Refund of Non-Resident Tax" (see in Appendix). This must be done within two years of the year in which you received the payment.

Question — 25% Withholding Tax, Non-domiciled/resident
I am a non-domiciled/resident of the United Kingdom. I earn dividends from a Canadian public corporation which are paid to an account in Jersey. The public company withholds 25% rather than 15%. Why?

Answer
A number of countries recognize the distinction between someone who is resident but not domicile. Under this tax regime, the country will tax a domicile/resident on his/her world income. However, if the individual is only resident and not domicile, the country only taxes him/her on income earned in the country or remitted to the country.

The tax treaty between Canada and the United Kingdom recognizes this tax treatment and reflects it in the tax treaty. In other words, if income (dividends) is paid from Canada to the Channel Islands for a resident/non-domicile of the United Kingdom, the payer should withhold 25% tax rather than 15%.

Treaty Withholding Tax Rates[*]

Current as at: June 1, 2016[**]

Treaty Country	Interest[3]	Dividends[4]	Royalties	Pensions/ Annuities
Algeria	15	15	0/15	15/25
Argentina	12.5	10/15	3/5/10/15	15/25
Armenia	10	5/15	10	15/25
Australia[1]	10	5/15	10	15/25
Austria	10	5/15	0/10	25
Azerbaijan	10	10/15	5/10	25
Bangladesh	15	15	10	15/25
Barbados[5]	15	15	0/10	15/25
Belgium[7]	10	5/15	0/10	25
Bolivia		25% imposed under ITA		
Brazil	15	15/25	15/25	25
Bulgaria[5]	10	10/15	0/10	10/15/25
Cameroon	15	15	15	25
Chile[5]	15	10/15	15	15/25
China[1]	10	10/15	10	25
Colombia[5]	10	5/15	10	15/25
Costa Ricia		25% imposed under ITA		
Croatia	10	5/15	10	10/15
Cuba		25% imposed under ITA		
Cyprus	15	15	0/10	15/25
Czech Republic	10	5/15	10	15/25
Denmark	10	5/15	0/10	25

Treaty Country	Interest[3]	Dividends[4]	Royalties	Pensions/ Annuities
Dominican Republic	18	18	0/18	18/25
Ecuador[5]	15	5/15	10/15	15/25
Egypt	15	15	15	25
Estonia[5]	10	5/15	10	10/15/25
Finland	10	5/15	0/10	15/20/25
France	10	5/15	0/10	25
Gabon	10	15	10	25
Germany	10	5/15	0/10	15/25
Greece	10	5/15	10	15/25
Guyana	15	15	10	25
Hong Kong	0/10	5/15	10	25
Hungary	10	5/15	0/10	10/15/25
Iceland	10	5/15	0/10	15/25
India	15	15/25	10/15/20	25
Indonesia	10	10/15	10	15/25
Ireland	10	5/15	0/10	0/15/25
Israel[1]	15	15	0/15	15/25
Italy	10	5/15	0/5/10	15/25
Ivory Coast	15	15	10	15/25
Jamaica	15	15	10	15/25
Japan	10	5/15	10	25
Jordan	10	10/15	10	25
Kazakhstan[5]	10	5/15	10	15/25
Kenya	15	15/25	15	15/25
Korea, Republic of	10	5/15	10	10/15/25
Kuwait	10	5/15	10	15/25

Treaty Country	Interest[3]	Dividends[4]	Royalties	Pensions/ Annuities
Kyrgyzstan	15	15	0/10	15/25
Latvia[5]	10	5/15	10	10/15/25
Lebanon[6]	[10]	[5/15]	[5/10]	[15/25]
Lithuania[5]	10	5/15	10	10/15/25
Luxembourg	10	5/15	0/10	25
Madagascar[1]		25% imposed under ITA		
Malaysia[1]	15	15	15	15/25
Malta	15	15	0/10	15/25
Mexico	10	5/15	0/10	15/25
Moldova	10	5/15	10	15/25
Mongolia	10	5/15	5/10	15/25
Morocco	15	15	5/10	25
Namibia[6]	[10]	[5/15]	[0/10]	[0/15]
Netherlands[1]	10	5/15	0/10	15/25
New Zealand	10	5/15	5/10	15/25
Nigeria	12.5	12.5/15	12.5	25
Norway	10	5/15	0/10	15/25
Oman	10	5/15	0/10	15/25
Pakistan	15	15	0/15	25
Papua New Guinea	10	15	10	15/25
Peru[5]	15	10/15	15	15/25
Philippines	15	15	10	25
Poland	10	5/15	0/5/10	15/25
Portugal	10	10/15	10	15/25
Romania	10	5/15	5/10	15/25
Russian	10	10/15	0/10	25

Treaty Country	Interest[3]	Dividends[4]	Royalties	Pensions/ Annuities
Federation				
Senegal	15	15	15	15/25
Serbia	10	5/15	10	15/25
Singapore	15	15	15	25
Slovak Republic	10	5/15	0/10	15/25
Slovenia	10	5/15	10	15/25
South Africa	10	5/15	6/10	25
Spain	[10]	5/15	0/10	15/25
Sri Lanka	15	15	0/10	15/25
Sweden	10	5/15	0/10	25
Switzerland	10	5/15	0/10	15/25
Taiwan[6]	[10]	[10/15]	[10]	[15/25]
Tanzania	15	20/25	20	15/25
Thailand	15	15	5/15	25
Trinidad & Tobago	10	5/15	0/10	15/25
Tunisia	15	15	0/15/20	25
Turkey	15	15/20	10	15/25
Ukraine	10	5/15	0/10	25
United Arab Emirates	10	5/15	0/10	25
United Kingdom	10	5/15	0/10	0/10/25
United States[8]	0[2]	5/15	0/10	15/25
Uzbekistan	10	5/15	5/10	25
Venezuela[5]	10	10/15	5/10	25
Vietnam	10	5/10/15	7.5/10	15/25
Zambia	15	15	15	15/25

Treaty Country	Interest[3]	Dividends[4]	Royalties	Pensions/ Annuities
Zimbabwe	15	10/15	10	15/25

Notes:

The rates in the table apply to payments made by a resident of Canada to a person resident in the particular treaty country. The particular treaty should be consulted to determine if specific conditions, exemptions, etc. apply.

1   Under negotiation/re-negotiation.

2   Canada and the U.S. signed the Fifth Protocol to the treaty on September 21, 2007. The Fifth Protocol entered into force on December 15, 2008, and its provisions will have effect according to the rules specified in Article 27 of the Protocol. Generally, withholding tax on interest paid or credited on non-participating debt is eliminated as follows: where paid or credited to an unrelated person, the rate is nil after December 31, 2007, and where paid or credited to a related person, the rate is 7% in 2008, 4% in 2009, and nil after 2009.

3   Part XIII of the *Income Tax Act* (Canada) was amended to eliminate withholding tax on interest paid or credited to an arm's length nonresident on non-participating debt effective January 1, 2008.

4   The lower rate of withholding tax on dividends generally applies where the beneficial owner of the dividend owns a certain percentage of voting stock or voting power of the company paying the dividend.

5   The treaty currently in effect with these countries includes a Most Favoured Nation clause, which provides for reduced withholding rates if the other country signs a treaty with another OECD member country and that treaty includes a lower withholding rate. This clause allows the lower rate to apply to the Canadian treaty. The items of income to which the clause applies vary by treaty. The lower withholding rate in the other country's treaty will apply to Canada if that treaty is signed after the date that Canada's treaty with the particular country is signed.

6   A new treaty is signed but not yet ratified. Until ratification, the withholding tax rate is generally 25%. Rates that will apply once the treaty is ratified are indicated in square brackets.

7   A protocol or replacement treaty is signed but not yet ratified. Until ratification, the withholding tax rates are the rates specified in the existing treaty. New rates (if any) are indicated in square brackets.

8   An Intergovernmental Agreement (IGA) between Canada and the U.S. for the enhanced exchange of tax information under the Canada-U.S. Tax Convention entered into force on June 27, 2014. The IGA was signed on February 5, 2014. The provisions of the IGA have effect in Canada as of July 1, 2014.

Treaties signed but not yet in force: Lebanon, Namibia and Taiwan.

Treaties under Negotiation/Re-negotiation: Australia, China (PRC), Israel, Madagascar, Malaysia and Netherlands.

Tax Information Exchange Agreements (TIEAs)

Agreements in Force

As of June 1, 2016, TIEAs are in force with the following jurisdictions:

COUNTRY	Date TIEA Entered Into Force
Anguilla	October 12, 2011
Aruba	June 1, 2012
Bahamas	November 16, 2011
Bahrain	April 3, 2014
Bermuda	July 1, 2011
British Virgin Islands	March 11, 2014
Brunei	December 26, 2014
Cayman Islands	June 1, 2011
Costa Rica	August 14, 2012
Dominica	January 10, 2012
Guernsey	January 18, 2012
Isle of Man	December 19, 2011
Jersey	December 19, 2011
Liechtenstein	January 26, 2014
Netherlands Antilles	January 1, 2011
Panama	December 6, 2013
Saint Lucia	July 20, 2012
San Marino	October 20, 2011
St. Kitts and Nevis	November 21, 2011
St. Vincent and the Grenadines	October 4, 2011
Turks and Caicos	October 6, 2011
Uruguay	June 27, 2014

Signed Agreements Not Yet in Force

As of June 1, 2016, Canada has signed TIEAs with the following jurisdictions:

COUNTRY	Date TIEA Signed
Cook Islands	June 15, 2015

Ongoing Negotiations

As of June 1, 2016, Canada has entered into TIEA negotiations with the following jurisdictions:

COUNTRY	Date TIEA Negotiations Commenced
Antigua and Barbuda	November 26, 2010
Belize	June 26, 2010
Gibraltar	May 14, 2009
Grenada	November 27, 2010
Liberia	February 23, 2010
Montserrat	December 3, 2010
Vanuatu	July 21, 2010

Notes:

A "designated treaty country" for a taxation year of a foreign affiliate of a corporation is defined in subsection 5907(11) of the *Income Tax Regulations* as a country with which Canada has entered into a tax treaty or a country with which Canada has entered into a comprehensive tax information exchange agreement that has entered into force and has effect for that taxation year of the foreign affiliate.

The date that Canada has begun negotiations for a comprehensive tax information exchange agreement with a country is applicable for purposes of the definition "non-qualifying country" in subsection 95(1) of the *Income Tax Act*.

**   © Thomson Reuters Canada.

5

Immigration

The time may come when you decide to return to Canada. While immigration is a relatively simple event for most Canadian citizens, it should not occur without some planning. Remember, once you commence being a Canadian resident for income tax purposes you will be taxed on your world income.

TIMING

Planning the date when you re-establish Canadian residency will be important. Income earned in a foreign jurisdiction but received after your return to Canada could be taxed in Canada. This may include such items as retirement or termination payments, accrued but unpaid interest and declared but unpaid dividends. You should review all sources of income prior to your arrival to ascertain if the amounts should be received prior to entering Canada.

If you are currently taxed in a foreign jurisdiction and will be taxed when you arrive in Canada, it may be tax effective to arrive in the middle of the taxation year, around June 30. This may permit you to benefit from the various marginal tax rates in both countries. As noted on departure, various tax credits will be prorated for the number of days you are resident in Canada.

DATE OF ARRIVAL

The point of time when you commence residency can be as definite or as uncertain as your date of departure. Its determination will depend on the nature and quality of the ties you establish in Canada compared to those retained in the foreign jurisdiction. As well, if you are coming from a treaty country, the residency article of the treaty may dictate your status.

You will give formal tax notice of your arrival on the Canadian tax return you file for your year of arrival. Complete the area on page one of the personal tax return which requests the date of entry into Canada.

You may need to visit Canada prior to your formal return. Caution must be exercised to ensure that you do not establish ties on any earlier visit that would cause you to be a resident. For example, if you come to Canada and acquire a home, that purchase may be seen as a significant tie which could cause you to be a resident from that point on. It may be prudent to postpone such action or at least delay the closing until the date you plan to actually enter Canada for tax purposes.

Another situation that may be viewed as creating a significant tie would arise if your spouse and children precede you and take up residence in Canada. This event could cause you to be resident in Canada at that time rather than at some future date when you yourself arrive. I suggest that you review the discussion in Chapter 1 regarding the various ties which the Canada Revenue Agency considers to determine if you have retained your resident status. The same criteria will be used to establish whether you have reacquired resident status in Canada.

Question — Immigration

I left Canada on June 30, 2015, severed all my ties and intended to remain in Saudi Arabia for three years. My contract was cancelled prematurely, requiring me to return to Canada in August 2016. Will I be considered a non-resident of Canada for the period June 30, 2015 through August 2016?

Answer

If you severed all your ties with Canada and intended to remain in Saudi Arabia for up to three years, the fact that you returned to Canada for the reasons beyond your control should not cause you to be a resident of Canada for the period June 30, 2015 through August 2016.

Question — Immigration, Spouse Returns Early

I have been a non-resident of Canada for five years. I plan to return to Canada in December 2017. My spouse and my children will return in late August 2017. What date will I be considered to be a resident of Canada — August 2017 or December 2017?

Answer

The Canada Revenue Agency will consider you to commence being a resident when your spouse and children arrive in Canada to take up residency. You may be able to refute this position if you are coming from a country which has a treaty with Canada. (see Chapter 4 — Tax Treaties — Tie-Breaker Rules)

Question — Immigration, Vacation
I have been a non-resident of Canada for seven years. I plan to return to Canada in October 2017. I will cease my current employment in June 2017 and plan to travel prior to arriving in Canada. When will I be considered to be a resident of Canada?

Answer
As long as you have not established residential ties in Canada prior to your arrival in October 2017, you will not be a resident for Canadian tax purposes until that date.

CAPITAL PROPERTY

You will recall that you were deemed to have disposed of property that is not taxable Canadian property at its fair market value when you left Canada. The same rule applies when you arrive back in Canada. All property that is not taxable Canadian property is deemed to be disposed of at its fair market value and reacquired at that value. This rule causes you to realize all gains (or losses) on these properties prior to commencing to be a resident. Such gains will not be subject to Canadian tax. The losses cannot be applied against future capital gains realized by you as a resident of Canada.

Properties subject to this deemed disposition and reacquisition may include shares of public companies, shares of non-TCP private companies, mutual funds, foreign real estate, foreign partnership interests, exchange traded funds, segregated funds, income trusts and foreign business assets.

The deemed disposition rules will not apply to taxable Canadian property. The tax on gains arising from the properties will only be paid when you sell the property, assuming you elected to defer the payment of tax on departure. See Chapter 2 for the deemed disposition rules on departure.

Due to the amendments to the definition of taxable Canadian property (TCP) in the March 4, 2010 Federal Budget, a number of properties which were TCP before March 5, 2010 will now be deemed to have been disposed on re-entry. A review of these amendments and their transitional rules has raised questions regarding their impact on former returning residents.

For greater certainty, the following outlines the definition of TCP from March 4, 2010 until they change the definition again.

Effective after March 4, 2010, TCP includes the following assets:
- real or immovable property situated in Canada;
- property including goodwill, inventory used by you in a business carried on in Canada;
- shares of capital stock of a corporation (other than a mutual fund corporation) that is not listed on a designated stock exchange, an

interest in a partnership or an interest in a trust (other than a mutual fund trust or an income interest in a trust resident in Canada), if at any time during the past 60 months, more than 50% of the value of the corporation's shares or interest in a partnership or trust is derived from one or any combination of

i.   real or immovable property situated in Canada,
ii. Canadian resource property,
iii. timber resource property, and
iv. options or interests in any of the properties listed in i, ii and iii.

- shares of a corporation that is listed on a designated stock exchange, shares of a mutual fund corporation or units of a mutual fund trust, where you together with related persons own 25% or more of the issued shares of any class of capital stock or issued units of the trust and, at any time in the past 60 months, more than 50% of the value of those shares or units was derived from the items listed in i, ii, iii and iv above;
- an option in respect of, or an interest in any of the properties listed above, whether or not the property exists;
- Canadian resource property;
- timber resource property;
- income interest in a trust resident in Canada;
- retired partner's right to share income or losses from his/her former partnership, and
- a life insurance policy in Canada.

The new provisions are law. If you left Canada before March 5, 2010 with what was TCP under the former definition, it may not be TCP now. What impact if any does this have on you? First the bad news: the shares were deemed to be disposed off at the time you ceased to be a resident for tax purposes. The good news is that any appreciation arising after your departure and during your period of non-residency will not be taxable in Canada.

Question — Immigration, Mutual Funds
I own an investment in a mutual fund which has increased in value. I understand that I will be deemed to have disposed of my mutual fund investment when I return to Canada. The fair market value of this investment will be its tax cost for future determination of capital gain on redemption. Will the unrealized gains within the mutual fund also be realized on the date I arrive in Canada?

Answer
The investments within the mutual fund will not be realized when you arrive in Canada. As a result, you may have capital gains allocated to you from unrealized gains which existed within the mutual fund on the day of your arrival in Canada. On subsequent redemption of your units in the mutual fund, you will likely have a capital loss which may be applied against the allocated gains.

Question — Losses realized after returning to Canada
I returned to Canada in January 2015. I had a number of investments which were deemed to be disposed of at the FMV on the date of my becoming a resident of Canada for tax purposes. As a result, my new tax cost for these investments was the FMV on that date. I have subsequently sold some of these investments but at a loss. Do I have a problem with the so-called superficial loss rules?

Answer
As long as you did not reacquire the investments that you sold that created the loss within 30 days of selling them, the superficial loss rules do not apply.

TAXABLE CANADIAN PROPERTY

Certain TCPs were not taxable (unless you elected to have them realized) when you left Canada and no deemed realization occurs when you return to Canada. As noted in Chapter 2, TCP which is not deemed to be disposed of includes Canadian real or immovable property and capital property or inventory that is used in a business carried on by a person through a permanent establishment in Canada.

For most Canadian expatriates, the most commonly held taxable Canadian property is the former family home. While this property is not deemed to be disposed of when you return to Canada, the action of ceasing to lease the home and commencing to live in it will constitute a change of use and a deemed realization will occur unless you elected not to have a change of use when you started to lease the house. If the latter action was taken, terminating the lease and commencing to use the house as your home will not have any immediate tax consequences. The tax consequences will arise when you ultimately sell your property. Remember, even though you elected not to have a change of use, you cannot designate the house to be your principal residence for any year throughout which you were a non-resident.

If you did not elect not to have a change of use when you left, you will have a deemed disposition and reacquisition of the property when you cease leasing it and commence using it as your principal residence. If the value of the property is higher at that point, you will realize a capital gain which you must include in your income. This gain would be included in the tax return you file for the year you become a resident of Canada, assuming you commence using the house as your principal residence upon your return.

You may elect to defer the taxation of the gain arising from this change of use until you actually sell the property. This is accomplished by electing with the Canada Revenue Agency in writing on or before the earlier of the day that is 90 days after the Agency requests such an election and April 30 following the year in which the property is actually disposed of by you. This election applies only to rental property that becomes your principal residence.

TAX RETURN — YEAR OF IMMIGRATION

The Canadian tax return you file for your year of arrival will include not only world income earned after your arrival but employment and business income earned in Canada while you were a non-resident, and gains from both actual dispositions of taxable Canadian properties and deemed dispositions arising from a change in use.

If you have been filing a separate return for rental income, you will still file that return and report the rental income earned up to the date of return. The rental income received after your return will be declared in your regular tax return which includes your world income for the period after your arrival.

Timing

To the extent you can control your arrival in Canada, you may be able to eliminate or reduce your Canadian tax burden on certain income. For example, if you own a property in Canada and you plan to sell it in the year you return to Canada (before or after your return), you will be required to include the gain in your regular tax return for that year. This may cause you to pay more tax than you would have if you were able to sell the property in a year prior to your return. If you are able to do this, only the gain would be reported and a lower tax would be paid because of the application of lower marginal tax rates.

If you receive certain payments for work performed while you were a non-resident after you return to Canada, they may be taxed in Canada. In order to ensure this does not happen, you should request payment of the amount prior to your arrival in Canada. Or take a well deserved vacation to somewhere other than Canada until the payment has been received. Also, do not establish Canadian residential ties during that period. Bon Voyage!!

Returning Former Residents

If you return and still own the same TCP and/or non-TCP acquired before your departure date, you may elect to undo the deemed disposition of TCP and non-TCP that occurred when you left. This will cause the tax authorities to repay the tax paid or return the security provided when you left. The election may apply to TCP and/or non-TCP that you continue to hold upon your return. The election is an all or nothing event for both TCP and non-TCP. However you may elect only on the TCP and not on the non-TCP or vice versa.

Any gain that accrued on the non-TCP while you were a non-resident will remain tax-free even if you elect to undo the deemed disposition.

There are a number of complex rules that ensure that you don't receive undue benefits from tax when you make this election. As a result, I urge you to seek professional assistance before making this election.

Question — Immigration, Non-TCP

I left Canada in 2005. I was deemed to have disposed shares of a Canadian private corporation. I paid the departure tax on the capital gains that arose from the deemed disposition.

I plan to return to Canada next month. I still own the shares of the Canadian private corporation. However, the shares have ceased to be TCP because of the March 4, 2010 amendments. What are my options when I return to Canada?

Answer

You have two options. One, you can do nothing. Since the shares are no longer TCP, they will be deemed to be disposed and reacquired at their fair market value on the day you arrive back in Canada. The gain that accrued from the time you left until you return will not be taxable in Canada.

Or you can elect to undo the deemed disposition that occurred when you emigrated and receive a refund of the tax paid on the capital gain that arose on your departure. The good news is that the gain that occurred while you are a non-resident remains tax free in Canada.

RRSP

Deductions on your first year's tax return may include contributions to an RRSP for yourself or your spouse. Remember, you may not have any deduction limit in the year of arrival unless it arose from the year of departure or from Canadian income earned while you were a non-resident. Incomes which qualify as earned income for RRSP purposes include Canadian employment and business income but not capital gains or any income earned outside of Canada.

You will recall from Chapter 2 that your deductible RRSP contribution is based on the lesser of 18% of your earned income in the previous year or the RRSP dollar limit for the year ($26,010 for 2017) adjusted for the pension adjustment. If you examine your most recent assessment notice from the Canada Revenue Agency, you should find your current RRSP deduction limit on the deduction limit statement.

Over-Contribution

Caution should be exercised when you contribute to your RRSP. Previous amendments reduced the $8,000 over-contribution allowance to $2,000, effective for 1996 and subsequent years. In order to avoid paying a penalty tax of 1% per month on the excess over the over-contribution allowance, you must remove excess contributions from your account.

Withdrawal

If you have not withdrawn funds from your RRSP prior to returning to Canada, you may want to consider doing so prior to the date of your arrival. This action will permit you to receive amounts at a maximum tax of 25%, which is likely lower than the rate you would pay as a resident of Canada. It is important to remember that any such withdrawal must occur prior to the day you become resident in Canada.

While withdrawal of your RRSP prior to becoming a resident of Canada may appear to be a smart move, there are several consequences to consider. One, you may be taxed in your foreign country of residence. Two, you have less funds to invest (RRSP funds less Canadian non-resident withholding tax). Third, once you take the funds out of your RRSP, the income from the after-tax RRSP funds is no longer tax sheltered from Canadian taxation.

RRIF WITHDRAWAL

You may also wish to consider making your annual minimum withdrawal or perhaps an additional withdrawal from your RRIF before re-establishing Canadian residency. RRIF payments received by a non-resident are subject to a 25% withholding tax. Although the rate may be reduced by treaty, under most treaties, any payment in excess of the greater of 10% of the fair market value of the RRIF at the beginning of the year or two times the minimum amount will be subject to the 25% tax. The minimum amount is a defined amount that must be paid out annually.

The same consequences arise if you withdraw your RRIF prior to becoming a resident as noted above for RRSPs.

OFFSHORE INVESTMENTS

As a resident of Canada, you will be subject to tax on your world income. This will include income earned from bank accounts located in various tax havens, offshore trusts and corporations. You no doubt have read about establishing an offshore trust and hope to capitalize on its benefits. While this is a well recognized vehicle to achieve a five-year tax holiday, you may not be able to benefit from it. I have prepared the following outline regarding how offshore trusts work and suggest that you seek professional assistance if you feel that you are eligible to use one.

Offshore Trusts

An offshore trust is like any other trust except its trustees are resident in a country other than Canada. The fact that the trustees are resident in another country should cause the trust to be resident in that other country. The fact that the trust is resident in another country should cause its income to be taxed by that country, rather than Canada. And if as usually is the case, the country is a tax haven, no tax will be paid.

Too good to be true?

Well, with the exception of several situations, it is too good to be true. Like it or not, our government is quite concerned about the loss of tax revenue and goes out of its way to develop tax laws to quell the use of offshore entities for other than legitimate reasons. This position was reinforced with the introduction of revisions to the foreign trust rules which go far beyond the previous rules and may catch existing structures which were set up years ago.

First of all, Canadian residents are taxed on world income. That is the harsh reality. Some feel that if they don't receive the income, they should not pay tax on that income — now or at any time. For most Canadians, that is not true.

Immigration Trusts for Individuals

Canadian residents must pay Canadian income tax on their worldwide income. However, individuals immigrating to Canada for the first time could establish a non-resident trust for the benefit of themselves and their families. The assets in a non-resident trust would earn income and capital gains from foreign sources free of Canadian income tax for up to the first five years of an immigrant's Canadian residency.

The rules that allowed first time residents the privilege of not paying tax on income earned in an immigration trust have come to an end for trusts' taxation years that end after February 14, 2014. This rule applies to both current and future immigration trusts.

So what is left?

Granny Trusts

As noted under immigration trusts, new Canadians can no longer benefit from a five-year exemption from Canadian tax. But what happens if an individual who has never been a resident of Canada in the past and never plans to reside in Canada in the future creates a trust in an offshore jurisdiction? Under current trust rules, such a trust may never be taxable in Canada.

Income earned by the trust will be taxed in a beneficiary's hands if it is allocated to them as income. Care must be taken to only pay out capital, which is not taxable. As a result, if a Canadian resident has a non-Canadian relative who plans to give him/her substantial amounts of money, consideration should be given by the relative to settle an offshore trust with that gift. The long term benefits can far outpace any value of immediate joy of receiving such a gift.

The rich relative should check with his/her local tax professional to ensure that the creation of this trust does not cause him/her any problems in his/her country of residence.

Testamentary Offshore Trust

Another opportunity to use an offshore trust arises from the death of a non-resident. In particular, individuals who have never been resident in Canada and former Canadians who have been non-resident for more than 18 months preceding their death can create a testamentary offshore trust. The Will of the deceased will provide that his or her assets will be left to a trust in an offshore jurisdiction under the control of non-Canadian executors. As with the granny trust, the trust should never be taxable in Canada. And income earned by the trust will only be taxed in Canada if that income is allocated to a Canadian beneficiary. Check with your domestic lawyer to ensure that wording is correct.

Exempt Foreign Trust

Exceptions are also made for a number of specific situations. This includes offshore trusts set up for non-resident dependents who are mentally or physically infirm, marriage breakdown and several limited situations. The rules are quite strict and must be carefully reviewed to ascertain if they apply.

Former Canadian Residents

A number of Canadians leaving Canada set up trusts to avoid paying taxes in their new homeland. If these trusts contain Canadian-resident beneficiaries, under the new rules these trusts will be taxable in Canada. An exception to the rules applies where the trust is set up after the emigrant has been a non-resident of Canada for more than five years.

There is, however, one catch. If you ever become a Canadian resident again for tax purposes, the trust will be taxed as a Canadian trust. These rules are now law. As a result, check the rules to ensure they provide the relief you expect.

A further problem arises for existing trusts. These trusts may be subject to Canadian taxes in the future. If you feel that this is not a problem since the trust is not in Canada, be aware that the current rules will cause the Canadian-resident beneficiaries to be liable for the tax. As a result, if the Canadian-resident beneficiaries receive any money from the trust, the tax authorities could lay claim to it to the extent of any unpaid tax liability. Old trusts should be reviewed to ensure that this does not happen.

An additional problem which may arise concerns who in fact controls the trust. A recent court case raised the question of control and management (who made the decisions) of an offshore trust regardless of the fact that the trustees were not residents of Canada. (See Income Tax Folio S6-F1-C1, Residence of a Trust or Estate in the Appendix for CRA's views.)

The foregoing raises concern about another tax provision that applies to certain trusts that are residents in Canada for more than 21 years. The tax provision causes the trust's assets to be deemed disposed of at fair market value. The result — tax on any gain the deemed disposition causes.

Non-resident trusts that hold taxable Canadian property may have an issue with the 21-year rule unless the property is treaty protected.

Other Trusts

So, aside from the situations noted above, Canada will tax offshore trusts. This may include trusts that already exist. But, how will Canada ever know about these trusts? Unfortunately, there are several rules which will cause exposure. First, Canadian residents are taxed on world income. If an offshore trust is taxable, it is required to pay tax in Canada. If it does not pay tax, its Canadian-resident beneficiaries could be liable for the tax.

Current foreign property reporting rules noted hereinafter require Canadians to report transfers of money to a trust and also report the receipt of money. The reporting forms are required even though the money received from the trust is capital. The information contained on the form will notify the Canada Revenue Agency what is in the trust. Severe penalties will be applied if no form is filed.

Once again, our authorities have tightened the tax screws on offshore trusts in the hopes of plugging the leakage of government revenue.

So, if you encounter an offshore structure that promises either tax deferral or tax-free funds, pinch yourself and wake up to reality. Aside from the limited list outlined above, they don't exist for Canadian residents.

Foreign Accrual Property Income (FAPI)

Canada has a number of tax rules that were introduced to ensure that you pay tax on investment income located in foreign jurisdictions. The FAPI rules are one such set of provisions. These are very complex and intended to cause you to pay tax on various types of investment income even though you have not received them. You may not have received the FAPI due to the fact it was earned by an offshore trust or corporation. Regardless of whether you received this income or not, if you meet the conditions (which are far too complex for this book), you will be taxable thereon as a resident of Canada. This area requires specific professional assistance to ensure that you abide by Canadian tax law.

Offshore Investment Funds

Canadian investment funds are taxed annually on income and capital gains accumulated in the fund. Investors are taxed on income or capital gains allocated to them by such funds, as well as on capital gains realized on the disposition of such funds. Foreign investment funds are usually not subject to Canadian taxation. As such, they can accumulate income at local tax rates (usually low) providing Canadian investors with tax deferral and possibly the ability to convert ordinary income to capital gains taxable at lower rates.

The *Income Tax Act* contains rules that attempt to eliminate this advantage. However, these rules have been largely ineffective. The government introduced a new set of rules in 1999.

The 1999 modifications included a requirement that investors include in income, their share of the undistributed earnings of a foreign-based investment fund along with foreign tax credits for any taxes paid by the fund on this income. Alternatively, taxpayers would be required to annually report the increase or decrease in the market value of the investment and to add or subtract the market value fluctuations from their incomes. These rules would not apply where the foreign-based funds annually distribute or allocate all of the income to which the Canadian investor is entitled. Various exemptions would apply.

The 1999 proposed legislation never became law. It was too complex and likely applied to many structures that were completely above board. In addition, our legislators received a number of representatives from the Canadian tax community who lobbied against the complexity and all the inclusiveness of the proposals.

Finally, our legislators saw the light and eliminated most of the complexities. They did not abandon the concept of taxing Canadian residents on funds invested offshore. As a result, you should seek professional advice if you have as an immigrant or as a former Canadian resident, contemplated the creation of a non-resident trust or the use of an offshore investment fund.

Foreign Asset Reporting Requirements

The Canada Revenue Agency now requires you to report certain information concerning your foreign holdings. This includes details of transfers to and deposits with foreign corporations, partnerships, trusts or estates. If you make a transfer to a non-resident trust, you have to provide financial statements and details of transfers to and distributions from the trust on an annual basis. As a result, if you establish an immigration trust or any other offshore structure, you are required to provide details of its existence to the Canada Revenue Agency. This will no doubt cause the Agency to scrutinize the structure of the offshore entity and challenge its integrity.

Four forms were introduced to accumulate this information.

T1135-Foreign Income Verification Statement

The information required to complete a T1135 became far more complicated as compared to previous years. If you think that you may be required to complete a T1135, you should obtain a copy from the Revenue Canada website: www.cra-arc.gc.ca/tx/nnrsdnt/cmmn/frgn/1135.

The new filing requirements were only one year old when the Federal government got the word that what they required was overwhelming. As a result, the April, 2015 Federal Budget proposed to simplify the reporting system for taxation years after 2014. The proposed simplification will apply to taxpayers who have foreign properties that have a total cost of less than $250,000 throughout the year. If the taxpayer is under the $250,000 total cost throughout the year, he/she can report the properties under a new simplified foreign reporting system. The new T1135 Foreign Income Verification Statement (see Appendix) contains two parts — Part A and Part B. If the total cost of all your specified property held at any time during the year exceeds

$100,000 but was less than $250,000, you will complete Part A: Simplified reporting method. However, if the total cost of all specified foreign property held at any time during the year was $250,000 or more, you will complete Part B: Detailed reporting method.

T1135 must be completed and filed by all Canadian residents *if at any time in the year* the total cost of foreign investments exceeds $100,000. There are some exceptions but very few. But let me show you the reportable and non-reportable.

What Property do you have to Report?

- funds or intangible property (patents, copyrights, etc.) situated, deposited or held outside Canada;
- tangible property situated outside of Canada;
- a share of the capital stock of a non-resident corporation held by the taxpayer or by an agent on behalf of the taxpayer;
- shares of corporations resident in Canada held by you or for you outside of Canada; (*Author's Note: I believe this refers to shares of a Canadian corporation that you might have placed in a safety deposit box off shore.*)
- an interest in a non-resident trust that was acquired for consideration, other than an interest in a non-resident trust that is a foreign affiliate;
- an interest in a partnership that holds a Specified Foreign Property unless the partnership is required to file a T1135;
- an interest in, or right with respect to, an entity that is a non-resident;
- a property that is convertible into, exchangeable for, or confers a right to acquire a property that is Specified Foreign Property;
- a debt owed by a non-resident, including government and corporate bonds, debentures, mortgages, and notes receivable;
- an interest in a foreign insurance policy;
- precious metals, gold certificates, and futures contracts held outside Canada.

(Please note that it may also include virtual currency stored offshore.)

Specified Foreign Property **does not** include:
- a property used or held exclusively in carrying on an active business;
- a share of the capital stock or indebtedness of a foreign affiliate;
- an interest in an exempt trust;
- a personal-use property;
- an interest in, or a right to acquire, any of the above-noted excluded foreign property.

Penalties for Non-Reporting

There are substantial penalties for failing to complete and file the T1135 accurately and by the due date. For additional information regarding penalties, see the CRA website at: www.cra-arc.gc.ca/tx/nnrsdnts/cmmn/frgn/pnlts_grd-eng.html.

Voluntary Disclosures

To promote compliance with Canada's tax laws, CRA encourages you to correct your tax affairs through the Voluntary Disclosures Program. For more information, see Information Circular IC00-1R3, *Voluntary Disclosures Program* (VDP) or visit the CRA website.

Note: An individual does not have to file a T1135 for the year in which the individual first becomes a resident of Canada.

Foreign Affiliates

If you, together with persons related to you, own 10% or more of a non-resident corporation, it is considered to be a foreign affiliate. This is true whether you own your shares directly or through another entity such as a Canadian corporation another non-resident corporation or a non-resident trust.

Form T1134A or T1134B must be completed for all shares that you own in foreign affiliates. There is no dollar threshold; all foreign affiliate holdings must be reported to the Canada Revenue Agency no matter how small.

Transfer and Loans to Foreign Trusts

Non-resident trusts are set up for many reasons. Many Canadian residents who operate businesses offshore choose to do so through foreign trusts. Also, many Canadian residents who are concerned about protecting their assets have transferred investments to offshore trusts in jurisdictions that have strong asset protection legislation.

In order to accumulate information on these trusts, Form T1141 requires the reporting of all loans and transfers to foreign trusts that are done on a "non-arm's length basis". Usually, this means the beneficiaries of the trust are related to you, such as family members. However, other loans and transfers are also caught unless a market interest rate is charged on loans or fair market value consideration is taken back on transfers.

Distributions from Foreign Trusts

Are you a beneficiary of a foreign trust? Perhaps a non-resident relative has set up a trust for your benefit.

If so and you received a distribution from the trust, or the trust became indebted to you (likely because they issued you a promissory note rather than making a distribution), you have to report this to the Canada Revenue Agency on Form T1142. You are only taxed in Canada if the distribution is out of trust income; however, the Canada Revenue Agency still wants to know about it.

Dual Resident Status

Individuals who can still claim to be residents of both Canada and another jurisdiction will be required to comply with these filing requirements even though the tax treaty indicates that they are taxable in the other jurisdiction. As a result, they will not only have to file a Canadian tax return to claim the exemption from tax but will also have to complete any or all of the foreign property reporting forms.

What if the Returns Aren't Filed?

In order to encourage Canadians to comply with these reporting requirements, severe penalties have been introduced if the required forms are not filed by their due dates. For all the returns except Form T1142 (Distributions From Foreign Trusts), the late filing penalty is $500 per month up to a maximum of $12,000. If the return is not filed within 24 months of its due date, an additional amount can be levied which increases the penalty to 5% of the total cost of foreign property that should have been reported. The late filing penalty for Form T1142 is $25 per day up to a maximum of $2,500.

Addition of a Due Diligence Test

Taxpayers required to file Form T1141 (Loans or Transfers to a Non-Resident Trust), Form T1135 (Information Return in Respect of Foreign Property) and Form T1134 (Information Return for Foreign Affiliates), will be excepted from the penalties for omissions in the return if they can prove that they exercised due diligence in attempting to obtain the required information. Note that to qualify for the due diligence exception, a taxpayer must give reasonable disclosure in the information return of the unavailability of the required information and must have made diligent attempts to get the information. In addition, if the information subsequently becomes available to the taxpayer, it must be filed with the Canada Revenue Agency within 90 days. Note that the due diligence exception does not apply to Form T1142 (Distributions From a Non-Resident Trust).

March 21st, 2013 Federal Budget

The Federal March 21st, 2013 Budget proposed a number of measures to address international tax evasion and aggressive tax avoidance.

The Budget of March 21st, 2013 proposed the following:

- Require certain financial intermediaries including banks to report international electronic funds transfers of $10,000 or more to the CRA. Funding of $15 million over five years will be provided to the CRA for this initiative;
- Streamline the process for the CRA to obtain information concerning unnamed persons from third parties such as banks.
- The CRA will also launch the Stop International Tax Evasion Program aimed at reducing international tax evasion and avoidance. Under this program, the CRA will pay rewards to individuals with knowledge of major international tax non-compliance when they provide information to the CRA that leads to the collection of outstanding taxes due. The CRA will pay a reward to an individual only if the information results in total additional assessments exceeding $100,000 in federal tax. In this way, the CRA will target high-income taxpayers who attempt to evade or avoid tax using complex international legal arrangements.

A number of other countries that are members of the Organisation for Economic Co-operation and Development (OECD), including the United States, the United Kingdom and Germany, already provide rewards for information regarding taxpayer non-compliance.

In addition to the implementation of these new measures, the CRA will increase compliance and audit efforts and activities to combat international tax evasion and aggressive tax avoidance.

February 11, 2014 Federal Budget

As noted earlier, the most significant change relates to the cessation of the eligibility to create an immigration trust. In addition, our government is beefing up the rules relating to treaty shopping.

New Canada USA Border Crossing Rules

Both Canada and the United States implemented the final phase of an Entry/ Exit Initiative. Under this initiative, both counties will share information on people entering or leaving either country. This information will be used to determine how many days an individual spent in the U.S.A. or Canada. It could be used to determine if someone is a resident for income tax purposes. The bottom line is keep track of the days or part days (because part of a day can count as a full day) you spend in the U.S.A.

The Panama Papers

This headline graced the front page of the Toronto Star on April 4th, 2016. It likely raised a few eyebrows. No doubt, Canada Revenue Agency (CRA) will want to get their hands on the information that is contained in those papers. This is a prime example of how secret financial information can suddenly create a headline at the height of tax season.

Aside from the news media or taxation authority receiving secret financial information from a disgruntled employee or an ambitious hacker, how do our governments keep an eye on us. Let us look at some of those ways.

The Financial Transactions and Reports Analysis Centre of Canada (FINTRAC)

Never heard about FINTRAC or been involved with it? Well, if you crossed the border into the United States or entered Canada, you were likely asked if you were carrying $10,000 or more in cash. This is a FINTRAC question.

What is FINTRAC?

The Financial Transactions and Reports Analysis Centre of Canada (FINTRAC) is an independent government agency. It operates at arm's length from law enforcement agencies, and collects, analyzes and discloses information to help detect, prevent and deter money laundering and the financing of terrorist activities in Canada and abroad.

FINTRAC receives and analyzes reports from reporting entities. It can also receive and analyze information from various other sources, such as similar agencies in other countries, law enforcement agencies, or government institutions and agencies. In addition, FINTRAC can receive and analyze any information about suspicions of money laundering or of the financing of terrorist activities that is provided voluntarily.

FINTRAC also receives and analyzes information from the Canada Border Services Agency about exports and imports of currency and monetary instruments.

FINTRAC relies on financial analysts and analytical technologies to produce high-quality analyses and assessments about suspicions of money laundering or terrorist financing.

Tax Information Exchange Agreements (TIEA)

Why is Canada signing tax information exchange agreements?

The signature of a tax information exchange agreement (TIEA) is consistent with the efforts of the Organisation for Economic Co-operation and Development (OECD) to implement the effective exchange of tax information to combat international tax evasion — an initiative endorsed by the G-20.

The Government of Canada regards the ability to exchange tax information between countries as an important means of improving the ability of tax authorities to administer and enforce tax laws in order to prevent international tax evasion.

TIEAs also strengthen bilateral ties between signatory countries by enabling the tax authorities of both jurisdictions to co-operate in the exchange of tax information.

How does a TIEA work?

A TIEA is a bilateral agreement pursuant to which two countries undertake to exchange tax information relevant to the administration and enforcement of their domestic tax laws as a way of fighting international tax evasion. Under a TIEA, a jurisdiction can be requested to exchange tax information if it is needed by the other country to administer its own tax laws.

In Canada, TIEAs are administered by the Canada Revenue Agency.

(See a list of countries that signed a Tax Information Exchange Agreement with Canada at the end of Chapter 4 — Tax Treaties.)

Foreign Account Tax Compliance Act (FATCA)

FATCA requires non-U.S. financial institutions to enter into an agreement with the U.S. Internal Revenue Service (IRS) to report to the IRS accounts held by U.S. residents and U.S. citizens (including U.S. citizens that are residents or citizens of Canada). If a financial institution is not compliant with FATCA, FATCA requires U.S. payors (i.e., corporations and others that pay amounts, such as interest or a dividend) making certain payments of U.S.-source income to the non-compliant financial institution to withhold a tax equal to 30 percent of the payment. The 30 percent FATCA withholding tax can also be levied in respect of a compliant financial institution, on individual accountholders that fail to provide documentation as to whether they are U.S. residents or U.S. citizens, and on passive entities (i.e., entities whose business purpose is to generate passive income) that fail to identify their substantial U.S. owners, if any. In some circumstances, FATCA could require financial institutions to close the accounts of certain clients.

March 22, 2016 Federal Budget

Improving Tax Compliance

To help ensure that all taxpayers pay their fair share of taxes, Budget 2016 proposed a number of measures to prevent evasion and improve tax compliance.

Cracking Down on Tax Evasion and Combating Tax Avoidance

Tax evasion and aggressive tax avoidance by individuals and businesses entail a fiscal cost to governments and taxpayers, and reduce the fairness and integrity of the tax system. Budget 2016 proposes to invest $444.4 million over five years for the CRA to enhance its efforts to crack down on tax evasion and combat tax avoidance by: hiring additional auditors and specialists; developing robust business intelligence infrastructure; increasing verification activities; and improving the quality of investigative work that targets criminal tax evaders.

And then, there is the nosy neighbour!

6

Miscellaneous Tax Relief, Residents of Canada

If you are a resident of Canada for tax purposes and earn income from a foreign source, it will be included in your Canadian income tax return and taxed accordingly. Generally, tax relief will be in the form of credits or a deduction of tax paid on such income in the foreign jurisdiction. As noted in Chapter 4, specific provisions of a treaty may reduce or eliminate double taxation through exemptions or tax credits.

There are, however, a number of types of income earned by residents of Canada which receive special tax treatment through tax credits or complete exemption.

OVERSEAS EMPLOYMENT TAX CREDIT (OETC)

(*Author's Note: This tax relief was used by a number of Canadians in the past. It helped introduce Canadian expertise to many foreign countries. But, 2015 was the last year that a Canadian could benefit from the OETC.*)

TREATIES

Our tax laws allow you in arriving at taxable income to deduct from income any income that is exempt from Canadian tax by virtue of a tax treaty. This provision appears to eliminate any Canadian tax on income exempted by treaty provisions. However, a closer look at the relief discloses that the provision allows you to deduct the exempt income to arrive at taxable income rather than net income. This may not be detrimental unless your net income causes you to lose certain benefits. For example, if your net income is over $35,927 (2016), you will lose part or all of your age credit; if your net income is over $73,756 (2016), your Old Age Security may be subject to clawback or not paid to you. So, even though you may not be taxed on certain types of foreign income because of a treaty provision, you may still face tax consequences.

EMPLOYMENT INCOME — PRESCRIBED INTERNATIONAL ORGANIZATIONS

If you are either a deemed or factual resident of Canada, you will pay Canadian tax on world income. However, if you earn employment income from an employer referred to by our tax laws as a "prescribed international organization", you may deduct it from your calculation of taxable income. In other words, you include the income from a prescribed international organization to determine your net income, then deduct the same amount from net income to arrive at taxable income.

The Canada Revenue Agency prescribes that the United Nations and any specialized agency that is brought into relationship with the United Nations in accordance with Article 63 of the Charter of the United Nations will qualify.

Question — U.N. Income
I am a factual resident of Canada and work for the U.N.'s Food and Agriculture Organization. This is my only source of income. Do I have to file a Canadian tax return?

Answer
Based on the fact that you are a resident of Canada, you should file a Canadian tax return and report your world income regardless of whether you will be required to pay Canadian tax on this income. Since this is employment income, it will establish your contribution room for purposes of your RRSP.

INTERNATIONAL NON-GOVERNMENTAL ORGANIZATIONS

As mentioned numerous times throughout this book, if you become a resident of Canada, you will be taxed on your world income. Certain world income may not be subject to Canadian tax either because a treaty exempts it from Canadian tax or it came from a prescribed international organization. A further exception is provided for employment income received from so called prescribed international non-governmental organizations. Unfortunately, this exception will only apply if you meet all of the following conditions:

1. you are not a Canadian citizen;
2. you were a non-resident of Canada immediately before commencing your employment in Canada; and
3. you became a resident of Canada solely for the purpose of employment.

To date, this exception will only apply if you meet the foregoing conditions and you are employed by the International Air Transport Association, the International Society of Aeronautical Telecommunications or the World Anti-Doping Agency.

The Canada Revenue Agency's guidelines are contained in its memorandum "Employees of International Organizations: Departmental Guidelines".

FOREIGN TAX CREDITS/DEDUCTIONS

If you earn income from a source outside of Canada, it may be taxable in the country from which it originates. Unless there is an exception which may be available under a treaty or our own tax law, it will be included in your income and subject to Canadian tax. If this income has already been taxed by a foreign jurisdiction, it would be subject to double taxation if not for certain provisions in the tax treaties and in our own domestic tax laws which allow you to reduce your Canadian tax on such income by tax paid in the other country. This relief may come in the form of a tax credit, a deduction or a combination of a credit and deduction.

ITF-S5-F2-C1 (see in Appendix) discusses the foreign tax credit, which is a deduction from Canadian tax otherwise payable. This foreign tax credit may be claimed in respect of income or profits tax you paid to a foreign country. You must calculate this credit on a country-by-country basis. In general terms, it is limited to the lesser of the income and profits tax paid by you to the particular foreign country and the Canadian tax otherwise payable for the year on income from sources within that particular country.

There may be occasions when you work in a foreign country while you continue to be a resident of Canada. As well, even though all your income is paid to you by your Canadian employer, the foreign country taxes you as well. You will claim a foreign tax credit to reduce the Canadian tax on that foreign earned income.

A problem arises when your Canadian T4 slip includes both Canadian and foreign income. CRA needs to know how much of your total annual income was earned and taxed in that foreign country. This information needs to be forwarded to CRA with your tax information along with proof that foreign tax was paid.

As you can appreciate, you may have tax withheld and remitted on all your income by your Canadian employer while foreign tax is paid on the same income. This can be avoided by requesting CRA to allow your employer to reduce its employee income tax deduction.

You, the employee must complete form T1213 — Request to Reduce Tax Deductions at Source for Year(s) _____ (See appendix). This should be completed and sent to CRA before your offshore assignment begins. The CRA will review your request and send you a letter agreeing or disagreeing with your request. Your request may be denied if you owe tax for another year.

If they agree, give the letter to your employer who will cease or reduce the amount of tax withheld at source.

If you have income from Canadian employment and foreign employment, it is important to have your employer indicate on the T4, Statement of Remuneration Paid, what was earned outside Canada. This is indicated by recording "ZZ" in Box 10 — Province of Employment. The employer will have to issue two T4 slips if you earned income in both Canada and the foreign country.

Foreign tax credits come in two forms: business and non-business. While the basic formula to determine your tax relief is similar for each, the results differ. Business foreign tax credits may only be claimed to reduce federal tax while non-business foreign tax credits may reduce both federal and provincial tax. If you incurred more foreign business tax than you are allowed to claim, you may carry the unapplied balance over for up to five years to be applied against tax on foreign business income in those years. There is no carryover for non-business foreign tax. However, to the extent it is not utilized, non-business foreign tax may be deducted as an expense in determining your net income. Please refer to Interpretation Bulletin IT-506 — Foreign Income Taxes as a Deduction from Income (www.cra-arc.gc.ca) for a more thorough discussion of this deduction.

RELOCATION

Relocation within Canada or outside can prove to be a very stressful event. In addition, the cost can be astronomical. Needless to say, you will want all reasonable moving expenses to be reimbursed or paid in the most tax effective manner. The relocation package may also include any number of employment benefits to ease the pain and reward your decision to move. The tax cost of the benefits must be reviewed to ensure that you are indeed not out of pocket. With this in mind, I prepared the following summary of moving expenses and relocation benefits to give you a better understanding of the tax consequences of moving.

Moving Expenses and Relocation Benefits[1]

When your employer transfers you from one place of business to another, the amount your employer pays or reimburses you for certain moving expenses is not a taxable benefit. This includes any amounts your employer incurred to move you, your family and household effects. This also applies when you accept

---

[1]   Adapted from the Canada Revenue Agency's publication T4130, Employers' Guide — Taxable Benefits and Allowance 2015.

employment at different locations from the locations of your former residences. Also, if your employer pays certain expenses to move you, your family and your household effects out of a remote work location when you have completed your employment duties there, the amount your employer pays is not a taxable benefit.

The following expenses are not a taxable benefit to you if your employer paid or reimbursed them:

- the cost of house-hunting trips to the new location, which includes child and pet-care expenses while you are away;
- travelling costs (including a reasonable amount spent for meals and lodging) while you and members of your household were moving from the old residence to the new residence;
- the cost to you of transporting or storing household effects while moving from the old residence to the new residence;
- costs to move personal items such as automobiles, boats or trailers;
- charges and fees to disconnect telephones, television aerials, water, space heaters, air conditioners, gas barbecues, automatic garage doors and water heaters;
- fees to cancel leases;
- the cost to the employee of selling the old residence;
- charges to connect and install utilities, appliances and fixtures that existed at the old residence;
- adjustments and alterations to existing furniture and fixtures to arrange them in the new residence, which include plumbing and electrical changes in the new residence;
- automobile licences, inspections and drivers' permit fees, if you owned these items at the former location;
- legal fees and land transfer tax to buy the new residence;
- the cost to revise legal documents to reflect the new address;
- reasonable temporary living expenses while waiting to occupy the new, permanent accommodation;
- long-distance telephone charges that relate to selling the old residence, and
- amounts the employer paid or reimbursed for mortgage interest, property taxes, heat, hydro, insurance and grounds maintenance costs to keep up the old residence after the move, when all reasonable efforts to sell have not been successful.

If your employer pays or reimburses moving costs that are not listed above, the amounts may be considered as a taxable benefit to you.

Eligible Housing Loss

The relocation of an employee usually involves the sale of a house. As long as the employee sells the house for more than he or she paid for it, no problem. However, what happens if the house sold at a loss? And the employer reimburses the employee for that loss?

Currently, if the reimbursement is for a loss that is an eligible housing loss, only one-half of the amount that exceeds $15,000 is a taxable benefit. If the loss is not an eligible housing loss, the entire reimbursement is a taxable benefit.

An eligible housing loss will only arise from an eligible relocation.

An eligible relocation is a move from one work place to another. Generally, if you moved more than 40 kilometres to live near the new work place, it will be an eligible relocation.

Home Relocation Loans

Relocation benefits may include low interest loans from your employer. If these loans meet certain conditions, the benefit caused by the low interest loan may be reduced or eliminated. The relocation must be an eligible relocation as required to qualify for the treatment under the eligible housing loss provision. If the relocation qualifies, the benefit arising from a low interest rate will be reduced or eliminated.

Non-Accountable Allowances

Allowances that you do not have to account for are called non-accountable allowances. The Canada Revenue Agency considers a non-accountable allowance for incidental relocation or moving expenses of up to $650 to be a reimbursement of expenses that you incurred because of the move. Therefore, this type of allowance is not taxable. For the Agency to consider it as a reimbursement for incidental expenses, you have to certify in writing that you incurred expenses for at least the amount of the allowance, up to a maximum of $650.

Benefits

COUNSELLING SERVICES

The fees your employer pays to provide services such as financial counselling or income tax preparation are usually considered a taxable benefit. Your counselling services are exempt from tax if they relate to:

- the mental or physical health (e.g. tobacco, drug and alcohol abuse, as well as stress management) of you or a person related to you (this does not include amounts for using recreational or sporting facilities and club dues);
- your re-employment; and
- your retirement.

EDUCATIONAL ALLOWANCES FOR CHILDREN

If your employer pays any amounts to you as an educational allowance for your child, your employer has to include these amounts in your income for the year. However, the educational allowance may not be taxable when you have to live in a specific location, by reason of your employment, where educational instruction is not available in your official language. The language of educational instruction primarily used in the school must be one of the two official languages of Canada. Other conditions are also related to this exemption.

GROUP TERM LIFE INSURANCE POLICIES: EMPLOYER-PAID PREMIUMS

This benefit applies to both current and former employees (retirees) who receive group term life insurance benefits from their employer or former employer.

Where premiums are paid on a regular basis and the premium rate for each individual is not dependent on age or sex, the taxable benefit is the total of:
- the premiums payable for term insurance on the individual's life; and
- the total of all sales taxes and excise taxes that apply to the individual's insurance coverage;

less
- the premiums and any taxes the employee paid, either directly or through reimbursements to the employer.

Premiums paid by an employer for employees' group life insurance (that is not group term insurance) is also a taxable benefit.

HOUSING, BOARD AND LODGING

Housing

If your employer provides you with a house, apartment or similar accommodation rent-free or for less than the fair market value of such accommodation, you are considered as receiving a taxable benefit. Your employer has to estimate a reasonable amount for the benefit. This is usually the fair market value for the same type of accommodation minus any rent you paid.

If your employer gives you cash for rent or utilities, the value of the housing benefit is the amount of the cash payment. This is the amount that your employer includes in your income.

Special Circumstances that Reduce the Value of a Housing Benefit

The following two factors may reduce the value of a housing benefit your employer provides to you:
- **Suitability of size.** You may have to occupy a dwelling larger than you need (e.g. a single person in a three-bedroom house). To determine the taxable housing benefit, your employer can reduce the value of the accommodation to equal the value of accommodation that is appropriate to your needs (in this case, a one or two-bedroom apartment or house).
- Note: If the dwelling your employer provides is smaller than you need, the Canada Revenue Agency cannot allow any reduction in value.
- **Loss of privacy and quiet enjoyment.** If the dwelling your employer provides to you contains things like equipment, public access or storage facilities which infringe on your privacy or quiet enjoyment of the dwelling, your employer can reduce the value of the housing benefit. The reduction has to reasonably relate to the degree of disturbance that affects you.

These two factors apply in the above order. If both circumstances apply to a dwelling, your employer should first reduce the value of the dwelling to equal the value of accommodation that suits your needs. Then, your employer should apply any reduction for loss of privacy and quiet enjoyment to that reduced value.

Free or Subsidized Board and Lodging

If your employer provides free board and lodging, you receive a taxable benefit. As a result, your employer must add to your remuneration, the fair market value of the board and lodging your employer provides.

If your employer provides subsidized board and lodging to you, the value of the benefit for board should be determined as described in the next section, "subsidized meals". The lodging benefit is the fair market value of the accommodation, minus any amount you paid.

SUBSIDIZED MEALS

If your employer provides subsidized meals to you (e.g. in an employee dining room or cafeteria), these meals are not considered a taxable benefit if you pay a reasonable charge. A reasonable charge is one that covers the cost of the food, its preparation and service. The value of the benefit is the cost of the meals minus any payment you make.

EXCEPTION TO THE RULES

There is an exception to these rules when your employer provides board and lodging to you at a remote location or a special work site.

This can arise when your employer sends you to a foreign country and provides you with room and board or an allowance for same. Under normal circumstances, this would be a taxable benefit. However, if you meet certain conditions, you will not be taxed on this "perk." As usual, you require a form — TD4, *Declaration of Exemption — Employment at Special Work Site.*

INTEREST-FREE AND LOW-INTEREST LOANS

Your employer has to include in income, any benefit that you receive as a result of an interest-free or low-interest loan because of an office, employment or shareholdings. The benefit is the amount of interest that you would have paid on the loan for the year at the prescribed rates minus the amount of interest that you paid on the loan in the year (or no later than 30 days after the end of the year).

Loans Received because of Employment

You receive a taxable benefit if you receive a loan because of an office or employment or intended office or employment. The loan can be received by you or your spouse. A loan includes any other indebtedness (e.g. The unpaid purchase price of goods or services).

The taxable benefit you receive in the taxation year is the total of the following two amounts:
   a)   the interest on each loan and debt, calculated at the prescribed rate for the period in the year during which it was outstanding; and
   b)   the interest on the loan or debt that was paid or payable for the year by the employer (for this purpose, an employer is a person or partnership that employed or intended to employ the individual, and also includes a person related to the person or partnership);

minus the total of the following two amounts:

c) the interest for the year that any person or partnership paid on each loan or debt no later than 30 days after the end of the year; and

d) any part of the amount in b) that the employee pays back to the employer no later than 30 days after the end of the year.

MEDICAL EXPENSES

If the employer pays for or provides an amount to pay for your medical expenses in a taxation year, these amounts are considered as a taxable benefit to you.

Premiums under a Private Health Service Plan

If your employer makes contributions to private health services plans for you, there is no taxable benefit to you.

Premiums under Provincial Hospitalization, Medical Care Insurance and Certain Government of Canada Plans

The amount an employer pays in premiums or contributes to a provincial hospital or medical care insurance plan for you is considered a taxable benefit to you if your employer:
- pays all or part of these amounts out of the employer's own funds, or
- pays an amount to the employee for these premiums.

PROFESSIONAL MEMBERSHIP DUES

If your employer pays or reimburses professional membership dues because membership in the organization or association is a condition of employment, there is no taxable benefit to you. Whether or not membership is a condition of employment depends on each situation. Your employer is responsible for making this determination. Your employer must be prepared to justify his/her position if the Canada Revenue Agency asks them to do so. In all other situations when your employer pays or reimburses your professional membership dues, there is a taxable benefit to you.

RECREATIONAL FACILITIES

If your employer supplies recreational facilities (e.g. exercise rooms, swimming pools, gymnasiums) for your general use, the value of any benefit you receive when you use the facilities is not taxable. This applies whether your employer provides the facilities free of charge or for a fee.

If your employer supplies recreational facilities to select groups or categories of employees for free or for a minimal fee while other employees are required to pay full fee, the Canada Revenue Agency considers that a taxable benefit is conferred to the employees who do not have to pay full fee.

CLUB DUES

If your employer pays fees for you to be a member of a social or athletic club and it is clear that these memberships are primarily to your advantage, the fees your employer pays are not taxable benefits to you.

REGISTERED RETIREMENT SAVINGS PLANS

Contributions your employer makes to your RRSP are considered as a taxable benefit to you. This does not include an amount your employer withheld from your remuneration and contributed for you.

STOCK OPTIONS

When a corporation agrees to sell or issue its shares to you, you may receive taxable benefits. The taxable benefit is the difference between the fair market value of the shares when you acquire them, and the amount paid, or to be paid, for them. In addition, a benefit can accrue to you if their rights under the agreement become vested in another person, or if they transfer or sell the rights.

TAX EQUALIZATION AND PROTECTION

The concept of tax equalization and protection is relevant for employees who move from one tax jurisdiction to another. If the relative tax cost is higher in the homeland, your employer may take steps to compensate you for the extra cost. As well, you may incur a number of costs such as relocation expenses, increase in cost of living, housing cost and foreign exchange fluctuation. You may require assistance in purchasing a home. All or some of the foregoing may be subsidized wholly or partially by the employer. From a Canadian point of view, a portion or all of the payments could be considered a taxable benefit.

Over the years, it was the Canada Revenue Agency's position that tax equalization or protection payments were subject to tax. For example, if a person received $100,000 in a foreign jurisdiction and paid $35,000 tax and moved to Canada and paid $45,000, they would have less after-tax funds.

If the employer paid the $10,000 additional tax, the Canada Revenue Agency would consider the $10,000 as additional income. Recent court cases have confirmed this position causing tax equalization or protection payments to be taxable. This reality should be taken into consideration when you negotiate a contract for employment in Canada.

7

Safeguarding Your Health

National Post, March 28, 2012 — "Australia couple gets $1-million hospital bill after baby's early birth in Vancouver"

Toronto Star, April, 2012 — "Premature birth on trip to U.S. costs Aussie $1M"

Canada Journal, November 19, 2014 — "Canadian mother Faces million-dollar medical bill for giving birth in US"

You may have seen these stories. Three separate families travelling with travel insurance. None received compensation from their travel insurance policies. I gather the Vancouver birth was not specifically covered while the U.S. ones failed because of "pre-existing conditions".

The B.C. Medical Services Plan did not cover the costs.

The foregoing events are examples that stress the need for health insurance while you travel. Albeit, these are unusual examples and deal only with tourists. But it raises the issue of coverage when you leave Canada to go to a new homeland and after having been a non-resident of Canada, returning.

One should look very carefully at the relevant health coverage a province or territory provides and when it kicks in. And don't forget, most plans require you to be a "resident" of that province or territory to receive coverage. Most jurisdictions have a waiting period before coverage occurs.

So emigrant or immigrant beware — an unexpected illness, etc., can be a disastrous financial event. Make sure that you are covered.

HEALTH INSURANCE

Some time ago, the Ontario Ministry of Health placed notices in airports warning, "Don't Leave the Country Without Reading This...Whether you are a business traveller, a student or a vacationer — whether you plan to be out of Canada for half a day or a half a year — you need extra health coverage."

Because of restrictions on the amounts which provincial/territorial health insurance plans will reimburse for medical expenses incurred outside of Canada, Canadians who spend even a short time abroad now require supplementary private health insurance coverage. If you plan to live outside Canada for an extended period, you will need a complete package of private medical and hospital benefits.

LEAVING CANADA

I have already stated that Canadians wishing to establish non-resident status for income tax purposes must cancel their government health insurance because participation in such a plan constitutes a significant residential tie with Canada.

If you leave Canada to reside elsewhere and do not cancel your government health insurance, you will likely find yourself ineligible for coverage in any case. Whether you qualify for provincial/territorial health insurance is determined by whether you are a resident of the jurisdiction in question. However, since residency regulations vary widely across Canada (and, by the way, are totally unrelated to the residency rules for income tax purposes), you should never assume that your coverage is continuing or has lapsed without checking with provincial/territorial authorities. While the consequences with regard to provincial health insurance for a family who pack up all their belongings and head overseas for five years may be fairly predictable, other cases involving, for example, rotational employment or a pattern of seasonal migration in search of warmer weather, may be less clear cut. In some instances (if you are not concerned about the residency implications for tax purposes), you may be able to apply for an extension of provincial/territorial coverage.

PROVINCIAL/TERRITORIAL INSURANCE

If you plan to live outside Canada, it is essential that you investigate the impact on your government health insurance both at the time you leave Canada and upon your return. Government regulations are, of course, subject to change. In every instance I strongly recommend that you contact your provincial or territorial health insurance authorities at the addresses given to confirm current rules and their effect on your particular situation.

CONTACTS

I recommend that you contact your provincial/territorial health insurance office with any questions regarding coverage:

Alberta
www.health.alberta.ca

British Columbia
www.health.gov.bc.ca

Manitoba
www.gov.mb.ca

New Brunswick
www.gnb.ca

Newfoundland and Labrador (Avalon Region)
www.gov.nl.ca/

Northwest Territories
www.gov.nt.ca

Nova Scotia
www.novascotia.co/

Nunavut
www.gov.nu.ca/health

Ontario
www.health.gov.on.ca

Prince Edward Island
www.healthpei.ca

Québec
www.ramq.gouv.qc.ca/en

Saskatchewan
www.saskatchewan.ca

Yukon Territory
www.hss.gov.yk.ca

PRIVATE HEALTH PLANS

Private Health Insurance While Living Abroad

While we are gradually becoming more accustomed to the idea, the average Canadian has little experience in purchasing medical and hospital insurance coverage. If you accept an international posting, your employer may provide health insurance for yourself and your dependents. If no such benefit package is available to you, you may be responsible for choosing and purchasing your own insurance. In some instances, it may also be possible to obtain coverage under a government-sponsored scheme in your new country of residence.

In any case, you would be wise to review your coverage options carefully with a professional insurance advisor familiar with the needs of expatriates.

While the author is not an insurance expert, a little research has enabled him to identify some of the concerns you will want to keep in mind when consulting an insurance professional. As is the case with insurance policies generally, expatriate medical coverage will have a maximum coverage limit, either per year or by type of benefit. Policies frequently also have territorial limits, largely because of the high cost of medical expenses incurred in North America. The premium for a policy which covers your family not only in your new country of residence but also on visits home or while travelling in the United States may be as much as double the cost of a similar policy excluding North America. Some policies are designed to accommodate business travel and visits home by allowing North American coverage for a limited number of days in each year.

Insurers may offer a range of benefits depending on whether you choose the economy or luxury version of their coverage. For example, one policy may cover in-patient hospital care only while another may cover out-patient care and even home nursing or visits to a general practitioner. Services may also be subject to a deductible or user fee. Medical care related to a pre-existing condition may or may not be covered. Policies can sometimes be supplemented with coverage for pregnancy and delivery (there may be a waiting period before coverage commences), prescription drugs, dental care (emergency and/or routine), long-term disability and income replacement, accidental death or dismemberment, life insurance and even insurance of personal liability and possessions.

A 24-hour helpline, access to English or French-speaking doctors and air evacuation service may be essential if you will be living or travelling to areas of the world where medical care is inadequate. Provision for a family member to travel with the patient, especially if the patient is a child, may also be a concern. You will want to give some thought to the specific evacuation provisions, bearing in mind that evacuation may simply take you to the nearest source of adequate care, not necessarily to the location of your choice. If your work involves travel to any of the world's "hot spots", you will also want to enquire as to whether war and other similar risks are excluded.

An insurance company's reputation for prompt processing and payment of claims is an important consideration but one which is difficult to assess. You may have to rely on the recommendations of colleagues. However, you should be able to investigate questions such as whether the policy provides for payment directly to the hospital and whether efforts have been made to eliminate any difficulty with currency exchange in the payment process.

Returning to Canada

Until recently, a Canadian who fell ill while living overseas could return to Canada and count on virtually immediate acceptance into a provincial/territorial health insurance plan. You should be aware, however, that in an effort to ensure that only those individuals genuinely resident in their jurisdiction receive coverage, certain provinces/territories have instituted waiting periods for returning Canadians.

You should investigate whether any waiting period will be covered by the provisions of the policy which insured you and your family while you lived overseas. Three-month extensions are becoming routine for Canadian companies with expatriate clients but will be less familiar to insurers based outside Canada. Never assume you will be covered without checking with your insurance provider. Always discuss how coverage would be handled in unusual circumstances, such as a sudden return to Canada part way through your employment contract or a prolonged round the world vacation at the end of your assignment. If you cannot arrange continuation of your overseas policy to cover a provincial/territorial waiting period, some assistance is available from insurance companies who offer insurance for travellers. These companies will provide you with the same type of "emergency" coverage you can buy for visitors to Canada. Policies are likely to cover emergency care but not treatment for pre-existing conditions, checkups and the like.

If you are considering "visitor to Canada" medical insurance, take note that most insurers require that coverage begin within a few days of entry into the country. Delay in applying may make you ineligible. Depending on the company, it may be possible to arrange in advance for coverage to commence on your date of arrival. Payment can generally be made by credit card.

SAFEGUARDING YOUR HEALTH

There are many resources in Canada to assist the prospective expatriate to maintain good health while abroad. Numerous travellers' clinics, public service organizations and a variety of books provide information on the risks associated with travel to all areas of the world and advice regarding precautionary measures such as immunization, prophylactic drugs and portable medical supplies.

Travellers' Clinics

The Canadian Society for International Health publishes a list of Travellers' Health Centres in Canada. Clinics may offer pre-travel advice, post-travel or both. The full list is available on their web site or by writing to:

Canadian Society for International Health
1 Nicholas St.
Suite 726
Ottawa, Ontario
K1N 7B7
Canada
Tel: 613-241-5785
www.csih.org

Information on travellers' clinics is also available from your local Public Health Unit (www.phac-aspc.gc.ca). For a list of travel clinics worldwide, visit www.istm.org, the web site of the International Society of Travel Medicine.

IAMAT

The International Association for Medical Assistance to Travellers was established a number of years ago by a Toronto doctor. The Association's stated aim is "to make competent care available to the traveller around the world (even in very remote places) by doctors who usually speak either English or French and have had medical training in Europe or North America."

While membership in IAMAT is free, donations are appreciated to support the work of the association, which is funded solely through voluntary contributions.

Members receive the IAMAT Directory, which lists physicians in countries worldwide who have agreed to IAMAT's standard fee schedule. IAMAT has reviewed their professional qualifications and determined that all speak English or another language in addition to their native tongue.

IAMAT also publishes detailed information regarding the world risk of malaria, schistosomiasis and Chagas' disease. If you make a substantial donation, you can also request the "24 World Climate Charts" which provide information on climate and the sanitary conditions of water, milk and food for hundreds of locations worldwide. The Association also sells a free-standing bed "mosquito" net.

For further information contact: IAMAT
                                          www.iamat.org

Canadian Medic Alert Foundation

If you have a medical condition such as diabetes, hypertension or asthma, a drug allergy, or an implant such as a pacemaker, a Medic Alert bracelet or necklet could save your life. If you are ill or injured and cannot communicate, the Medic Alert "ident", engraved with your primary medical information, your membership number and the 24-hour Medic Alert Hotline number, will give emergency personnel essential information. A collect call to Medic Alert will enable medical staff to obtain information on your medical history, the medications you take, your allergies and how to reach your physician and other emergency contacts.

For further information contact:

Canadian Medic Alert
2005 Sheppard Avenue East
Suite 800
Toronto, Ontario
Canada
M2J 5B4
Tel: 416-696-0267
Toll Free: 1-800-668-1507
www.medicalert.ca

HEALTHY READING

There are numerous health guides for travellers available. Reference to other sources can be found in the bibliographies of the following books:

International Travel Health Guide
Stuart R. Rose, M.D. and Jay S. Keystone, M.D.
www.travmed.com/health-guide

Travel Health Guide
Mark Wise, M.D.
www.drwisetravel.com

HEALTH SUPPLIES

If you will be travelling to areas where sanitation and medical care may be inadequate, you may wish to check out the following source for water filters and purifiers, mosquito nets and a wide variety of medical kits ranging from basic first aid needs to sterile syringes, hypodermic needles and other supplies designed to reduce the risk from contaminated medical equipment.

Travel Medicine, Inc.
www.travmed.com

HEALTHY PETS

If you plan to take family pets to live with you outside Canada, you should, of course, check with the relevant authority on your new country of residence regarding vaccination requirements, import restrictions, quarantine periods and so on.

For information on bringing animals back into Canada, contact:

Canadian Food Inspection Agency
www.inspection.gc.ca

CANADIAN CONSULAR ASSISTANCE

Canada's embassies, consulates and other missions abroad provide assistance to Canadian residents travelling in their areas. A full listing of Canadian missions is contained in the Appendix.

Enquiries Service
Global Affairs Canada
125 Sussex Drive
Ottawa, Ontario
K1A 0G2
Canada
Tel: 613-944-6788
Toll Free: 1-800-267-6788 (within Canada)
Fax: 613-996-9709
www.international.gc.ca

Canadian missions offer 24-hour assistance. For emergency assistance, you can also call Foreign Affairs, Trade and Development Canada in Ottawa at 613-996-8885 or e-mail using the online form at the Department's web site or at enqserv@international.gc.ca and sos@international.gc.ca.

The web site is an excellent source of information on a wide range of travel-related topics, from passports, visas and customs requirements to advice for the woman traveller. There are publications on working and retiring abroad, as well as on a number of more specialized topics. You can also access Travel Reports on 220 destinations, as well as weekly Travel Bulletins highlighting current hot spots. The U.S. Department of State also posts information and travel warnings on its web site at www.travel.state.gov.

HEATHY TRAVEL WEB SITES

The following web sites provide very useful health-related information for travellers, ranging from immunization recommendations and regional disease outbreaks to food and water safety.

www.cdc.gov/travel	National Center for Infectious Diseases (U.S. Travelers' Health)
www.phac-aspc.gc.ca	Public Health Agency of Canada
www.travelhealth.gc.ca	Health Canada Travel Medicine Program

8

Canadian Driver's Licences

Canadians planning to live overseas frequently ask us whether they must relinquish their provincial/territorial driver's licences. Most are concerned that retention of a Canadian licence might jeopardize their non-resident status for taxation purposes. In fact, a Canadian driver's licence represents only a minor tie with Canada which should not, in the absence of other ties, affect non-resident status.

However, it is the responsibility of each province or territory to determine whether a person living outside Canada can continue to hold a valid provincial driver's licence. Our research indicates that provincial policies vary widely. For further information, contact the relevant authority listed below:

ALBERTA
www.alberta.ca

BRITISH COLUMBIA
www.icbc.com

MANITOBA
www.gov.mb.ca

NEW BRUNSWICK
Service New Brunswick
www.gnb.ca

NEWFOUNDLAND AND LABRADOR
www.gov.nl.ca

NORTHWEST TERRITORIES
www.gov.nt.ca

NOVA SCOTIA
www.gov.ns.ca

NUNAVUT
www.gov.nu.ca

ONTARIO
www.mto.gov.on.ca

PRINCE EDWARD ISLAND
www.gov.pe.ca

QUEBEC
www.saaq.gouv.qc.ca

SASKATCHEWAN
www.gov.sk.ca

YUKON
www.gov.yk.ca

9

Goods and Services Tax (GST)/ Harmonized Sales Tax (HST)

WHAT IS THE GST/HST?

The goods and services tax (GST) is a tax that applies to most supplies of goods and services made in Canada. The GST also applies to supplies of real property (for example, land, buildings and interests in such property) and intangible property such as trademarks, rights to use a patent, and digitized products downloaded from the internet and paid for individually.

The participating provinces harmonized their provincial sales tax with the GST to implement the harmonized sales tax (HST) in those provinces. Generally, the HST applies to the same base of goods and services as the GST. GST/HST registrants who make taxable supplies (other than zero-rated supplies) in the participating provinces collect tax at the applicable HST rate. GST/HST registrants collect tax at the 5% GST rate on taxable supplies they make in the rest of Canada (other than zero-rated supplies).

GST/HST Rates	
	On or after April 1, 2013
Ontario	HST at 13%
Nova Scotia	HST at 15%
New Brunswick	HST at 15%
Newfoundland and Labrador	HST at 15%
Prince Edward Island	HST at 14%
Territories and other provinces in Canada	GST at 5%

Who Pays the GST/HST?

Almost everyone has to pay the GST/HST on purchases of taxable supplies of goods and services (other than zero-rated supplies). The GST/HST also applies to most supplies of intangible personal property and certain supplies of real property. However, Native Indians and some groups and organizations, such as certain provincial and territorial governments, do not always pay the GST/HST on their purchases.

TAXABLE SUPPLIES

Most property and services supplied in or imported into Canada are subject to GST/HST.

Supplies Taxable at 5%, 13%, 14% or 15%

Examples of supplies taxable at 5%, 13%, 14% or 15% include:
- sales of new housing (certain sales of new housing may be subject to a previous rate of GST/HST);
- sales and rentals of commercial real property;
- sales and leases of automobiles;
- car repairs;
- soft drinks, candies, and potato chips;
- clothing and footwear
- taxi and limousine transportation;
- legal and accounting services;
- franchises;
- hotel accommodation; and
- barber and hairstylist services.

Zero-Rated Supplies

Some supplies are zero-rated under the GST/HST — that is, GST/HST applies at a rate of 0%. This means that you do not charge GST/HST on these supplies, but you may claim input tax credits for the GST/HST paid or payable on purchases and expenses made to provide these supplies. Examples of supplies taxable at 0% (zero-rated) include:
- basic groceries such as milk, bread, and vegetables;
- agricultural products such as grain, raw wool, and dried tobacco leaves;
- most farm livestock;
- most fishery products such as fish for human consumption;

- prescription drugs and drug-dispensing services;
- medical devices such as hearing aids and artificial teeth;
- exports (most goods and services for which you charge and collect the GST/HST in Canada are zero-rated when exported); and
- many transportation services where the origin or destination is outside Canada.

Exempt Supplies

Some supplies are exempt from the GST/HST — that is, no GST/HST applies to them. This means that you do not charge the GST/HST on these supplies of property and services, and you do not claim input tax credits.

Examples of exempt supplies include:
- a sale of housing that was last used by an individual as a place of residence;
- long-term rentals of residential accommodation (of one month or more) and residential condominium fees;
- most health, medical and dental services performed by licensed physicians or dentists for medical reasons;
- child care services, where the primary purpose is to provide care and supervision to children 14 years of age or under for periods of less than 24 hours per day;
- most domestic ferry services;
- legal aid services;
- certificate or a diploma that certifies the ability of individuals to practise or perform a trade or vocation or tutoring services made to an individual in a course that follows a curriculum designed by a school authority;
- music lesions;
- most services provided by financial institutions such as lending money or operating deposit accounts;
- arranging for and the issuance of insurance policies by an insurer and the arranging for the issuance of insurance policies by insurance agents;
- most goods and services provided by charities; and
- certain goods and services provided by non-profit organizations, governments, and public service bodies such as municipal transit services and standard residential services such as water distribution.

Should You Register?

You have to register for GST/HST if:
- you provide taxable supplies in Canada; and
- you are not a small supplier.

You do not have to register if:
- you are a small supplier (that does not carry on a taxi business);
- your only commercial activity is the sale of real property, other than in the course of a business. Although you do not have to register for the GST/HST in this case, your sale of real property may still be taxable and you may have to charge and collect the tax; or
- you are a non-resident who does not carry on business in Canada (see Guide RC4027, *Doing Business in Canada — GST/HST Information for Non-Residents*).

If your business is registered for the GST, your business is also registered for the HST.

Small Supplier

You are a small supplier and do not have to register if you meet one of the following conditions:
- you are a **sole proprietor** and your total revenues from taxable supplies (before expenses) from all your businesses are $30,000 or less in the last four consecutive calendar quarters or in any single calendar quarter;
- you are a **partnership or a corporation** and your total revenues from taxable supplies (before expenses) are $30,000 or less in the last four consecutive calendar quarters or in any single calendar quarter; or
- you are a **public service body** (charity, non-profit organization, municipality, university, public college, school authority or hospital authority) and your total revenues from taxable supplies from all of the activities of the organization are $50,000 or less in the last four consecutive calendar quarters or in any single calendar quarter. A gross revenue threshold of $250,000 also applies to charities and public institutions. For more information, see Guide RC4082, *GST/HST Information for Charities*.

10

Canada Pension Plan and Old Age Security

CANADA PENSION PLAN (CPP)

The Canada Pension Plan (CPP) came into effect on January 1, 1966 and became fully effective January 1, 1976. Pensions are paid to persons in retirement and to widows, widowers, orphans, the disabled and children of disabled contributors. The retirement pension is earnings-related and payable in addition to Old Age Security payments. There is also a death benefit which is payable to the estate of a contributor.

Contributions are required from employees, the self-employed and employers. These are required from individuals from age 18 to age 65 (or to age 70 if the individual continues to work and does not apply for his or her retirement pension).

Since January 1, 1978, a contributor may collect his or her retirement pension as early as age 60, subject to an actuarial adjustment, if he or she has wholly or substantially ceased working.

No benefit is payable unless you make an application in writing and payment of the benefit has been approved. Applications are made on a prescribed form (Application for Retirement Pension Canada Pension Plan) addressed to Service Canada (see address below).

To be eligible for a retirement pension, you must have:
• contributed to CPP for at least one year;
• reached the age of 60; and
• substantially ceased working, if under 65 years of age.

The amount of your retirement pension is calculated on the basis of your pensionable earnings. This amount may be determined by making an inquiry to Service Canada (www.servicecanada.gc.ca). In general terms, as long as you have contributed to the CPP for at least one year, you will be eligible for a retirement pension of some amount. As well, your surviving spouse or orphaned children may be eligible for a survivor's pension. You do not have to be resident in Canada to apply for or to receive this retirement pension.

Since January 1, 1996, CPP payments made to non-residents of Canada have been subject to non-resident withholding tax of 25%. The rate may be reduced where there is a tax treaty between Canada and your country of residence. Some non-residents with relatively modest amounts of income, substantially from Canadian sources, may be able to obtain a reduction of the non-resident tax.

Please Note: Changes to the Canada Pension Plan (CPP)

These changes will affect you if you are:
- an employee who contributes to the Canada Pension Plan (CPP), whether you are just starting your career or you are planning to retire soon;
- a self-employed person who contributes to the CPP;
- between the ages of 60 and 70 and you work while receiving your CPP retirement pension (or if you work outside of Quebec while receiving a Quebec Pension Plan (QPP) retirement pension); or
- an employer who contributes to the CPP on behalf of your employees.

You will not be affected by these changes if you started receiving a CPP retirement pension before December 31, 2010, and you remain out of the work force.

The CPP operates throughout Canada, expect in Quebec, where the Quebec Pension Plan (QPP) provides benefits. These changes do not apply to the QPP.

What are the Changes?

The following changes to the CPP will be phased in gradually between 2011 and 2016, with the first major change occurring in January 2011 for people retiring after age 65:
- Your monthly CPP retirement pension amount will increase by a larger percentage if you take it after age 65 (gradually from 2011 to 2013).
- Your monthly CPP retirement pension amount will decrease by a larger percentage if you take it before age 65 (gradually from 2012 to 2016).
- The number of years of low or zero earnings that are automatically dropped from the calculation of the CPP retirement pension will increase (in 2012 and 2014).
- You will be able to begin receiving your CPP retirement pension without any work interruption (starting in 2012).
- If you are under 65 and you work while receiving your CPP retirement pension, you and your employer will have to make CPP contributions (or if you work outside of Quebec while receiving a QPP retirement pension) (starting in 2012). These contributions will increase your CPP retirement benefits (starting in 2013).

- If you are age 65 to 70 and you work while receiving your CPP retirement pension, you can choose to make CPP contributions (or if you work outside of Quebec while receiving a QPP retirement pension) (starting in 2012). These contributions will increase your CPP benefits (starting in 2013).

These changes will improve retirement flexibility for working individuals in Canada, enhance pension coverage, and improve equity in the CPP.

Remember, your CPP benefits may also be subject to tax in your country of residence.

OLD AGE SECURITY (OAS)

OAS is payable in addition to CPP. It is a flat-rate pension, escalated quarterly according to any increase in the Canadian Consumer Price Index, and payable at age 65. Application for OAS may be made to Service Canada (www. servicecanada.gc.ca) (see address below).

In order to qualify for OAS payments while living outside of Canada, you must have resided in Canada for at least 20 years after your 18th birthday. The 20 years need not have been consecutive. The amount of your OAS pension may be less than the maximum, however, if certain conditions relating to the period or periods you have been resident in Canada are not met. A current pensioner who has not completed 20 years Canadian residency will continue to receive payments for six months after leaving Canada, whereupon payments will be suspended until the individual resumes residence in Canada.

Since January 1, 1996, OAS payments have been subject to non-resident withholding tax of 25%. The rate of tax may be reduced where there is a tax treaty between Canada and your country of residence. As in the case of CPP benefits, some non-residents with relatively modest amounts of income, substantially from Canadian sources, may be able to obtain a reduction of the non-resident tax.

Also effective January 1, 1996, OAS payments to non-residents became subject to a "recovery tax" or clawback designed to reduce payments to higher-income pensioners. Non-resident recipients of OAS must report their world income to the Canada Revenue Agency by submitting the OAS Return of Income (T1136) (see Appendix), due April 30 of each year. Recovery tax will be applied at a rate of 11.25% of the amount by which your net income after certain allowable deductions exceeds $73,756 (2016) (this figure may change from year to year). OAS payments for the current year will be based on the previous year's income.

The recovery tax may be reduced or, in some cases eliminated, by a social security agreement between Canada and your country of residence. Only those who reside in countries which are "recovery tax exempt" (slightly less than half of the countries with which Canada has a tax treaty) are not required to report.

For all other countries (including other tax treaty countries) the full amount of
the OAS payment will be withheld if the report is not filed.

Once again, I hate to remind you, but any amount you do receive may be
subject to non-resident withholding tax in Canada and may also be taxed in your
country of residence.

By the same token, tax paid to Canada may qualify for a foreign tax credit
in your country of residence.

Please Note: Changes to Old Age Security

Eligibility for the Old Age Security Pension and the Guaranteed Income Supplement

The Government of Canada proposes to gradually increase the age old eligibility
for the OAS pension and the Guaranteed Income Supplement (GIS) between the
years 2023 and 2029, from 65 to 67. **People currently receiving OAS benefits will
not be affected by the proposed changes**. Select your birth year from the following
list to see how your eligibility may change for the OAS pension and the GIS:

* 1957 or earlier
* 1958
* 1959
* 1960
* 1961
* 1962
* 1963 or later

The Government of Canada also proposes to gradually increase the ages at
which the Allowance and the Allowance for the Survivor are provided, from 60-
64 today to 62-66.

Voluntary Deferral of the Old Age Security Pension

Changes to Old Age Security

The Government of Canada also proposes a voluntary deferral of the Old Age
Security (OAS) pension that will give people the option to defer take- up of their
OAS pension by up to five years past the age of eligibility, and subsequently
receive a higher, actuarially adjusted pension.

Proactive Enrolment for OAS Benefits

To improve services for seniors, the Government of Canada proposes to start a proactive enrolment process that will remove the need for many seniors to apply for the OAS pension and the GIS. This means that eligible seniors will no longer need to complete an OAS pension or GIS application.

Proactive enrolment will be implemented in a phased-in approach from 2013 to 2016. People who are eligible for proactive enrolment will be notified personally by mail. Service Canada will continue to send applications to those seniors who cannot be proactively enrolled for OAS benefits. Applications are also available on the Service Canada website. Further information on proactive enrolment will be provided as it becomes available.

I question whether non-resident seniors will be notified personally by mail. If you live outside of Canada, you will likely have to apply. Good luck!

Lived or Living Outside Canada — Pensions and Benefits

If you have lived or worked in Canada and in another country, or you are the survivor of someone who has lived or worked in Canada and in another country, you may be eligible for pensions and benefits from Canada and/or from the other country because of a social security agreement.

What is a social security agreement?

A social security agreement is an international agreement between Canada and another country that is designed to coordinate the pension programs of the two countries for people who have lived or worked in both countries.

Canada has signed social security agreements with a number of other countries that offer comparable pension programs.

The requirements under the social security agreements vary from agreement to agreement. It is important to check the details of the agreement that relates to you.

How can a social security agreement help me qualify for benefits?

A social security agreement can help you qualify for benefits by allowing you to combine your periods of contribution or periods of residency in Canada with your periods of contribution or periods of residency in the other country to meet the minimum eligibility criteria. It can also reduce or eliminate restrictions based on citizenship or on payment of pensions abroad.

Note: Possible eligibility for more than one benefit

You may be eligible for a foreign pension, a Canadian pension, or both.

Canadian benefits

If you have lived and/or worked in Canada and in another country, and do not meet the contributory or residence requirement for a Canada Pension Plan or Old Age Security benefit, a social security agreement may help you qualify. It might also provide benefits to your surviving spouse, common-law partner or children.

The Canadian benefits included in Canada's international social security agreements are those paid under the Old Age Security program and the Canada Pension Plan program.

Foreign benefits

The foreign benefits covered by Canada's international social security agreements vary from agreement to agreement. It is important to check the details of the agreement that relates to you.

Applying for Benefits

To learn about the benefits covered under a social security agreement, whether you might be eligible, and how to apply, you can go to the Service Canada (http://www.servicecanada.gc.ca/eng/services/pensions/international) and select a country from the drop-down menu under "Applying for Benefits".

Note: A country without a social security agreement

If you live or lived in another country that doesn't have a social security agreement with Canada, you must apply for your foreign benefits directly to that country's social security authorities and apply for your Canadian pensions and benefits using the application forms and procedures found through the links from the Pensions in Canada page.

Canada's Social Agreements with other Countries

Currency: March 4, 2013

Social security agreement and CPT form number

(The CPT form referred to above can be downloaded from the Canada Revenue Agency website. CRA has a list of all the countries that have a social security agreement with Canada. The same list is below with the relevant CPT form numbers. The CPT is an application for a certificate of coverage under a social security agreement.)

Country	Date in force	CPT form number
Antigua and Barbuda	January 1, 1994	111
Austria	November 1, 1987	112
Barbados	January 1, 1986	113
Belgium	January 1, 1987	121
Brazil	August 8, 2011	168
Bulgaria	March 1, 2014	170
Chile	June 1, 1998	114
Croatia	May 1, 1999	115
Cyprus	May 1, 1991	116
Czech Republic	January 1, 2003	137
Denmark	January 1, 1986	117
Dominica	January 1, 1989	118
Estonia	November 1, 2006	142
Finland	February 1, 1988	128
France	March 1, 1981	52
Germany	April 1, 1988	130
Greece	December 1, 1997	54
Grenada	February 1, 1999	119
Guernsey	January 1, 1994	120

Country	Date in force	CPT form number
Hungary	October 1, 2003	141
Iceland	October 1, 1989	49
India	August 1, 2015	169
Ireland	January 1, 1992	50
Israel	September 1, 2003	140
Italy	January 1, 1979	51
Jamaica	January 1, 1984	57
Japan	March 1, 2008	122
Jersey	January 1, 1994	120
Korea (South)	May 1, 1999	58
Latvia	November 1, 2006	143
Lithuania	November 1, 2006	144
Luxembourg	April 1, 1990	60
Macedonia	November 1, 2011	163
Malta	March 1, 1992	61
Mexico	May 1, 1996	62
Morocco	March 1, 2010	166
Netherlands	April 1, 2004	63
Norway	January 1, 1987	127
Philippines	March 1, 1997	64
Poland	October 1, 2009	161
Portugal	May 1, 1981	55
Romania	November 1, 2011	165
St. Kitts and Nevis	January 1, 1994	65
Saint Lucia	January 1, 1988	67
Saint Vincent and the Grenadines	November 1, 1998	66

Country	Date in force	CPT form number
Serbia	April 12, 2013	162
Slovakia	January 1, 2003	138
Slovenia	January 1, 2001	68
Spain	January 1, 1988	125
Sweden	April 1, 2003	129
Switzerland	October 1, 1995	69
Trinidad and Tobago	July 1, 1999	70
Turkey	January 1, 2005	72
United Kingdom	April 1, 1998	71
United States	August 1, 1984	56
Uruguay	January 1, 2002	136

(*Author's Note: Two other countries have a social Agreement with Canada: Australia – July 26, 2001 (last update) and New Zealand – April 9, 1996. For some reason beyond my knowledge there does not seem to be a CPT form assigned to these two countries.*)

FURTHER INFORMATION

For further information regarding CPP or OAS, contact:

Service Canada
www.servicecanada.gc.ca

11

Customs and Excise

RESIDENTS RETURNING TO CANADA

(Author's Note: The following has been adapted from the Canada Border Service Agency's web site (www.cbsa.gc.ca) and Memorandum D2-3-2. If you are in the process of planning to return to Canada, I recommend that you go to the web site to determine if the rules have changed.)

The following will be helpful if you are:
- entering Canada with the intention of establishing, for the first time, a residence for a period of not less than one year;
- coming to Canada for temporary employment for a period of more than three years;
- moving back to Canada to resume residence after an absence of at least one year, or after being a resident of another country for at least one year.

The CBSA considers one year to be one calendar year from your date of departure.

For example, if you leave on January 1, 2010, and return on January 1, 2011, you are considered to have been absent for one year.

In all cases, you may qualify for duty- and tax-free importation of your personal and household goods, if you meet the conditions outlined herein after.

Before leaving for Canada

Before you leave for Canada, you should prepare **two copies** of a list (preferably typewritten) of **all** the goods you intend to bring into Canada as part of your personal effects. The list should indicate the value, make, model and serial number (when applicable) of all the goods.

You should describe each item of jewellery you plan to bring into Canada on the list of goods you submit. Since jewellery is difficult to describe accurately, it is best to use the wording from your insurance policy or jeweller's appraisal and to include photographs that have been dated and signed by the jeweller or a gemologist. This information makes it easier to identify the jewellery when you first enter Canada, and later on when you return from a trip abroad with this jewellery.

Divide the list into **two** sections. In the first section, list the goods you are bringing with you; in the second, list the **goods to follow**. Goods that arrive later will **only** qualify for duty- and tax-free importation under your entitlement as a settler or former resident **if they are on your original list**.

Who are considered Settlers?

Under customs legislation, "Settlers" means all individuals who enter Canada with the intention of establishing, for the first time, a residence for a period of not less than 12 months.

It is important to know that the status of a person for customs purposes is not always the same as the person's status for immigration purposes.

For example,

• Persons coming to Canada for the purposes of employment for a period **exceeding** 36 months (other than United States Preclearance personnel) are at first arrival considered to be Settlers to Canada even though they may be considered Temporary Residents for immigration purposes;

• Persons entering Canada to become Permanent Residents without the intention of residing immediately in Canada are not considered Settlers to Canada since they do not have any intention of remaining in Canada at that time, and will live outside Canada for an undetermined period of time. Therefore, under customs legislation, these persons are considered visitors to Canada, even if they are Permanent Residents for immigration purposes.

Who are considered Former Residents?

• Former Residents of Canada are persons who are returning to Canada to resume residence in Canada after having been residents of another country for a period of not less than one year. Persons who establish themselves as residents of another country for a period of at least one year may make return visits to Canada (as non-resident visitors) without jeopardizing their former resident entitlement.

• However, persons who do **not** establish themselves as residents of another country during their absence from Canada, such as those on extended vacations, voyages or world cruises, are only eligible to the former resident entitlement if the duration of their absence is a continuous period of at least one year, without any return to Canada having been made during that time. Should these persons make return visits to Canada, they will be entitled to a personal exemption as described in the publication called "*I Declare*".

Items you can import duty- and tax-free

Settlers and Former Residents can include the following personal and household effects in their duty- and tax-free entitlement:
- clothing and linen;
- furniture;
- furnishings;
- appliances;
- silverware;
- jewellery;
- antiques;
- family heirlooms;
- private collections of coins, stamps and art;
- personal computers;
- books;
- musical instruments;
- hobby tools and other hobby items;
- personal vehicles;
- pleasure boats and the trailers to carry them (trailers are subject to Transport Canada requirements);
- mobile trailers, not exceeding 2.6 metres (9 feet) in width, that the owner is capable of moving on his or her own;
- utility trailers;
- motor homes;
- private aircraft; and
- tool sheds or garages that do not attach to or form part of a dwelling.

A house, a large trailer you use as a residence and any goods you use or will use commercially **are not** eligible as personal or household effects. These goods are subject to regular duty and taxes.

Value limitation (CAN$10,000)

If you are a **former resident** of Canada, any single personal or household item (including an automobile) that is worth more than CAN$10,000 on the date you import it is subject to applicable duty and taxes on the amount that is over CAN$10,000. This applies to items acquired after March 31, 1977.

Additional personal exemption

If you are a **former resident** who is returning to resume residence in Canada, you are entitled to claim a duty- and tax-free personal exemption of a maximum value of CAN$800 for goods you acquired abroad or while in transit. You do not have to own, possess or use these goods before you return to Canada to resume residence.

Wedding gifts

If you got married within three months of coming to Canada or if you plan to marry no later than three months after arriving in this country, you can bring in your wedding gifts free of duty and taxes. However, you must have owned and possessed the gifts before you arrived in Canada. In this instance, the requirement to have used the goods does not apply. These same conditions apply to household goods you bring in as part of a bride's trousseau.

Ownership, possession and use requirements

To import goods duty- and tax-free, Settlers must have owned, possessed and used the goods prior to their arrival in Canada and Former Residents must have owned, possessed and used the goods for at least six months before returning to resume residence.

It is important that you meet these three requirements. For example, if you owned and possessed the goods without using them, the goods will be subject to duty and taxes. Please note that leased goods are subject to duty and taxes because the CBSA does not consider that you own them. If you have bills of sale and registration documents, they can help you prove that you meet these requirements.

Even if your goods meet the ownership, possession and use requirements, they must still meet other government department requirements. For information on other restrictions and/or requirements for goods being imported into Canada, see the section called "Restrictions".

Exceptions to ownership, possession and use requirements

If you are a **former resident**, the six-month stipulation will be waived if you have been absent from Canada for five years or more. Therefore, you only need to have owned, possessed and used your personal and household effects (for a period of time) before you return.

Replacement goods

Replacement goods imported by Former Residents are also exempt from the six-month requirement. However, they must have owned, possessed and used the goods abroad before returning to Canada to resume residence. To qualify for the exemption, the goods must be replacements for goods that would have met the six-month ownership, possession and use requirements, except for the fact that they were lost or destroyed as a result of a fire, a theft, an accident or another unforeseen circumstance.

In addition, replacement goods must be of a similar class and about the same value as the goods they are replacing. You will need to show proof of this. If you intend to claim replacement goods, to ensure that the goods qualify, call the BIS at one of the telephone numbers listed in the section called "Additional information".

Declaring your goods

When you arrive, **even** if you have no goods with you at the time, you must give your list of goods to the border services officer **at your first point of arrival in Canada**. Based on the list of goods you submit, the officer will complete a Form B4, *Personal Effects Accounting Document*, assign a file number to it and give you a copy of the completed form as a receipt. You will need to present your copy of this form to claim free importation of your unaccompanied goods when they arrive. Goods to follow may be subject to import restrictions before you can import them.

To facilitate the clearance process, you can complete Form B4, in advance of your arrival at the first port of entry in Canada. You can obtain a copy of the form on the CBSA web site at www.cbsa.gc.ca.

Disposing of goods you imported duty- and tax-free

If you import goods duty- and tax-free into Canada and if you sell or give the goods away within the first year of importing them into Canada, you will have to pay any applicable duty and taxes immediately. If you divert the goods for commercial use, the same rule applies.

Public health

If you are suffering from a communicable disease upon your arrival/return in Canada, or if you have been in close contact with someone with a communicable disease, you are obligated to inform a border services officer or a quarantine officer who can determine if you require further assessment. If you have been ill while travelling or become ill after you arrive/return in Canada, consult a Canadian doctor and inform the doctor that you have travelled abroad, where you were and what, if any, treatment or medical care you have received (e.g. medications, blood transfusions, injections, dental care or surgery).

Alcoholic beverages

Alcoholic beverages are products that exceed 0.5% alcohol by volume. If you meet the minimum age requirements of the province or territory where you enter Canada, you can include limited quantities of alcoholic beverages in your personal entitlement. These items **must be in your possession** upon your arrival/ return. Minimum ages for the importation of alcoholic beverages as prescribed by provincial or territorial authorities are 18 years for Alberta, Manitoba and Quebec; and 19 years for the remaining provinces and territories.

You are allowed to import only **one** of the following amounts of alcohol free of duty and taxes:

• 1.5 litres (53 imperial ounces) of wine;
• a total of 1.14 litres (40 ounces) of alcoholic beverages; **or**
• up to a maximum of 8.5 litres of beer or ale.

Note

The CBSA classifies "cooler" products according to the alcoholic beverage they contain. For example, alcohol coolers are considered to be alcoholic beverages and wine coolers are considered to be wine. Beverages not exceeding 0.5% alcohol by volume are not considered to be alcoholic beverages.

The quantities of alcohol you bring in must be within the limit set by the province or territory where you will enter Canada. If the value of the goods is more than the free allowance, you will have to pay duty and taxes as well as provincial/territorial assessments. In Nunavut and the Northwest Territories, you cannot bring in more than the free allowance. For more information, contact the appropriate provincial or territorial liquor control authority **before** coming to Canada.

If you intend to ship alcoholic beverages to Canada (e.g. the contents of a bar or wine cellar), contact the appropriate provincial or territorial liquor control authority beforehand so you can pay the provincial or territorial fees and assessments in advance. To obtain release of the shipment in Canada, you have to produce a copy of the provincial or territorial receipt and pay all of the applicable federal assessments.

Tobacco products

You are allowed to bring **all** of the following amounts of tobacco into Canada
free of duty and taxes if these products are **in your possession** upon arrival:
* 200 cigarettes;
* 50 cigars;
* 200 grams (7 ounces) of manufactured tobacco; **and**
* 200 tobacco sticks.

Note

If you include cigarettes, tobacco sticks or manufactured tobacco in your
personal exemption allowance, a partial exemption may apply. You will have to
pay a special duty on these products **unless** they are marked "**CANADA DUTY
PAID — DROIT ACQUITTÉ**." You will find Canadian-made products sold at a
duty-free shop marked this way. You can speed up your clearance by having
your tobacco products available for inspection when you arrive.

If you bring in more than your personal allowance, you will have to pay
regular assessments on the excess amount. These regular assessments can include
duty and taxes as well as provincial or territorial fees. In certain cases, provincial
and territorial limits may apply.

In addition, the *Excise Act, 2001* limits the quantity of tobacco products that
may be imported (or possessed) by an individual for personal use if the tobacco
product is not packaged and stamped "**CANADA DUTY PAID — DROIT
ACQUITTÉ**." The limit is currently five units of tobacco products. **One** unit of
tobacco products consists of one of the following:
* 200 cigarettes;
* 50 cigars;
* 200 grams (7 ounces) of manufactured tobacco; **or**
* 200 tobacco sticks.

Travelling with CAN$10,000 or more

If you have currency or monetary instruments equal to or greater than
CAN$10,000 (or the equivalent in a foreign currency) in your possession when
arriving in or departing from Canada, you must report this to the CBSA.
Monetary instruments include items such as stocks, bonds, bank drafts, cheques,
and travellers' cheques.

CBSA reminds all travellers that this regulation applies to currency and
monetary instruments you have on your person, in your baggage and in your
vehicle.

Upon your arrival in Canada with CAN$10,000 or more in your possession, it must be reported on the CBSA Declaration Card (if one was provided to you), or in the verbal declaration made to a border services officer.

When departing Canada by air with CAN$10,000 or more in your possession, you must report to the CBSA office within the airport, prior to clearing security or, if departing by land or boat, report your intent to export to the CBSA at one of our offices.

Settlers' effects acquired with blocked currencies

Some countries limit the amount of money you can take out of the country. You should check with your banker, lawyer or financial advisor. If this is the case, you may be able to take advantage of a special provision that may allow you to claim free importation of certain goods.

To claim free importation of goods under the provisions of the *Settlers' Effects Acquired With Blocked Currencies Remission Order*, it will be necessary for you to satisfy the CBSA at the time of importation that the country from which you emigrated does in fact apply restrictions on the transfer of capital by emigrants to Canada and that, due to such restrictions, the currency on deposit could not be exported at the time of emigration.

Settlers from countries that apply currency restrictions may have up to three years to import goods purchased with blocked funds on deposit in the former country of domicile prior to their arrival in Canada without reference to the ownership, possession and use requirements abroad.

Restrictions

The importation of certain goods is restricted in Canada. The following are examples of some of these goods. Make sure you have the information you require before attempting to import these items into Canada.

Firearms and weapons

You must declare all weapons and firearms at the port of entry when you enter Canada. **If not, you could face prosecution and the goods may be seized**.

For more detailed information on importing a firearm into Canada, see the publication called *Importing a Firearm or Weapon Into Canada*.

For information about applying for a Canadian firearms licence or a firearms registration certificate, or to obtain an *Application for an Authorization to Transport Restricted Firearms and Prohibited Firearms* (Form CAFC 679) **in advance**, please contact:

Canadian Firearms Program
Ottawa ON K1A 0R2
Telephone: 1-800-731-4000 (toll-free in Canada and the United States)
506-624-5380 (from all other countries)
Fax: 613-825-0297
E-mail: cfp-pcaf@rcmp-grc.gc.ca
web site: www.rcmp.gc.ca/cfp

Explosives, fireworks and ammunition

You are required to have written authorization and permits to bring explosives, fireworks and some types of ammunition into Canada. For more information, contact Natural Resources Canada:

Explosives Regulatory Division
Natural Resources Canada
1431 Merivale Road
Ottawa ON K1A 0G1
Telephone: 613-948-5200

Vehicles

Vehicles include any kind of pleasure vehicles such as passenger cars, pickup trucks, camper trucks, vans, Jeeps, chassis cabs, motorcycles, snowmobiles and motor homes, as long as you use them for non-commercial purposes. However, you should be aware that Transport Canada has many requirements that apply to vehicles.

Transport Canada defines a vehicle as any vehicle that is capable of being driven or drawn on roads, by any means other than muscular power exclusively, but not including a vehicle designed to run exclusively on rails. Trailers such as recreational, boat, camping, horse and stock trailers are considered vehicles as are wood chippers, generators or any other equipment mounted on rims and tires.

For Transport Canada requirements on the importation of any vehicle, refer to the CBSA publication "*Importing a Vehicle Into Canada*" which is available on the CBSA web site at www.cbsa.gc.ca, or visit the Transport Canada web site at www.tc.gc.ca.

Import restrictions apply to most used or secondhand vehicles that are not manufactured in the current year and are imported from a country other than the United States.

Before you import a vehicle, you **should** also contact the Registrar of Imported Vehicles at:

Telephone: **1-888-848-8240** (toll-free in Canada and the United States)
416-626-6812 (from outside Canada and the United States)
web site: www.riv.ca

This is an agency which is contracted by Transport Canada to administer a
national program to ensure that imported vehicles are brought into compliance
with Canada's safety standards.

web site: www.nrcan.gc.ca

Restrictions on temporary importing

You are only allowed to bring temporarily into Canada a vehicle for the purpose
of transporting your household or personal effects into or out of Canada. In all
other circumstances, if you buy, lease, rent or borrow a vehicle while outside
Canada, Transport Canada and border services legislation does not allow you to
bring a vehicle into Canada for your personal use, even temporarily, unless it
meets all Transport Canada requirements and you pay the duty and federal taxes
that apply. For exceptions, consult Memorandum D2-4-1, Temporary
Importation of Conveyances by Residents of Canada, and Memorandum D8-
1-1, Amendments to Temporary Importation (Tariff Item No. 9993.00.00)
Regulations, which are available on the CBSA web site at www.cbsa.gc.ca under
"Publications and forms". You can also call the Border Information Service
(BIS) at one of the telephone numbers listed in the section called "Additional
information".

The duty and taxes, as well as the Registrar of Imported Vehicles fee, are not
refunded when the vehicle leaves Canada.

Goods subject to import controls

To monitor the effects of imports on Canadian manufacturers, there are import
controls on items such as clothing, handbags and textiles. These controls are
outlined in the *Export and Import Permits Act*. Depending on the value, quantity
or type of goods you intend to import, you may need an import permit even if
you qualify for a personal exemption.

For more information, call the BIS at one of the telephone numbers listed in
the section called "Additional information", or contact the Export and Import
Controls Bureau:

Export and Import Controls Bureau
Foreign Affairs and International Trade Canada
125 Sussex Drive
Ottawa ON K1A 0G2
web site: www.international.gc.ca

Prohibited consumer products

The *Hazardous Products Act* prohibits the importation of consumer products that could pose a danger to the public (e.g. baby walkers and jequirity beans that are often found in art or beadwork). Settlers and Former Residents should be aware of the consumer products that have safety requirements in Canada. Many of these safety requirements are stricter than requirements for other countries. For more information about prohibited and restricted products, contact Health Canada:

Telephone: 1-866-662-0666 (toll-free in Canada)
613-952-1014 (from all other countries)
web site: www.healthcanada.gc.ca

Food, plants, animals and related products

All food, plants, animals and related products must be declared. Food can carry diseases such as E. coli. Plants and plant products can carry invasive alien species such as the Asian long-horned beetle. Animals and animal products can carry diseases such as avian influenza and foot and-mouth disease. Furthermore, certain species of plants and animals are protected under the *Convention on International Trade in Endangered Species of Wild Fauna and Flora* (CITES) and their trade is carefully controlled. Because of these risks, the Government of Canada regulates the import and export of certain food, plants, animals and related products to and from Canada.

Based on emerging threats, import requirements for food, plants, animals and related products are subject to change on a daily basis. For the most up-to-date import requirements for these items, refer to the Canadian Food Inspection Agency's (CFIA) Automated Import Reference System (AIRS) at www.inspection.gc.ca. AIRS is an automated reference tool that will lead you through a series of questions about food, plants, animals or related products you wish to import to determine the applicable regulations, policies and import requirements.

Note

CITES import requirements do not appear in the AIRS. If you have questions about importing a CITES species, visit www.ec.gc.ca or call the Canadian Wildlife Service at 1-800-668-6767.

In addition to the import requirements established by the CFIA and CITES, Foreign Affairs and International Trade Canada has set limits on the quantity and/or dollar value of certain food products you can bring into Canada duty-free or that you can include in food, plants, animals and related products.

All food, plants, animals and related products must be declared. Food can carry diseases such as E. coli. Plants and plant products can carry invasive alien species such as the Asian long-horned beetle. Animals and animal products can carry diseases such as avian influenza and foot and-mouth disease. Furthermore, certain species of plants and animals are protected under the *Convention on International Trade in Endangered Species of Wild Fauna and Flora* (CITES) and their trade is carefully controlled. Because of these risks, the Government of Canada regulates the import and export of certain food, plants, animals and related products to and from Canada.

Based on emerging threats, import requirements for food, plants, animals and related products are subject to change on a daily basis. For the most up-to-date import requirements for these items, refer to the Canadian Food Inspection Agency's (CFIA) Automated Import Reference System (AIRS) at www.inspection.gc.ca. AIRS is an automated reference tool that will lead you through a series of questions about food, plants, animals or related products you wish to import to determine the applicable regulations, policies and import requirements.

Note

CITES import requirements do not appear in the AIRS. If you have questions about importing a CITES species, visit www.ec.gc.ca or call the Canadian Wildlife Service at **1-800-668-6767**.

In addition to the import requirements established by the CFIA and CITES, Foreign Affairs and International Trade Canada has set limits on the quantity and/or dollar value of certain food products you can bring into Canada duty-free or that you can include in your personal entitlement.

Unless you have an import permit from Foreign Affairs and International Trade Canada for quantities over the established limits, you will have to pay duty and taxes ranging from 150% to 300% of the value of the goods.

For more information, refer to the "Food, Plant and Animal Inspections" section of the CBSA web site at www.cbsa.gc.ca or call the BIS at one of the telephone numbers listed in the section called "Additional information".

Prohibited goods

You cannot import prohibited goods such as obscene material, hate propaganda and child pornography into Canada.

Health products (prescription drugs)

In Canada, health products may be regulated differently than they are in other countries. For example, what is available without a prescription in one country may require a prescription in Canada. Canada, like many other countries, has restrictions on the quantities and types of health products that can be brought in. For more information regarding health products and their importation into Canada, please consult Health Canada's web site at www.hc-sc.gc.ca.

Cultural property

Certain antiquities or cultural objects considered to have historical significance to their country of origin cannot be brought into Canada without the appropriate export permits. Before you import such items, you should contact Canadian Heritage:

Movable Cultural Property Program
Canadian Heritage
15 Eddy Street, 3rd Floor
Gatineau QC K1A 0M5
Telephone: 819-997-7761
Fax: 819-997-7757
web site: www.pch.gc.ca

Items you import for commercial use

If you import vehicles, farm equipment or other capital equipment to use in construction, contracting or manufacturing, or other goods for use in a trade, you have to pay the goods and services tax and any applicable duty on these items.

Additional information

For more information, within Canada call the Border Information Service at **1-800-461-9999**. From outside Canada, call 204-983-3500 or 506-636-5064 (long distance charges will apply). Agents are available Monday to Friday (08:00-16:00 local time / except holidays). TTY is also available within Canada at **1-866-335-3237**.

You may obtain further information by consulting the publications (Guides and Brochures) available on the CBSA web site at www.cbsa.gc.ca.

12

Death and Taxation

WILLS

Whether you venture abroad, or, after reading all of this, opt to live out your days in Canada, it is essential that you ensure the smooth administration of your affairs should you die or become disabled. As a first step, you need a Will. To cite only the most basic advantages, a Will allows you to choose the executors who will administer your estate and, within certain legal limitations, your beneficiaries. If you die without a Will, these matters will be decided according to prescribed legal formulae which may result in ongoing government involvement in your affairs. I strongly recommend that you seek appropriate legal advice in making these decisions and drawing up the necessary documents.

Canadians who plan to live abroad should also prepare for the possibility they may die abroad. You would be well advised to seek legal counsel in every jurisdiction where you reside, have assets or other connections to determine the precise legal consequences of your demise. You may, for example, need to have a Will in more than one jurisdiction.

Your death will also have tax consequences. Your estate or heirs may be responsible for inheritance tax outside of Canada. If you die as a non-resident for Canadian tax purposes, you should be aware that the various tax deferred transfers to a spouse do not apply. As a result, your taxable Canadian property (TCP) will be deemed to be disposed of at fair market value on the date of your death. Your executor will be required to file a Canadian tax return to report this gain and pay the resulting tax.

Non-residents for tax purposes may be concerned that maintaining a Will in a province/territory of Canada would constitute a significant residential tie with Canada. In fact, such a document would be viewed as a minor tie only, necessary for the administration of your property.

DEATH OF A NON-RESIDENT

All your TCP will be deemed to be disposed at its fair market value at the date of death. This occurs even if you leave your property to your spouse. Death will trigger the payment of tax you elected to defer at the date of departure. This includes the tax deferred on both TCP and non-TCP.

As noted in previous chapters, the definition of Taxable Canadian Property (TCP) was changed on March 4, 2010. You may have had a property that was TCP if you left Canada prior to March 5, 2010. Now due to the amendments, the property is no longer TCP.

On the other hand, you may have acquired property after your departure from Canada that may now qualify as TCP under the new rules. As well, you may have a property that was non-TCP when you acquired it, but later became TCP. As a result, it is worthwhile to review what now qualifies as TCP.

Effective after March 4, 2010, TCP includes the following assets:

- real or immovable property situated in Canada;
- property including goodwill, inventory used by you in a business carried on in Canada;
- shares of capital stock of a corporation (other than a mutual fund corporation) that is not listed on a designated stock exchange , an interest in a partnership or an interest in a trust (other than a mutual fund trust or an income interest in a trust resident in Canada), if at any time during the past 60 months, more than 50% of the value of the corporation's shares or interest in a partnership or trust is derived from one or any combination of
  i.   real or immovable property situated in Canada,
  ii. Canadian resource property,
  iii. timber resource property, and
  iv. options or interests in any of the properties listed in i, ii and iii.
- shares of a corporation that is listed on a designated stock exchange, shares of a mutual fund corporation or units of a mutual fund trust, where you together with related persons own 25% or more of the issued shares of any class of capital stock or issued units of the trust and, at any time in the past 60 months, more than 50% of the value of those shares or units was derived from the items listed in i, ii, iii and iv above;
- an option in respect of, or an interest in any of the properties listed above, whether or not the property exists;
- Canadian resource property;
- timber resource property;
- income interest in a trust resident in Canada;
- retired partner's right to share income or losses from his/her former partnership, and
- a life insurance policy in Canada.

As you can see, TCP could be shares of a foreign corporation that in turn owns shares in a Canadian private corporation loaded (more than 50%) with Canadian real estate (real or immovable).

RRSPs/RRIFs enjoy some protection, if they are transferred directly to a surviving spouse or dependent child. The rules are similar to those applied if you are a resident. If there is no spouse or dependent child, the value of the RRSPs/RRIFs/LIFs at date of death will be subject to non-resident withholding tax. Care must be taken in this area to ensure that the tax burden is minimized.

Life insurance proceeds remain tax-free to the beneficiary regardless of whether they are resident or non-resident.

Death benefits will be tax-free up to $10,000. The excess will be subject to non-resident withholding tax if paid by a Canadian employer to a non-resident. The excess will be included in the recipient's income if they are resident at the time of payment.

Mutual funds and other non-TCP will be deemed to be disposed at fair market value. Fortunately, aside from triggering the payment of the tax-deferred on departure, no further gain is taxable by Canada.

The former family home or cottage can create tax consequences. Since there is no tax-deferred rollover to a surviving spouse, they will be deemed to be disposed of at fair market value. The tax may be reduced if the estate can claim a principal residence exemption on a portion of the gain. Remember, your executors can only use those years that you were a resident to get this protection.

The foregoing is a brief overview of some of the issues that arise on the death of a non-resident. Due to the complexity of this area, I recommend you seek professional assistance to ensure that your final tax bill is minimized. Good news! I have recently created an interactive workbook which will assist you to compile all your relevant documentation into an easily searchable format. It is called *When I Die: Financial Planning for Life and Death*.

When I Die is an essential tool to help you understand how to minimize the costs that may arise on your death and the various aspects of the financial impact of dying. It can be used as a guide to facilitate the organization of your estate while you are still alive and act as a source of information for your loved ones after your final departure.

When I Die: Financial Planning for Life and Death 2017 can be acquired from Carswell online: www.carswell.com.

POWERS OF ATTORNEY

When you visit your lawyer, you should also inquire about the benefit of giving powers of attorney to the person you wish to manage your affairs in the event you are no longer able to do so yourself. While some jurisdictions recognize powers of attorney for both property and financial affairs and for personal care, you will need legal advice in each place where you reside, have assets or other connections to determine whether powers given in one jurisdiction will be valid in another.

Appendix

The following Canada Revenue Agency forms and documents are available from the Agency's website: *www.cra-arc.gc.ca*.

I✦I Canada Revenue   Agence du revenu
Agency   du Canada

**Application by a non-resident of Canada
for a reduction in the amount of
non-resident tax required to be withheld
for tax year** _____

Protected B
when completed

▶ **NEW – Effective January 2011, a non-resident will only be required to file one Form NR5 every five taxation years and the non-resident would retain their original reduction coverage throughout this five year approval period.**

Section 1 – Information and terms of agreement

- As a non-resident, it may be beneficial for you to elect under section 217 of the Canadian *Income Tax Act* to pay tax at the same rate as residents of Canada on your Canadian-source pensions or other benefits described in Section 2 below. If you wish to elect under section 217, we will use the information you give on this application to determine if the election may benefit you. If we process your application and it indicates that an election under section 217 may be beneficial, we will authorize your Canadian payer(s) to reduce the amount of non-resident tax withheld from your benefits. Your reduction will be valid for **five years**.

- If we approve this application, you will have to file a Canadian income tax return within six months of the end of every taxation year covered under the five year approval period to benefit from the election under section 217. If you do not file your return within that time, you will have to pay the full amount of tax that your payer(s) should have withheld. We cannot process a return if it is filed late.

- If you are a resident of Algeria, Azerbaijan, Brazil, Croatia, Cyprus, Ecuador, Greece, Ireland, Italy, the Philippines, Portugal, Romania, Senegal, Slovenia or Turkey and are applying only to receive a treaty exemption on qualifying income, complete all sections of this form and report all your Canadian-source benefits. Although you are not electing under section 217 and need not to file a Canadian income tax return, we also require information on your net world income. **We will apply the treaty exemption on qualifying income.**

- If you have questions about this application, contact the International and Ottawa Tax Services Office by writing to P.O. Box 9769, Station T, Ottawa ON K1G 3Y4, or by telephone, toll free, at **1-855-284-5946** (in Canada or the United States), or from elsewhere at **613-940-8499**. The fax number is 613-941-6905.

Section 2 – Types of Canadian benefits you have to report in Section 4 below

1. Canada Pension Plan (CPP) or Quebec Pension Plan (QPP) benefits
2. Old Age Security (OAS) pension
3. Superannuation or pension benefits including registered pension plan (RPP) benefits*
4. Retiring allowance*

5. Death benefits
6. Benefits under the *Employment Insurance Act*
7. Registered retirement savings plan (RRSP) payments*
8. Registered retirement income fund (RRIF) payments

*Do not use this application for amounts 3, 4, or 7 that you are transferring to your RRSP or RPP. Instead, use Form NRTA1, *Authorization for Non-Resident Tax Exemption*. For additional Canadian benefits, refer to guide T4145 – *Electing Under Section 217 of the Income Tax Act*

Section 3 – Applicant identification (please print)

First name	Last name	*Your Canadian Social Insurance Number (SIN) or Individual Tax Number (ITN)
Address (street number and name)		Your date of birth Y M D
City	Country	Zip or postal code	Date of departure from Canada Y M D
Telephone number	Spouse's name	Spouse's SIN or ITN

***If you do not have a SIN or ITN, please complete Form T1261,
*Application for a Canada Revenue Agency Individual Tax Number (ITN) for Non-Residents.***

Section 4 – Canadian benefits described in Section 2 above that you will receive in the year

a) Social security benefits (in CAN$)	Account number	Estimated gross annual amount (CAN$)
☐ CPP benefits (do not include death benefits).....	_____	$
☐ QPP benefits (do not include death benefits).....	_____	$
☐ CPP/QPP death benefits	_____	$
☐ OAS benefits*	_____	$

*Do not report OAS Guaranteed Income Supplement in this section. Report it on line (b) of Section 5.

b) Other Canadian benefits (in CAN$) (please indicate any additional benefits on a separate sheet)		$
☐ Pension payment (☐ periodic or ☐ lump-sum payment)		
☐ RRSP payment	$	
☐ RRIF payment (please give minimum amount)	$	
☐ Other (please specify type) _____		

Payer's name	Policy plan number
Payer's mailing address (street number and name)	City	Province	Postal code

NR5 E (15)   (Ce formulaire existe en français.)

Canadä

Section 5 – Net world income information (in CAN$)*

a) **Estimated other Canadian-source income (employment and business income, and taxable Canadian capital gains) for which you have to file a Canadian income tax return** (including amounts that are exempt under the Canadian *Income Tax Act* or by virtue of a treaty between Canada and your country of residence). Please give details on a separate sheet, indicating type and amount of income and allowable deductions .... $ _____ |

b) **Estimated other Canadian-source income** (e.g. interest, dividends, net rental, Guaranteed Income Supplement) ... $ _____ |

c) **Will you receive income from sources outside Canada?** ☐ Yes ☐ No
If **yes**, please indicate the estimated amount for the upcoming year
(e.g. interest, dividends, pensions, income from employment, social security, other)

Total income from sources outside Canada .... $ _____ |

* If there are changes to your estimated world income for the year, please file an amended application no later than 30 days after these changes occur.

Member of a recognized religious order. Will you be giving your total superannuation, pension, and earned income to the religious order and claiming a vow of perpetual poverty deduction on your Canadian income tax return?........... Yes ☐   No ☐

Section 6 – Non-refundable tax credit information

1. If you are married or have a common-law spouse, are you supporting your spouse? .... Yes ☐ No ☐

   A common-law spouse is a person with whom you live in a common-law relationship for any continuous period of at least 12 months, or with whom you live in a common-law relationship and who is the natural or adoptive parent of your child.

2. Are you single, divorced, separated, or widowed, and supporting a relative who, on December 31 of the tax year, will be under 19, except for a relative who has a mental or physical disability*? .... Yes ☐ No ☐

   If you claim a person here, you cannot claim that person again in question 3 below.

3. Do you support a disabled* dependent relative who, on December 31 of the tax year, will be 18 years old or older, and who has a physical or mental infirmity? .... Yes ☐ No ☐

4. During the tax year, will you pay tuition fees for yourself or will you be a full-time student? .... Yes ☐ No ☐

   If **yes**, please give the following information:
   • amount of your tuition fees, for courses you will take in the year, to attend a university or a college .... $ _____ |
   • number of months in the year that you will be enrolled full-time in a qualifying educational program at a Canadian university, college, or a school offering job retraining courses or correspondence courses, or a university outside of Canada ....
   • amount of any scholarships, fellowships, or bursaries you will receive in the tax year .... $ _____ |

5. Do you have a prolonged disability*?.. Yes ☐ No ☐

* The disability must markedly restrict the activities of daily living and should have lasted or be expected to last for at least 12 consecutive months. If you make a claim for the disability tax credit or a claim for a disabled dependant, you will have to file a completed Form T2201, Disability Tax Credit Certificate, with your Canadian income tax return.

Section 7 – Dependent information
If you answered **yes** in questions 1, 2, or 3 of Section 6 above, please give the following information (attach a list if you need more space):

Dependant's name
Residential address

Relationship to you	Date of birth Y M D	Nature of disability, if any
Estimated annual world income (CAN$)		

Section 8 – Certification

I, _____ , certify that the information given on this form is, to the best of my knowledge, correct and complete. I understand and agree with the terms outlined in Section 1. *Information and terms of agreement.*

_____   _____
Non-resident's signature   Date

Note
If you are signing for the applicant, you have to include a copy of the power of attorney document with this application.

I✦I Canada Revenue Agency   Agence du revenu du Canada

Protected B when completed

UNDERTAKING TO FILE AN INCOME TAX RETURN BY A NON-RESIDENT RECEIVING RENT FROM REAL OR IMMOVABLE PROPERTY OR RECEIVING A TIMBER ROYALTY

for tax year _____

Before completing this form, please read the instructions on the back.

Section 1 – Non-resident identification

Last name or, if applicable, complete name of the corporation, trust, or estate	First name	Social insurance number or Canadian individual tax number
Address (street number and name)		Date of birth Year Month Day
City Country Postal or zip code		Canadian, corporation, trust, or estate tax account number
Area code and telephone number ( )		Fiscal year end for corporation, trust, or estate Year Month Day
Mailing address if different than above C/O		**Do not write in this area**
Street number and name		
City Country Postal or zip code		

Section 2 – Rental property information

Addresses of all rental properties (list additional properties on a separate sheet) Address			Gross rents	Total expenses *	Net income
City Province Postal code					
Address					
City Province Postal code					
Address					
City Province Postal code					
* Provide a breakdown of expenses for each property on a separate sheet (see Section 2 on the back). **Total ▶**					

Section 3 – Undertaking by non-resident

I, the undersigned, undertake to file an income tax return under subsection 216(4) of the Canadian *Income Tax Act* for the tax year indicated above, within six months of the tax year, to include all rents from my real or immovable property and timber royalties, and to pay any additional tax owing. If I do not fulfill these obligations, I will have to pay to the Receiver General for Canada, the full amount of tax that I would otherwise have been required to remit in the year, as well as applicable interest charges.

_____ _____ _____
Non-resident's signature   Name of representative* (please print)   Date

* If you sign for the non-resident, print your name on this line and provide a copy of the power of attorney document.

Section 4 – Canadian agent* identification

Name (individual or company)	Non-resident tax account number **N R** ☐☐☐☐☐☐
Address (street number and name)	Date the first rental payment is due Year Month
City Province Postal code	Area code and telephone number ( )

* For purposes of this form, the "agent" must be a resident of Canada to whom the rental payments are paid or credited on behalf of the non-resident when this form is signed.

I, the undersigned, declare that I am the Canadian agent of the non-resident indicated in Section 1. If the non-resident does not file an income tax return or pay tax according to the undertaking, I understand that I will have to pay to the Receiver General for Canada the full amount of tax that would otherwise have been required to be remitted for the year, as well as applicable penalty and interest charges.

_____ _____ _____
Agent's signature   Name of individual signing on the agent's behalf (please print)   Date

* If the agent is a company, print the name of the person signing on the agent's behalf.

NR6 E (13)   (Ce formulaire existe en français.)   **Canada**

Instructions

General

- Use this form if you are a non-resident receiving rent from real or immovable property or a timber royalty and you want your agent to be able to elect to deduct and remit tax at the applicable rate on the net amounts available to you. Your agent must be a resident of Canada to whom the rental payments are paid or credited on your behalf when this form is signed.

- File a separate form for each tax year. For individuals, the tax year corresponds to the calendar year (January 1 to December 31). For corporations, estates, and trusts, the tax year can differ from the calendar year, therefore, for these entities, indicate the fiscal year end.

- File this form on or before the first day of each tax year, or when the first rental payment is due.

- Complete all applicable sections on this form. An incomplete form will not be accepted as a valid undertaking and will be returned.

- The non-resident individual, corporation, trust, estate, or member of a partnership should forward one completed copy of this form to the Canadian agent who, after completing Section 4, will file it with the International Tax Services Office, P.O. Box 9769, Station T, Ottawa ON, K1G 3Y4.

- We will advise both the non-resident and the agent in writing when a valid undertaking is approved.

- Your agent must continue to withhold and remit non-resident tax based on the gross rental income until we approve a valid undertaking in writing. If a valid NR6 is approved, the non-resident withholding tax must be determined when the actual rental payment is made taking into account expenses (excluding CCA). We must receive any non-resident tax withheld by the 15th day of the month following the month during which the rental payment was paid or credited to the agent on the non-resident's behalf.

- The non-resident undertakes to file an income tax return, whether there is a profit or a loss situation, under subsection 216(4) of the Canadian *Income Tax Act* within six months of the end of the tax year for which the undertaking is filed. Each non-resident member of a partnership who files a valid undertaking must file a separate income tax return. For information on how to complete a Section 216 return, see the *Income Tax Guide for Non-Residents Electing Under Section 216*.

- The agent has to file an NR4 return before March 31 of the year after the year in which the rental income was paid or credited, or within 90 days of the fiscal year end for estates and trusts. For information on how to complete the NR4 return, see the *Non-Resident Withholding Tax Guide*.

- For more information, see Information Circular 77-16R4, *Non-Resident Income Tax* and Interpretation Bulletin 393R2, *Election Re: Tax on Rents and Timber Royalties – Non-Residents*, contact the International Tax and Non-Resident Enquiries line at **1-855-284-5946** (within Canada and the United States), or at **613-940-8495**.

Section 1 – Non-resident identification

- Print your name and address, including your country of residence, and telephone number.

- For individuals, provide your Canadian social insurance number (SIN) or individual tax number (ITN) and your date of birth. If you don't have a SIN or ITN please complete Form T1261, *Application for a Canada Revenue Agency Individual Tax Number (ITN) for Non-Residents*.

- For corporations, trusts, and estates, provide your Canadian tax account number as well as your fiscal year end.

- Provide your mailing address if it is different from your residential address.

Section 2 – Rental property information

- List all rental properties and provide the address of each rental property. Include the street number and name, apartment or suite number (lot and concession if a rural property), town or city, province or territory, and postal code. List additional properties on a separate sheet.

- Provide the estimated gross income, total expenses, and net income for the year for each property.

- On a separate sheet, provide an itemized estimate of the expenses you expect to incur during the year for each property. (**You have to provide this information.**) Include the current and prepaid expenses that relate to the day to day management of your property. Do not include capital cost allowance, depreciation, and amortization. You can claim these amounts when you file your income tax return.

- Each non-resident member of a partnership filing an undertaking should report only his or her share of the gross rents, total expenses, and net income.

- Rent on real or immovable property includes crop-sharing proceeds.

Section 3 – Undertaking by non-resident

- Sign and date in the designated area.

- You must sign this form for the undertaking to be valid.

- If a representative signs on your behalf, he or she must print his or her name in the space provided and attach a copy of the power of attorney document.

- **If you do not fulfill your obligations as specified in the undertaking, you will have to pay to the Receiver General for Canada, the full amount of tax that you would otherwise have been required to remit in the year, as well as applicable interest charges. We calculate the required amount of tax at the statutory rate of 25% of the gross rental income, unless reduced to a lesser rate by the provisions of a bilateral tax treaty, minus the amount of tax already remitted for the year.**

Section 4 – Canadian agent identification

- To be considered an agent for the purposes of this form, you must be a resident of Canada to whom the rental payments are paid or credited on behalf of the non-resident when this form is signed.

- Print your name, address, city or town, province, postal code, and telephone number.

- Provide your non-resident tax account number. If you do not have one, we will assign one to you when we process this form.

- Provide the first month of the year for which you expect to receive rental income.

- Sign and date in the designated area.

- **If the non-resident does not file the income tax return or pay tax according to the conditions of the undertaking, you as agent will have to pay to the Receiver General for Canada the full amount of tax that would otherwise have been required to be remitted in the year, as well as applicable penalty and interest charges. We calculate the required amount of tax at the statutory rate of 25% of the gross rental income, unless reduced to a lesser rate by the provisions of a bilateral tax treaty, minus the amount of tax already remitted for the year.**

- If you fail to file the NR4 return by the due date, you may be charged a penalty and interest.

I✦I Canada Revenue Agency / Agence du revenu du Canada

Protected B when completed

Application For Refund of Part XIII Tax Withheld

NR7-R Control Number

Applicant

Name

Canadian Tax Identification Number (SIN,ITN,BN, etc.)

Mailing address (authorized) C/O

Details of payment and tax withheld

Gross Amount	$ _____	☐ $ U.S. or ☐ _____	Tax Year: _____
Tax remitted (____ %) Rate	$ _____	☐ $ U.S. or ☐ _____	**IMPORTANT**: Check boxes only if tax was **remitted** in a currency other than $Cdn. funds. See notes on back for instructions on foreign currency refunds and other information for this section.
Tax payable (____ %) Rate	$ _____	☐ $ U.S. or ☐ _____	
Refund (____ %) Rate	$ _____	☐ $ U.S. or ☐ _____	

Type of payment:
☐ Interest Repayable in: ☐ $ U.S. or ☐ $ Cdn. Security lending arrangement: ☐ Yes or ☐ No
   Bond: ☐ Yes or ☐ No   Bond (purchase) price: $ _____
☐ Dividend security name: _____   CUSIP number: _____
   Payable date: | Year | Month | Day | Number of shares: _____ (At Record Date)
☐ Periodic pension ☐ OAS ☐ CPP/QPP ☐ RPP ☐ RRSP ☐ Lump sum pension ☐ Annuity ☐ Retiring allowance
☐ RRIF FMV _____ (beginning of year) Minimum amount _____ (for the year)
☐ Other payment (specify): _____

Reason for refund

The beneficial owner is:
☐ A holder of a comfort letter or Letter of Exemption (treaty Article XXI (Cdn. – U.S.), Canadian Securities Dealer etc.), # _____
☐ Entitled to a lower rate under treaty Article # _____ of ____ % as resident of _____ (country) at the time of payment
☐ Entitled to a treaty exemption under Article # _____ as a resident of _____ (country) at the time of payment
☐ A person resident in the US who is considered to have derived the income through an entity that is fiscally transparent under the laws of the US, in accordance with paragraphs 6 and 7 of Article IV of the Canada-United States tax treaty. As such, the person is entitled to a lower rate under treaty Article # _____ of _____ % at the time of payment.
☐ Entitled for another reason. (Specify details.)

Participants (name and address):
Canadian payer or agent (who paid the amount): _____
Canadian payer or agent (who withheld tax): _____
Registered owner or nominee: _____
Custodian #1: _____
Custodian #2: _____
Beneficial Owner: _____

Mandatory attachments (if applicable):
☐ (Notarized) Affidavit of Registered Ownership or (authorized) D.T.C. Statement
☐ (Notarized) Affidavit of Beneficial Ownership
☐ Structure chart(s) and any other pertinent information explaining treaty rate entitlement
☐ Security Lending Arrangement
☐ Other agreement(s) (Specify. such as Royalty Agreement, etc.) _____
☐ NR4 slip or Canadian tax slip

Certification

• I certify that the information given above and in any documents attached is correct and complete; and
• I certify that the non-resident taxpayer is entitled to the benefits on the income listed. in accordance with the Limitation on Benefits provision, if such provision exists, between Canada and the country listed above

Authorized person's name (print)	Position or office	
Authorized person's signature	Date	Telephone number

Certificate of tax withheld

I, _____ (payer/agent's name) certify that the non-resident
tax of $ _____ ☐ $ Cdn. ☐ $ U.S. or _____ (specify currency) was withheld from
_____ (registered owner's name) and remitted under non-resident account
number NR _____ , and included in the amount of $ _____ ☐ $ Cdn. ☐ $ U.S.
or _____ (specify currency) and remitted on _____ (date of remitance).

Authorized person's name (print)	Position or Office	
Authorized person's signature	Date	Telephone number

Privacy Act, Personal Information Bank number CRA PPU 094

NR7-R E (15)   (Ce formulaire existe en français.)

Canadä

INSTRUCTIONS

Follow the instructions below that apply to you as a Non-resident of Canada or a Canadian Resident. Please complete all applicable sections in detail, provide all supporting documentation and a letter of explanation where necessary to avoid returning the refund application to you unprocessed. Retain a photocopy of this form for your records. In addition, please read the important instructions below in their entirety.

Residents of Canada

- Attach the NR4 slip(s) or Canadian tax slip(s) to your T1, T2 or T3 Income Tax Return if third party participants were not involved in the transaction. If your return is already processed, send an amendment request with the tax slip(s) to your local Tax Centre.

- You must complete the NR7-R application if you do not have an NR4 tax slip issued in your name, or, if third parties participated in the transaction. Attach this completed form, the appropriate affidavits and other documents to your T1, T2 or T3 Income Tax Return for the year of payment to claim a credit for any tax withheld.

Non-Residents of Canada

Applicant

- The only person/entity entitled to the refund is typically the beneficial owner. A refund will only be issued in another name, if a qualifying situation arises (e.g., partnership, multiple beneficial owners, Canadian Securities Dealers etc.). One (1) NR7-R application per year, per income type, per beneficial owner, per Canadian payer or agent's non-resident tax account number is required.

Details of payment and tax withheld

- Where tax was remitted to us in Canadian currency, you must enter the "Refund applied for" in Canadian currency. We will then issue only a Canadian currency refund. You may need to contact the Canadian payer or agent to confirm the remittance currency.

- We will issue refunds in a foreign currency only if the tax was remitted in that same foreign currency. If we approve a refund in foreign funds, we will use the exchange rate that applies on the date we issue the refund cheque. As a result, the amount refunded may be different from the amount remitted.

- You must verify the "Tax payable" rate to ensure it agrees with the rate provided under Section 212 of the *Income Tax Act* or with the relevant tax treaty rate provided within Information Circular 76-12R5 (or later) based on the non-resident's country of residence at the time of payment.

- For security payments, such as dividends or interest, we require only one (1) NR7-R application per year, per income type, per beneficial owner, per CUSIP number, per Canadian payer or agent's non-resident tax account number.

- We only issue current year refunds to clients for security payments that flowed through custodians or nominees. Otherwise, you may request a current year refund directly from the Canadian payer or agent where an NR4 slip or Canadian tax slip has not yet been issued.

- If you want to have your refund deposited directly into your bank account at a Canadian financial institution, you must attach a completed Form NR304, *Direct Deposit Request for Non-Resident Account Holders and NR7-R Refund Applicants*.

- We do not issue refunds for less than $2.00.

Reason for refund

- Ensure the appropriate "Reason for refund" is identified and any relevant exemption number for the beneficial owner is entered.

- Where there are third party participants, such as a custodian, we require an **(notarized) affidavit of beneficial ownership** linking the custodian and beneficial owner. The affidavit must include: the name of the registered owner of the security, the name of the custodian, the number of units held by the custodian, the name of the security, the payable date of the security and the notary or lawyer's seal and signature.

- Where there are third party participants, such as a custodian, we also require an **(notarized) affidavit of registered ownership** linking the custodian and the registered owner. The affidavit must include: the name of the registered owner of the security, the name of the custodian, the number of units held by the custodian, the name of the security, the payable date of the security and the notary or lawyer's seal and signature. If the transaction flowed through the Depository Trust Company (D.T.C.) in the United States, a (authorized) D.T.C. Statement, specifically a Final Detail Report, CSH SDFS Settlement Stmt Div. or Dividend Cash Settlement Items List, are *mandatory* substitutions for the "affidavit of registered ownership."

- A combined (notarized) affidavit of registered ownership and affidavit of beneficial ownership may be submitted where payments flow through one (1) third party participant other than D.T.C.

- Where more than three (3) participants are involved, we require multiple affidavits. Specify all custodians names on the front of this form.

- Only the notary or lawyer for the custodian and/or registered owner directly involved in the transaction may provide the relevant affidavits.

- U.S. Residents must ensure that they meet the requirements as stipulated in the 5th Protocol of the Canada/U.S. Tax Convention.

- You may provide forms NR301, NR302 or NR303 to support your entitlement to treaty benefits.

Certification

- Only a person authorized by the beneficial owner may sign this area.

Certificate of tax withheld

- Attach an original (or photocopy) of the NR4 slip or Canadian tax slip issued in either the beneficial owner or nominee's name.

- If an NR4 slip or Canadian tax slip was not issued in the beneficial owner's name, the Canadian payer or agent must complete this area. For security payments, such as dividend and interest, we require a certificate of tax withheld for each payable date.

General information

- The six (6)-digit Control Number printed on the front of this form will appear on the refund cheque. If you complete the form without the six (6)-digit Control Number, Canada Revenue Agency (CRA) will assign one for you.

- Send this original, signed NR7-R application form with all required documentation to the CRA, no later than two (2) years after the end of the calendar year in which the non-resident tax was remitted, to the International and Ottawa Tax Services Office, Non-Resident Withholding Division, P.O. Box 9769, Station T, Ottawa ON, K1G 3Y4, Canada.

- If you need help, please contact the International Tax and Non-Resident Enquiries line at **1-855-284-5946** (within Canada and the United States) or **613-940-8499** (outside North America). You may also send a facsimile transmission to us at **613-941-6905**.

Canada Revenue Agency   **Agence du revenu du Canada**

DETERMINATION OF RESIDENCY STATUS
(LEAVING CANADA)

- Complete all areas of this form if you plan to leave or have left Canada, either permanently or temporarily. Give all the facts about your residency status while living inside and outside Canada.
- Mail only one completed copy of this form for the tax years in question (an additional form is not necessary for each tax year unless your situation changes, or directed otherwise) to the International Tax Services Office, Post Office Box 9769, Station T Ottawa ON K1G 3Y4 CANADA. If you prefer, you can send the form by fax to 613-941-2505.
- If you need help completing this form, see Interpretation Bulletin IT-221, *Determination of an Individual's Residence Status*, or call the International tax and non-resident enquiries line at:
  - Calls from anywhere in Canada and the United States 1-855-284-5942
  - Calls from outside Canada and the United States (we accept collect calls) 1-613-940-8495
- You can find most of our forms and publications, as well as information on taxes, programs and credits, on our Web site at www.cra.gc.ca.

Attach any necessary additional information to this form.

Identification

Last name	Usual first name and initial	Social insurance number (SIN)	Tax year

Address while outside Canada	Telephone number

Do you want us to change our records to show this as your mailing address for all future correspondence? ☐ Yes ☐ No

Mailing address ONLY (if different from above)	Citizenship	In what province did you reside?	In what country will you live?

Date of departure			Marital status			Date of birth		
Day	Month	Year	☐ Married ☐ Divorced	☐ Separated ☐ Widowed	☐ Living common-law ☐ Single	Day	Month	Year

Outside Canada

How long do you expect to live outside Canada?

Number of days: ____ Number of months: ____ Number of years: ____   ☐ Leaving or left Canada permanently and no plan to return to Canada

General Information

Indicate which one of the following situations apply to you by ticking (✓) the appropriate box:

☐ You usually live in another country and you were temporarily living in Canada for ____ days in the year, but will leave, or have left Canada during the year (we will calculate the number of days if you give us the dates you were, or will be, in Canada);

☐ You usually live in another country, but enter and leave Canada on the same day to work, shop, or study.

☐ You usually live in Canada, but you leave Canada during the day to work, shop, or study in another country, and return to Canada the same day.

☐ You are vacationing outside Canada and will return to Canada after your vacation.

☐ None of the above — explain: ____

Leaving Canada

Indicate why you are leaving Canada by ticking (✓) the appropriate box:

☐ Employment   ☐ Professional or improvement leave

☐ Retirement   ☐ Spouse (or common-law partner) of an individual leaving Canada

☐ Studying or doing research   ☐ Descendant of an individual leaving Canada

☐ Self-employment   ☐ None of the above — specify: ____

Relationship

If you are a spouse (or common-law partner), child, or other dependant of an individual who has left Canada, or will be leaving, indicate whether your spouse (or common-law partner), parent, or individual you are dependent on after the person has left Canada, has been determined to be a

☐ Factual resident of Canada   ☐ Deemed resident of Canada   ☐ Non-resident of Canada   ☐ Residency status not determined

Give the name, SIN, and address of this individual: ____

If you do not know the residency status of your spouse (or common-law partner), parent, or the individual you are dependent on, have the individual complete Form NR73, *Determination of Residency Status (Leaving Canada)*, and file it with this request.

If you are the spouse (or common-law partner) of a person leaving Canada:

Are you, or were you, a resident of Canada in the current year, before leaving Canada?	☐ Yes	☐ No
Were you a resident of Canada in a previous year?	☐ Yes	☐ No
Will you live with your spouse (or common-law partner) at any time in the year?	☐ Yes	☐ No
Will you be exempt from tax in the foreign country because of your relationship to your spouse (or common-law partner)?	☐ Yes	☐ No

NR73 E (12)   (Ce formulaire est disponible en français.)

Canada

Are you the spouse (or common-law partner) of an individual employed by the Canadian Forces who has been posted abroad?	☐ Yes	☐ No

If yes, what is the length of the posting? _____ and,

Will you be returning to Canada at the end of the posting?	☐ Yes	☐ No

If you are a child or dependant of a person leaving Canada, tick (✓) the appropriate box:

☐ you are under 18 years old at any time during the year

☐ you are 18 or older and you are dependent because of a mental or physical disability

Enter your net world income for the current year _____

Employment

If you will be employed while you live abroad, tick (✓) the boxes that apply to you

☐ You are a member of the Canadian Forces

☐ You are a member of the overseas Canadian Forces school staff.

Will you choose to file a Canadian income tax return each year to report your world income?	☐ Yes	☐ No
Were you living in the province of Quebec immediately prior to your departure?	☐ Yes	☐ No

☐ You are a locally engaged employee (you lives outside of Canada after severing ties and were then hired locally) of a Canadian embassy or mission abroad

☐ You are an ambassador, a high commissioner, an agent general of a province or territory of Canada, or an officer or servant (employee) of Canada or of a province or territory of Canada

Will you receive a recommitment allowance for the year?	☐ Yes	☐ No
Were you a Canadian resident (including factual or deemed) just before your appointment or employment by Canada, the province, the territory, or the Crown corporation?	☐ Yes	☐ No

☐ You are an employee or officer of a Canadian Crown corporation, other federal or provincial, where:

☐ the corporation is designated as an agent of Canada,

☐ the employees of the corporation have been given the status of servants of Canada, or

☐ none of the above apply - explain _____

Will you receive a recommitment allowance for the year?	☐ Yes	☐ No
Were you a Canadian resident (including factual or deemed) just before your appointment or employment by Canada, the province, the territory, or the Crown corporation?	☐ Yes	☐ No

☐ You are performing services as an employee, cooperant, advisor, contractor, or sub-contractor under a prescribed international development assistance program of the Government of Canada that is financed with Canadian funds.

Specify _____

Were you a resident (including factual or deemed) at any time during the three months before the day you started your service abroad?	☐ Yes	☐ No

☐ You are a missionary.

Will you file a Canadian income tax return for each year you are living outside Canada to report your world income?	☐ Yes	☐ No
Are you a Canadian citizen or landed immigrant?	☐ Yes	☐ No
Will you be employed by a Canadian religious organization while you are outside Canada?	☐ Yes	☐ No

How many years will you be outside Canada _____

☐ You are an employee of an employer or an organization other than those described above

Give your employer's name and address _____

Is this a Canadian employer?	☐ Yes	☐ No
Do you expect to return to reside in Canada because of a contract with your employer, or because you have a specific date to report back to work in Canada?	☐ Yes	☐ No

If you have a contract with your employer, attach a copy of the contract

If you do not have a contract with your employer or a return date to Canada specified by your employer, will your job in Canada be kept available for you on your return to Canada?	☐ Yes	☐ No

STATEMENT OF RESIDENCY

Are you, under a tax treaty with another country, considered resident in the other country and not resident in Canada?	☐ Yes	☐ No
Are you subject to income tax in that country on your world income? (total income from inside and outside Canada).	☐ Yes	☐ No
Are you considered resident of a country that does not have a tax treaty with Canada?	☐ Yes	☐ No

We may ask you for confirmation from that government that you are considered resident and are subject to tax as a resident for the year in question

We may also ask you to give us proof that your income is subject to tax in that country. (e.g. Copy of the foreign tax return, notice of tax assessment, a statement from the foreign authorities with the equivalent information as the tax return. Form 6166)

Ties in Canada

Which of the following ties will you have in Canada while living in another country? Tick (✓) the boxes that apply to you

☐ Your spouse or common-law partner will stay in Canada. Give the name, SIN, citizenship, and current address of your spouse or common-law partner. If you are legally separated, this item does not apply to you. List any reason for your spouse or common-law partner to stay in Canada

☐ You will leave children or dependants in Canada. Give their names, ages, citizenship, and current address, as well as the name and address of the school they attend and the grade in which they are enrolled. List any reasons why they are staying in Canada

Which of the following ties will you have in Canada while living in another country? Tick (✓) the boxes that apply to you. (continued)

- ☐ You will continue to support a person in Canada who lives in a dwelling (e.g., a house, apartment, trailer, room, suite) that you occupied before your departure.
- ☐ You did not own but you rented a dwelling in Canada. You will sublet it for the period of your absence from Canada, and you intend to renew the lease when it expires.

You will continue to own a dwelling in Canada that is suitable for year-round occupancy and:

   a) ☐ keep the dwelling vacant;

   b) ☐ rent the dwelling to a related person;

   c) ☐ rent the dwelling on non-arm's length terms, for example, under fair market value;

   d) ☐ rent the dwelling without a written lease; or

   e) ☐ rent the dwelling at arm's length, at fair market value, and with a written lease. Explain: _____

- ☐ You will keep the majority (or a significant part) of such things as your furniture, furnishings, appliances, and utensils) in Canada.
- ☐ You will have personal possessions in Canada such as your clothing or personal items or pets.
- ☐ You will keep vehicles in Canada that are registered in a province or territory of Canada.
- ☐ You will keep your driver's licence from a province or territory of Canada.
- ☐ You will have a valid Canadian passport.
- ☐ You will have a guaranteed job available on your return to Canada.
- ☐ You will be employed by a Canadian employer while outside Canada.
- ☐ You will stay eligible for medical coverage from a province or territory of Canada for more than three months after you leave Canada. To find out whether or not you will be eligible for provincial or territorial medical coverage while living outside Canada, contact the provincial or territorial health authorities where you live.
- ☐ You will keep memberships in Canadian social, recreational, or religious organizations. List these memberships: _____
- ☐ You will keep professional or union memberships in Canada that depend on Canadian residency. List these memberships: _____
- ☐ You will keep bank accounts in Canada. Explain why you keep these accounts: _____
- ☐ You will keep and use credit cards or debit cards issued by Canadian financial institutions.
- ☐ You will have investments (RRSPs, securities, accounts, etc.) in Canada. Describe these investments: _____
- ☐ You will keep a seasonal residence in Canada (e.g., a cottage or chalet).
- ☐ You will have a telephone listing or service in Canada. Even if it is not listed, give the address for any telephone service and indicate if it is a personal or business service: _____
- ☐ You will use personal stationery or business cards with a Canadian address. Give the address you will use: _____
- ☐ You will keep a mailing address, a post office box, or a safety deposit box in Canada. Give the address for these items: _____
- ☐ You will have newspaper or magazine subscriptions sent to a Canadian address.
- ☐ You will have subscription for life or general insurance, including health insurance, through a Canadian insurance company.
- ☐ You will be involved with and have responsibilities in partnerships, corporate or business relationships, or endorsement contracts in Canada. Specify: _____
- ☐ You will keep landed immigrant status (if you are a landed immigrant) or a temporary work permit in Canada. Give the date of application for landed immigrant status or list the type of visa you have and the expiry date: _____
- ☐ You will have other ties with Canada. Describe them: _____
- ☐ None of the items in this section apply to you.

Intention

Do you intend to return to Canada to live? ☐ Yes ☐ No

Please state your long-term career goals: _____

Note – If it is determined that you are a non-resident of Canada you are expected to pay or post acceptable security for departure tax and advise Canadian financial institutions making payments to you that you may be subject to non-resident withholding taxes on certain income, i.e. dividends. For more information see form T1161 and guide T4061.

Visiting Canada

You will make return visits to Canada ☐ Yes ☐ No

If yes, select which of the following best describes your visits to Canada:

- ☐ Lengthy
- ☐ Regular
- ☐ Frequent
- ☐ None of the above

Please provide details _____

Ties in another country

a) If your spouse (or common-law partner) will not stay in Canada, give: Social Insurance Number: _____

     Spouse's (or common-law partner's) name   Citizenship: _____

     Spouse's (or common-law partner's) current address

     Spouse's (or common-law partner's) date of departure (day/month/year)

     Number of months your spouse (or common-law partner) expects to live outside of Canada

b) If you have children or dependants not staying in Canada, give their name, age, citizenship, and current address, as well as the name and address of the school they attend and the grade in which they are enrolled

c) If you have children and dependants who will follow you at a later date, give

     Their date of departure (day/month/year)

     Number of months they expect to live outside of Canada

d) If you support individuals, other than through a charitable organization, give the name and current address of these people and financial details of your support.

e) Describe the dwelling in which you live in the other country. Include details such as address, type, size, and whether you rent or own the dwelling. If you rent the dwelling, give the length of time you have agreed to be a tenant.

f) Describe the personal possessions (e.g. clothing, furniture, personal items, pets) you will have in the other country.

g) If you have a driver's licence issued in a country other than Canada, state for which country it is issued, the expiry date, and whether you will renew it.

h) If you have a foreign passport, give details as to which country it is for and if you will renew it when it expires.

i) If applicable, give the name of the insurer of your medical and hospitalization coverage while living outside Canada and the length of the coverage.

j) List the professional, social, or recreational organizations in which you will be a member in countries other than Canada.

k) Describe the investments you will have in countries other than Canada. Include details of chequing and savings accounts, pension and retirement plans, property, and shares in companies you will have in these countries. Explain why these investments are kept outside Canada.

l) Give details of other consumer relationships, such as lines of credit and credit cards, you will have in other countries.

m) Give the address for your telephone service in other countries, even if it is not listed, and indicate if it is a personal or business service.

n) Give the address you use for any personal stationery and business cards in other countries.

o) Give the address for any post office boxes and safety deposit boxes you use in other countries.

p) Give details of your involvement and responsibilities in any partnerships, corporate or business relationships, and endorsement contracts you have in other countries.

q) List the countries, other than Canada, you have visited in this calendar year, the length of time spent in each country, and the reason for visiting these countries. Include the dates of entry and departure for each country visited.

Certification

We use this form as a starting point to get the facts we need in order to give an opinion on your residency status. Contact us if your situation changes since your residency status could also change.

I, _____ (print) certify that the information given on this form is to the best of my knowledge, correct and complete.

Date _____   Signature _____

More Information

If there is more information that we have not asked for and that you feel will help us determine your residency status, give this information here

_____

_____

_____

_____

_____

Privacy Act, Personal Information Bank number CRA PPU 005

■◆■ Canada Revenue Agency / Agence du revenu du Canada

Protected B when completed

NR301

Declaration of eligibility for benefits (reduced tax) under a tax treaty for a non-resident person
(NOTE: Partnerships should use Form NR302 and hybrid entities should use Form NR303)

Use this form if you are a non-resident taxpayer resident in a country that Canada has a tax treaty with and you are eligible to receive the reduced rate of tax or exemption provided by the treaty on all or certain income and you:

- receive income subject to Part XIII withholding tax, such as investment income, pension, annuities, royalties, and estate or trust income, and the withholding tax rate is reduced by the tax treaty, or

- are completing forms T2062, *Request by a Non-Resident of Canada for a Certificate of Compliance Related to the Disposition of Taxable Canadian Property* or T2062A, *Request by a Non-Resident of Canada for a Certificate of Compliance Related to the Disposition of Canadian Resource or Timber Resource Property, Canadian Real Property (Other Than Capital Property), or Depreciable Taxable Canadian Property* to request a certificate of compliance for the disposition of treaty protected property, or

- derive income of any kind through a partnership or hybrid entity and it asks you to complete Form NR301 to support a declaration by the partnership or hybrid entity.

Please refer to the instruction pages for more information.

Part 1. **Legal name of non-resident taxpayer** (for individuals: first name, last name)

Part 2. **Mailing address:** P.O. box, apt no., street no., street name and city

State, province or territory	Postal or zip code	Country

Part 3. **Foreign tax identification number**

Part 4. **Recipient type**

☐ Individual   ☐ Corporation   ☐ Trust

Part 5. **Tax identification number**

Enter your Canadian social insurance number or Canadian individual tax number, if you have one:

Enter the corporation's Canadian business number, if it has one: R C

Enter the trust's Canadian account number, if it has one: T

Part 6. **Country of residence for treaty purposes**

Part 7. **Type of income for which the non-resident taxpayer is making this declaration**

☐ Interest, dividends, and/or royalties   ☐ Trust income   ☐ Other – specify income type or indicate "all income" _____

Part 8. **Certification and undertaking**

- I certify that the information given on this form is correct and complete.
- I certify that I am, or the non-resident taxpayer is, the beneficial owner of all income to which this form relates.
- I certify that to the best of my knowledge and based on the factual circumstances that I am, or the non-resident taxpayer is, entitled to the benefits of the tax treaty between Canada and the country indicated in part 6 on the income listed in part 7.
- I undertake to immediately notify whoever I am submitting this form to (whether it is the payer, agent or nominee, CRA, or the partnership or hybrid entity through which the income is derived) of any changes to the information provided on this form.

Signature of non-resident taxpayer or authorized person	Name of authorized person (print)	Position/title of authorized person	Telephone number	Date (YYYY/MM/DD)

Expiry date – For Part XIII tax withholding purposes, this declaration expires when there is a change in the taxpayer's eligibility for treaty benefits or three years from the end of the calendar year in which this form is signed and dated, whichever is earlier.

NR301 E (13)   (Ce formulaire est disponible en français.)   Canadä

Do not use this form:

- to support exemptions from tax under Article XXI of the Canada-U.S. tax treaty. You must apply to the CRA for a Letter of Exemption. Refer to guide T4016, *Exempt U.S. Organizations – Under Article XXI of the Canada-United States Tax Convention*.

- to support exemptions under a tax treaty that does not tax pension income if the total amount received from all payers is less than a certain threshold amount, or in other situations where Form NR5, *Application by a non-resident of Canada for a reduction in the amount of non-resident tax required to be withheld*, is applicable. See guide T4061, NR4 – *Non-resident tax withholding, remitting, and reporting* for more information on pension exemptions. In these cases, you have to file Form NR5 to receive a letter authorizing a reduction in withholding tax on pension income.

- to support exemptions from Part XIII withholding tax that are provided for in the *Income Tax Act*, such as fully exempt interest as defined in subsection 212(3); to support arm's length interest payments that are not captured by paragraph 212(1)(b); or to support reductions of the Part XIII withholding tax on rental income when the non-resident makes an election under Section 216. In these circumstances, the exemption or reduction is in the *Income Tax Act* rather than in one of Canada's tax treaties.

Business profits and disposition gains

For exemptions pertaining to services provided in Canada, including those provided by artists and athletes who are exempt from tax under a tax treaty, see Rendering services in Canada at **www.cra.gc.ca/tx/nnrsdnts/cmmn/rndr/menu-eng.html** or Film Advisory Services at **www.cra.gc.ca/tx/nnrsdnts/flm/menu-eng.html**. These pages contain links to information for non-residents, including how to apply for a waiver of withholding tax. You may need to attach Form NR302, *Declaration of eligibility for benefits (reduced tax) under a tax treaty for a partnership with non-resident partners* or NR303, *Declaration of eligibility for benefits (reduced tax) under a tax treaty for a hybrid entity* to an application for a waiver in certain circumstances, such as when the applicant for the waiver is a partnership or hybrid entity. The payer of income for services provided in Canada must withhold tax on these payments unless the non-resident provides the payer with a copy of a tax waiver or reduction issued by the CRA for those services.

For exemptions pertaining to dispositions of taxable Canadian property, see Disposing of or acquiring certain Canadian property at **www.cra.gc.ca/nrdispositions/** Vendors and purchasers will find information on filing forms T2062, T2062A, and T2062C on this page. Generally, the purchaser of taxable Canadian property has to withhold tax on the purchase price unless the vendor receives a certificate of compliance from the CRA, or other rules apply.

Information and instructions for the non-resident taxpayer

Part XIII tax

Part XIII tax is a withholding tax imposed on certain amounts paid or credited to non-residents of Canada. Subject to certain exceptions specified in the law, the rate of Part XIII tax is generally 25%. However, an income tax treaty between Canada and another country may provide for complete exemption from Part XIII tax or may reduce its rate.

It is the payer's responsibility to withhold and remit Part XIII tax at the appropriate rate and the payer is liable for any deficiency. For this reason, the payer may request a completed Form NR301 or equivalent information before applying a reduced rate of withholding tax. Without Form NR301, the payer may not be satisfied of your entitlement to treaty benefits for the application of less than the full 25% Part XIII tax rate.

Foreign tax identification number

Enter the tax identification number that you use, if you have one, in your country of residence. For individuals who are resident in the United States, this is your social security number.

Recipient type

Tick the appropriate type of non-resident taxpayer.

A foreign partnership that is treated as fiscally transparent under the laws of a foreign country, resulting in the partners paying tax on the partnership's worldwide income, should use Form NR302 to claim treaty benefits the partners are entitled to.

Hybrid entities (see "Amounts derived through hybrid entities" below) should use Form NR303 if they are considered "fiscally transparent" by a country that Canada has a tax treaty with and that treaty contemplates extending treaty benefits for income derived through the entity to the residents of that country who have an interest in the entity (e.g., see paragraph 6 of Article IV of the Canada-U.S. tax treaty). A foreign entity that is taxed as a corporation on its worldwide income under the laws of the foreign country completes Form NR301.

For other entity types, such as government entities and professional unincorporated associations, go to the CRA website at **www.cra.gc.ca/formspubs/frms/nr301-2-3-eng.html**

Canadian tax number

Provide a Canadian tax number, if you have one.

Country of residence

Indicate your country of residence. You must be a resident of the country as defined in the tax treaty between Canada and that country. For more information, consult the publication *Income Tax Technical News No. 35* at **www.cra-arc.gc.ca/E/pub/tp/itnews-35/**, published February 26, 2007.

Type of income

Enter the types of income being paid for which you are eligible for tax treaty benefits (such as an exemption from tax in Canada or a reduced withholding tax rate).

> **Note:** Income, including interest and dividend income, paid by a trust (other than a deemed dividend paid by a SIFT trust to which subsection 104(16) applies) to a non-resident is considered "trust income" under the *Income Tax Act* and Canada's tax treaties.

Some tax treaties only reduce the Part XIII withholding tax on specific income types, such as interest or trust income, if the amount is taxable in the non-resident taxpayer's country of residence. To check if this applies to the income you receive, go to the Department of Finance website at **www.fin.gc.ca/treaties-conventions/treatystatus_-eng.asp**, or try the non-resident tax calculator at **www.cra.gc.ca/partxiii-calculator/** For example, the Canada-United Kingdom tax treaty contains such a provision in paragraph 2 of Article 27.

Limitation on benefits

Limitation on benefits provisions prevent the unintended use of treaties by residents of a third country. Tax treaty benefits will be refused if any applicable limitation on benefits provision is not satisfied.

For example, Article XXIX-A of the Canada-U.S. tax treaty generally restricts full treaty benefits to "qualifying persons" as defined in that article. U.S. resident individuals are "qualifying persons." Corporations, trusts, and other organizations resident in the United States should consult the tax treaty article to find out if they meet the criteria. The document "CRA guidelines for taxpayers requesting treaty benefits pursuant to paragraph 6 of article XXIX-A of the Canada-U.S. Tax Convention" at **www.cra.gc.ca/tx/nnrsdnts/rtc/29-eng.html**, provides the Canada-U.S. tax treaty in Appendix II and information for those who do not meet the criteria.

Certification and undertaking

This area should be completed and signed by:

- the non-resident taxpayer in the case of an individual;
- an authorized officer in the case of a corporation;
- the trustee, executor, or administrator if the person filing the form is a trust;
- an authorized partner in the case of a partnership.

A non-resident who does not satisfy the requirements of the limitation on benefits provisions, if any, contained in the tax treaty will not be entitled to all the benefits of the tax treaty. By signing this form you are certifying that the non-resident is entitled to a reduced rate of tax under a tax treaty.

During an audit or review, or while processing a related request, the CRA may ask you for more information to support the tax treaty benefit you claimed.

Change in circumstances

If a change in circumstances makes any information on the form incorrect, notify the payer immediately and fill out a new form.

Amounts derived through hybrid entities

A hybrid entity is in general a foreign entity (other than a partnership) whose income is taxed at the beneficiary, member, or participant level. For example, the United States resident members/owners of a Limited Liability Company (that is treated as a fiscally transparent entity under U.S. tax laws) may be entitled to treaty benefits if all the conditions in paragraph 6 of Article IV of the Canada-U.S. treaty are met. Under paragraph 6, an amount of income, profit or gain is considered to be derived by a resident of the United States if:

1) the amount is derived by that person through an entity (other than an entity that is a resident of Canada); and

2) by reason of that entity being considered fiscally transparent under U.S. tax laws, the treatment of the amount under U.S. tax laws is the same as it would be if that amount had been derived directly by that person. Paragraph 7 of Article IV contains additional restrictions on this look-through provision.

Entities that are subject to tax, but whose tax may be relieved under an integrated system, are not considered hybrid entities.

Where do I send this form?

Depending on your circumstances, send this form to one of the three areas noted below.

- If you receive income subject to Part XIII tax from a Canadian payer, or from an agent, nominee, or other financial intermediary who requested that you complete this form, send this form and your completed worksheets directly to the person who requested it, to reduce the Part XIII withholding tax on income being paid to you.
- If you derive income through a partnership or hybrid entity, and that partnership or hybrid entity asked you to complete Form NR301, send it to that partnership or hybrid entity.
- If requesting a certificate of compliance for the disposition of treaty-protected property, send this form, along with forms T2062 or T2062A, to the CRA according to the instructions on those forms.

Agents and nominees, or financial intermediaries

If you are an agent or nominee providing financial intermediary services as a part of a business, you should collect Form NR301, NR302, or NR303, or equivalent information, from the beneficial owner. See the instructions in Information Circular 76-12, *Applicable rate of part XIII tax on amounts paid or credited to persons in countries with which Canada has a tax convention*, and published updates to this information on the CRA website, for the suggested format to use for submitting the information to the Canadian payer or withholding agent. If you are an agent or nominee providing financial intermediary services as part of a business and you pay another agent or nominee amounts for non-resident beneficial owners, collect an agent/nominee certification from them as described in Information Circular 76-12 and published updates.

Instructions for payers

To determine the appropriate reduced rate of withholding, see the relevant Canadian tax treaty on the Department of Finance website at **www.fin.gc.ca/treaties-conventions/treatystatus_-eng.asp**, or try the non-resident tax calculator at **www.cra.gc.ca/partxiii-calculator/**.

Do not apply a reduced rate of withholding in the following circumstances:

- the non-resident taxpayer has not provided Form NR301 or equivalent information and you are not sure if the reduced rate applies;
- the form is incomplete (see note below);
- a tax treaty is not in effect with the taxpayer's country of residence; or
- you have reason to believe that the information provided in this declaration is incorrect or misleading.

   Note: The foreign and Canadian tax number fields may be blank because not all non-residents will have these tax numbers.

Expiry date

For Part XIII tax withholding purposes, this declaration expires when there is a change in the taxpayer's eligibility for the declared treaty benefits or three years from the end of the calendar year in which the form is signed and dated, whichever is earlier. For example, if the taxpayer's mailing address has changed to a different country, you should ask the taxpayer for a revised Form NR301.

If you need more information, see Part XIII withholding tax at **www.cra.gc.ca/tx/nnrsdnts/pyr/prtxiii/wthhldng/menu-eng.html** and select Beneficial ownership or Rates for part XIII tax.

◆◆ Canada Revenue   Agence du revenu
Agency   du Canada

Protected B when completed

For departmental use.

Foreign Income Verification Statement

* This form must be used for the 2015 and later taxation years.
* Complete and file this form if at any time in the year the total cost amount to the reporting taxpayer of all specified foreign property was more than $100,000 (Canadian).
* If an election has been made to use a functional currency (see attached instructions), state the elected functional currency code. . . . . └─┴─┴─┘
* See attached instructions for more information about completing this form.

If this is an amended return check this box. ☐

Identification

Check (✓) a box to indicate who you are reporting for, and complete the areas that apply

☐ Individual	First name	Last name	Initial	Social insurance number	Individual code ☐ 1 ☐ 2
☐ Corporation	Corporation's name			Business number (BN)	R │ C
☐ Trust	Trust's name			Account number T └─┴─┴─┘ –	
☐ Partnership	Partnership's name	Partnership code ☐ 1 ☐ 2 ☐ 3	Partnership's account number	R │ Z	

Reporting taxpayer's address

Number _____   Street _____

City _____   Province or territory _____   Postal or zip code _____   Country code

For what taxation year are you filing this form?   From Year Month Day to Year Month Day

Check (✓) the appropriate box that applies for the taxation year:

☐ If the total cost of all specified foreign property held at any time during the year exceeds $100,000 but was less than $250,000, you are required to complete either Part A or Part B;

☐ If the total cost of all specified foreign property held at any time during the year was $250,000 or more, you are required to complete Part B.

Part A: Simplified reporting method

For each type of property that applies to you, check (✓) the appropriate box.

Type of property:

Funds held outside Canada . . . . ☐
Shares of non-resident corporations (other than foreign affiliates) . . . . ☐
Indebtedness owed by non-resident . . . . ☐
Interests in non-resident trusts . . . . ☐
Real property outside Canada (other than personal use and real estate used in an active business) . . . . ☐
Other property outside Canada . . . . ☐
Property held in an account with a Canadian registered securities dealer or a Canadian trust company . . . . . . ☐

Country code:

Select the top three countries based on the maximum cost amount of specified foreign property held during the year. Enter the country codes in the boxes below:

└──────┘ └──────┘ └──────┘

Income from all specified foreign property $ _____

Gain(loss) from the disposition from all specified foreign property $ _____

Privacy Act, personal information bank number CRA PPU 035
T1135 E (16)   (Ce formulaire existe en français.)

Canadä

Part B: Detailed reporting method

Categories of specified foreign property

In each of the tables below, provide the required details of each specified foreign property held at any time during the particular tax year. If you need additional space, please attach a separate sheet of paper using the same format as the tables.

A taxpayer who held specified foreign property with a Canadian registered securities dealer or a Canadian trust company is permitted to report the aggregate amount, on a country-by-country basis, of all such property in Category 7, *Property held in an account with a Canadian registered securities dealer or a Canadian trust company*. See attached instructions for Category 7 for details as to how to report under this method.

1. Funds held outside Canada

Name of bank/other entity holding the funds	Country code	Maximum funds held during the year	Funds held at year end	Income
		Total		

2. Shares of non-resident corporations (other than foreign affiliates)

Name of corporation	Country code	Maximum cost amount during the year	Cost amount at year end	Income	Gain (loss) on disposition
		Total			

3. Indebtedness owed by non-resident

Description of indebtedness	Country code	Maximum cost amount during the year	Cost amount at year end	Income	Gain (loss) on disposition
		Total			

4. Interests in non-resident trusts

Name of Trust	Country code	Maximum cost amount during the year	Cost amount at year end	Income recieved	Capital received	Gain (loss) on disposition
		Total				

5. Real property outside Canada (other than personal use and real estate used in an active business)

Description of property	Country code	Maximum cost amount during the year	Cost amount at year end	Income	Gain (loss) on disposition
		Total			

6. Other property outside Canada

Description of property	Country code	Maximum cost amount during the year	Cost amount at year end	Income	Gain (loss) on disposition
		Total			

7. Property held in an account with a Canadian registered securities dealer or a Canadian trust company

Name of registered security dealer/Canadian trust company	Country code	Maximum fair market value during the year	Cost amount at year end	Income	Gain (loss) on disposition
		Total			

Privacy Act, personal information bank number CRA PPU 035

Certification

I certify that the information given on this form is, to my knowledge, correct and complete, and fully discloses the reporting taxpayer's foreign property and related information.		If someone other than the taxpayer or the partnership prepared this form, provide their:	
Print name		Name	
Sign here (It is a serious offence to file a false statement.)		Address	
Position/title			
Telephone number	Date (YYYYMMDD)	Postal or zip code	Telephone number

Instructions

All legislative references on this form refer to the *Income Tax Act* (the Act).

If the reporting taxpayer is a partnership, references to year or taxation year should be read as fiscal period and references to taxpayer should be read as partnership.

Do you have to file this form?

All Canadian resident taxpayers (including non-resident trusts deemed resident in Canada by section 94 of the Act) are required to file the Form T1135, *Foreign Income Verification Statement* if at any time in the year the total cost amount of all specified foreign property to the taxpayer was more than $100,000 (Canadian).

An individual (other than a trust) does **not** have to file Form T1135 for the year in which the individual first becomes a resident of Canada (section 233.7 of the Act).

The following entities **do not** have to file this form:

- a mutual fund corporation or mutual fund trust;
- a non-resident-owned investment corporation;
- a person all of whose taxable income is exempt from Part I tax;
- a registered investment under section 204.4 of the Act;
- a trust described in any of paragraphs (a) to (e.1) of the definition of trust in subsection 108(1) of the Act;
- a trust in which all of the persons beneficially interested are persons described above;
- a partnership in which all the members are persons described above; and
- a partnership where the share of the partnership's income or loss attributable to non-resident members is 90% or more of the income or loss of the partnership.

What property do you have to report?

You are required to report all specified foreign property in accordance with subsection 233.3(1) of the Act which includes:

- funds or intangible property (patents, copyrights, etc.) situated, deposited or held outside Canada;
- tangible property situated outside of Canada;
- a share of the capital stock of a non-resident corporation held by the taxpayer or by an agent on behalf of the taxpayer;
- an interest in a non-resident trust that was acquired for consideration, other than an interest in a non-resident trust that is a foreign affiliate for the purposes of section 233.4 of the Act;
- shares of corporations resident in Canada held by you or for you outside Canada;
- an interest in a partnership that holds a specified foreign property unless the partnership is required to file Form T1135;
- an interest in, or right with respect to, an entity that is a non-resident;
- a property that is convertible into, exchangeable for, or confers a right to acquire a property that is specified foreign property;
- a debt owed by a non-resident, including government and corporate bonds, debentures, mortgages, and notes receivable;
- an interest in a foreign insurance policy; and
- precious metals, gold certificates, and futures contracts held outside Canada.

Specified foreign property **does not** include:

- a property used or held exclusively in carrying on an active business;
- a share of the capital stock or indebtedness of a foreign affiliate;
- an interest in a trust described in paragraph (a) or (b) of the definition of "exempt trust" in subsection 233.2(1) of the Act;
- a personal-use property as defined in section 54 of the Act; and
- an interest in, or a right to acquire, any of the above-noted excluded foreign property.

For frequently asked questions or examples, check our web site at www.cra-arc.gc.ca/tx/nnrsdnts/cmmn/frgn/1135_fq-eng.html.

How to complete this form

If the total cost of all specified foreign property held at any time during the year exceeds $100,000 but was less than $250,000, the form has been designed to provide you with the option of completing either Part A or Part B.

Where a particular specified foreign property has been reported all of the other fields associated with that particular property must also be completed. All nil amounts should be reported by indicating "0" in the corresponding field rather than leaving it blank. Amounts should be rounded to the nearest dollar.

Functional currency

If an election has been made under paragraph 261(3)(b) of the Act to report in a functional currency, state all monetary amounts in that functional currency, otherwise state all monetary amounts in Canadian dollars. The codes for the functional currencies are as follows:

AUD – for Australian dollar
USD – for U.S. dollar
GBP – for U.K. pound
EUR – for Euro

Identification

Check the appropriate box to identify the category of taxpayer filing this form. Provide the taxpayer's name, address, and identification number. Provide the taxation year for which this form is being filed.

Reporting individual/partnership identification

For individual code, check (✓):

1. If the individual or the individual's spouse (common-law partner) is self-employed.
2. If the individual and the individual's spouse (common-law partner) are both not self-employed.

For partnership code, check (✓):

1. If end partners are individuals or trusts.
2. If end partners are corporations.
3. If end partners are a combination of 1 and 2 mentioned above.

An end partner is the final recipient (corporation, trust or individual) that receives an allocation of income from the partnership after the income has flowed through the various levels of a tiered partnership.

Categories of specified foreign property

This form contains seven tables corresponding to different categories of specified foreign property. Report the detail of each particular property that was held at any time during the year in the appropriate category.

Country codes

For the list of country codes, see the CRA website at www.cra-arc.gc.ca/E/pub/tg/t4061/t4061-e.html#P482_43418.

The country code for each category should identify:

- Category 1 – the country where the funds are located;
- Category 2 – the country of residence of the non-resident corporation;
- Category 3 – the country of residence of the non-resident issuer;
- Category 4 – the country of residence of the trust;
- Category 5 – the country where property is located;
- Category 6 – the country where property is located;
- Category 7 – depending on the type of property, use the instructions above from categories 1 to 6.

If you are uncertain of the appropriate country code for a particular specified foreign property, select "Other".

Cost amount/Maximum cost amount

Cost amount is defined in subsection 248(1) of the Act and generally would be the acquisition cost of the property. If you immigrate to Canada, the cost amount is the fair market value of the property at the time of immigration. Similarly, if you received specified foreign property as a gift, or inheritance, the cost amount is its fair market value at the time of the gift or inheritance.

The maximum cost amount during the year can be based on the maximum month-end cost amount during the year.

Foreign currency conversion

The amounts to be reported on Form T1135 should be determined in the foreign currency then translated into Canadian dollars. Generally, when converting amounts from a foreign currency into Canadian dollars, use the exchange rate in effect at the time of the transaction (i.e. the time the income was received or the property was purchased). If you received income throughout the year, an average rate for the year is acceptable.

The following summarizes how other amounts of the form should be translated:

- Maximum funds held during the year – the average exchange rate for the year.
- Funds held at year end – the exchange rate at the end of the year.
- Maximum fair market value during the year – the average exchange rate for the year.
- Fair market value at year end – the exchange rate at the end of the year.

Tables

Specified foreign property has been divided into seven (7) categories and should be reported in one of the following tables:

1. Funds held outside Canada

Funds held outside Canada include money on deposit in foreign bank accounts, money held with a foreign depository for safekeeping and money held by any other foreign institution at any time during the year. Prepaid debit or credit cards and negotiable instruments, such as cheques and drafts, are also included in this category. Marketable securities should be reported in category 3.

2. Shares of non-resident corporations (other than foreign affiliates)

Report all shares of non-resident corporations whether or not they are physically held in Canada.

Do not report shares of a foreign affiliate corporation. Generally, a foreign affiliate is a non-resident corporation (or certain non-resident trusts) of which you hold at least 1% of the shares individually, and, either alone or with related persons, hold 10% or more of the shares. If you have a foreign affiliate, you may have to file Form T1134, *Information Return Relating to Controlled and Not Controlled Foreign Affiliates*.

3. Indebtedness owed by non-residents

Report all amounts owed to you by a non-resident person (other than a foreign affiliate corporation) whether the indebtedness is held inside or outside Canada. Include all promissory notes, bills, bonds, commercial paper, debentures, loans, mortgages, and other indebtedness owed to you by a non-resident person. Marketable securities, such as guaranteed investment certificates, government treasury bills and term deposits issued by a non-resident, should be reported under this category.

4. Interests in non-resident trusts

Report all interests in non-resident trusts acquired for consideration, other than a non-resident trust that is a foreign affiliate for the purposes of section 233.4 of the Act.

If you contributed to, or received a distribution or loan from, a non-resident trust you may be required to file Form T1141, *Information Return in Respect of Contributions to Non-Resident Trusts, Arrangements or Entities* or Form T1142, *Information Return in Respect of Distributions from and Indebtedness to a Non-Resident Trust*.

5. Real property outside Canada

Report all real property located outside of Canada other than real property used in an active business or used primarily for personal use (such as a vacation property used primarily as a personal residence). Rental property outside Canada should be included in this category.

6. Other property outside Canada

This category should include any property that does not correspond to any of the other categories.

Other property includes:

- shares of corporations resident in Canada held by you or for you outside Canada;
- an interest in a partnership that holds specified foreign property where the partnership is not required to file the Form T1135;
- foreign insurance policies;
- precious metals or bullion (e.g., gold and silver) situated outside Canada;
- commodity or future contracts, options or derivatives that constitute a right to, a right to acquire, or an interest in, specified foreign property; and
- any other rights to, rights to acquire, or interests in, specified foreign property.

7. Property held in an account with a Canadian registered securities dealer or a Canadian trust company

A taxpayer who held specified foreign property with a Canadian registered securities dealer (as defined in subsection 248(1) of the Act) or with a Canadian trust company (as determined under paragraph (b) of the definition of restricted financial institution in subsection 248(1) of the Act) is permitted to report the aggregate amount of all such property in this category.

The table for this category should be completed as follows:

- all of the property held with a particular securities dealer or trust company should be aggregated on a country-by-country basis;
- it is also acceptable to provide aggregate totals for each particular account on a country-by-country basis;
- refer to the "country code" instructions above to determine the appropriate country for each property; and
- the maximum fair market value during the year may be based on the maximum month-end fair market value.

Certification

This area should be completed and signed by:

- the person filing this form in the case of an individual;
- an authorized officer in the case of a corporation;
- the trustee, executor or administrator in the case of a trust; or
- an authorized partner in the case of a partnership.

Due dates for filing this form

Form T1135 must be filed on or before the due date of your income tax return or, in the case of a partnership, the due date of the partnership information return, even if the income tax return (or partnership information return) is not required to be filed.

Filing by internet (EFILE or NETFILE)

Individuals and corporations can file Form T1135 electronically. Individuals can file Form T1135 electronically (Efile or Netfile) for the 2014 and subsequent taxation years. Corporations can Efile Form T1135 electronically for the 2014 and subsequent taxation years. Trusts and partnerships are required to file a paper copy of this form.

- **EFILE** – Your EFILE service provider, including a discounter, can complete and file your Form T1135 for you if prepared with tax preparation software certified by the CRA for the internet filing of Form T1135. For more information or to file your Form T1135, go to EFILE at **www.cra.gc.ca/efile**.

- **NETFILE** – You can file your Form T1135 by Internet if prepared with tax preparation software certified by the CRA for the internet filing of Form T1135. Most individuals are eligible to NETFILE. For more information or to file your Form T1135, go to NETFILE at **www.cra.gc.ca/netfile**.

Filing a paper return

Form T1135 can be attached to your income tax return, or partnership information return, and mailed to your tax centre. Alternately, Form T1135 can be mailed separately to the following address:

Ottawa Technology Centre
Data Assessment and Evaluations Program
Validation and Verification Section
Foreign Reporting Returns
875 Heron Road
Ottawa ON K1A 1A2

Penalties for non-reporting

There are substantial penalties for failing to complete and file Form T1135 accurately and by the due date. For additional information regarding penalties, see the CRA website at www.cra-arc.gc.ca/tx/nnrsdnts/cmmn/frgn/pnlts_grd-eng.html.

Voluntary disclosures

To promote compliance with Canada's tax laws, we encourage you to correct your tax affairs through the Voluntary Disclosures Program. For more information, see Information Circular IC00-1R3, *Voluntary Disclosures Program* (VDP) or visit the CRA website.

More information

If you need more information visit our website at www.cra-arc.gc.ca. Alternatively you can call general enquires at:

- **1-800-959-5525** for businesses, self-employed individuals and partnerships; or
- **1-800-959-8281** for individuals (other than self-employed individuals) and trusts.

You may also contact your local tax services office. Our addresses and fax numbers are listed on our website and in the government section of your telephone book.

Privacy notice

Personal information is collected under the authority of section 233.3 of the Act and is used to monitor compliance with the foreign reporting requirements related to offshore investments. Information may also be used for the administration and enforcement of the Act, including audit, enforcement action, collections, and appeals, and may be disclosed under information-sharing agreements in accordance with the Act. Incomplete or inaccurate information may result in various compliance actions, including the assessment of monetary penalties.

Your Social Insurance Number is the authorized number for income tax purposes under section 237 of the Act and is used under certain federal programs.

Information is described in personal information bank CRA PPU 035 in the Canada Revenue Agency (CRA) chapter of the *Info Source* publication at www.infosource.gc.ca. Personal information is protected under the *Privacy Act* and individuals have a right of protection, access to, and correction of their personal information. Further details regarding requests for personal information at the CRA can be found at www.cra-arc.gc.ca/atip.

Canada Revenue Agency / **Agence du revenu du Canada**

Protected B when completed   **2015** [10]

Old Age Security Return of Income

Identification

Information about you

Enter your Canadian social insurance number (SIN):

Enter your date of birth: [Year Month Day]

Your language of correspondence:
Votre langue de correspondance :

☐ English   ☐ Français

First name and initial

Last name

Mailing address: Apt No - Street No Street name

PO Box	RR

City	Prov./Terr.	Postal Code

Country

Is this return for a deceased person?

If this **return** is for a **deceased person**, enter the date of death: [Year Month Day]

I understand that by providing an email address, I am **registering** for online mail and I have read and **accept the terms and conditions** on page 8 of the guide.

Enter an email address:

Tick the box that applies to your marital status on December 31, 2015:

1 ☐ Married   2 ☐ Living common-law
3 ☐ Widowed   4 ☐ Divorced
5 ☐ Separated   6 ☐ Single

Information about your residence

Enter your country of residence on **December 31, 2015**:

If you **became** or **ceased** to be a **resident of Canada** for income tax purposes **in 2015**, enter the date of:

Month Day   Month Day
entry [ ] or **departure** [ ]

Tax or pension account number in your country of residence:

Information about your spouse or common-law partner (if you ticked box 1 or 2 above)

Enter his or her SIN:

Enter his or her first name:

Your old age security number

Enter your old age security number:

Do not use this area

Include your world income on this return.
World income is income from all sources both inside and outside Canada.

Income

Old age security pension (read line 113 in the guide)	113	
Canada or Quebec Pension Plan benefits (read line 114 in the guide)	114 +	
Other pensions or superannuation (read line 115 in the guide)	115 +	
Interest and other investment income (from the worksheet on page 2)	121 +	
Net rental income (read line 126 in the guide)	126 +	
Registered retirement savings plan income (read line 129 in the guide)	129 +	
Other income (read line 130 in the guide) Specify:	130 +	
Net business income (read line 135 in the guide)	135 +	
Add lines 113 to 135 This is your **total world income.**	150 =	

T1136 E (15)   Please do not use this area | 171

Deductions

Carrying charges and interest expenses
(read line 221 in the guide)   **221**

Other deductions (read line 232 in the guide)

Specify: _____   **232 +**

Add lines 221 and 232   **233 =**   ▶ –

Line 150 minus line 233 (if negative, enter "0")   This is your **net world income. 242 =**

Refund or balance owing

Old age security recovery tax (read line 235 in the guide).
If line 242 is CAN$72,809 or less, enter "0"   **235**   •

Recovery tax withheld from box 27 of your NR4-OAS slip   **437 –**   •

Line 235 minus line 437.   This is your **refund** or **balance owing.**   =

If the result is negative, you have a **refund**. If the result is positive, you have a **balance owing.**

┌─ Enter the amount below on whichever line applies.

Generally, we do not charge or refund a difference of $2 or less.

Refund 484 _____ •   **Balance owing 485** _____ •

Do not use this area   **486**   •

For more information on how to make your payment, see line 485 in the guide or go to **www.cra.gc.ca/payments.** Your payment is due no later than April 30, 2016.

I certify that the information given on this return and in any documents attached is correct, complete, and fully discloses all my income.

Sign here _____ _____ _____
     It is a serious offence to make a false return.   Date   Telephone number

Interest and Other Investment Income Worksheet

State the names of the payers below, and attach any information slips you received. Attach a separate sheet of paper if you need more space.

Interest and dividend income

_____

_____ +

_____ +

_____ +

Total interest and dividend income =   1

Capital gains (see line 121 in the guide)

Description of property: _____

1. Proceeds of disposition	2. Adjusted cost base	3. Outlays and expenses (from dispositions)	4. Capital gain (or loss) Box 1 minus boxes 2 and 3

Taxable capital gains (50% of the amount in box 4 above)
If the amount in box 4 is negative, enter "0" +   2

Add lines 1 and 2. Enter this amount on line 121 on page 1. =   3

Protected B when completed

[■◆■] Canada Revenue Agence du rven.
Agency   du Canada

2015

Income Tax Return for Electing Under Section 216

11

Identification

Print your name and address below.

First name and initial

Last name

Mailing address: Apt No – Street No Street name

PO Box	RR
City	Prov./Terr.	Postal code

Country

Email address

I understand that by providing an email address, I am **registering** for online mail. I **have read** and I **accept the terms and conditions** on page 7 of the Income Tax Guide for Electing Under Section 216.

Enter an email address:

Information about you

Enter your social insurance number (SIN), temporary tax number (TTN), or individual tax number (ITN):

Enter your date of birth: | Year | Month | Day |

Your language of correspondence: English   Français
Votre langue de correspondance :   ☐   ☐

Is this return for a deceased person?

If this return is for a **deceased person**, enter the date of death: | Year | Month | Day |

Do not use this area.

Income

Rental income and timber royalties   Gross **160** | Net **126**
Total income **150**

Deductions

RRSP/pooled registered pension plan (PRPP) deduction (attach receipts)	**208**	
Support payments made Total **230**	Allowable deduction **220** +
Other deductions (see line 232 in the guide) Specify:	**232** +
Add lines 208, 220, and 232.	**233** =	► –
Line 150 minus line 233 (if negative, enter "0")	This is your taxable income **260** =	1

Federal tax

Part 1 – Federal tax on taxable income

Complete the appropriate column depending on the amount on line 1.	Line 1 is **$44,701** or less	Line 1 is more than **$44,701** but not more than **$89,401**	Line 1 is more than **$89,401** but not more than **$138,586**	Line 1 is more than **$138,586**	
Enter the amount from line 1.					2
Line 2 minus line 3 (cannot be negative)	– 0 00	– 44,701 00	– 89,401 00	– 138,586 00	3
	=	=	=	=	4
Multiply line 4 by line 5.	× 15%	× 22%	× 26%	× 29%	5
	=	=	=	=	6
Add lines 6 and 7.	+ 0 00	+ 6,705 00	+ 16,539 00	+ 29,327 00	7
Enter this amount on line 9.	=	=	=	=	8

Continue on the next page.

| Do not use this area. | 171 | 172 | | 5524 |

T1159 E (15)

Part 2 – Federal tax

Enter the amount from line 8.		9
Minimum tax carryover (see line 427 in the guide)	427 –	•10
Line 9 minus line 10	=	11

Surtax for non-residents of Canada: enter the amount from line 11.   × 48 % =   +   12

Add lines 11 and 12.   Federal tax =   13

Refund or balance owing

Enter the amount from line 13. This is your total payable.	435	•
Total non-resident tax withheld (from your NR4 slips; see line 437 in the guide)	437	•
Total tax remitted for the recapture of capital cost allowance (from Form T2064 or Form T2068)	476 +	•
Add lines 437 and 476.	482 =	▶ –
Line 435 minus line 482. This is your refund or balance owing.	=	

If the result is negative, you have a **refund**. If the result is positive, you have a **balance owing**.

Enter the amount below on whichever line applies.

Generally, we do not charge or refund a difference of $2 or less.

Refund 484   •   Balance owing 485   •

Do not use this area.   486   •

For more information on how to make your payment, see line 485 in the guide or go to **www.cra.gc.ca/payments**. Your payment is due no later than April 30, 2016.

Direct deposit – Enrol or update (see line 484 in the guide)

You do not have to complete this area every year. Do not complete it this year if your direct deposit information has not changed. To **enrol** for direct deposit to a financial institution **in Canada** or to **update** account information, complete lines 460, 461, and 462 below. By providing my banking information **I authorize** the Receiver General to deposit in the bank account number shown below **any amounts payable** to me by the CRA, until otherwise notified by me. I understand that this authorization will replace all of my previous direct deposit authorizations.

Branch number 460 _____   Institution number 461 _____   Account number 462 _____
        (5 digits)   (3 digits)   (maximum 12 digits)

I certify that the information given on this return and in any documents attached is correct and complete and fully discloses all my income from rents and timber royalties on which I am electing under section 216 of the *Income Tax Act*.

490

If a fee was charged for preparing this return, complete the following:

Sign here _____

It is a serious offence to make a false return.

Telephone _____   Date _____

Name of preparer: _____

Telephone: _____

Personal information is collected under the *Income Tax Act* to administer tax, benefits, and related programs. It may also be used for any purpose related to the administration or enforcement of the Act such as audit, compliance and the payment of debts owed to the Crown. It may be shared or verified with other federal, provincial/territorial government institutions to the extent authorized by law. Failure to provide this information may result in interest payable, penalties or other actions. Under the *Privacy Act*, individuals have the right to access their personal information and request correction if there are errors or omissions. Refer to Info Source at **www.cra.gc.ca/gncy/tp/nfsrc/nfsrc-eng.html**, Personal Information Bank CRA PPU 005.

I+I Canada Revenue Agence du revenu
Agency du Canada

List of Properties by an Emigrant of Canada

Protected B
when completed

Last name (print)	First name (print)	Social insurance number		
Mailing address (print)		Date of emigration from Canada	Year	Month	Day

Complete this form if you ceased to be a resident of Canada in the year and the fair market value of **all** the properties you owned when you left Canada was more than $25,000, **excluding** the following properties:

1) cash (including bank deposits);

2) pension plans, annuities, registered retirement savings plans, pooled registered pension plans, registered retirement income funds, registered education savings plans, registered disability savings plans, tax-free savings accounts, deferred profit-sharing plans, employee profit-sharing plans, employee benefit plans, salary deferral arrangements, retirement compensation arrangements, employee life and health trusts, and rights or interests in certain other trusts. For a complete list, refer to the definition of "excluded right or interest" in Subsection 128.1(10) of the *Income Tax Act* read without reference to paragraphs (c), (j) and (l);

3) property you owned when you last became a resident of Canada, or property you inherited after you last became a resident of Canada, if you were a resident of Canada for 60 months or less during the 10-year period before you emigrated and the property is not taxable Canadian property; and

4) any item of personal-use property (such as your household effects, clothing, cars, collectibles) that has a fair market value of less than $10,000.

Attach a copy of this form to your tax return. Even if you do not have to file a return, you **must** send this form on or before your filing due date. The penalty for failing to file this form by the due date is $25 for each day you are late. There is a minimum penalty of $100, and a maximum penalty of $2,500.

List of properties

List in the table below all properties and their fair market value. Indicate either (C) for Canadian properties or (F) for foreign properties (outside of Canada), that you owned on the date you ceased to be a resident of Canada.

Property includes shares (both public and private), bonds, debentures, promissory notes, treasury bills, interests in trusts, interests in partnerships, personal-use property, business property (including inventory), real or immovable property, and security options.

Do not list any property described on lines 1 to 4 above. If you need more space, attach a separate sheet of paper.

Number of shares (if applicable)	Description of property (such as name of corporation and class of shares (stock symbol), address or location for buildings or land)	Canadian (C) or foreign (F)	Fair market value on the date you emigrated

To calculate and report any capital gains (or losses) on property that you are deemed to have disposed of on the date you ceased to be a resident of Canada, complete Form T1243, *Deemed Disposition of Property by an Emigrant of Canada.*

To defer the payment of tax on income relating to the deemed disposition of property, complete Form T1244, *Election, Under Subsection 220(4.5) of the Income Tax Act, to Defer the Payment of Tax on Income Relating to the Deemed Disposition of Property.*

See the privacy notice on your return.

T1161 E (15)   (Vous pouvez obtenir ce formulaire en français à **www.arc.gc.ca/formulaires**.)

Canadä

Canada Revenue Agency   Agence du revenu du Canada

Request to Reduce Tax Deductions at Source

Year _____

- Use this form to ask for reduced tax deductions at source for any deductions, credits, or non-refundable tax credits that are not part of the Form TD1, *Personal Tax Credits Return*.
- **Before you send us your request**, make sure that your income tax returns for the previous years are filed and all amounts owing are paid in full.
- You usually have to file this request every year. However, if you have deductible support payments that are the same or greater for more than one year, you can make this request for two years.
- Send the filled out form with all supporting documents to the Taxpayer Services Division of your tax services office. You can find the address on our website at **www.cra.gc.ca/tso** or by calling us at **1-800-959-8281**.

Identification

First name	Last name	Social insurance number

Address

City	Province or territory	Postal code	Residence	Telephone Business

Employer/Payer Name	Contact person	Telephone and fax numbers

Address

Request to reduce tax on

☐ Salary   ☐ Lump sum* – if lump sum, give payment amount and details (for example, a bonus or vacation pay)

$ _____

* If you are using a lump sum amount for an RRSP and the amount is unknown, enter your expected RRSP contribution without exceeding your RRSP deduction limit.

Deductions from income and non-refundable tax credits

Registered retirement savings plan (RRSP) contributions . . . . $ _____
- Give details or a copy of the payment arrangement contract.
- Do not include contributions deducted from your pay by your employer.

Child care expenses . . . . $ _____
- Give details on a separate sheet.

Support payments . . . . $ _____
- Attach a copy of your court order or written agreement and Form T1158, *Registration of Family Support Payments* (if not previously filed).
- Recipient's name and social insurance number:

_____ |__|__|__|__|__|__|__|__|__|

Employment expenses . . . . $ _____
- Attach a filled out Form T2200, *Declaration of Conditions of Employment*, and Form T777, *Statement of Employment Expenses*.

Carrying charges and interest expenses on investment loans . . . . $ _____
- Attach a copy of statements from the lender confirming the purpose and amount of the loan(s) and the interest payments to be made in the year.

Medical expenses . . . . $ _____
- Attach a list identifying the medical expenses and indicate the amount

Donations . . . . $ _____
- Attach a list that names the registered charities or other qualified donees and indicates the amount.

Continued on next page

T1213 E (15)   (Vous pouvez obtenir ce formulaire en français à **www.arc.gc.ca/formulaires** ou en composant le **1-800-959-7383**.)

Canadä

Deductions from income and non-refundable tax credits (continued)

Clergy residence . . . . $ _____
- Attach a filled out and signed T1223, *Clergy Residence Deduction.*

RPP buying back contributions for past service . . . . $ _____
- Indicate if the buying back is for past service contributions for 1989 or earlier years and the deductible amount.
- Indicate if the buying back is for past service contributions made for 1990 or later years and attach a copy of the Past Service Pension Adjustment (PSPA) certification.

Foreign tax credit . . . . $ _____
- Attach a completed Form T2209, *Federal Foreign Tax Credits,* or a letter that includes the calculations.
- Attach pro forma Schedule 1 or a letter that includes the calculations.

Other . . . . $ _____
(for example, moving expenses, carrying forward tuition, education, and textbook amounts, or rental loss)
- Attach all supporting documents*. Use a separate sheet to give details if necessary.
  Specify: _____

* Refer to the General Income Tax and Benefit Guide for information on which
  supporting documents are needed to justify the deductions and credits you requested.

Total amounts to be deducted from income $ _____

Subtract income not under tax deductions at source (interest, net rental or self-employed income) = _____

Net amount requested for **tax waiver** $ _____

Certification

I request authorization for my employer/payer to reduce my tax deductions at source based on the information given.

I certify that the information given on this form and in any attached documents is correct and complete.

_____   _____
                  Signature   Date

I✦I Canada Revenue   Agence du revenu
Agency   du Canada

Deemed Disposition of Property by an Emigrant of Canada

Protected B
when completed

Last name (print)	First name (print)	Social insurance number
Mailing address (print)	Date of emigration from Canada	Year Month Day

Complete this form if you ceased to be a resident of Canada in the year and you were deemed to have disposed of property when you left Canada, **excluding** properties such as:

1) Canadian real or immovable property, Canadian resource property, and timber resource property;

2) Canadian business property (including inventory) if the business is carried on through a permanent establishment in Canada;

3) pension plans, annuities, registered retirement savings plans, pooled registered pension plans, registered retirement income funds, registered education savings plans, registered disability savings plans, tax-free savings accounts, deferred profit-sharing plans, employee profit-sharing plans, employee benefit plans, salary deferral arrangements, retirement compensation arrangements, employee life and health trusts, rights or interests in certain other trusts, employee security options (exercised) subject to Canadian tax, interests in certain personal trusts resident in Canada, and interests in life insurance policies in Canada (other than segregated fund policies). For a complete list, refer to the definition of "excluded right or interest" in Subsection 128.1(10) of the *Income Tax Act*; and

4) property you owned when you last became a resident of Canada, or property you inherited after you last became a resident of Canada, if you were a resident of Canada for 60 months or less during the 10-year period before you emigrated.

Note
If you ceased to be a resident of Canada and you elected to declare the deemed disposition of properties listed on lines 1 or 2 above, include those properties when calculating your deemed dispositions and complete Form T2061A, *Election by an Emigrant to Report Deemed Dispositions of Property and Any Resulting Capital Gain or Loss.*

Use the table below to calculate your capital gains (or losses) for the properties you were deemed to have disposed of. Indicate either (C) for Canadian properties or (F) for foreign properties (outside of Canada). If some or all of your investments are in a portfolio, please provide a complete breakdown. Make sure you include those capital gains (or losses) on your Schedule 3, *Capital Gains (or Losses).*

Note
You can elect to defer the payment of tax on income relating to the deemed disposition of property by completing Form T1244, *Election, Under Subsection 220(4.5) of the Income Tax Act, to Defer the Payment of Tax on Income Relating to the Deemed Disposition of Property.*

Attach your Form T1243 and Schedule 3 to your tax return.

(1) Number of shares (if applicable)	(2) Description of property (such as name of corporation and class of shares (stock symbol), address or location for buildings or land)	(3) Canadian (C) or foreign (F)	(4) Year of acquisition	(5) Fair market value on the date you emigrated	(6) Adjusted cost base	(7) Gain (or loss) (column 5 minus column 6)

See the privacy notice on your return.

T1243 E (15)   (Vous pouvez obtenir ce formulaire en français à **www.arc.gc.ca/formulaires**.)   **Canadä**

I✶I Canada Revenue Agency   Agence du revenu du Canada

Election, Under Subsection 220(4.5) of the *Income Tax Act*, to Defer the Payment of Tax on Income Relating to the Deemed Disposition of Property

Protected B when completed

Last name (print)	First name (print)	Social insurance number

Mailing address (print)	Date of emigration from Canada	Year	Month	Day

Complete and attach a copy of this form to your tax return if you ceased to be a resident of Canada in the year and you are electing to defer the payment of tax on income relating to the deemed disposition of a property indicated on Form T1243, *Deemed Disposition of Property by an Emigrant of Canada*. If your election to defer the payment of tax is not for all properties, list the properties for which you would like to defer the payment of tax. You must file this election by April 30 of the year after you emigrate from Canada.

If you make this election and the amount of federal tax owing on income from the deemed disposition of property is more than $14,500 ($12,107.50 for former residents of Quebec), you have to provide us with adequate security acceptable to cover the amount. You may also be required to provide security to cover any applicable provincial or territorial tax payable. Contact us as soon as possible to make acceptable arrangements before April 30. For more information, go to **www.cra.gc.ca/tx/nnrsdnts/ndvdls/dspstn-eng.html**.

Notes

If the amount of federal tax on income relating to the deemed disposition of property is $14,500 or less ($12,107.50 or less for former residents of Quebec), security is not required. You must however complete this form and attach it to your tax return. If your election to defer payment of tax is only for some of the properties you included on Form T1243, *Deemed Disposition of Property by an Emigrant of Canada*, attach a separate sheet of paper to list the properties for which you would like to defer the payment of tax.

If you resided in Quebec prior to ceasing Canadian residency, do not complete lines 10 to 12 of this form.

Tax on income relating to the deemed disposition of property

Taxable income from line 260 of your return		1
Amount of taxable capital gains on emigration from Canada	2	
Other income relating to the deemed disposition of property on emigration from Canada	+ 3	
Any deductions claimed that are related to this deemed disposition	− 4	
Line 2 plus line 3, minus line 4	= ▶6890 −	5
Line 1 minus line 5 (if negative, enter "0") **Adjusted taxable income**	=	6
Federal tax on your taxable income (from line 1 above) calculated using Schedule 1, *Federal Tax* (minus the Quebec abatement, if applicable)	7	
Federal tax on your adjusted taxable income (from line 6 above) calculated using Schedule 1, *Federal Tax* (minus the Quebec abatement, if applicable)	− 8	
Line 7 minus line 8 **Federal tax relating to the deemed disposition of property**	= ▶	9
Provincial or territorial tax on your taxable income (from line 1 above) calculated using Form 428 included in your forms book	10	
Provincial or territorial tax on your adjusted taxable income (from line 6 above) calculated using Form 428 included in your forms book	− 11	
Line 10 minus line 11 **Provincial or territorial tax relating to the deemed disposition of property**	= ▶ +	12
Add lines 9 and 12. **Total tax on income relating to the deemed disposition of property**	=	13

Election

I ELECT under subsection 220(4.5) of the *Income Tax Act* to defer the payment of tax according to the amounts of tax specified below:

Federal tax relating to the deemed disposition of property (up to the maximum on line 9)   6891   •

Provincial or territorial tax relating to the deemed disposition of property (up to the maximum on line 12)   6892   •

Signature   Date

Do not use this area	Amount of security provided	Type of security	Security expiry date

See the privacy notice on your return.

T1244 E (15)   (Vous pouvez obtenir ce formulaire en français à **www.arc.gc.ca/formulaires**.)   **Canada**

◆◆ Canada Customs   Agence des douanes
and Revenue Agency   et du revenu du Canada

**ELECTION BY AN EMIGRANT TO REPORT DEEMED
DISPOSITIONS OF PROPERTY AND ANY RESULTING
CAPITAL GAIN OR LOSS**

	Do not use this area

- Use this form if you are an individual, other than a trust, who ceased at any time in the year to be a resident of Canada, and you want to elect under subparagraph 128.1(4)(d) of the *Income Tax Act* to recognize the deemed disposition of any of the following property:
  - real property in Canada, Canadian resource property, or timber resource property; or
  - capital property used in, eligible capital property in respect of, or property described in the inventory of a business you carried on through a permanent establishment in Canada at the time you ceased to be a resident of Canada.

- File one copy of this election and attach it to your tax return for the year in which you ceased to be resident in Canada.

- Complete Schedule 3 of your Canadian income tax return and whichever of forms T657, T657A, and T936 apply to your situation to calculate and report the capital gain or loss from the elected deemed dispositions. Include the schedule or forms with your tax return for the year in which you ceased to be resident in Canada.

Full name (print)		
Present address		
Address while resident in Canada		
Date Canadian residence ceased	(year, month, day)	Canadian social insurance number

Details of property to which this election applies

Description	Adjusted cost base	Fair market value at date Canadian residence ceased
	$	$

- Attach a sheet of paper if you need more space.

CERTIFICATION

I, _____ (Please print), certify that the information given on this form is, to the best of my knowledge, correct and complete.

_____ Date   _____ Signature of authorized person   _____ (Position or office)

T2061A E (05)   Form authorized by the Minister of National Revenue   **Canada**

I✦I Canada Revenue   Agence du revenu
Agency   du Canada

Request by a Non-Resident of Canada for a Certificate of Compliance Related to the Disposition of Taxable Canadian Property

INSTRUCTIONS – T2062

All legislative references are to the *Canadian Income Tax Act.*

When and How to file the Form

Use this form if you are a non-resident of Canada to give notice of the proposed disposition of, or the completed disposition of, certain taxable Canadian property. Taxable Canadian property is property described in subsection 248(1) of the Act. A disposition of taxable Canadian property includes any interest or option for such property, whether or not the property exists.

Use Form T2062A for proposed or completed dispositions of Canadian resource or timber resource property, Canadian real property (other than capital property), or depreciable taxable Canadian property. However, when disposing of depreciable taxable Canadian property, use this form to report the gain on the disposition and Form T2062A to report the recapture of capital cost allowance or terminal loss. If both forms T2062 and T2062A are required for a disposition, the forms must be filed together.

File a separate T2062 for each disposition or proposed disposition. However, if you are disposing of, or proposing to dispose of, several properties to the same purchaser at the same time, only one T2062 is required for all the properties. A separate T2062 must be filed by each person indicating an interest in a joint tenancy, tenancy in common, or co-ownership.

If you file a request for a proposed disposition under subsection 116(1) and the completed disposition complies with the requirements of paragraphs 116(3)(d), (e), and (f), you do not have to file a separate request under subsection 116(3) for the completed disposition.

We issue a certificate of compliance after tax is paid or security acceptable to the Minister is submitted in respect of the proposed or completed disposition. You may have to file a Canadian income tax return to report the disposition of property listed on this form. Final settlement of the tax liability is made when you file your Canadian income tax return. **Failure to attach this certificate of compliance to your income tax return may result in a delay in processing. For further information related to the filing requirements, please refer to the CRA website.**

Penalties for Failure to Comply

If you are giving notice of a completed disposition under subsection 116(3), you must notify us by registered mail not later than **10 days after the date of disposition**. The penalty, under subsection 162(7), for failing to file or submit a notice on time is $25 a day. There is a minimum penalty of $100 and a maximum penalty of $2,500.

Completing the Form

Send this notice along with all supporting documents (see list attached), to the Centre of Expertise (CoE) for the area where the property is located. If there is more than one property and the properties are located in several areas and more than one CoE is affected, the notification should be sent to the CoE where the majority of the properties are located. If the property is real property, the CoE is determined based on the property's legal or municipal address. If the property is shares or assets in a business, the CoE is determined based on the head office address of the corporation whose shares are being disposed of, or where the business is located. If the property is a capital interest in an estate or a trust (pursuant to the distribution of capital), the CoE is determined by the location of the trustee. The CoEs are listed on the CRA's website: **www.cra.gc.ca.**

Vendor Information

Country of residence – indicate the country where you normally, customarily, or routinely live.

Identification number – Enter the appropriate identification number. This will ensure that security or payment made for tax is credited to the correct account. Identification numbers must be used when filing your Canadian income tax return and on all correspondence with us.

Social insurance number (SIN)	– applies if an individual was formerly a resident or a deemed resident of Canada.
Individual Tax Number (ITN)	– is a number assigned to a non-resident individual who filed a Canadian income tax return in previous years.
Subsidiary ledger number	– is a number assigned to a non-resident individual who has made a remittance but does not have a Canadian tax account number.
Business number (BN)	– is a registration number for businesses such as corporations, partnerships, and sole proprietorships.
Trust account number	– is a number assigned to a trust that filed a Canadian income tax return in previous years.

If you do not have a SIN or ITN, please complete Form T1261, *Application for a Canada Revenue Agency Individual Tax Number (ITN) for Non-Residents,* available on the Internet at **www.cra.gc.ca. Include the completed form and supporting documentation with your T2062.**

Applying for a BN

Complete Form RC1, *Request for a Business Number (BN).* Form RC1 and our pamphlet, *The Business Number and Your Canada Revenue Agency Accounts,* are available on the Internet at: **www.cra.gc.ca**

Send the completed RC1 with a copy of the certification of incorporation to the tax services office where you filed the Form T2062

Details of property – If a disposition includes more than one property, attach a piece of paper providing the details for each property. All amounts must be in Canadian dollars.

Property jurisdiction – include the city/municipality, province/territory, and postal code for the street address requested below in "Property description".

Property description	– include the following details:
Land or buildings	– street address, plan number, lot number, registration number, municipal value, and use of property (e.g., personal residence, rental or business property).
Business property	– identification of business assets, business name, and street address.
Shares	– name and street address of corporation, number of shares, certificate numbers, and par value or stated capital.
Partnership property	– name, street address, and identification number of partnership.
Trusts	– name and address, if any, of trust; otherwise name(s) and street address(es) of trustee(s).
Designated insurance property	– identification of insurer's business asset, business name, and street address.

Gross Proceeds of Disposition

Enter the gross proceeds of disposition from the sale of the property. Enter the vendor's share of the gross proceeds in Column (1).

Exemption (column 4)

If you are claiming an exemption from tax, such as under a tax treaty or a principal residence exemption, enter the exempt portion in column (4). If the amount claimed is pursuant to a tax treaty, the vendor has to certify that they are resident in the stated country of residence and, if the tax treaty contains a limitation on benefits provision (e.g., Article XXIX A of the Canada – U.S. treaty) the vendor has to provide certification that they meet the requirements of the provision in relation to the property described in this form. Form NR301, NR302 and NR303 can be used for this purpose. Please attach a note detailing any calculations involved in determining the exemption amount.

Note: You cannot claim outlays and expenses related to the disposition of property, including real estate commissions, brokerage fees, and legal and notary fees, when you file this form. However, you can claim these amounts when you file your Canadian income tax return.

Certification

Authorizing a representative

By checking the authorization boxes in the Certification section you are authorizing the person named as your representative in the Vendor's section to act on your behalf for matters concerning this T2062 and the T1261 only.

If you want to authorize the representative to deal with the CRA on additional tax matters, you will need to complete a T1013, Authorizing or Cancelling a Representative.

Authorization Expiry Date

Your authorization will stay in effect until you or your representative cancels it. Otherwise, the authorization will expire within six months from the date of the issuance of a Certificate of Compliance or the finalization of the T2062, whichever comes first.

Signature and Date

To protect the confidentiality of your tax information, we will not deal with a representative on any information given on this form unless you or a legal representative has signed and dated the form.

This area should be completed and signed by:

- the vendor in the case of an individual;
- an authorized officer in the case of a corporation;
- the trustee, executor or administrator if the person is filing the statement for a trust; or
- an authorized partner in the case of a partnership.

More information

You can get more information about residency status in Canada from Interpretation Bulletin S5-F1-C1: *Determining an Individual's residence status*, or by contacting our General Enquiries line as follows: From inside Canada or the United States **1-800-959-8281** (for non-resident individuals and trusts) or **1-800-959-5525** (for non-resident corporations), From outside Canada or the United States **613-940-8495** (for non-resident individuals and trusts) or **613-940-8497** (for non-resident corporations). You can also visit our website at **www.cra.gc.ca**.

You can also get information from:

Information Circular:	IC72-17 – *Procedures Concerning the Disposition of Taxable Canadian Property by Non-Residents of Canada – Section 116*
Interpretation bulletins:	IT 176 – *Taxable Canadian Property – Interests in and Options on Real Property and Shares*
	IT 419 – *Meaning of Arm's Length*
Guide:	T4058 – *Non-Residents and Income Tax.*

Supporting Document List

When you send us your completed Form T2062, you must attach supporting documents so we can process your request. To help you, we have provided the following reference list. You can tick (✓) the boxes that apply to you.

Transactions

Sale of land or buildings

If you sell land or buildings, include copies of:

- [ ] the offer to purchase (proposed disposition);
- [ ] the sales agreement (actual disposition);
- [ ] the purchase agreement (when property was acquired); and
- [ ] the registered deeds on purchase and sale.

Principal residence

If the property is your principal residence, also include:

- [ ] Form T2091(IND), *Designation of a Property as a Principal Residence by an Individual (Other than a Personal Trust)*; and
- [ ] Form T2091(IND)-WS, *Principal Residence Worksheet*.

Personal use property

If you sell other personal use property, include a copy of:

- [ ] a letter describing the use of the property for the ownership period; and
- [ ] a list of adjustments to the adjusted cost base with supporting documentation.

Rental property

If you sell rental property, include:

- [ ] the capital cost allowance (CCA) schedules for all years;
- [ ] a list of adjustments to the adjusted cost base with supporting documentation;
- [ ] documents to support the allocation of the proceeds of disposition between land and building;
- [ ] documents to support subsection 21(1) and (3) elections regarding capitalization of interest; and
- [ ] a completed Form T2062A. *Request by a Non-Resident of Canada for a Certificate of Compliance Related to the Disposition of Canadian Resource or Timber Resource Property, Canadian Real Property (other than Capital Property), or Depreciable Taxable Canadian Property.*

Leases

If you grant an interest in property, or dispose of an interest in property, include copies of:

- [ ] the right-of-way agreement;
- [ ] the surface lease agreement; or
- [ ] the leasehold interest agreement.

Vendor takes back mortgage

If the vendor takes back the mortgage include:

- [ ] a copy of the mortgage agreement.

Mortgage foreclosures and power of sale

If the transaction is a result of a mortgage foreclosure or power of sale, include copies of:

- [ ] the power of sale or court order; and
- [ ] the mortgage agreement.

Sale of business assets

If you sell business assets including but not limited to accounts receivables and prepaid expenses, include copies of:

- [ ] the sale agreement (actual disposition);
- [ ] the most recent financial statements;
- [ ] if the proceeds are included in a bundled payment, ensure that the proper value has been attributed to assets; and
- [ ] the offer to purchase (proposed dispositions).

Sale of depreciable property (other than rental property)

For this type of transaction, include copies of:

- [ ] the sales agreement;
- [ ] the CCA schedules for all years;
- [ ] documentation to support the cost amount; and
- [ ] a completed Form T2062A.

Sale of shares

If you sell shares, please provide:

- [ ] documentation supporting the adjusted cost base of the shares;
- [ ] documentation supporting the proceeds of disposition; and
- [ ] the most recent financial statements of the corporation, and if they were not prepared on a consolidated basis, the most recent financial statements of any subsidiary corporations (if applicable).

Sale of partnership property

If you sell partnership property, include copies of:

- [ ] the sale agreement (actual disposition);
- [ ] the listing of partners (including their names, addresses, Canadian identification number, percentage ownership and each partner's portion of payment;
- [ ] the partnership agreement; and
- [ ] the offer to purchase (proposed disposition).

Partnership interest

If the property is a partnership interest, include a copy of:

- [ ] the calculation of the adjusted cost base (ACB);
- [ ] the partnership capital account balance; and
- [ ] the purchase agreement (if interest was originally acquired from another partnership).

Partnership residual interest

If the property is a partnership residual interest, include a copy of:

- [ ] a calculation of the ACB.

Partnership continuing income right

If the property is a continuing income right, include:

- [ ] a calculation of the ACB; and
- [ ] documents to support the partner's share of income.

Interest in a Trust

If you are disposing of interest in a trust, include:

- [ ] the name and account number of the trust;
- [ ] Sale documents if interest was sold;
- [ ] FMV of any property received from the trust in settlement of the capital including any evaluations; and
- [ ] A calculation of proceeds and adjusted cost base.

Tax Treaty Exemptions

If you are claiming an exemption under a tax treaty, you have to give us proof of residency.

The vendor has to provide sufficient information to establish that they met the requirement of the treaty and that they are eligible for tax treaty benefits under the treaty. In this regard, the vendor should complete and submit Form 301, *Declaration of eligibility for benefits under a tax treaty for a nonresident taxpayer*, Form 302, *Declaration of eligibility for benefits under a tax treaty for a partnership with non-resident partners*, Form 303, *Declaration of eligibility for benefits under a tax treaty under a hybrid entity*, or equivalent information. For partnerships and hybrid entities, each partner or member in respect of whom treaty benefits are claimed must provide a summary declaration to the CRA as indicated below.

Individuals should include:

☐ copies of their most recent income tax returns from the treaty country; and
☐ a letter from the tax authority in the treaty country confirming their residency status.

Corporations should include:

☐ a copy of their charter;
☐ a letter from the tax authority in the treaty country confirming their residency status; and
☐ copies of their most recent income tax returns from the treaty country.

Hybrid entities should include:

☐ Complete and submit NR303, *Declaration of eligibility for benefits under a tax treaty for hybrid entity*, and Worksheet B or equivalent information; or
☐ proof of the election to be taxed as a corporation.

Note: A treaty exemption can only be claimed on the portion of income derived by residents of the United States who are entitled to treaty benefits under paragraph 6 of Article IV of the Canada – United States tax treaty and to whom paragraph 7 of the same article does not apply. These persons must also meet the limitation on benefits provision of Article XXIX A.

Partnerships should include:

☐ Complete and submit NR302, *Declaration of eligibility for benefits under a tax treaty for a partnership with non-resident persons*; or
☐ proof of the election to be taxed as a corporation.

Trusts and estates should include:

☐ a copy of the trust agreement, indenture or will; and
☐ a letter from the tax authority in the treaty country confirming the trust's residency status; or
☐ copies of the most recent income tax returns from the treaty country.

Fresh start rule

If you are claiming an exemption under the *Canada-US Tax Convention*, Article XIII paragraph 9 (Fresh Start Rule), include:

☐ proof that you were a continuous resident of the United States from September 26, 1980, to the date of sale;
☐ the value of the property on December 31, 1971 (for property acquired before January 1, 1972);
☐ the calculation of the exempt portion of the gain accrued to December 31, 1984; or
☐ an appraisal report for the fair market value of the property on December 31, 1984.

Non arm's length transactions

If the transaction is between non arm's length parties, include:

☐ an appraisal report determining the fair-market value of the property at the time of disposition; or
☐ a letter of opinion from an appraiser.

Gift of property

If the transaction is a gift of property, include:

☐ a copy of the transfer deed.

Section 85 elections (rollovers)

If a section 85 election is made on the transaction, include a copy of:

☐ Form T2057, *Election on Disposition of Property by a Taxpayer to a Taxable Canadian Corporation*; or
☐ Form T2058, *Election on Disposition of Property by a Partnership to a Taxable Canadian Corporation*; and
☐ all supporting documents including variations, appraisals, and calculations showing how the agreed amounts were determined.

Corporate reorganization

If the transaction is a result of a corporate reorganization, include:

☐ copies of documents explaining the reorganization;
☐ a list of steps involved in the reorganization; and
☐ a corporate organization chart.

Deemed dividends – section 212.1 or subsection 84(3)

If a section 212.1 or subsection 84(3) deemed dividend results from the transaction, include the calculation of the:

☐ deemed dividend or paid-up capital reduction;
☐ tax paid-up capital; and
☐ non-resident tax account number.

Trusts and estates

If the vendor is a trust or estate, include the following information as well as documents related to the transaction:

☐ name and address of the trustee, executor, administrator, or other representative of the trust or estate;
☐ proof of residency of the trustee, executor, administrator, or other representative of the trust or estate;
☐ list of beneficiaries and their residences;
☐ the trust or estate's country of residence; and
☐ disclosure that a trust is a party to the transaction.

Charities and non-profit organizations

If the vendor is a charity or non-profit organization, include the following information as well as specific documents related to the transaction:

☐ proof that the organization is registered as a charity for tax purposes in the country of residence.

Joint tenancy, tenancy in common, or co-ownership

If the vendor is a member of a joint tenancy, tenancy in common, or co-ownership, include the following information as well as specific documents related to the transaction:

☐ a list of names and addresses of all members; and
☐ the percentage of ownership of each member.

Elections

If you previously made an election on the property, include a copy of the election form such as:

☐ Form T2061A, *Election by an Emigrant to Report Deemed Dispositions of Taxable Canadian Property and Any Resulting Capital Gain or Loss.*
☐ Electing under subsection 45(2), deems the change in use from personal to income producing not to have occurred.
☐ Electing under subsection 45(3), deems the change in use from income producing to personal not to have occurred.

Note: If there was a change in use and no election was made provide the fair market value of the property at the time the change occurred.

Payment of tax or security

If you are making a payment of tax, include:

☐ the trust cheque, certified cheque, bank draft, or money order;
☐ the bank guarantee; or
☐ proof that acceptable security has been provided to the Minister.

I✦I Canada Revenue   Agence du revenu
Agency   du Canada

Protected B when completed

Request by a Non-Resident of Canada for a Certificate of Compliance Related to the Disposition of Taxable Canadian Property

Note: The information you provide on this form is collected under the authority of the *Income Tax Act* (ITA) and is protected by the provisions of the *Privacy Act*. It is used to process requests for certificates of compliance under Section 116 of the ITA and is retained in information bank number CRA-OPPU 111.

Vendor (non-resident)

☐ Corporation   ☐ Trust   ☐ Partnership   ☐ Individual

Business number	Trust account number	Social insurance, individual tax, or subsidiary ledger number

Last name (print)	First name and initial (print)	Date of Birth YYYY MM DD	Date of departure from Canada (if applicable) YYYY MM DD

Present address	Telephone number
Country of residence (see the instructions on page 1)	Fax number
Representative name	Telephone number
Representative address	Fax number

Check the box where correspondence is to be sent (if no box is ticked, correspondence will be sent to vendor)   ☐ Vendor   ☐ Representative

Purchaser

Last name (print)	First name and initial (print)	Telephone number
Present address		Fax number
Representative's name		Telephone number
Representative address		Fax number

Check the box where correspondence is to be sent (if no box is ticked, correspondence will be sent to purchaser)   ☐ Purchaser   ☐ Representative

Details of property (see the instructions on page 1 for more information)

☐ Real property   ☐ Business property   ☐ Shares   ☐ Partnership property   ☐ Trusts   ☐ Designated insurance property

Date or proposed or completed disposition ▶	YYYY MM DD	Vendor's acquisition date ▶	YYYY MM DD
Property jurisdiction ▶	City/ Municipality	Province/territory	Postal code

Property description

Gross proceeds of disposition. Tick the box that applies to you   ☐ Proposed disposition   ☐ Completed disposition

(1) Vendor's Share of Gross Proceeds of Disposition	(2) Adjusted cost base	(3) Gain or (loss) Column (1) less column (2)	(4) Exemptions	(5) Net gain or (loss) Column (3) less column (4)
$	$	$	$	$
			Payment of tax. Enter 25% of net gain. ▶	$

T2062 E (06/2016)   (Ce formulaire existe en français.)   **Canadä**

Protected B when completed

1. Is the disposition subject to an election under section 85 (transfer of property to a company)?	☐ Yes ☐ No

2. Did you rent or lease the property during the period of ownership?   ☐ Yes   ☐ No
   If **yes**, complete the following:

   ☐ Non-resident tax was withheld. Provide name and address of person who withheld the tax. ▶

   ☐ Non-resident tax was not withheld. State the period during which income was received from the property (attach statements that show the amount of gross income).

From: YYYY	MM	DD	To: YYYY	MM	DD

   If no, state the use of the property during the period of ownership. ▶

3. If you have outstanding balances for taxes, including income or excise taxes, custom duties, or the goods and services tax/harmonized sales tax (GST/HST), provide the identification or account number(s) for the outstanding balances. ▶

4. Indicate the last tax year for which you filed a Canadian income tax return, if applicable. ▶

5. Is the disposition of property to a person with whom you are not dealing with at arm's length, or a gift inter-vivos?   ☐ Yes   ☐ No
   If **yes**, to either or both, and the disposition is at less than fair market value, enter the vendor's share of the fair market value at the time of the disposition in the vendor's share of gross proceeds of disposition column (1) above.

Certification

Please check the box(es) that apply if you are authorizing the CRA to deal with your representative concerning:

☐ T2062, *Request by a Non-Resident for a Certificate of Compliance Related to the Disposition of Taxable Canadian Property*

☐ T1261, *Application for a CRA Individual Tax Number (ITN) for Non-Residents*

I, _____ , certify that the information given on this form is, to the best of my knowledge, correct and complete.
     Name

_____	_____	_____
Date	(Authorized person's signature)	(Position or office)

Canada Revenue **Agence du revenu**
Agency **du Canada**

Request by a Non-Resident of Canada for a Certificate of Compliance Related to the Disposition of Canadian Resource or Timber Resource Property, Canadian Real Property (Other than Capital Property), or Depreciable Taxable Canadian Property

INSTRUCTIONS – T2062A

All legislative references are to the Canadian *Income Tax Act.*

When and How to file the Form
Use this form if you are a non-resident of Canada to give notice of the proposed disposition of, or the completed disposition of, Canadian resource property, Canadian real property (other than capital property), Canadian timber resource property, or depreciable Canadian taxable property. A disposition of taxable Canadian property includes any interest or option for such property, whether or not the property exists.

Use Form T2062 for the proposed or completed disposition of other taxable Canadian property, including the gain on the disposition of depreciable property. If both forms T2062A and T2062 are required for a disposition, the forms must be filed together.

If you are reporting a proposed or completed disposition of Canadian resource property, you must also complete Form T2062A, Schedule 1, *Disposition of Canadian Resource Property by Non-Residents.*

File a separate T2062A for each disposition or proposed disposition. However, if you are disposing of, or proposing to dispose of, several properties to the same purchaser at the same time, only one T2062A is required for all the properties. A separate T2062A must be filed by each person indicating an interest in a joint tenancy, tenancy in common, or co-ownership.

We issue a certificate of compliance after tax is paid or security acceptable to the Minister is submitted. You may have to file a Canadian income tax return to report the disposition of property listed on this form. Final settlement of the tax liability is made when you file your Canadian income tax return. Failure to attach the certificate of compliance to your income tax return may result in a delay in processing. For further information related to the filing requirements, please refer to the CRA website.

Completing the Form
Send this notice along with all supporting documents (see list attached), to the tax services office (TSO) or Centre of Expertise (CoE) for the area where the property is located. If there is more than one property and the properties are located in several areas and more than one TSO or CoE is affected, the notification should be sent to the TSO or CoE where the majority of the properties are located. If the property is real property, the TSO or CoE is determined based on the property's legal or municipal address. If the property is shares or assets in a business, the TSO is determined based on the head office address of the corporation whose shares are being disposed of, or where the business is located. If the property is a capital interest in an estate or a trust (pursuant to the distribution of capital), the TSO or CoE is determined by the location of the trustee. The TSOs and CoEs are listed on the CRA's website: **www.cra.gc.ca**

Vendor Information

Country of residence – Indicate the country where you normally, customarily, or routinely live.

Identification number – Enter the appropriate identification number. This will ensure that security or payment made for tax is credited to the correct account. Identification numbers must be used when filing your Canadian income tax return and on all correspondence with us.

Social insurance number (SIN)	– applies if an individual was formerly a resident or a deemed resident of Canada.
Individual Tax Number (ITN)	– is a number assigned to a non-resident individual who filed a Canadian income tax return in previous years.
Subsidiary ledger number	– is a number assigned to a non-resident individual who has made a remittance but does not have a Canadian tax account number.
Business number (BN)	– is a registration number for businesses such as corporations, partnerships, and sole proprietorships.
Trust account number	– is a number assigned to a trust that filed a Canadian income tax return in previous years.

If you do not have a SIN or ITN, please complete Form T1261, *Application for a Canada Revenue Agency Individual Tax Number (ITN) for Non-Residents,* available on the Internet at **www.cra.gc.ca**. Include the completed form and supporting documentation with your T2062.

Applying for a BN
Complete Form RC1, *Request for a Business Number (BN).* Form RC1 and our pamphlet called *The Business Number and Your Canada Revenue Agency Accounts* are available on the Internet at: **www.cra.gc.ca**.
Send the completed Form RC1 with a copy of the certificate of incorporation to the tax services office where you filed the Form T2062.

Details of property – If a disposition includes more than one property, attach a piece of paper providing the details for each property. All amounts must be in Canadian dollars.

Property jurisdiction – include the city/municipality, province/territory, and postal code for the street address requested below in "Property description".

Property description – Include the following details:
Depreciable property, real property (other than capital property) and timber resource property – street address, plan number, lot number, registration number, serial number, and use of property (rental, lease, or business); a written description and the applicable class of asset according to Schedule II of the *Income Tax Regulations.*

Resource property – well or mine location, legal description, and street address.

Gross Proceeds of Disposition
Enter the gross proceeds of disposition from the sale of the property. Enter the vendor's share of the gross proceeds in Column (1).

Proceeds of disposition (Column 1) and Capital Cost (Column 2)
For dispositions of depreciable property, enter amounts in columns (1) and (2) and enter the lesser of columns (1) and (2) in column (3).
For dispositions of timber resource property and real property (other than capital property), enter the proceeds of disposition in column (1) and in column (3).

Undepreciated capital cost or cost amount (Column 4)
For dispositions of depreciable property and timber resource property, use the undepreciated capital cost. For dispositions of real property (other than capital property), use the cost amount.

Exemption (Column 6)
If you are claiming an exemption from tax, such as under a tax treaty or a principal residence exemption, enter the exempt portion in column (6). If the amount claimed is pursuant to a tax treaty, the vendor has to certify that they are resident in the stated country of residence and, if the tax treaty contains a limitation on benefits provision (e.g., Article XXIX A of the Canada – US treaty) the vendor has to provide written certification that they meet the requirements of the provision in relation to the property described in this form. Please attach a note detailing any calculations involved in determining the exemption amount.

T2062A E (16)   (Ce formulaire existe en français.)

Note: You cannot claim outlays and expenses related to the disposition of property, including real estate commissions, brokerage fees, and legal and notary fees, when you file this form. However, you can claim these amounts when you file your Canadian income tax return.

Certification

This area should be completed and signed by:

- The vendor in the case of an individual;
- An authorized officer in the case of a corporation;
- The trustee, executor or administrator if the person is filing the statement for a trust; or
- An authorized partner in the case of a partnership.

More information

You can get information about residency status in Canada from Interpretation Bulletin S5-F1-C1: *Determining an Individual's residence status*, or by contacting our general enquiries line as follows: From inside Canada or the United States **1-800-959-8281** (for non-resident individuals and trusts) or **1-800-959-5525** (for non-resident corporations), From outside Canada or the United States **613-940-8495** (for non-resident individuals and trusts) or **613-940-8497** (for non-resident corporations). You can also visit our website at **www.cra.gc.ca**.

You can also get information from:

Information Circular:	IC72-17 – *Procedures Concerning the Disposition of Taxable Canadian Property by Non-Residents of Canada – Section 116*
Interpretation bulletins:	IT-176 – *Taxable Canadian Property – Interests in and Options on Real Property and Shares*
	IT-419 – *Meaning of Arm's Length*
Guide:	T4058 – *Non-Residents and Income Tax*

Supporting Document List   Protected B when completed

When you send us your completed Form T2062A, you must attach supporting documents so we can process your request. To help you, we have provided the following reference list. You can tick (✓) the boxes that apply to you.

Transactions

Sale of depreciable property
If you sell depreciable property, include copies of:
☐ the sales agreement (actual disposition);
☐ the capital cost allowance (CCA) schedules for all years;
☐ documentation to support the cost amount and capital cost;
☐ a completed Form T2062, *Request by a Non-Resident of Canada for a Certificate of Compliance Related to the Disposition of Taxable Canadian Property*; and
☐ the offer to purchase (proposed disposition).

Rental Property
If you sell rental property, include:
☐ documentation to support the allocation between land and building;
☐ documents to support subsection 21(1) and (3) elections regarding capitalization of interest.

Leases
If you grant an interest in property, or dispose of an interest in property, include copies of:
☐ the right of-way agreement;
☐ the surface lease agreement; or
☐ the leasehold interest agreement.

Vendor takes back mortgage
If the vendor takes back the mortgage, include:
☐ a copy of the mortgage agreement.

Mortgage foreclosures and power of sale
If the transaction is a result of a mortgage foreclosure or power of sale, include copies of:
☐ the power of sale or court order; and
☐ the mortgage agreement.

Sale of Canadian resource property
If you sell Canadian resource property, include copies of:
☐ the petroleum and natural gas lease;
☐ the offer to purchase and conveyance agreement;
☐ Form T2062A, Schedule 1; Disposition of Canadian resource property by non-residents
☐ documents to support pool balances;
☐ the sales agreement (actual disposition); and
☐ the purchase agreement (when property was acquired).

Sale of Canadian timber resource property
If you sell timber resource property, include copies of:
☐ the CCA schedules for all years;
☐ documents to support any revenue received (e.g., logging contract, payments from sawmills);
☐ your Canadian income tax returns for the last three years;
☐ the offer to purchase (proposed disposition);
☐ the sales agreement (actual disposition);
☐ the purchase agreement (when property was acquired); and
☐ the calculation of the ACB.

Sale of partnership property
If you sell partnership property, include copies of:
☐ the sales agreement (actual disposition);
☐ the listing of partners (including their names, addresses, Canadian identification number, percentage ownership and each partner's portion of payment;
☐ the partnership agreement; and
☐ the offer to purchase (proposed disposition).

Partnership interest
If the property is a partnership interest, include:
☐ a calculation of the ACB;
☐ a copy of the partnership capital account balance; and
☐ the purchase agreement (if interest was originally acquired from another partnership).

Partnership residual interest
If the property is a partnership residual interest, include a copy of:
☐ a calculation of the ACB.

Partnership continuing income right
If the property is a continuing income right, include:
☐ the calculation of the ACB; and
☐ documents to support the partner's share of income.

Tax Treaty Exemptions
If you are claiming an exemption under a tax treaty, you have to give us proof of residency.
The vendor has to provide sufficient information to establish that they met the requirement of the treaty and that they are eligible for tax treaty benefits under the treaty. In this regard, the vendor should complete and submit Form NR301, *Declaration of eligibility for benefits under a tax treaty for a nonresident taxpayer*, Form NR302, *Declaration of eligibility for benefits under a tax treaty for a partnership with non-resident partners*, Form NR303, *Declaration of eligibility for benefits under a tax treaty under a hybrid entity*, or equivalent information. For partnerships and hybrid entities, each partner or member in respect of whom treaty benefits are claimed must provide a summary declaration to the CRA as indicated below.

Individuals should include:
☐ copies of their most recent income tax returns from the treaty country; and
☐ a letter from the tax authority in the treaty country confirming their residency status.

Corporations should include:
☐ a copy of their charter;
☐ a letter from the tax authority in the treaty country confirming their residency status; and
☐ copies of their most recent income tax returns from the treaty country.

Hybrid entities should include:
☐ Complete and submit NR303, Declaration of eligibility for benefits under a tax treaty for hybrid entity, and Worksheet B or equivalent information; or
☐ proof of the election to be taxed as a corporation.

Note: A treaty exemption can only be claimed on the portion of income derived by residents of the United States who are entitled to treaty benefits under paragraph 6 of Article IV of the Canada – United States tax treaty and to whom paragraph 7 of the same article does not apply. These persons must also meet the limitation on benefits provision of Article XXIX A.

Partnerships should include:
- ☐ Complete and submit NR302, *Declaration of eligibility for benefits under a tax treaty for a partnership with non-resident persons*; or
- ☐ proof of the election to be taxed as a corporation.

Trusts and estates should include:
- ☐ a copy of the trust agreement, indenture, or will; and
- ☐ a letter from the tax authority in the treaty country confirming the trust's residency status;
- ☐ copies of the most recent income tax returns from the treaty country.

Fresh start rule

If you are claiming an exemption under the *Canada-US Tax Convention*, Article XIII paragraph 9 (Fresh Start Rule), include:
- ☐ proof that you were a continuous resident of the United States from September 26, 1980, to the date of sale;
- ☐ the value of the property on December 31, 1971 (for property acquired before January 1, 1972);
- ☐ the calculation of the exempt portion of the gain accrued to December 31, 1984; or
- ☐ an appraisal report for the fair market value of the property on December 31, 1984.

Non arm's length transactions

If the transaction is between non arm's length parties, include:
- ☐ an appraisal report determining the fair-market value of the property at the time of disposition; or
- ☐ a letter of opinion from an appraiser or agent.

Gift of property

If the transaction is a gift of property, include:
- ☐ a copy of the transfer deed.

Section 85 elections (rollovers)

If a section 85 election is made on the transaction, include a copy of:
- ☐ a Form T2057, *Election on Disposition of Property by a Taxpayer to a Taxable Canadian Corporation*; or
- ☐ a Form T2058, *Election on Disposition of Property by a Partnership to a Taxable Canadian Corporation*; and
- ☐ all supporting documents including variations, appraisals, and calculations showing how the agreed amounts were determined.

Corporate reorganization

If the transaction is a result of a corporate reorganization, include:
- ☐ copies of documents explaining the reorganization;
- ☐ a list of steps involved in the reorganization;
- ☐ a corporate organization chart.

Deemed dividends – section 212.1 or subsection 84(3)

If a section 212.1 or subsection 84(3) deemed dividend results from the transaction, include the calculation of the:
- ☐ deemed dividend or paid-up capital reduction; and
- ☐ tax paid up capital;
- ☐ non-resident tax account number.

Trusts and estates

If the vendor is a trust or estate, include the following information as well as documents related to the transaction:
- ☐ name and address of the trustee, executor, administrator, or other representative of the trust or estate;
- ☐ proof of residency of the trustee, executor, administrator, or other representative of the trust or estate;
- ☐ list of beneficiaries and their residences;
- ☐ the trust or estate's country of residence; and
- ☐ disclosure that a trust is a party to the transaction.

Charities and non-profit organizations

If the vendor is a charity or non-profit organization, include the following information as well as specific documents related to the transaction:
- ☐ proof that the organization is registered as a charity for tax purposes in the country of residence.

Joint tenancy, tenancy in common, or co-ownership

If the vendor is a member of a joint tenancy, tenancy in common, or co-ownership, include the following information as well as specific documents related to the transaction:
- ☐ a list of names and addresses of all members; and
- ☐ the percentage of ownership of each member.

Elections

If you previously made an election on the property, include a copy of the election form such as:
- ☐ Form T2061A, *Election by an Emigrant to Report Deemed Dispositions of Taxable Canadian Property and Any Resulting Capital Gain or Loss.*
- ☐ Electing under subsection 45(2), deems the change in use from personal to income producing not to have occurred.
- ☐ Electing under subsection 45(3), deems the change in use from income producing to personal not to have occurred.

Note: If there was a change in use and no election was made, provide the fair market value of the property at the time the change occurred.

Payment of tax or security

If you are making a payment of tax, include:
- ☐ the trust cheque, certified cheque, bank draft, or money order;
- ☐ the bank guarantee; or
- ☐ proof that acceptable security has been provided to the Minister.

I✦I Canada Revenue Agency   Agence du revenu du Canada   **Protected B** when completed

Request by a Non-Resident of Canada for a Certificate of Compliance Related to the Disposition of Canadian Resource or Timber Resource Property, Canadian Real Property (Other than Capital Property), or Depreciable Taxable Canadian Property

Note: The information you provide on this form is collected under the authority of the *Income Tax Act* (ITA) and is protected by the provisions of the *Privacy Act*. It is used to process requests for certificates of compliance under section 116 of the ITA and is retained in information bank number CRA-OPPU 111.

Vendor (non-resident)

☐ Corporation   ☐ Trust   ☐ Partnership   ☐ Individual

Business number	Trust account number	Social insurance, individual tax, or subsidiary ledger number

Last name (print)	First name and initial (print)	Date of birth YYYY MM DD	Date of departure from Canada (if applicable) YYYY MM DD

Present address	Telephone

Country of residence (see the instructions on page 1)	Fax

Representative name	Telephone

Representative address	Fax

Check the box where correspondence is to be sent (if no box is ticked, correspondence will be sent to vendor)   ☐ Vendor   ☐ Representative

Purchaser

Last name (print)	First name and initial (print)	Telephone

Present address	Fax

Representative name	Telephone

Representative address	Fax

Check the box where correspondence is to be sent (if no box is ticked, correspondence will be sent to purchaser)   ☐ Purchaser   ☐ Representative

Details of property (see the instructions on page 1 for more information)

☐ Depreciable property   ☐ Real property (other than capital property)   ☐ Canadian resource property   ☐ Timber resource property

Date of proposed or completed disposition ▶	YYYY MM DD	Vendor's acquisition date ▶	YYYY MM DD

Property jurisdiction ▶	City/Municipality	Province/territory	Postal code

Property Description

Gross proceeds of disposition. Tick the box that applies to you   ☐ Proposed disposition   ☐ Completed disposition

(1) Vendor's Share of Gross Proceeds of Disposition	(2) Capital Cost	(3) Lesser of Column (1) and column (2)	(4) Undepreciated Capital Cost or Cost Amount	(5) Income or (loss) Column (1) minus column (2)	(6) Exemptions	(7) Net gain or (loss) Column (3) less column (4)
$	$	$	$	$	$	$

Payment of tax. Enter Part 1 federal tax on net income. (For resource property, enter the amount from line (H) of Form T2062A, Schedule 1.) ▶ $

T2062A E (16)   (Ce formulaire existe en français.)   **Canadä**

Protected B when completed

1. Is the disposition subject to an election under section 85 (transfer of property to a company)?		☐ Yes ☐ No

2. Did you rent or lease the property during the period of ownership?   ☐ Yes ☐ No
If *yes*, please complete the following:

☐ Non-resident tax was withheld. Provide name and address of person who withheld the tax. ▶

☐ Non-resident tax was not withheld. State the period during which income was received from the property (attach statements that show the amount of gross income).

From: YYYY	MM	DD	To: YYYY	MM	DD

If no, state the use of the property during the period of ownership. ▶

3. If you have outstanding balances for taxes, including income or excise taxes, custom duties, or the goods and services tax/harmonized sales tax (GST/HST), provide the identification or account number(s) for the outstanding balances. ▶

4. Indicate the last tax year for which you filed a Canadian income tax return, if applicable. ▶

5. Is the disposition of property to a person with whom you are not dealing with at arm's length, or a gift inter-vivos?   ☐ Yes ☐ No
If *yes*, to either or both, and the disposition is at less than fair market value, enter the vendor's share of the fair market value at the time of the disposition in the vendor's share of gross proceeds of disposition column (1) above.

Certification

Please check the box(es) that apply if you are authorizing the CRA to deal with your representative concerning:

☐ T2062A, *Request by a Non-Resident of Canada for a Certificate of Compliance Related to the Disposition of Canadian Resource or Timber Resource Property, Canadian Real Property (Other than Capital Property), or Depreciable Taxable Canadian Property*

☐ T1261, *Application for a CRA Individual Tax Number (ITN) for Non-Residents*

I,_____ , certify that the information given on this form is, to the best of my knowledge, correct and complete.
       Name

_____	_____	_____
Date	(Authorized person's signature)	(Position or office)

I✦I Canada Revenue   Agence du revenu
       Agency   du Canada

DESIGNATION OF A PROPERTY AS A PRINCIPAL RESIDENCE
BY AN INDIVIDUAL (OTHER THAN A PERSONAL TRUST)

Use this form to designate a property as a principal residence and to calculate the capital gain for the year you
 - disposed of, or were considered to have disposed of, your principal residence, or any part of it; or
 - granted someone an option to buy your principal residence, or any part of it.

Attach one copy of this form to your return **only** if a capital gain has to be reported. If the property is designated as your principal residence for **all the years** in which you owned it, there is no capital gain.

Note
If you were not a resident of Canada for the entire time you owned the designated property, call **1-800-959-8281**.
Your period of non-residence may reduce or eliminate the availability of the principal residence exemption.

The term **spouse** used throughout this form applies to a person to whom you are legally married. For 1993 to 2000, a spouse included a common-law spouse. For 2001 and future years, the reference to spouse is replaced with **spouse** or **common-law partner** as defined in the "Definitions" section in Guide T4037, *Capital Gains*.

Note
If you made an election to have your same-sex partner considered your common-law partner for 1998, 1999, and/or 2000, then, for those years, your common-law partner also could not designate a different housing unit as his or her principal residence.

If you disposed of, or were considered to have disposed of, a property for which you or your spouse or common-law partner filed Form T664 or T664(Seniors), *Election to Report a Capital Gain on Property Owned at the End of February 22, 1994*, use this form to calculate the capital gain for the year if:
 - the property was your principal residence for 1994; or
 - you are designating the property in this form as your principal residence for any tax year.

You may be entitled to a reduction as a result of the capital gains election. To calculate this reduction, use Form T2091(IND)-WS, *Principal Residence Worksheet*. To get this form, go to **www.cra.gc.ca/forms** or call **1-800-959-8281**.

For more information about designating a principal residence and what qualifies as a principal residence, see Income Tax Folio S1-F3-C2, *Principal Residence*, or the "Principal residence" chapter in Guide T4037, *Capital Gains*.

┌─ **Designation** ───

For the purpose of this form, the **acquisition date** is the date on which you acquired or last reacquired the property, or December 31, 1971, whichever is later. However, if you or your spouse or common-law partner filed Form T664 or T664(Seniors), you or your spouse or common-law partner are not considered to have disposed of and immediately reacquired the property as a result of that election.

Note
If the property was designated as a principal residence for the purpose of filing Form T664 or T664(Seniors), you have to include those previously designated tax years as part of this principal residence designation.

Description of property designated: _____

I, _____ , hereby designate the property described above to have been my principal residence for the
   (print your name)
following tax years ending after the **acquisition date**:

a) _____
      (specify which tax years after 1971 and before 1982)

b) _____
         (specify which tax years after 1981)

For those years before 1982, I confirm that I have not designated any other property as my principal residence.

For those years after 1981, I also confirm that neither I, nor my spouse or common-law partner (who was not separated and living apart from me throughout the year under a judicial separation or written separation agreement), nor any of my children (who were under 18 and unmarried or not in a common-law partnership throughout the year) designated any other property as a principal residence. For any tax year after 1981 for which I am designating the property and throughout which I was under 18 and unmarried or not in a common-law partnership, I also confirm that neither my mother, father, nor any of my brothers and sisters (who were under 18 and unmarried or not in a common-law partnership throughout the year) designated any other property as a principal residence.

Signature	Social insurance number	Date
	⎵ ⎵ ⎵ ⎵ ⎵ ⎵ ⎵ ⎵ ⎵	

───

Information needed to calculate the capital gain

Number of tax years for which the property is designated as a principal residence:
 - Before 1982 (as per designation above) 1
 - After 1981 (as per designation above) .... + ___ 2
 - Total number of years designated (line 1 **plus** line 2) .... = ___ 3

Number of tax years ending after the **acquisition date** in which you owned the property
(jointly with another person or otherwise):
 - Before 1982 4
 - After 1981 .... + ___ 5
 - Total number of years owned (line 4 **plus** line 5) .... = ___ 6

Proceeds of disposition or deemed disposition 7
Outlays and expenses related to the disposition 8
Adjusted cost base at the time of disposition (If you or your spouse or common-law partner filed Form T664 or T664(Seniors) for this property, do not take into consideration any increase to the adjusted cost base as a result of that election.) 9
Adjusted cost base on December 31, 1981 10
Fair market value on December 31, 1981 11
Adjustments to the cost base made after 1981 (for example, capital expenditures) 12

Canada

Calculation of the capital gain

Part 1

Proceeds of disposition or deemed disposition (line 7)		13
Adjusted cost base at the time of disposition (line 9)	14	
Outlays and expenses (line 8)	+ 15	
Line 14 **plus** line 15	= ► −	16
Capital gain before principal residence exemption (line 13 minus line 16)	=	17
Amount from line 17	18	
Line 3 **plus** 1 (one year is granted by law)	× 19	
Multiply line 18 by line 19	= 20	
Line 6	+ 21	
Divide line 20 by line 21	= ► −	22
Net capital gain from Part 1 (line 17 **minus** line 22; if negative, enter "0")	=	23

Part 2

Complete Part 2 **only** if the property disposed of is one of two or more properties that qualify as principal residences a family member owned on December 31, 1981, and continuously thereafter until its disposition. You will find a definition of **family** in the "Principal residence" chapter in Guide T4037, *Capital Gains*. **In all other cases**, do not complete Part 2 and enter the amount from line 23 above on line 53 in Part 3 below.

a) Pre-1982 gain – If you designated the property as a principal residence for all the years you owned it before 1982, do not complete lines 24 to 31 and enter "0" on line 32.

Fair market value on December 31, 1981 (line 11)		24
Adjusted cost base on December 31, 1981 (line 10)	−	25
Pre-1982 gain before principal residence exemption (line 24 minus line 25)	=	26
Amount from line 26	27	
Line 1 **plus** 1 (one year is granted by law)	× 28	
Multiply line 27 by line 28	= 29	
Line 4	+ 30	
Divide line 29 by line 30	= ► −	31
Pre-1982 gain (line 26 **minus** line 31; if negative, enter "0")	=	32

b) Post-1981 gain – If you designated the property as a principal residence for all the years you owned it after 1981, enter "0" on line 44 and complete area d) below.

Proceeds of disposition or deemed disposition (line 7)		33
Fair market value on December 31, 1981 (line 11). If the fair market value of the property on December 31, 1981, is more than the amount on line 33, enter "0" on line 44 and complete areas c) and d) below	34	
Adjustments made to the cost base after 1981 (line 12)	+ 35	
Outlays and expenses (line 8)	+ 36	
Add lines 34 to 36	= ► −	37
Post-1981 gain before principal residence exemption (line 33 minus line 37)	=	38
Amount from line 38	39	
Line 2	× 40	
Multiply line 39 by line 40	= 41	
Line 5	+ 42	
Divide line 41 by line 42	= ► −	43
Post-1981 gain (line 38 **minus** line 43; if negative, enter "0")	=	44

c) Post-1981 loss

Fair market value on December 31, 1981 (line 11)		45
Proceeds of disposition or deemed disposition (line 7)	−	46
Post-1981 loss (line 45 **minus** line 46; if negative, enter "0")	=	47

d) Net capital gain from Part 2

Pre-1982 gain, if any (line 32)	48	
Post-1981 gain, if any (line 44)	+ 49	
Line 48 **plus** line 49	= 50	
Post-1981 loss, if any (line 47)	− 51	
Net capital gain from Part 2 (line 50 **minus** line 51; if negative, enter "0")	= ►	52

Part 3

Total capital gain (If you completed Part 2, enter the amount from line 23 or line 52, **whichever is less**. Otherwise, enter the amount from line 23) ... | 53

Complete Part 4 **only** if you or your spouse or common-law partner filed Form T664 or T664(Seniors) for this property. In all other cases, enter the amount from line 53 on line 158 of Schedule 3, *Capital Gains (or Losses)*, for dispositions or deemed dispositions.

Part 4

Total capital gain before reduction (line 53)		54
Reduction as a result of the capital gains election (line 66 of Form T2091(IND)-WS)	−	55
Capital gain (line 54 **minus** line 55; if negative, enter "0")	=	56

Enter the amount from line 56 on line 158 of Schedule 3, *Capital Gains (or Losses)*, for dispositions or deemed dispositions.

See the privacy notice on your return.

Procedures concerning the disposition of taxable Canadian property by non residents of Canada Section 116

No. : **IC72-17R6**

Date: **September 29, 2011**

Subject: **Procedures concerning the disposition of taxable Canadian property by non residents of Canada — Section 116**

This version is only available electronically.

This circular cancels and replaces Information Circular 72 17R5, dated March 15,2005. Unless otherwise stated all references to a statute herein are to the Income Tax Act (the "Act").

General Information

1. Under section 116, non resident vendors (from now on referred to as vendors) who dispose of certain taxable Canadian property (see paragraph 2 below) have to notify the Canada Revenue Agency (CRA) about the disposition either before they dispose of the property or within ten days after the disposition. When the CRA has received either an amount to cover the tax on any gain the vendor may realize upon the disposition of property, or appropriate security for the tax, the CRA will issue a certificate of compliance to the vendor. A copy of the certificate is also sent to the purchaser. If the purchaser does not receive such certificate, the purchaser is required to remit a specified amount to the Receiver General for Canada and is entitled to deduct the amount from the purchase price. Any payments or security provided by the vendor and/or purchaser will be credited to the vendor's account. A final settlement of tax will be made when the vendor's income tax return for the year is assessed.

2. For dispositions after March 4, 2010, taxable Canadian property (referred to in paragraph 1 above) is described in subsection 248(1). While this is not a complete list, taxable Canadian property includes:

    a.   real or immovable property situated in Canada;

    b.   property used or held in, or eligible capital property in respect of, a business carried on in Canada;

    c.   designated insurance property of an insurer;

    d. a share of the capital stock of a corporation (other than a mutual fund corporation) that is not listed on a designated stock exchange, if, at any time in the last 60 months more than 50% of the fair market value of the share was derived directly or indirectly from one or any combination of,

        i.   real or immovable property situated in Canada;

        ii. Canadian resource properties;

        iii. timber resource properties, and;

        iv. options in respect of, or interests in, or for civil law, rights in a property described in i), ii) or iii) above, whether or not the property exists.

    e. an interest in a partnership if, at any time in the last 60 months, more than 50% of the fair market value of the interest, was derived directly or indirectly from one or any combination of the properties listed in (d)(i) to (d)(iv) above;

    f. an interest in a trust (other than a unit of a mutual fund trust or an income interest in a trust resident in Canada) if, at any time in the last 60 months, more than 50% of the fair market value of the interest was derived directly or indirectly from one or any combination of the properties listed in (d)(i) to (d)(iv) above;

    g. a share of the capital stock of a corporation that is listed on a designated stock exchange if at any time in the last 60 months,

        i.   25% or more of the issued shares of any class of capital stock of the corporation were owned or belonged to one or a combination of,

           A. the taxpayer; and

           B. persons with whom the taxpayer did not deal with at arm's length and

        ii. more than 50% of the fair market value of the share was derived directly or indirectly from one or any combination of properties described in (d)(i) to (d)(iv) above.

    h. a share of the capital stock of a mutual fund corporation if at any time in the last 60 months,

        i.   25% or more of the issued shares of any class of capital stock of the corporation were owned by or belonged to one or a combination of,

           A. the taxpayer; and

           B. persons with whom the taxpayer did not deal with at arm's length and

        ii. more than 50% of the fair market value of the share was derived directly or indirectly from one or any combination of properties described in (d)(i) to (d)(iv) above.

    i. a unit of a mutual fund trust if at any time in the last 60 months,

      i.   25% or more of the issued units of the trust were owned by or belonged to one or a combination of,

          A. the taxpayer; and

          B. persons with whom the taxpayer did not deal with at arm's length and

      ii. more than 50% of the fair market value of the unit was derived directly or indirectly from one or any combination of properties described in (d)(i) to (d)(iv) above.

j. an option in respect of, or an interest in, or for civil law a right in, a property described in any of paragraphs (a) to (i) above.

3. Certain types of taxable Canadian property fall into the category of excluded property as defined in subsection 116(6) and, as such, are not subject to the requirements of section 116. The disposition of excluded properties by a non resident person may result in tax payable under subsections 2(3) and 115(1). Excluded property consists of:

a. a property that is a taxable Canadian property solely because a provision of the Act deems it to be a taxable Canadian property;

b. a property that is inventory of a business carried on in Canada (other than real or immovable property situated in Canada, a Canadian resource property or a timber resource property);

c. shares of capital stock of a corporation that are listed on a recognized stock exchange;

d. a unit of a mutual fund trust;

e. a bond, debenture, bill, note, mortgage, hypothecary claim or similar obligation;

f. property of a non resident insurer that is licensed to carry on an insurance business in Canada and does so;

g. property of an authorized foreign bank that is used or held in the bank's Canadian banking business;

h. an option in respect of property (whether or not such property is in existence) referred to in any of items (a) to (g);

i. an interest in, or for civil law any right in property referred to in any of items (a) to (h); and

j. a treaty-exempt property (see paragraph 27).

4. Subsection 116(5.2) specifies that where a non resident disposes or proposes to dispose of a life insurance policy in Canada, a Canadian resource property, a property (other than capital property) that is real property situated in Canada, a timber resource property, a depreciable property that is a taxable Canadian property, or any interest in or option in respect of these properties, and the non resident has paid the tax or provided acceptable security, the Minister will issue a certificate stating the proceeds or proposed proceeds of disposition.

5. Section 116 applies when the vendor is a non resident or considered to be a non resident under the Act (e.g., subsection 250(5) *Deemed non resident*). If a vendor is contemplating selling the property to which section 116 applies, and the vendor is a Canadian resident before the property is disposed of, but will be a non resident when the property is finally disposed of, section 116 will apply. The purchaser's domicile or country of residence is not relevant in determining if section 116 applies. The purchaser may be either a Canadian resident or a non resident.

Vendor Notification Process

6. Under subsection 116(1), a vendor may submit a notice to the CRA for a proposed disposition. The vendor should send this notice at least 30 days before the property is actually disposed of to permit sufficient time to review the transaction and verify that the vendor's payment or security is adequate. If possible, the CRA will issue a T2064, *Certificate — Proposed Disposition of Property by a Non-Resident of Canada* before the actual date the vendor disposes of the property. Where notification of a proposed disposition was not made or if the transaction was completed in a manner different from the proposed disposition, the vendor must send the CRA a notice of the actual disposition, as required by subsection 116(3), by registered mail, not later than 10 days after the date the property was disposed of.

There are three principal reasons for differences between the proposed and actual transaction:

a. The actual purchaser is different from the one originally reported. This may occur, for example, if the purchaser assigns the purchase and sale agreement to a related party or takes title in joint tenancy with another person.

b. The actual proceeds of disposition to the non resident are higher than the estimated amount reported.

c. Prior to the disposition, there is a decrease to the vendor's adjusted cost base. In view of the diverse events which may reduce the adjusted cost base, as described in subsection 53(2), careful attention must be given to this situation.

However, where the actual proceeds of disposition are lower than the stated amount on the notice of proposed disposition or where the adjusted cost base is higher than previously reported on the notice of proposed disposition, the vendor does not have to send a notice regarding the actual disposition.

7. A vendor should use the appropriate authorized form to notify the CRA about a section 116 disposition. The forms outline the procedures to follow for

reporting the transaction, calculating the gain or loss, income, recapture or terminal loss, and making the required payment on account of tax. The vendor must also provide all required information and documentation as described in the "Supporting Document List" attached to the authorized form. This information is essential to the issuance of the certificate in a timely manner. The notification form must be signed by the vendor. However, a notification signed by the vendor's representative will be accepted if a letter authorizing the CRA to deal with the representative is provided. For information regarding our forms, visit the CRA website www.cra.gc.ca/forms. Refer to the section on Authorized Forms below for the form numbers.

8. The vendor may also notify the CRA by a letter stating that it is a notification of a disposition for section 116 purposes. In this case, the vendor must report the transaction, calculate the capital gain or loss, income, recapture or terminal loss, make the required payment on account of tax or provide security for it, and provide all required information and documentation as described in the "Supporting Document List" (available on the authorized form), along with the following information:

  a. the vendor's complete name and address, including country of residence;
  b. if an individual, date of birth, and departure date from Canada if applicable;
  c. identification number (social insurance number, business number, trust account number or individual tax number);
  d. the complete name and address of the proposed or actual purchaser;
  e. a description that will enable the Minister to identify the property;
  f. the estimated or actual amount of the proceeds of disposition (if applicable, an appraisal or valuation report); and
  g. the vendor's adjusted cost base at the time the notice was filed.

9. The vendor's identification number is required to ensure that any payment the vendor makes is credited to the proper account. These payments are then matched with the information filed on the vendor's income tax return for the year. The identification number is also required as it is entered on the certificate of compliance issued by the CRA. An identification number is required in order for a certificate of compliance to be issued.

If an individual does not have an identification number, they should complete Form T1261, *Application for a Canada Revenue Agency Individual Tax Number (ITN) for Non Residents* and submit it with the notification.

If a non-resident corporation does not have an identification number, Form RC1, *Request for a Business Number (BN)* should be completed and submitted with a copy of the certification of incorporation. The RC1 should be sent to the Tax Services Office (TSO) where the notification is sent.

A non-resident trust should provide the account number issued by CRA from a previous year tax assessment. If a tax return was not filed in a previous year, an account number will be assigned to the trust when the notification is submitted.

10. When there is more than one vendor, each vendor must file a separate notification indicating his or her interest in the property. For partnership dispositions, it is CRA policy to accept one notification of disposition filed on behalf of all partners. However, along with the notice, a complete listing of the non resident partners who are disposing of the property along with their Canadian and foreign addresses, identification numbers, percentage of ownership, and their portion of the payment or security is required. If no account information is available for a non resident partner, the CRA will assign an identification number. Generally, each partner is required to file a tax return and, as such, each partner's final tax liability will be determined when the tax returns are filed and assessed.

11. The vendor should complete the applicable notification and send it with the required payment on account of tax or acceptable security to the TSO serving the area in which the property is located. If the properties are located in several areas and more than one TSO is affected, the vendor should send the notice to the TSO that serves the area where the majority of the properties are located.

If the property is real property, the TSO is based on the property's legal or municipal address.

If the property is shares or assets in a business, the TSO is determined based on the head office address of the corporation whose shares are being disposed of, or where the business is located.

If a property is a capital interest in an estate or trust (pursuant to the distribution of capital), the TSO is determined by the location of the trustee.

12. A vendor who fails to report a disposition under subsection 116(3) may be assessed a penalty pursuant to subsection 162(7) plus any applicable interest. Subsection 162(7) provides that every person or partnership that fails to comply with a duty or obligation imposed by the Act or its regulations is liable to a penalty equal to the greater of $100 and $25 per day up to a maximum of $2,500.

Authorized Forms

13. Vendors should use Form T2062, *Request by a Non Resident of Canada for a Certificate of Compliance Related to the Disposition of Taxable Canadian*

Property to notify the CRA of an actual or proposed disposition of taxable Canadian property as described in paragraph 2 above. Except as otherwise noted below, the notification process for Form T2062 is as outlined in paragraphs 6 to 12 above.

14. Form T2062A, *Request by a Non Resident of Canada for a Certificate of Compliance Related to the Disposition of Canadian Resource or Timber Resource Property, Canadian Real Property (Other than Capital Property), or Depreciable Taxable Canadian Property*, is to be used for reporting the proposed or actual dispositions of properties identified in paragraph 4 above. Except as otherwise noted below, the notification process for Form T2062A is the same as the process outlined for Form T2062 in paragraphs 6 to 12 above.

15. In some cases, vendors may have to file both Form T2062 and Form T2062A for one disposition. When vendors dispose of depreciable taxable Canadian property, they should use Form T2062 to declare the gain or loss. The recapture of capital cost allowance or terminal loss should be reported on Form T2062A. Depreciable property is property for which a taxpayer is entitled to claim capital cost allowance, which is deductible when calculating income from business or property. Form T2062A should be filed even if capital cost allowance has not been claimed on a depreciable property. In these instances two certificates of compliance will be issued.

16. Vendors should use Form T2062A Schedule 1, *Disposition of Canadian Resource Property by Non Residents* to determine the balances in the various "pools" and the payment on account of tax (if any) when they dispose of Canadian resource properties. To support the amounts reported, vendors should also submit Form T2062A along with any other supporting documents. Vendors cannot use unrelated outlays and expenses and losses carried forward from previous years to reduce the balance in the "pools" and thus lower the amount subject to payment on account of tax under section 116.

17. Life insurance companies should use Form T2062B, *Notice of Disposition of a Life Insurance Policy in Canada by a Non Resident of Canada.* and Form T2062B Schedule 1, *Certification and Remittance Notice* to report the disposition of life insurance policies in Canada on behalf of a vendor. In these instances, the insurer requests a letter of authorization from the vendor in order to establish an agency relationship. The insurer then submits a copy of this letter with Form T2062B and the appropriate payment on account of tax to the CRA.

18. Form T2062C, *Notification of an Acquisition of Treaty-Protected Property from a Non-Resident Vendor* may be used by a purchaser of taxable Canadian property,where the vendor is a non-resident and the property is treaty protected property.

Technical Applications

19. A "disposition" is defined in subsection 248(1) as including "any transaction or event entitling a taxpayer to proceeds of disposition of the property." Therefore, the disposition of real property normally occurs at the time the deed, in properly executed form, is delivered to the purchaser. This is usually the closing date. If the disposition is in the form of a vendor's agreement for sale, then the disposition normally occurs when the properly executed agreement for sale is delivered to the person acquiring the property.

20. The definition of "proceeds of disposition" in section 54 is used for calculating the proceeds amount for section 116 reporting. If the disposition is not at arm's length and the consideration is less than fair market value, proceeds will be considered to be equal to fair market value, in accordance with subsection 116(5.1).

21. The adjusted cost base reported on Form T2062, T2062A, or T2062B must be calculated in accordance with the relevant sections of the Act and the *Income Tax Application Rules*. If the CRA determines that the adjusted cost base differs from the amount reported by the vendor, the CRA will take the position that the vendor has not provided the required information, and will then withhold the certificate until the vendor provides the correct information.

22. When a foreign currency is involved, the adjusted cost base is converted into Canadian dollars at its historical rate while the proceeds of disposition are converted at the exchange rate in effect at the date of disposition.

23. The rules for determining whether a disposition of a life insurance policy in Canada has occurred, as well as the amount of the proceeds and the adjusted cost base are set out in section 148. For more information, refer to the current version of IT 87, *Policy holders' Income from Life Insurance Policies*.

Real Estate Appraisals or Business Equity Valuations

24. To reduce delays, the CRA may request copies of the vendor's financial statements for the previous year, as these are usually not readily available in the TSOs. These statements may be used by the CRA's Business Equity Valuation or Real Estate Appraisal Sections to review the vendor's reported values.

25. If the CRA determines that a detailed real estate appraisal or business equity valuation is required, an attempt will be made to establish an "estimated value" on which a required payment on account of tax may be based. If the vendor wishes to make a payment based on this "estimated value," the CRA will issue the certificate of compliance to enable the vendor to complete the transaction

without having to wait for the results of the appraisal or valuation, which may take several months.

Once the business equity valuation or real estate appraisal has been completed, any changes in the values will be discussed with the vendor or the vendor's representative. The values established as a result of the appraisal or equity valuation should be used when the vendor files a return of income for the year in which the disposition occurs.

If the valuation or appraisal is finalized in the vendor's favour before the income tax return for the year in which the disposition occurs may be filed, the vendor may request a refund of any excess payment on account of tax. The request must be made in writing to the TSO that processed the section 116 notification and an amended Certificate of Compliance will be issued.

Treaty-Protected and Treaty-Exempt Property

26. A property is considered a treaty-protected property of the vendor, if all of the income or gain derived from the disposition of that property is exempt from tax under Part I of the Act, due to a provision in a tax treaty that Canada has with the country of residence of the vendor.

27. Where the vendor and purchaser are related, a treaty protected property of the vendor is considered a treaty exempt property only if the purchaser submits Form T2062C or a similar notification to the CRA within 30 days after the date of the acquisition of the property. A treaty-exempt property is an excluded property for the purposes of section 116, (see paragraph 3).

28. A late-filed notification submitted by the purchaser will not be accepted by the CRA as a valid notification.

Where the purchaser and vendor are related, and the purchaser notification is late-filed, the property will not be considered a treaty-exempt property and is not an excluded property. In this situation, the regular vendor notification requirements will apply.

Where the purchaser and vendor are not related, there is no requirement for the purchaser to file a notification in order to qualify the property as a treaty-exempt property and thus an excluded property. However, the purchaser may want to reduce the potential for purchaser's liability by sending Form T2062C or a similar notification to the CRA within 30 days after the acquisition date of the property.

For further information on purchaser's liability, refer to paragraphs 50 to 58.

Tax Treaty Exemptions

29. If Form T2062 and/or T2062A is submitted by the vendor and there is a claim under a tax treaty, the vendor must provide the applicable provision of the tax treaty that Canada has with their country of residence and submit the necessary documentation to support the claim. The documentation must be based on the particular tax treaty under which the exemption is claimed, and would include items such as proof of residency, or proof that the gain has been or will be reported in the vendor's country of residence. Tax officials in some countries may supply the necessary certification of residency required to claim the exemption. The vendor has to provide sufficient information to establish that they meet the requirements of the provision and that they are eligible for tax treaty benefits under the tax treaty. In this regard, the vendor should complete and submit Form NR301, *Declaration of Eligibility for Benefits Under a Tax Treaty for a Non-Resident Taxpayer*, Form NR302, *Declaration of Eligibility for Benefits Under a Tax Treaty for a Partnership with Non-Resident Partners*, or Form NR303, *Declaration of Eligibility for Benefits Under a Tax Treaty for a Hybrid Entity*, or equivalent information. Refer to the Supporting Document List in the instructions to Forms T2062 and T2062A for a complete list of the required documentation and forms.

30. The United States Department of the Treasury, Internal Revenue Service will provide certification of residency for corporations, exempt organizations and individuals. Requests for certification of residency should be sent to the appropriate service centre. The IRS provides residency certification on Form 6166. Please contact the the IRS or visit their website for further information on the certification process.

31. If the CRA and the vendor cannot agree as to whether the exemption of a particular tax convention applies, the vendor must provide the required payment or security before a certificate of compliance is issued. A letter of undertaking is not considered acceptable security. Once the matter is resolved, the vendor may request a refund or release of security based on the final decision and an amended certificate of compliance will be issued.

32. The vendor must provide documents to support the proceeds of disposition and the adjusted cost base of the property. The certificate of compliance will indicate that the disposition is treaty exempt.

33. For the purpose of Article XIII, paragraph 9 of the Canada-United States Tax Convention, the reduction of the capital gain for properties owned on September 26, 1980 and disposed of after December 31, 1984, is normally calculated by using the following ratio:

A ¼ B = ratio

Where, A equals the number of months between the date of acquisition or January 1, 1972 (whichever is later), and December 31, 1984;

and, B equals the number of months between the date of acquisition or January 1, 1972 (whichever is later), and the date of disposition.

This is so because capital gains in Canada became taxable after 1971, and under the Canada's-United States Tax Convention the gains derived in Canada were exempt in Canada until December 31, 1984, provided the property was owned on September 26, 1980. It is reasonable to view the gain as accruing evenly over the total period of ownership. The gain may be allocated unevenly over the period if the vendor satisfies the Canadian Competent Authority that such an allocation is appropriate. If the vendor wants to use this method, a valuation of the property at December 31, 1984 must be submitted with the notification.

For more information, refer to the current version of IT 173, *Capital Gains Derived in Canada by Residents of the United States*.

34. If a partnership has disposed of taxable Canadian property, and is claiming a tax treaty exemption based on its partners' entitlements to tax treaty benefits, the partnership should complete and submit Form NR302 along with Worksheet B, or equivalent information. The partnership should have on file Forms NR301, NR302, or NR303 (or equivalent information), whichever is applicable, for each partner resident in a treaty country regarding their eligibility for tax treaty benefits, or a declaration from each Canadian resident partner regarding their residency. A partnership that has elected to be taxed as a corporation on its world income in a treaty country can claim a tax treaty exemption on its own entitlement to tax treaty benefits or that of its partners, whichever is more beneficial. For exemptions to which the partnership is entitled due to its election to be taxed as a corporation, proof of the election is required.

35. If a hybrid entity has disposed of taxable Canadian property, and is claiming a tax treaty exemption based on the entitlement to tax treaty benefits of U.S. residents who derive income from the entity in accordance with paragraphs 6 and 7 of Article IV of the Canada's-United States Tax Convention, the hybrid entity should complete and submit Form NR303 along with Worksheet B, or equivalent information. The hybrid entity should have on file Forms NR301 or NR303 (or equivalent information), whichever is applicable, for each person (other than a partnership) regarding their eligibility for tax treaty benefits. In the case of a partnership that derives income through the hybrid entity, the hybrid entity should have on file a statement from each partnership listed in Worksheet B of what information the partnership would have certified on their Form

NR302 had all of its partners, other than those that reside in the U.S., resided in a country that Canada does not have a tax treaty with.

A hybrid entity that has elected to be taxed as a corporation on its world income in a treaty country claims a tax treaty exemption based on its own entitlement to tax treaty benefits, and not that of its members/shareholders. Proof of the election will be required.

Inventory of Land

36. Before February 20, 1990, inventory of land was excluded from section 116 requirements. For dispositions after February 20, 1990, the CRA has a discretionary exemption policy for certain vendors who operate a business involving inventory of land. To qualify, the vendor must satisfy the CRA that:

    a.   property transactions of this kind have been previously reported on income account; and/or
    b.   the vendor is making regular instalment payments.

If at the time of filing the notification of disposition, the vendor and the CRA disagree as to the nature of the transaction, i.e. whether proceeds are on account of income or capital, the request for exemption will be referred to the International Audit Section in the applicable TSO. The vendor has to supply any necessary supporting documentation or representation as to why the nature of the transaction should be considered as in respect of income rather than capital. If the International Audit Section is satisfied that the vendor meets the established criteria, and has no outstanding tax liabilities, a certificate of compliance stating "qualified business exemption" will be issued. Refer to the Supporting Document List in the instructions to forms T2062 and T2062A for a complete list of the required documentation.

Section 85 Elections

37. For a disposition that is subject to an election under section 85, the vendor must submit the prescribed section 85 election Form T2057, *Election on Disposition of Property by a Taxpayer to a Taxable Canadian Corporation* or Form T2058, *Election on Disposition of Property by a Partnership to a Taxable Canadian Corporation* along with Form T2062 or Form T2062A.

38. The vendor must provide supporting documentation, such as business equity valuations, real estate appraisals or calculations showing how the reported values were determined. Refer to the Supporting Document List attached to forms T2062 and T2062A for a list of the required documentation.

Corporate Reorganizations

39. In a corporate reorganization, where multiple taxpayers are involved in a share for share exchange and/or an exchange of stock options, and there is no gain on the exchange, one notification for a disposition may be filed. The transactions must not result in any gains or any benefit conferred on any person and there must be absolutely no non share consideration involved. Along with the notification, a complete listing of the non resident shareholders and/or option holders who are disposing of the property, together with their Canadian and foreign addresses, identification number, adjusted cost base and the valuation of shares or options must be provided. The CRA will review the group of transactions as one transaction and may issue one or more certificates of compliance.

40. Where a share of the capital stock of a corporation that is taxable Canadian property is exchanged for another share of the corporation and paragraph 51(1)(c) applies so as to deem the exchange not to be a disposition, the holder of the share has no obligation under subsections 116(1) and 116(3). However, the corporation has an acquisition and therefore may have obligations as a purchaser under subsection 116(5). Therefore, to prevent a purchaser's liability assessment under subsection 116(5), a certificate of compliance may be requested for the exchange. The cost to the corporation would be the stated capital of the shares issued. The TSO may, at its discretion, require nominal security in order to issue a certificate of compliance. For more information on purchaser's liability, refer to paragraphs 50 to 58 below.

Security or Payments on Account of Tax

41. For a certificate of compliance to be issued under subsection 116(2) or 116(4), the required payment on account of tax or security acceptable to the Minister on the disposition or proposed disposition of property, is a flat rate of 25% of the excess of the proceeds of disposition over the adjusted cost base of the property. Outlays and expenses incurred for the purpose of making the disposition are not taken into account in this calculation. These amounts are deductible in calculating the gain on the disposition, which should be reported on the income tax return for the year in which the disposition occurred.

42. For a certificate of compliance to be issued under subsection 116(5.2), for either an actual or a proposed disposition, a payment on account of tax or security acceptable to the Minister must be provided. The amount subject to a payment on account of tax from the disposition of property described in paragraph 4 above recognizes the fact that those amounts are fully included in

income. Therefore individual, trust or corporate tax rates will be used in calculating the amount of payment on account of tax or security.

43. The CRA's policy is as follows regarding payments on account of tax or security for the disposition of depreciable taxable Canadian property, and any resulting gains and recapture of capital cost allowance.

     a.   Where no capital cost allowance has ever been claimed or a correct amount subject to recapture of capital cost allowance can be determined, the required payment on account of tax is determined as follows:
         i.   25% of the gain on the land and building (the amount determined should be reported on Form T2062); and
         ii.   the applicable individual, trust or corporate federal tax rate applied to the amount of recapture, because this amount will be fully taxable when the vendor files a return of income for the year in which the disposition occurred. Recapture of capital cost allowance should be reported on Form T2062A.

     b.   When the amount of recapture of capital cost allowance or terminal loss cannot be determined at the time of disposition or proposed disposition, the required payment on account of tax is determined as follows:
         i.   25% of the gain on the land and building (the amount determined should be reported on Form T2062); and
         ii.   the applicable federal tax rate applied to the estimated recapture based on the assumption that the full capital cost allowance was claimed from the time of purchase to the date of disposition. This procedure ensures that a sufficient payment is provided to cover any amount subject to recapture. The final settlement of tax will be made when the return of income, for the year in which the disposition occurs, is assessed. Form T2062A should be used for the notification.

This procedure will only be used after all efforts to determine the correct amount subject to recapture of capital cost allowance have been exhausted and an agreement for the amount subject to recapture of capital cost allowance cannot be reached with the CRA, and it is imperative that the certificate of compliance be issued. Income tax returns for previous years should be made available to support the recapture reported or the terminal loss claimed.

44. Payment of tax should be made by a certified cheque, a cheque drawn on a lawyer's trust account, a bank draft or money order. Where a personal cheque is submitted, the certificate will be issued once the cheque has cleared the bank account. As an alternative to immediate payment of the tax, the CRA may

accept security for the tax as an interim arrangement. In such a case, the vendor should contact the Revenue Collections Division at the TSO processing the notification to negotiate the security that the CRA is prepared to accept.

Certificate of Compliance

45. The CRA will issue the certificate of compliance at the earliest possible date once the necessary information and supporting documentation have been received and validated, and acceptable payment or security has been received.

46. A copy of the certificate of compliance will be issued to both the vendor and the purchaser. The certificate protects the purchaser from any further tax liability in respect of the particular notice filed for that particular disposition. The vendor's final tax liability in respect of the particular notice will be determined when the vendor files a tax return, as is required under the Act, for the year the disposition took place.

47. Form T2064, *Certificate — Proposed Disposition of Property by a Non Resident of Canada* will be issued in accordance with subsection 116(2) if the conditions of subsection 116(1) are met, and the required payment on account of tax or acceptable security is provided.

Form T2068, *Certificate — The Disposition of Property by a Non Resident of Canada* will be issued in accordance with subsection 116(4) if the conditions of subsection 116(3) are met, and the required payment on account of tax or acceptable security is provided.

48. Form T2064, *Certificate — Proposed Disposition of Property by a Non Resident of Canada* or Form T2068, *Certificate — The Disposition of Property by a Non Resident of Canada*, will be issued for proposed or actual dispositions respectively, in accordance with subsection 116(5.2), provided that the vendor has paid any required amount on account of tax or provided acceptable security for the properties described in paragraph 4 above.

49. A certificate is not issued when Form T2062C, *Notification of an Acquisition of Treaty-Protected Property from a Non-Resident Vendor* is submitted by a purchaser.

Purchaser's Liability

50. If the vendor does not comply with the requirements of subsection 116(3), and the CRA has not issued a certificate of compliance, the purchaser may become liable under subsection 116(5) to pay a specified amount of tax on behalf

of the vendor. The purchaser is then entitled to withhold that amount from the purchase price.

The purchaser is liable to pay and remit 25% of either:

    a. the cost of the property acquired by the purchaser; or

    b. if a certificate of compliance has been issued under subsection 116(2), the amount by which the cost of the property acquired by the purchaser exceeds the certificate limit fixed by a proposed disposition.

Purchaser liability assessments are not subject to any time restrictions. Therefore, an assessment may be issued at any time the CRA becomes aware that a vendor or purchaser has not adhered to the requirements of section 116.

51. For dispositions of properties described in paragraph 4 above, the purchaser may become liable under the provisions of subsection 116(5.3) to pay to the CRA, on behalf of the vendor, an amount equal to 50% of either:

    a. where a certificate of compliance under subsection 116(5.2) has not been issued, the purchase amount, or

    b. where a certificate of compliance has been issued, the amount by which the purchase price of the property exceeds the amount fixed in the certificate.

The purchaser is then entitled to withhold that amount from the purchase price.

52. Since the purchaser's liability under subsection 116(5) does not apply to the disposition of excluded property, there is no purchaser's liability in respect of such property. An excluded property includes a treaty-exempt property. To qualify as a treaty-exempt property, the property must be a treaty-protected property and if the vendor and purchaser are related, Form T2062C must be submitted by the purchaser. If Form T2062C is not submitted by a purchaser who is related to the vendor, a treaty-protected property will not be considered an excluded property and the regular purchaser's liability and vendor notification requirements will apply.

In addition, the purchaser's liability does not apply if all of the following conditions are met:

    a. after reasonable inquiry, the purchaser has determined the vendor's country of residence;

    b. the property is treaty protected under the tax treaty that Canada has with the vendor's declared country of residence; and

    c.   where the vendor and purchaser are related, a T2062C is submitted by the purchaser within 30 days after the date of acquisition.

If Form T2062C is not used, the purchaser must provide the following information with the notice of acquisition of treaty-protected property:

    a.   the date of the acquisition;
    b.   the name and address of the non-resident person;
    c.   a description of the property;
    d.   the amount paid or payable by the purchaser of the property; and
    e.   the name of the country with which Canada has a tax treaty under which the property is a treaty protected property for the purposes of subsection 116(5.01) or 116(6.1).

53. The purchaser's liability for tax under subsection 116(5) or 116(5.3) does not extend to a mortgagee who acquired a property by an Order of Foreclosure, unless the transactions of mortgage and foreclosure were used as a device to sell the property to a mortgagee or a third party. Where the purchaser is the mortgagee, the amount paid will be the amount of the mortgage that is set off because of the purchase. When the mortgagee is not liable under section 116 to pay tax, and requests that the CRA issue a certificate of compliance, the CRA may issue a letter to that effect.

54. If a mortgagee exercises a power of sale pursuant to the terms of the mortgage, a court order or the provisions of the relevant Mortgage Act, rather than foreclosing, title to the property passes directly from the mortgagor to a third party purchaser. Thus the provisions of subsections 116(5) or (5.3) apply if the vendor/mortgagor was a non resident. Where title to the property has passed from a Canadian resident vendor/mortgagor to a Canadian resident purchaser, albeit through a power of sale by a non resident mortgagee, the provisions of section 116 will not apply to any of the three parties.

55. Any tax remittances payable by the purchaser must be remitted to the Receiver General for Canada within 30 days from the end of the month in which the property was acquired. The purchaser should give particulars of the transaction, identify the remittances, and specify that the payment concerned pertains to subsection 116(5) or 116(5.3). The full name and address of the vendor and the purchaser should be indicated.

56. Any purchaser who fails to remit or pay an amount required under subsection 116(5) or 116(5.3) may be assessed a penalty under the authority of subsection 227(10.1), calculated under the provisions of subsection 227(9). Paragraph 227(9)(a) provides for a penalty for the failure to pay or remit an amount required to be deducted or withheld. The penalty is calculated as a percentage of the tax payment required under Section 116. The penalty is 3% if

it is one to three days late, 5% if it is four or five days late, 7% if it is six or seven days late, and 10% if it is more than seven days late. For second and subsequent failures during the same year, if the failure to remit or pay was made knowingly or under circumstances amounting to gross negligence, the penalty under paragraph 227(9)(b) will be 20% of the amount required to be deducted or withheld. Subsection 227(9.3) provides for levying interest on the payment or remittance required by subsections 116(5) and 116(5.3).

57. For penalties and interest, the Minister has the discretion under subsection 220(3.1) to waive or cancel all or any portion of any penalty or interest if it is found that the penalty or interest resulted from circumstances beyond the control of the purchaser. For more information, refer to the current version of IC07-1, *Taxpayer Relief Provisions*.

58. The purchaser incurs no obligation to pay tax if, after reasonable inquiry, there was no reason to believe the vendor was a non resident of Canada. There is a question as to what constitutes "reasonable inquiry." The purchaser must take prudent measures to confirm the vendor's residence status. The CRA will review each case on an individual basis whenever a purchaser assessment is being considered. The purchaser may become liable if, for any reason, the CRA believes that the purchaser could have or should have known that the vendor was a non resident or did not take reasonable steps to find out the vendor's residence status. The CRA will not make inquiries on behalf of a purchaser in this regard.

Filing a Tax Return — Refund of Excess Payment

59. A vendor is not required to file a Canadian tax return in respect of the disposition if all of the following apply:

    i.   the vendor is a non-resident at the time of the disposition;

    ii. the vendor has no Part I tax payable for the year;

    iii. the vendor does not owe any amounts under the Act for any prior year (other than amounts for which the CRA has accepted and holds adequate security); and

    iv. all of the taxable Canadian property disposed of by the vendor is either excluded property as defined in subsection 116(6) of the Act, or property for which the CRA has issued a certificate of compliance in accordance with subsection 116(2), 116(4) or 116(5.2) of the Act.

60. If all of the criteria in paragraph 59 are not met, a tax return is required to be filed by the vendor for the taxation year in which the disposition took place. After the return is assessed, any excess payment is refunded or provision is made

for the release of security once the established debt has been satisfied. Income tax returns filed before the end of the taxation year will be processed only after the end of the taxation year.

61. Generally, for individuals, the income tax return is due on April 30th of the year following the year in which the disposition occurred. For corporations, the return is due six months after the end of the taxation year in which the disposition took place. Trust returns are due 90 days after the end of the trust's taxation year in which the disposition took place. Returns that are filed late are subject to interest and applicable penalties. Copies of the income tax returns and the related guides can be obtained from any TSO or from the CRA website, www.cra.gc.ca. Individuals should request guide 5013 G, *General Income Tax and Benefit Guide for Non Residents and Deemed Residents of Canada.*

62. These returns must be sent to the:

International Tax Services Office
Canada Revenue Agency
Post Office Box 9769, Station T
Ottawa ON K1G 3Y4
Canada

Any questions concerning the assessment of the return should also be forwarded to this office.

63. Delays in processing a vendor's income tax return occur for many reasons. However, if the proper information is provided at the time of filing, the return will be processed as quickly as possible.

Vendors should ensure that:

    a.   the information area is completed in detail;
    b.   their identification number is entered as requested;
    c.   Copy 2 of the certificate of compliance (form T2064 or T2068) is enclosed. This information slip is invaluable in tracing payments, security or exemptions in respect of the disposition, and
    d.   if, for any reason, circumstances have changed and the amount reported on the vendor's income tax return differs substantially from the amount reported for the disposition on the certificate of compliance, a note should be attached to the income tax return along with the appropriate documentation.

64. The Minister has the discretion to assess returns of individuals and testamentary trusts that are filed more than three years after the end of the taxation year in which the disposition occurred in order to issue refunds or to

reduce taxes payable. This discretion may be exercised where the request is in writing and the Minister is satisfied that the refund would have been issued or tax payable reduced had the returns been filed on time.

Misallocated or Lost Payments

65. The CRA makes every effort to ensure that a payment made for a section 116 disposition is matched to the income tax return filed. If vendors follow the instructions for filing income tax returns in paragraphs 59 to 64 above, the problem of misallocated or lost payments will be alleviated.

66. If the payment is not properly credited on the Notice of Assessment, the vendor should contact:

International Tax Services Office
Canada Revenue Agency
Post Office Box 9769, Station T
Ottawa ON K1G 3Y4
Canada

Vendors should also provide the following information:

a. a brief description of the disposition;
b. the date of the payment;
c. the TSO that processed the certificate of compliance; and
d. a photocopy of the front and back of the cancelled cheque, if applicable.

General Comments

67. Section 116 does not apply to a deemed disposition on death under subsection 70(5). However, the executor acting on behalf of a non resident decedent must file an income tax return for the year of death and pay any tax that may be necessary on the deemed disposition.

68. Section 116 does not apply to property that is transferred or distributed on or after death and as a consequence thereof.

69. If compensation is received for damages to property, consideration must be given as to whether any part of the compensation involves a transfer of title or an interest therein to which section 116 would apply. It is unlikely that a transfer of title or an interest therein has taken place when compensation has been paid to the owner of property for damages claimed in a tort action. However, when

such a payment is made according to a contractual arrangement between the parties, the terms of the contract should be examined to determine whether title or an interest in the property has been received in exchange for the compensation.

70. A deemed dividend is triggered under section 212.1 in cases when a non resident disposes of shares of a corporation resident in Canada to another corporation resident in Canada in a non arm's length transaction; this deemed dividend is subject to Part XIII withholding tax under subsection 212(2). The CRA will accept a calculation of proceeds of disposition of the shares, for purposes of section 116, which includes a reduction for the section 212.1 deemed dividend. Vendors should submit a letter of explanation and a copy of the section 212.1 calculation along with Form T2062 when requesting a certificate of compliance in these cases. The CRA may request payment of Part XIII tax before a certificate of compliance is issued.

71. Under the Doctrine of Sovereign Immunity, the Government of Canada may grant exemption from tax on certain Canadian source investment income paid or credited to the government of a foreign country. Capital gains on the disposition of taxable Canadian property may be eligible for this exemption, subject to the conditions described in the current version of IC77 16, *Non Resident Income Tax*. When the vendor of taxable Canadian property is a foreign government, the CRA will issue a certificate of compliance once it is substantiated that the property is, in fact, wholly owned by that government. The request should be sent to:

Canada Revenue Agency
22nd floor, Tower A, 320 Queen Street
Ottawa ON K1A 0L5
Canada
Attention: International Legislative Affairs
Legislative Policy Directorate

72. The disposition of mineral rights in Canada is considered to be a disposition of a Canadian resource property, and as such, is subject to the requirements of subsection 116(5.2). In the case of a Petroleum and Natural Gas Lease, the bonus portion (bonus consideration) is subject to the provisions of subsection 116(5.2). The annual rental payment is subject to withholding tax under paragraph 212(1)(d).

73. When a non-resident disposes of a principal residence, the non-resident may qualify for an exemption in accordance with paragraph 40(2)(b) or (c) of the Act. However, pursuant to paragraph 40(2)(b), the exemption is limited by the number of years ending after the acquisition date during which the taxpayer was resident in Canada. If a property owned in Canada by a non-resident qualifies as

the non-resident's principal residence, the period of non residence may reduce or eliminate the availability of the principal residence exemption.

Paragraph 40(2)(b) provides the formula for computing the taxable portion of a gain from the disposition of a principal residence in a year. A - [A æ (B/C) - D] where:

A is the calculated gain

B is one plus the number of taxation years ending after the acquisition date for which the property was the taxpayer's principal residence and during which the taxpayer was resident in Canada (both the year of acquisition [if after 1971] and the year of disposition can be included if the property qualified as a principal residence in the year).

C is the number of taxation years ending after the acquisition date. The acquisition date is defined as the later of December 31, 1971, the date on which the taxpayer last acquired or reacquired the property during which the taxpayer owned the property, whether jointly with another person or otherwise (both the year of acquisition [if after 1971] and the year of disposition will be included).

D is the "capital gains reduction amount" (this only occurs if the taxpayer's acquisition date is before February 23, 1994 and the taxpayer, or his or her spouse, made a subsection 110.6(19) capital gains election for the property).

When a non-resident disposes of a principal residence, a T2062 or similar notification must be submitted to report the disposition. The tax or security required may be reduced accordingly where the gain is reduced by the principal residence exemption. For the purposes of Section 116, the request for a principal residence exemption can be made by completing and submitting Form T2091 (IND), *Designation of a Property as a Principal Residence by an Individual (other than a Personal Trust)* or by a letter signed by the taxpayer attached to the notification. When completing Form T2091 to calculate the exemption at line 22, ensure that lines 1 to 3 do not include any tax years during which the taxpayer was not resident in Canada. If a letter is sent with the notification, the letter should contain a calculation of the portion of the gain otherwise determined that is or will be eliminated by the principal residence exemption.

74. Many of Canada's income tax conventions contain provisions dealing with cross border reorganizations that allow, through its interaction with section 115.1 of the Act, for the Canadian Competent Authority and the person who is acquiring the taxable Canadian property to agree to defer the recognition of the vendor's profit, gain or income on what would otherwise be a taxable disposition under the Act (e.g., paragraph 8 of Article XIII of the Canada - U.S. Income

Tax Convention). These dispositions may be subject to the provisions of section 116. The vendor must file the appropriate form to report a disposition along with a copy of the request made to the Canadian Competent Authority. The requirement for payment or security on account of tax may be waived when the Canadian Competent Authority accepts the non-resident's request for relief. For more information, refer to the current version of IC71-17, *Guidance on Competent Authority Assistance under Canada's Tax Conventions.*

S1-F3-C2: Principal Residence

Date: November 24, 2015

Series 1: Individuals

Folio 3: Family Unit Issues

Chapter 2: Principal Residence

Summary

This chapter discusses the principal residence exemption, which can eliminate or reduce (for income tax purposes) a capital gain on the disposition of a taxpayer's principal residence.

In order for a property to qualify for designation as the taxpayer's principal residence, he or she must own the property. Joint ownership with another person qualifies for this purpose.

The housing unit representing the taxpayer's principal residence generally must be inhabited by the taxpayer or by his or her spouse or common—law partner, former spouse or common—law partner, or child. A taxpayer can designate only one property as his or her principal residence for a particular taxation year. Furthermore, for a taxation year that is after the 1981 year, only one property per family unit can be designated as a principal residence.

Table of contents

o Land contributing to the use and enjoyment of the housing unit as a residence
o Land in excess of one-half hectare
o Disposition of part of a principal residence
o Disposition of a property where only part of it qualifies as a principal residence
o Principal residence on land used in a farming business
o Complete change in use of a property from principal residence to income-producing
o Complete change in use of a property from income-producing to principal residence
o Partial changes in use
o Change in use rules regarding CCA, deemed capital cost, and recapture
o Personal trusts
o Transfer of a principal residence
o Partnership property
o A principal residence outside Canada
o Non-resident owner of a principal residence in Canada
o Section 116 certificate for a disposition of a principal residence in Canada by a non-resident owner
o Beneficial ownership
o Ownership issues in the province of Quebec
o Sole or joint ownership
o Ownership in dispute
o Share in the capital stock of a co-operative housing corporation
o Interest in a property under an enforceable agreement for sale
o Ownership issues with condominium units
o Property on leased land
o Acquisition of a property by way of gift or inheritance
o Appendix A
o Appendix B

• Application
• Reference

Discussion and interpretation

Introduction

2.1 Various topics concerning the principal residence exemption are discussed in this chapter, as indicated in the Contents section. It should be noted that some of these topics are not relevant for all taxpayers. For example, a resident of Canada who owns only one housing unit which is situated in Canada on land of one-half hectare or less and which has been used since its acquisition strictly as his or her residence, will usually find that ¶2.32-2.78 have no particular relevance.

2.2 If a property qualifies as a taxpayer's principal residence, he or she can use the principal residence exemption to reduce or eliminate any capital gain otherwise occurring, for income tax purposes, on the disposition (or deemed disposition) of the property. The term **principal residence** is defined in section 54. The principal residence exemption is claimed under paragraph 40(2)(*b*), or under paragraph 40(2)(*c*) where land used in a farming business carried on by the taxpayer includes his or her principal residence.

2.3 Unless otherwise stated, any reference in this chapter to a tax year or year means a particular tax year for which the principal residence exemption is being claimed.

2.4 Various references are made throughout this chapter to a taxpayer's spouse or common-law partner and child. For the 1993 to 2000 tax years, former subsection 252(4) extended the meaning of the term spouse to include a common-law spouse of the opposite sex. Effective in 2001, the extended meaning of spouse in subsection 252(4) has been replaced with the term common-law partner in subsection 248(1) which can now also include a person of the same sex. A transitional rule for the 1998, 1999 and 2000 tax years allowed same-sex couples to elect to be treated as common-law partners under the Act for those years. For more information about the meaning of the terms spouse and common-law partner, see the current version of the Guide 5000-G, General Income Tax and Benefit Guide. For purposes of applying the rules in subsections 70(6) and 73(1) as discussed in ¶2.69, see also the extended meaning of spouse and former spouse in subsection 252(3), as it reads for the particular tax year being considered. Subsection 252(1), as it reads for the particular tax year being considered, extends the meaning of child for purposes of applying all the rules in the Act, including the principal residence exemption rules, for that year.

2.5 It is also possible for a personal trust to claim the principal residence exemption on the disposition of a property. This is discussed in ¶ 2.65-2.66 and ¶2.69.

When the sale of a property results in business income

2.6 Where the gain from the sale of a taxpayer's personal residence results in business income (as opposed to a capital gain), the gain cannot be exempt from income tax as a result of the principal residence exemption under paragraph 40(2)(*b*). An individual does not have to be involved in the housing construction industry to have business income from the sale of houses, and the sale of one house can result in business income. For more information about taxpayers buying and selling their own houses for the purpose of earning income, see the current version of Income Tax Info Sheet TI-001, Sale of a Residence by an Owner Builder, Interpretation Bulletin IT-218R, Profits, capital gains and losses from the sale of real estate, including farmland and inherited land and conversion of real estate from capital property to inventory and vice versa, and Interpretation Bulletin IT-459, Adventure or concern in the nature of trade.

Types of property that can qualify as a principal residence

2.7 As indicated in the definition in section 54, the following types of property can qualify as a principal residence:

- a housing unit, which the CRA has accepted could include:
  - o   a house;
  - o   an apartment or unit in a duplex, apartment building or condominium;
  - o   a cottage;
  - o   a mobile home;
  - o   a trailer; or
  - o   a houseboat.
- a leasehold interest in a housing unit; or
- a share of the capital stock of a co-operative housing corporation, if such share is acquired for the sole purpose of obtaining the right to inhabit a housing unit owned by that corporation. The term co-operative housing corporation means an association, incorporated subject to the terms and conditions of the legislation governing such incorporation, and formed and operated for the purpose of providing its members with the right to inhabit, by reason of ownership of shares therein, a housing unit owned by the corporation.

2.8 Land on which a housing unit is situated can qualify as part of a principal residence, subject to certain restrictions (see ¶ 2.32-2.46).

Ownership is required

2.9 For a property to be a taxpayer's principal residence for a particular year, he or she must own the property in the year. This requirement is met where the taxpayer is the legal owner or the beneficial owner of the property. The taxpayer's ownership of the property qualifies for purposes of the section 54 definition of principal residence whether such ownership is **jointly with another person or otherwise**. These latter words include sole ownership or a form of co-ownership such as joint tenancy or tenancy-in-common. The meaning of **ownership of property** is discussed in more detail in ¶ 2.79-2.80. The meaning of beneficial ownership of property as applied in the Province of Quebec is discussed in more detail in ¶2.83-2.85.

The ordinarily inhabited rule

2.10 Another requirement is that the housing unit must be ordinarily inhabited in the year by the taxpayer or by his or her spouse or common-law partner, former spouse or common-law partner, or child.

2.11 The question of whether a housing unit is ordinarily inhabited in the year by a person (that is, the taxpayer, the taxpayer's spouse, common-law partner, former spouse, former common-law partner or child) must be resolved on the basis of the facts in each particular case. Even if a person inhabits a housing unit only for a short period of time in the year, this is sufficient for the housing unit to be considered ordinarily inhabited in the year by that person. For example, even if a person disposes of his or her residence early in the year or acquires it late in the year, the housing unit can be considered to be ordinarily inhabited in the year by that person by virtue of his or her living in it in the year before such sale or after such acquisition, as the case may be. If the main reason for owning a housing unit is to gain or produce income then that housing unit will not generally be considered to be ordinarily inhabited in the year by the taxpayer where it is only inhabited for a short period of time in the year. With regard to whether the main reason for owning a housing unit is to earn income, a person receiving only incidental rental income from a housing unit is not considered to own the property mainly for the purpose of gaining or producing income. However, if the main reason for owning a housing unit is to earn income but the housing unit is rented to the taxpayer's child who also ordinarily inhabits the housing unit in that year, the taxpayer could still designate that housing unit as the taxpayer's principal residence provided the other conditions are met.

2.12 If the housing unit is not ordinarily inhabited in the year by any of the above-mentioned persons, it is still possible for the property to be considered to be the taxpayer's principal residence for the year, by means of an election under subsection 45(2) or (3). For a discussion of these provisions, see ¶ 2.48-2.56.

Designation of a property as a principal residence

2.13 For a property to be a taxpayer's principal residence for a particular year, he or she must designate it as such for the year and no other property may have been so designated by the taxpayer for the year. Furthermore, no other property may have been designated as the principal residence of any member of the taxpayer's family unit for the year. For purposes of the latter rule, which applies if the taxpayer is designating a property as his or her principal residence for 1982 or a subsequent year, the taxpayer's family unit for the year includes, in addition to the taxpayer, the following persons (if any):

- the taxpayer's spouse or common-law partner throughout the year, unless the spouse or common-law partner was throughout the year living apart from, and was separated under a judicial separation or written separation agreement from, the taxpayer;
- the taxpayer's children, except those who were married, in a common-law partnership or 18 years of age or older during the year; and
- where the taxpayer was not married, in a common-law partnership or 18 years of age or older during the year:
  o the taxpayer's mother and father; and
  o the taxpayer's brothers and sisters who were not married, in a common-law partnership or 18 years of age or older during the year.

2.14 As discussed in ¶2.4, for the 1993 to 2000 tax years, a spouse included a common-law spouse of the opposite sex. Accordingly, these individuals will be considered a family unit for the purposes of the principal residence exemption for the 1993 and subsequent tax years (see Example 2 in Appendix A). In the case of same-sex common-law partners, they will be considered a family unit for the 2001 and subsequent tax years. However, if a same-sex couple filed a joint election to be treated as common-law partners for the 1998, 1999 and/or 2000 tax years, then they will be considered a family unit for those years.

2.15 According to section 2301 of the Regulations, a taxpayer's designation of a property as a principal residence for one or more tax years is to be made in his or her income tax return for the tax year in which he or she has disposed of the property or granted an option to another person to acquire the property. The designation form used for this purpose is Form T2091 (IND), Designation of a Property as a Principal Residence by an Individual (Other Than a Personal Trust). However, in accordance with CRA practice, Form T2091(IND) need not be completed and filed with the taxpayer's income tax return unless:

a) a taxable capital gain on the disposition of the property remains after using the principal residence exemption formula (as shown in ¶2.17-2.26); or
b) form T664 or T664(Seniors), *Election to Report a Capital Gain on Property Owned at the End of February 22, 1994* was filed with respect to the property by the taxpayer, or his or her spouse or common—law partner; and the property was the taxpayer's principal residence for 1994, or it was designated in the year as the principal residence for any tax year.

2.16 Note that if a taxpayer using the principal residence exemption formula to eliminate a gain on the disposition of a property is not, because of the above—mentioned practice in ¶2.15, required to complete and file Form T2091(IND), he or she is still considered to have designated the property as his or her principal residence (that is, to have claimed the principal residence exemption for that property) for the years in question as far as the limitations discussed earlier in ¶2.13-2.14 are concerned.

Calculating the gain on the disposition of a principal residence — the principal residence exemption

2.17 Under the principal residence exemption provision contained in paragraph 40(2)(*b*), a taxpayer's gain from the disposition (or deemed disposition) of any property that was his or her principal residence at any time after his or her **acquisition date** (see definition below) with respect to the property, is equal to his or her **gain otherwise determined** (see explanation below) less two amounts, which are described ¶2.20-2.26.

2.18 The taxpayer's **acquisition date** with respect to the property is the later of the following two dates:

- December 31, 1971; and
- the date on which:
  o the taxpayer last acquired or reacquired the property; or
  o the taxpayer is deemed to have last acquired or reacquired it.

Note that, by virtue of subsection 40(7.1), if a subsection 110.6(19) capital gains election was made in respect of the property, the deemed reacquisition of the property under that election is not considered to be a reacquisition for purposes of determining the acquisition date used in paragraph 40(2)(*b*).

2.19 The taxpayer's **gain otherwise determined** means the amount that the gain (if any) from the taxpayer's disposition (or deemed disposition) of the property would be — before the two reductions described in ¶2.20-2.26 — if the capital gains election provision in subsection 110.6(19) and the related provision in subsection 110.6(21) were not taken into account. Thus, if a subsection 110.6(19) capital gains election has been made in respect of the property, the taxpayer's gain otherwise determined is calculated without reference to the deemed disposition and reacquisition of the property under that election. That is, the gain otherwise determined is calculated without taking into account the increase to the adjusted cost base of the property under subsection 110.6(19) or the decrease to that adjusted cost base under subsection 110.6(21).

2.20 The first amount by which the taxpayer's gain otherwise determined is reduced under paragraph 40(2)(*b*) is calculated by using the following formula:

A × (**B** ÷ **C**)

The variables in the above formula are as follows:

A is the taxpayer's gain otherwise determined, as described above.

B is 1 + the number of tax years ending after the acquisition date for which the property was the taxpayer's principal residence and during which he or she was resident in Canada. (Note that both these conditions must be satisfied for a particular year in order for that year to qualify for inclusion in variable **B**.)

C is the number of tax years ending after the acquisition date during which the taxpayer owned the property (whether jointly with another person or otherwise — see ¶2.9).

2.21 For a discussion of the meaning of **resident in Canada**, refer to Income Tax Folio S5-F1-C1, Determining an Individual's Residence Status. The word **during** in reference to a tax year means **at any time in** rather than **throughout the whole of** the tax year.

2.22 The second amount by which the taxpayer's gain otherwise determined is reduced is shown in paragraph 40(2)(*b*) as variable **D** and it is referred to in this Chapter as the **capital gains election reduction amount**. It occurs only if:

- the taxpayer's acquisition date with respect to the property (as described above) is before February 23, 1994; and
- the taxpayer, or his or her spouse, or common-law partner made a subsection 110.6(19) capital gains election for the property or for an interest in the property, or for civil law, a right therein — if such an election was made, Form T664 or T664(Seniors), would have been filed.

Proposed legislative change

On July 16, 2010, the Department of Finance released *Legislative Proposals to Amend the Income Tax Act and Related Legislation to Effect Technical Changes and to Provide for Bijural Expression in that Act*. This document contains a proposal to amend subparagraph (i) of the description D in paragraph 40(2)(b) to add the civil law concept of **right** in the property together with the common law concept of **interest** in the property, which is already found in this provision.

2.23 The inclusion of the 110.6(19) election amount of a spouse or common-law partner of the taxpayer, when calculating the capital gains election reduction amount for the taxpayer, ensures that any elected gain reported by the spouse or common-law partner in 1994 with respect to a property that was subsequently transferred to the taxpayer through a spousal or common-law partner rollover provision after February 1994, is properly reflected in the ultimate disposition of the property by the taxpayer. In other words, in situations where a spouse or common-law partner has transferred property to the taxpayer subsequent to 1994 and pursuant to the roll-over provisions of subsection 73(1) or 70(6), the calculation of the capital gains reduction amount of the taxpayer at the time the property is sold, must include any 1994 elected gain reported by the spouse or common-law partner with respect to the transferred property. Qualifying transfers of property under these subsections are discussed in ¶2.69.

2.24 The capital gains election reduction amount essentially represents the total amount of the gains that resulted from the taxpayer's and his or her spouse or common-law partner's capital gains elections for the property, after taking into account any reduction in calculating those gains by virtue of the property having been designated as the principal residence of the taxpayer or his or her spouse or common-law partner for any tax year up to and including the tax year that included February 22, 1994. The capital gains election reduction amount cannot, however, be more than such gains — after taking into account any reduction thereto by virtue of the property having been the principal residence of the taxpayer or his or her spouse or common law partner for any tax year up to and including the tax year that included February 22, 1994 — that would have resulted from such capital gains elections if the fair market value of the property as at the end of February 22, 1994 had been used as the designated proceeds for the property.

2.25 The taxpayer calculates the capital gains election reduction amount on Form T2091(IND)-WS, Principal Residence Worksheet, which the taxpayer files with the T2091(IND) designation form (see ¶2.15-2.16).

2.26 The remaining discussions in this Chapter regarding paragraph 40(2)(*b*) are concerned with the first reduction to the gain otherwise determined, that is, the reduction provided for by means of the above-mentioned formula, A × (B ÷ C). Unless stated to the contrary, it is assumed for purposes of those discussions that the taxpayer did not make a capital gains election and thus that there is no second reduction to the gain otherwise determined, that is, no capital gains election reduction amount.

Ownership of a property by both spouses or common—law partners

2.27 Where there is a gain on the disposition of a property owned both by a taxpayer and his or her spouse or common-law partner in one of the forms of ownership described in ¶2.9, both spouses or common-law partners will generally have a gain on the disposition. It should be kept in mind that if one of the spouses or common-law partners designates the property as his or her principal residence for any tax year after the 1981 year, the other spouse or common-law partner will be able to designate only that same property as his or her principal residence for that year if the rule described in ¶ 2.13-2.14 prevents him or her from so designating any other property for that year.

More than one residence in a tax year

2.28 While only one property may be designated as a taxpayer's principal residence for a particular tax year, the principal residence exemption rules recognize that the taxpayer can have two residences in the same year, that is, where one residence is sold and another acquired in the same year. The effect of the one plus in variable B in the formula in ¶2.20 is to treat both properties as a principal residence in such a year, even though only one of them may be designated as such for that year.

Construction of a housing unit on vacant land

2.29 If a taxpayer acquires land in one tax year and constructs a housing unit on it in a subsequent year, the property may not be designated as the taxpayer's principal residence for the years that are prior to the year in which the taxpayer, his or her spouse or common-law partner, former spouse or common-law partner, or child commences to ordinarily inhabit the housing unit. Such prior years (when the taxpayer owned only the vacant land or the land with a housing unit under construction) would not be included in variable B in the formula in ¶2.20 (or in the years included in the statement in ¶2.43(b)). However, all years, commencing with the year in which the taxpayer acquired the vacant land, would be included in variable C. Therefore, it is possible that when the property is later disposed of, only part of the gain otherwise determined will be eliminated by the principal residence exemption.

Example 1

In 2002, Mr. A acquired vacant land for $50,000. In 2005, he constructed a housing unit on the land, costing $200,000, and started to ordinarily inhabit the housing unit. In 2011, he disposed of the property for $300,000. Mr. A's gain otherwise determined on the disposition of the property is equal to his $300,000 proceeds minus his $250,000 adjusted cost base = $50,000 (assume there were no costs of disposition). Mr. A can designate the property as his principal residence for the years 2005 to 2011 inclusive, but not for the years 2002 to 2004 inclusive because no one lived in a housing unit on the property during those years. The principal residence exemption formula cannot, therefore, eliminate his entire $50,000 gain otherwise determined, but rather can eliminate only $40,000 of that gain, as shown in the following:

Applying the formula $A \times (B \div C)$:

A is $50,000

B is $1 + 7$ (being tax years 2005 to 2011)

C is 10 (being tax years 2002 to 2011)

= $50,000 x (8 ÷ 10)

= $40,000

Property owned on December 31, 1981

2.30 A property may not be designated as a taxpayer's principal residence for any tax year after the 1981 year if another property has been designated for that year as the principal residence of another member of his or her family unit (for further particulars on this rule, see ¶ 2.13 - 2.14). If the taxpayer disposes of a property he or she has owned (whether jointly with another person or otherwise) continuously since before 1982 and the property cannot be designated as the taxpayer's principal residence for one or more years after the 1981 year because of the above-mentioned rule, a transitional provision in subsection 40(6) puts a cap on the amount of the taxpayer's gain (if any) on the disposition. Appendix A at the end of this Chapter provides examples which illustrate how the rule in subsection 40(6) works.

Loss on the disposition of a residence

2.31 A property which is used primarily as a residence (that is, for the personal use and enjoyment of those living in it) — or an option to acquire a property which would, if acquired, be so used — is **personal-use property**. Therefore, a loss on the disposition of such a property or option is deemed to be nil by virtue of subparagraph 40(2)(*g*)(iii).

Land contributing to the use and enjoyment of the housing unit as a residence

2.32 By virtue of paragraph (*e*) of the section 54 definition of **principal residence**, a taxpayer's principal residence for a tax year shall be deemed to include, except where the property consists of a share of the capital stock of a co-operative housing corporation, the land upon which the housing unit stands and any portion of the adjoining land that can reasonably be regarded as contributing to the use and enjoyment of the housing unit as a residence. Evidence is not usually required to establish that one-half hectare of land or less, including the area on which the housing unit stands, contributes to the use and enjoyment of the housing unit as a residence. However, where a portion of that land is used to earn income from business or property, such portion will not usually be considered to contribute to such use and enjoyment. Where the taxpayer claims a portion of the expenses related to the land (such as property taxes or mortgage interest) in computing income, the allocation of such expenses for this purpose is normally an indication of the extent to which he or she considers the land to be used to earn income.

Land in excess of one-half hectare

2.33 Where the total area of the land upon which a housing unit is situated exceeds one-half hectare, the excess land is deemed by paragraph (*e*) of the section 54 definition of principal residence not to have contributed to the use and enjoyment of the housing unit as a residence and thus will not qualify as part of a principal residence, except to the extent that the taxpayer establishes that it was necessary for such use and enjoyment. The excess land must clearly be necessary for the housing unit to properly fulfill its function as a residence and not simply be desirable. Generally, the use of land in excess of one—half hectare in connection with a particular recreation or lifestyle (such as for keeping pets or for country living) does not mean that the excess land is necessary for the use and enjoyment of the housing unit as a residence.

2.34 Land in excess of one-half hectare may be considered necessary where the size or character of a housing unit together with its location on the lot make such excess land essential to its use and enjoyment as a residence, or where the location of a housing unit requires such excess land in order to provide its occupants with access to and from public roads. Other factors may be relevant in determining whether land in excess of one-half hectare is necessary for the use and enjoyment of the housing unit as a residence, such as, for example, a minimum lot size or a severance or subdivision restriction (see ¶2.35). In all cases, however, it is a question of fact as to how much, if any, of the excess land is necessary for the use and enjoyment of the housing unit as a residence.

2.35 A municipal or provincial law or regulation may require, for example, a minimum lot size for a residential lot in a particular area that would be in excess of one-half hectare, or impose a severance or subdivision restriction with respect to a residential lot in a particular area restricting the lot from being one-half hectare or below. If such a law or regulation existed in any given year during which the taxpayer owned the property, the area that is in excess of one-half hectare would normally be part of the principal residence for that particular year.

Example 2

Mrs. B disposes of her principal residence which she owned for ten years for a total capital gain of $100,000. The portion of the gain attributable to the house and one-half hectare of land is $60,000, and the portion attributable to the excess land is $40,000. Assuming that Mrs. B's house and one-half hectare of land qualify as her principal residence for all the years during which she owned the property, and assuming that the excess land could not be subdivided from the remainder of the property because of a municipal regulation for five of the ten years ownership period (the third year to the seventh year of ownership), the formula would be applied as follows.

First, the application of the formula in paragraph 40(2)(*b*) results in the gain allocable to the house and the one-half hectare of land being entirely exempt. That is because variable B is 11 (that is, 1 plus the total number of years for which the house and the one-half hectare of land was Mrs. B's principal residence, which is ten years). The formula would give the following result: $60,000 – ($60,000 × 11 ÷ 10) = –$6,000 (this negative amount is deemed to be zero under section 257).

The gain on the excess land would however not be fully exempted under paragraph 40(2)(*b*) as variable B would be 6 (1 plus 5), with the formula providing the following result: $40,000 – ($40,000 × 6 ÷ 10) = $16,000

Disposition of part of a principal residence

2.36 Where only a portion of a property qualifying as a taxpayer's principal residence is disposed of (for example, the granting of an easement or the expropriation of land), the property may be designated as the taxpayer's principal residence in order to use the principal residence exemption for the portion of the property disposed of. It is important to note that such a designation is made on the entire property (including the housing unit) that qualifies as the principal residence, and not just on the portion of the property disposed of. Accordingly, when the remainder of the property is subsequently disposed of, it too will be recognized as the taxpayer's principal residence for the tax years for which the above-mentioned designation was made. No other property may be designated as a principal residence for any of those years by the taxpayer (or, for any of those years that are after the 1981 tax year, by the taxpayer or any of the other members of his or her family unit) as discussed in ¶ 2.13 - 2.14.

Disposition of a property where only part of it qualifies as a principal residence

2.37 In some cases, only a portion of a property that is disposed of for a gain will qualify as a principal residence (see ¶2.32 - 2.35). If such qualifying portion of the property is designated as the taxpayer's principal residence, it will be necessary to calculate the gain on such portion separately from the gain on the remaining portion of the property which does not qualify as the taxpayer's principal residence. This is because the gain otherwise determined on the portion of the property designated as the principal residence may be reduced or eliminated by the principal residence exemption, whereas the gain on the remaining portion of the property results in a taxable capital gain. The allocation of the proceeds of disposition and adjusted cost base of the total property between the two portions does not necessarily have to be on the basis of area — consideration should be given to any factors which could have an effect on the relative value of either of the two portions.

2.38 The comments in this section do not apply if the property includes land used in a farming business (see instead ¶2.39 - 2.46).

Example 3

Mr. A's house is on a property with a total land area of three-quarters of a hectare. He sells the property at fair market value and realizes an actual gain on the disposition. The house and one-half hectare of land qualify as his principal residence for all the years he has owned it. The extra one-quarter hectare does not qualify as part of his principal residence for these reasons:

- There has never been any law or regulation requiring the extra one-quarter hectare to be part of the property as a residence (see ¶2.35) — it has always been severable from the one-half hectare on which the house is situated.
- There has never been, as elaborated on below, any other valid reason for considering the extra one-quarter hectare to be necessary for the use and enjoyment of the house as a residence (see ¶2.33 - 2.34).
- If the extra one—quarter hectare were severed, it would still be accessible from the road by which the principal residence's one-half hectare is accessed. However, it would be difficult to sell the extra one-quarter hectare on its own because it forms part of a shallow gully through which a small brook flows. In fact, the only feasible use for the extra one-quarter hectare is to enhance the enjoyment of Mr. A's residence or, if severed, the residence of his next door neighbour, that is, by providing the owner with the enjoyment of such additional land with its natural beauty. Nevertheless, the extra one-quarter hectare is not necessary for the use and enjoyment of Mr. A's house as a residence. Note that in these circumstances, the portion of Mr. A's gain that is considered to pertain to the extra one-quarter hectare may not simply be one-third of the gain pertaining to the entire three-quarters of a hectare of land he sold, but would probably be a lower amount (a determination of the actual amount in such a case could require a real estate appraisal).

Principal residence on land used in a farming business

2.39 If a taxpayer disposes of land used in a farming business which he or she carried on at any time and such land includes property that was at any time his or her principal residence, paragraph 40(2)(*c*) provides that any gain on the disposition of the land may be calculated using either of the two methods discussed below. It should be noted that the reference to land in paragraph 40(2)(*c*) includes the buildings thereon.

2.40 First Method: The taxpayer may regard the property as being divided into two portions: the principal residence portion and the remaining portion, part or all of which was used in the farming business. The proceeds of disposition and adjusted cost base of the total property must be allocated on a reasonable basis between the two portions in order to determine the gain for each portion. The gain otherwise determined for the principal residence portion may be reduced or eliminated by the principal residence exemption provided for in paragraph 40(2)(*b*), as described in ¶ 2.17 - 2.26 (including, if applicable, the capital gains election reduction amount, that is, variable D in paragraph 40(2)(*b*)). The gain on the remainder of the property results in a taxable capital gain (see, however, ¶2.47). For purposes of determining what portion of the proceeds of disposition of the land may reasonably be allocated to the principal residence, it is our usual practice to accept the greater of the following two amounts:

a) the fair market value, as of the date of disposition of the land, of one-half hectare of land estimated on the basis of comparable sales of similar farm properties in the same area (the fair market value of more than one-half hectare could be used to the extent that such excess land was necessary for the use and enjoyment of the housing unit as a residence — see ¶2.33 - 2.35); and

b) the fair market value, as of the date of disposition of the land, of a typical residential lot in the same area.

2.41 Whichever basis is chosen, ¶2.40(a) or (b), for allocating a portion of the proceeds of disposition of the land to the principal residence, the same basis should be used to allocate a portion of the adjusted cost base of the land to the principal residence. For purposes of making this allocation of the land's adjusted cost base, the fair market value of the land referred to in (a) or (b), as the case may be, would be as of the taxpayer's acquisition date for the land rather than as of the date of its disposition.

2.42 Appendix B at the end of this Chapter provides an example which illustrates the use of the first method allowed under paragraph 40(2)(*c*).

2.43 Second Method: The taxpayer may elect under subparagraph 40(2)(*c*)(ii) to compute the gain on the disposition of the total property (including the property that was the principal residence) without making the allocations described above or using the principal residence exemption provided for in paragraph 40(2)(*b*) as described in ¶2.17 - 2.26. With regard to this election under subparagraph 40(2)(*c*)(ii), section 2300 of the Regulations requires that a letter signed by the taxpayer be attached to the income tax return filed for the tax year in which the disposition of the property took place. The letter should contain the following information:

a) a statement that the taxpayer is electing under subparagraph 40(2)(c)(ii);

b) a statement of the number of tax years ending after the acquisition date for which the property was the taxpayer's principal residence and during which he or she was resident in Canada (for the meanings of **resident in Canada** and **during**, see ¶2.21); and

c) a description of the property sufficient to identify it with the property designated as the taxpayer's principal residence.

2.44 Under the subparagraph 40(2)(c)(ii) election, the gain on the disposition of the total property is equal to the gain otherwise determined less the total of $1,000 plus $1,000 for each taxation year in ¶2.43(b) above. Two points should be noted for purposes of calculating the gain under subparagraph 40(2)(c)(ii):

- The **acquisition date** mentioned in ¶2.43(b) is the later of:
  o   December 31, 1971; and
  o   the date on which the taxpayer last acquired or reacquired the property or is deemed to have last acquired or reacquired it. If the taxpayer made a subsection 110.6(19) capital gains election in respect of the property, the deemed reacquisition of the property immediately after the end of February 22, 1994 under that election is considered to be a reacquisition for purposes of determining the acquisition date when calculating the gain otherwise determined. The reason for this is that, although subsection 40(7.1) prevents a subsection 110.6(19) deemed reacquisition from being considered a reacquisition for purposes of determining the acquisition date used in paragraph 40(2)(b), neither subsection 40(7.1) nor any other provision prevents a subsection 110.6(19) deemed reacquisition from being considered a reacquisition for purposes of determining the acquisition date used in subparagraph 40(2)(c)(ii).

- If the acquisition date is in fact the date of the deemed reacquisition under a subsection 110.6(19) capital gains election, that is, immediately after the end of February 22, 1994, the gain otherwise determined is calculated by taking into account the taxpayer's cost of the property under that deemed reacquisition rather than his or her actual cost at some earlier date. (Variable A in paragraph 40(2)(b) does not apply for the purposes of subparagraph 40(2)(c)(ii)).

2.45 Appendix B at the end of this Chapter provides an example which illustrates the use of the second method allowed under paragraph 40(2)(c).

2.46 When the second method is used, the exemption of $1,000 per year, which is to allow for the fact that a portion of the total property pertains to the principal residence rather than the farm, is not reduced where part of the residence itself is used to earn income (for example, there could be an office in the house which is used in connection with a business). However, any gain or recapture of capital cost allowance (CCA) pertaining to the portion of the residence (that is, building) so used to earn income (either or both of which can occur, for example, where the use of such portion of the residence is changed back from income-producing to non-income-producing — see ¶2.57 and ¶2.64) cannot be reduced by the $1,000 per year exemption.

2.47 Where an individual has a taxable capital gain from the disposition of a farm property, a section 110.6 capital gains deduction (which is a deduction in calculating taxable income) may be possible on the basis that the property is **qualified farm or fishing property**. For further particulars on this topic, see either Guide T4003, *Farming Income* or Guide RC4060, *Farming Income and the AgriStability and AgriInvest Programs Guide*.

Complete change in use of a property from principal residence to income-producing

2.48 If a taxpayer has completely converted his or her principal residence to an income-producing use, he or she is deemed by paragraph 45(1)(*a*) to have disposed of the property (both land and building) at fair market value and reacquired it immediately thereafter at the same amount. Any gain otherwise determined on this deemed disposition may be eliminated or reduced by the principal residence exemption. The taxpayer may instead, however, defer recognition of any gain to a later year by electing under subsection 45(2) to be deemed not to have made the change in use of the property. This election is made by means of a letter to that effect signed by the taxpayer and filed with the income tax return for the year in which the change in use occurred. For e-filers, see the Paper documentation page on the CRA Web site. If the taxpayer rescinds the election in a subsequent tax year, he or she is deemed to have disposed of and reacquired the property at fair market value on the first day of that subsequent year (with the above-mentioned tax consequences). If CCA is claimed on the property, the election is considered to be rescinded on the first day of the year in which that claim is made.

2.49 Subsection 220(3.2), in conjunction with section 600 of the Regulations, provides the authority for the CRA to accept a late-filed subsection 45(2) election. Such a late-filed election may be accepted under certain circumstances, one of which is that no CCA has been claimed on the property since the change in use has occurred and during the period in which the election is to remain in force. For further particulars on the acceptance of late-filed elections, see the current version of Information Circular IC07-1, Taxpayer Relief Provisions.

2.50 A property can qualify as a taxpayer's principal residence for up to four tax years during which a subsection 45(2) election remains in force, even if the housing unit is not ordinarily inhabited during those years by the taxpayer or by his or her spouse or common-law partner, former spouse or common-law partner, or child. However, the taxpayer must be resident, or deemed to be resident, in Canada during those years for the full benefit of the principal residence exemption to apply (see variable B in the formula in ¶2.20 or the years included in the statement in ¶2.43(b), as the case may be). It should also be noted that the rule described in ¶ 2.13-2.14 prevents the designation of more than one property as a principal residence for any particular year by the taxpayer (or, for any particular year after the 1981 tax year, by the taxpayer or any other member of his or her family unit). Thus, for example, a taxpayer's designation for the same year of one property by virtue of a subsection 45(2) election being in force, and another property by virtue of the fact that he or she ordinarily inhabited that other property, would not be permitted.

Example 4

Mr. A and his family lived in a house for a number of years until September 30, 2003. From October 1, 2003 until March 31, 2008 they lived elsewhere and Mr. A rented the house to a third party. On April 1, 2008, they moved back into the house and lived in it until it was sold in 2011. When he filed his 2011 income tax return, Mr. A designated the house as his principal residence for the 2004 to 2007 tax years inclusive (that is, the maximum four years) by virtue of a subsection 45(2) election (which he had already filed with his 2003 income tax return) having been in force for those years. (He was able to make this designation because no other property had been designated as a principal residence by him or a member of his family unit for those years.) He designated the house as his principal residence for all the other years in which he owned it by virtue of his having ordinarily inhabited it during those years, including the 2003 and 2008 years. Having been resident in Canada at all times, Mr. A's gain otherwise determined on the disposition of the house in 2011 was, therefore, completely eliminated by the principal residence exemption.

2.51 Any income in respect of a property (for example, the rental income in the above example), net of applicable expenses, must be reported for tax purposes. However, for tax years covered by a subsection 45(2) election, CCA should not be claimed on the property (see ¶2.48 - 2.49).

2.52 Section 54.1 removes the above-mentioned four-year limitation for tax years covered by a subsection 45(2) election if all of the following conditions are met:

a) the taxpayer does not ordinarily inhabit the housing unit during the period covered by the election because the taxpayer's or his or her spouse's or common-law partner's place of employment has been relocated;

b) the employer is not related to the taxpayer or his or her spouse or common-law partner;

c) the housing unit is at least 40 kilometers farther from such new place of employment than is the taxpayer's subsequent place or places of residence; and

d) either:

- the taxpayer resumes ordinary habitation of the housing unit during the term of employment by that same employer or before the end of the tax year immediately following the tax year in which such employment terminates; or
- the taxpayer dies during the term of such employment.

2.53 With regard to condition (d), two corporations that are members of the same corporate group, or are otherwise related, are not considered to be the same employer.

Complete change in use of a property from income-producing to principal residence

2.54 If a taxpayer has completely changed the use of a property (for which an election under subsection 45(2) is not in force) from income-producing to a principal residence, he or she is deemed by paragraph 45(1)(*a*) to have disposed of the property (both land and building), and immediately thereafter reacquired it, at fair market value. This deemed disposition can result in a taxable capital gain. The taxpayer may instead defer recognition of the gain to a later year by electing under subsection 45(3) that the above-mentioned deemed disposition and reacquisition under paragraph 45(1)(*a*) does not apply. This election is made by means of a letter to that effect signed by the taxpayer and filed with the income tax return for the year in which the property is ultimately disposed of (or earlier if a formal demand for the election is issued by the CRA). For e-filers, see the Paper documentation page on the CRA Web site. Also, subsection 220(3.2), in conjunction with section 600 of the Regulations, provides the authority for the CRA to accept a late-filed subsection 45(3) election. Such a late-filed election may be accepted under certain circumstances. For further particulars on the acceptance of late-filed elections, see the current version of Information Circular IC07-1.

2.55 Even if a subsection 45(3) election is filed in order to defer recognition of a gain from the change in use of a property from income-producing to principal residence, the net income from the property for the period before the change in use must still be reported. However, for purposes of reporting such net income, it should be noted that an election under subsection 45(3) is not possible if, for any tax year ending after 1984 and on or before the change in use of the property from income-producing to a principal residence, CCA has been allowed in respect of the property to:

- the taxpayer;
- the taxpayer's spouse or common-law partner; or
- a trust under which the taxpayer or his or her spouse or common-law partner is a beneficiary.

CCA so allowed would cause subsection 45(4) to nullify the subsection 45(3) election.

2.56 Similar to the treatment for a subsection 45(2) election (see ¶2.50 - 2.51), a property can qualify as a taxpayer's principal residence for up to four tax years prior to a change in use covered by a subsection 45(3) election, in lieu of fulfilling the ordinarily inhabited rule (discussed in ¶ 2.10 - 2.12) for these years. As in the case of a subsection 45(2) election, residence or deemed residence in Canada during these years is necessary for the full benefit of the principal residence exemption to apply. Furthermore, the rule described in ¶ 2.13 - 2.14 prevents the designation of more than one property as a principal residence for any particular year by the taxpayer (or, for any particular year after the 1981 tax year, by the taxpayer or any other member of his or her family unit).

Example 5

Mr. X bought a house in 2003 and rented it to a third party until mid-2009. Mr. X and his family then lived in the house until it was sold in 2011. Mr. X has been resident in Canada at all times. When he filed his 2011 income tax return, Mr. X designated the house as his principal residence for the 2009 to 2011 tax years inclusive, by virtue of his having ordinarily inhabited it during those years. He also designated the house as his principal residence for the 2005 to 2008 years inclusive (that is, the maximum 4 years) by virtue of a subsection 45(3) election, which he filed with his 2011 income tax return (he was able to make this designation because (i) no other property had been designated by him or a member of his family unit for those years, and (ii) he did not claim any CCA when reporting the net income from the property before the change in use). However, his gain otherwise determined on the disposition of the house in 2011 could not be fully eliminated by the principal residence exemption formula because he could not designate the house as his principal residence for the 2003 and 2004 years.

Partial changes in use

2.57 If a taxpayer has partially converted a principal residence to an income-producing use, paragraph 45(1)(c) provides for a deemed disposition of the portion of the property so converted (such portion is usually calculated on the basis of the area involved) for proceeds equal to its proportionate share of the property's fair market value. Paragraph 45(1)(c) also provides for a deemed reacquisition immediately thereafter of the same portion of the property at a cost equal to the very same amount. Any gain otherwise determined on the deemed disposition is usually eliminated or reduced by the principal residence exemption. If the portion of the property so changed is later converted back to use as part of the principal residence, there is a second deemed disposition (and reacquisition) thereof at fair market value. A taxable capital gain attributable to the period of use of such portion of the property for income-producing purposes can arise from such a second deemed disposition or from an actual sale of the whole property subsequent to the original partial change in use. An election under subsection 45(2) or (3) cannot be made where there is a partial change in use of a property as described above.

2.58 The above-mentioned deemed disposition rule applies where the partial change in use of the property is substantial and of a more permanent nature, that is, where there is a structural change. Examples where this occurs are the conversion of the front half of a house into a store, the conversion of a portion of a house into a self-contained domestic establishment for earning rental income (a duplex, triplex, etc.), and alterations to a house to accommodate separate business premises. In these and similar cases, the taxpayer reports the income and may claim the expenses pertaining to the altered portion of the property (that is, a reasonable portion of the expenses relating to the whole property) as well as CCA on such altered portion of the property.

2.59 It is the CRA's practice not to apply the deemed disposition rule, but rather to consider that the entire property retains its nature as a principal residence, where all of the following conditions are met:

a) the income-producing use is ancillary to the main use of the property as a residence;
b) there is no structural change to the property; and
c) no CCA is claimed on the property.

2.60 These conditions can be met, for example, where a taxpayer carries on a business of caring for children in the home, rents one or more rooms in the home, or has an office or other work space in the home which is used in connection with business or employment. In these and similar cases, the taxpayer reports the income and may claim the expenses (other than CCA) pertaining to the portion of the property used for income-producing purposes.

Certain conditions and restrictions are placed on the deductibility of expenses relating to an office or other work space in an individual's home — see Interpretation Bulletin IT-514, Work Space in Home Expenses (if the income is income from a business) or Interpretation Bulletin IT-352R2, Employee's Expenses, Including Work Space in Home Expenses. In the event that the taxpayer commences to claim CCA on the portion of the property used for producing income, the deemed disposition rule is applied as of the time at which the income-producing use commenced.

Change in use rules regarding CCA, deemed capital cost, and recapture

2.61 If a taxpayer has completely or partially changed the use of property from principal residence to income-producing, subsection 13(7) provides for a deemed acquisition of the property or portion of the property so changed that is depreciable property. For purposes of claiming CCA, the deemed capital cost of such depreciable property is its fair market value as of the date of the change in use unless that fair market value is greater than its cost to the taxpayer. In that case, the deemed capital cost of such depreciable property is equal to its cost to the taxpayer plus an amount which represents the taxable portion of the accrued gain on the property (before any reduction to that gain by means of the principal residence exemption) to the extent that a section 110.6 capital gains deduction has not been claimed in respect of that amount (this latter rule has no particular significance for dispositions of residence properties occurring after February 22, 1994, because of the elimination of the $100,000 lifetime capital gains exemption for dispositions after that date).

Example 6

Mr. A completely converted his house to a rental property in January 2011, at which time its cost to him and its fair market value were $160,000 and $200,000 respectively (both amounts pertain only to the housing unit and not the land). The change in use resulted in a deemed disposition of the property at fair market value (see ¶ 2.48 - 2.51 — assume that Mr. A did not make a subsection 45(2) election in respect of the property because he wanted to use the principal residence exemption for his cottage for the years after 2011). Mr. A was able to use the principal residence exemption to bring his gain on the January 2011 deemed disposition of the house to nil. Mr. A's deemed capital cost for the house (that is, for CCA purposes) at the time of its change in use to a rental property was $180,000. This amount was calculated by taking the $160,000 cost and adding $20,000, the latter amount being one-half of the excess of the $200,000 fair market value over the $160,000 cost. (Note that the $20,000 potentially taxable portion of the gain was included in Mr. A's deemed capital cost for CCA purposes even though he eliminated the gain by means of the principal residence exemption.)

2.62 In the case of a complete change in use of a property from principal residence to income-producing, a subsection 45(2) election will cause subsection 13(7), as described above, not to apply. However, if the election is rescinded in a subsequent tax year (for example, by claiming CCA on the property — see ¶2.48 - 2.49), a subsection 13(7) deemed acquisition of depreciable property will occur on the first day of that subsequent year.

2.63 Because a subsection 45(2) election is not available where there is only a partial change in use of a property from principal residence to income-producing, subsection 13(7) applies in such a situation in the manner described above (except where conditions (a) to (c) in ¶2.59 have been met, including the condition not to claim CCA on the portion of the property used to earn income).

2.64 If a taxpayer completely or partially changes the use of a property from income-producing to principal residence, there is a deemed disposition at fair market value, by virtue of subsection 13(7), of the portion of the property so changed that is depreciable property. This can result in a recapture of CCA previously claimed on the property. A subsection 45(3) election cannot be used to defer such a recapture (for example, a recapture of CCA claimed for a tax year ending before 1985 — see the comments regarding CCA in ¶ 2.54 - 2.55).

Personal trusts

2.65 It is possible for a **personal trust** (as defined in subsection 248(1)) to claim the principal residence exemption to reduce or eliminate a gain that the trust would otherwise have on the disposition of a property. For this purpose, the normal principal residence exemption rules generally apply, subject to the following modifications:

a) When a personal trust designates a property as its principal residence for one or more tax years, the trustee of the trust must complete and file Form T1079, Designation of a Property as a Principal Residence by a Personal Trust. For purposes of calculating a capital gains election reduction amount (see ¶ 2.17 - 2.26) for the trust, the trustee should complete Form T1079-WS, Principal Residence Worksheet, and file it with the T1079 designation form.

b) For each tax year for which the trust is designating the property as its principal residence, the trust must specify in the above-mentioned designation each individual who, in the calendar year ending in that tax year:
- was beneficially interested in the trust; and
- ordinarily inhabited the housing unit or who had a spouse or common—law partner, former spouse or common-law partner, or child who ordinarily inhabited the housing unit (a subsection 45(2) or (3) election can be used, however, in essentially the same manner as, and subject to the limitations discussed in, ¶ 2.50 - 2.51 and ¶2.56, to

remove the requirement that the ordinarily inhabited rule be fulfilled for the year by one of these persons).

Any individual specified by the trust to be an individual as described above is referred to as a **specified beneficiary** of the trust for the year.

c) For each tax year for which the trust is designating the property as its principal residence, there must not have been any corporation (other than a registered charity) or partnership that was beneficially interested in the trust at any time in the year.

d) For each tax year for which the trust is designating the property as its principal residence (including years before 1982), no other property may have been designated as a principal residence, for the calendar year ending in the year, by any specified beneficiary of the trust for the year, or by any person who throughout the calendar year ending in the year was a member of such a beneficiary's family unit. For this purpose, a specified beneficiary's **family unit** includes, in addition to the specified beneficiary, the following persons (if any):

- the specified beneficiary's spouse or common-law partner throughout the calendar year ending in the year, unless the spouse or common-law partner was throughout that calendar year living apart, and was separated pursuant to a judicial separation or written separation agreement, from the specified beneficiary;

- the specified beneficiary's children, except those who were married, in a common-law partnership or 18 years of age or older during the calendar year ending in the year; and

- where the specified beneficiary was not married, in a common-law partnership or 18 years of age or older during the calendar year ending in the year:
  o the specified beneficiary's mother and father; and
  o the specified beneficiary's brothers and sisters who were not married, in a common-law partnership or 18 years of age or older during that calendar year.

2.66 Furthermore, if a personal trust designates a property as its principal residence for a particular tax year, the property is deemed to be property designated, for the calendar year ending in the year, as the principal residence of each specified beneficiary of the trust. This deeming rule can be applied, in conjunction with the other principal residence exemption rules, to various situations not explicitly described in those rules.

Example 7

Personal Trust A owned a house in its tax year ended December 31, 2011. The house was ordinarily inhabited in 2011 by Mr. X, a specified beneficiary of Personal Trust A (and also by his spouse, Mrs. X). The trust has designated the house as its principal residence for its tax year ended December 31, 2011. The house is therefore deemed to have been designated as Mr. X's principal residence for 2011.

Personal Trust B owned a cottage in its tax year ended December 31, 2011. The cottage was ordinarily inhabited in 2011 by Mrs. X, a specified beneficiary of Personal Trust B (and also by Mr. X). As discussed in ¶ 2.13 - 2.14, a taxpayer and his or her spouse or common-law partner cannot designate different properties for the same year. Therefore, since the house has already been deemed to have been designated as Mr. X's principal residence for 2011, Personal Trust B cannot designate the cottage as its principal residence for 2011 because that would have resulted in the cottage being deemed to have also been designated as Mrs. X's principal residence for 2011.

2.67 Where a beneficiary acquired a property from a personal trust in satisfaction of all or any part of the beneficiary's capital interest in the trust, subsection 40(7) provides a deeming rule when the beneficiary disposes of the property provided the following two conditions were met:

- the rollover provision in subsection 107(2) applied (see discussion in ¶2.68 for an exception to this rollover provision); and
- subsection 107(4) did not apply.

For purposes of claiming the principal residence exemption, the beneficiary is deemed by subsection 40(7) to have owned the property since the trust last acquired it.

Example 8

A personal trust acquired a residential property on October 1, 2007 for $200,000. On January 10, 2009, the property was distributed to Mr. X in satisfaction of his capital interest in the trust. Subsection 107(4) did not apply with respect to this distribution, and the rollover provision in subsection 107(2) prevented the gain on the property accrued to January 10, 2009 from being taxed in the hands of the trust. Instead, the potential for taxing that gain was transferred to Mr. X because subsection 107(2) deemed him to have acquired the property at a cost equal to $200,000, that is, the cost amount of the property to the trust. Mr. X lived in the residence from October 15, 2007 until he disposed of the property on December 1, 2011 for $250,000, incurring no costs in connection with the disposition.

Mr. X's gain otherwise determined on the disposition of the property was equal to his $250,000 proceeds minus his $200,000 adjusted cost base, for a gain of $50,000. Subsection 40(7) deemed him to have owned the property from October 1, 2007 rather than from January 10, 2009. Since Mr. X ordinarily inhabited the residence in all of the years from 2007 to 2011 inclusive (that is, all of the years in which he either owned the property or was deemed to have owned it), he was able to designate the property as his principal residence for all those years. Thus, he was able to use the principal residence exemption to fully eliminate his $50,000 gain otherwise determined. However, if neither Mr. X nor his current or former spouse or common—law partner, or child had ordinarily inhabited the residence (see the rule discussed in ¶ 2.10 - 2.12) until it was distributed by the trust to Mr. X on January 10, 2009, he would have been able to designate the property as his principal residence only for 2009 to 2011. In other words, he would have been able to use the formula in ¶2.17 - 2.26 to eliminate only the following portion of his $50,000 gain otherwise determined:

Applying the formula $A \times (B \div C)$:

A is $50,000

B is $1 + 3$ (being tax years 2009 to 2011)

C is 5 (being tax years 2007 to 2011)

$= \$50,000 \times (4 \div 5)$

$= 40,000$

2.68 In order to prevent the rollover rule in subsection 107(2) from applying with respect to a trust's distribution, to a beneficiary, of a property that qualifies for designation as the trust's principal residence before the distribution, a personal trust can use an election under subsection 107(2.01). Under this election, the trust would instead be deemed, just before the distribution of the property to the beneficiary, to have disposed of and then to have reacquired the property at fair market value. This could be done, for example, in order for the trust to use the principal residence exemption to eliminate or reduce any gain on the property accrued to that point in time (see ¶2.65 - 2.66), ideal in circumstances where the recipient beneficiary is not the specified beneficiary and has owned another home during the period in which the trust owned the home being distributed. The cost of the property to the beneficiary would be that same fair market value, and the beneficiary would not be deemed by subsection 40(7) (see ¶2.67) to have owned the property during the period of time in which it was owned by the trust prior to the distribution.

Transfer of a principal residence

2.69 Subsection 40(4) can apply if a property of a taxpayer (hereinafter referred to as the **transferor**):

- has been transferred inter vivos to one of the following parties and the subsection 73(1) rollover rule has applied:
    o the transferor's spouse or common-law partner;
    o the transferor's former spouse or common-law partner;
    o a spousal or common-law partner trust;
    o a joint spousal or common-law partner trust; or
    o an alter ego trust.

or

- has been transferred or distributed, as a consequence of the transferor's death, to his or her spouse or common-law partner or to a spousal or common-law partner trust, and the subsection 70(6) rollover rule has applied.

2.70 If the spouse or common-law partner, former spouse or common-law partner, spousal or common-law partner trust, joint spousal or common-law partner trust, or alter ego trust (hereinafter referred to as the transferee) subsequently disposes of the property, subsection 40(4) can apply with respect to a principal residence exemption, claimed by the transferee, for the property. For purposes of the transferee's claiming the principal residence exemption under either paragraph 40(2)(*b*) (see the formula in ¶2.17 - 2.26) or paragraph 40(2)(*c*) (see ¶ 2.39 - 2.46), the following rules apply under subsection 40(4):

a) The transferee is deemed to have owned the property throughout the period that the transferor owned it.
b) The property is deemed to have been the transferee's principal residence:
   - in a case where the subsection 73(1) rollover rule applied — for any tax year for which it was the transferor's principal residence; and
   - in a case where the subsection 70(6) rollover rule applied — for any tax year for which it would have been the transferor's principal residence if he or she had so designated it.
c) If the transferee is a trust, it is deemed to have been resident in Canada during each of the tax years during which the transferor was resident in Canada.

2.71 Any year included in the period described in (a) is included by the transferee in variable C in the formula in ¶2.17 - 2.26. Any year described in (b) is included by the transferee in variable B in the formula in ¶2.17 - 2.26 or in the years included in the statement in ¶2.43(b), as the case may be, assuming that the transferee meets the residence requirement mentioned therein, as the case may be, for that year. (If the transferee is a trust, see (c) above with regard to this residence requirement.)

Example 9

Mr. X was the sole owner of a house in Canada, which he had acquired in 1995. In 2000, Mr. X got married and his spouse, Mrs. X, moved into the house with him. In 2005, Mr. X died and the house was transferred to a spousal trust for Mrs. X. The trust was a trust as described in subsection 70(6). The trust's tax year-end was December 31. If Mr. X had not died (and if he had sold his house in 2005), he could have designated it as his principal residence for any of the years 1995 to 2005 inclusive.

Under the rollover rule in subsection 70(6), Mr. X was deemed to have disposed of the house immediately before his death for proceeds equal to his cost of the house. Thus, Mr. X had no gain or loss on the deemed disposition of the house. The spousal trust for Mrs. X was deemed under subsection 70(6) to have acquired the house, at the time of Mr. X's death, at a cost equal to Mr. X's deemed proceeds, that is, at Mr. X's cost of the house.

In 2011, Mrs. X died and the trust sold the house at fair market value. Since this amount was greater than the trust's deemed cost of the house, the trust had a gain otherwise determined from the disposition, which the trust (that is, its trustee) wishes to eliminate by using the principal residence exemption.

Subsection 40(4) deems the trust to have owned the house in all the years in which Mr. X owned it, that is, 1995 to 2005 inclusive, in accordance with the rule described in ¶2.70(a) above. (The house was, of course, owned by the trust in 2005 in any event.) This means that the years that the trust must include in variable C in the principal residence exemption formula in ¶ 2.17 - 2.26 are 1995 to 2011 inclusive.

Since the trust is a personal trust resident in Canada and also since Mrs. X lived in the house and qualified as a specified beneficiary of the trust for the years 2005 to 2011 inclusive, the trust can designate the house as its principal residence for those years. The trust cannot designate the house as its principal residence for the years 1995 to 2004 inclusive; however, such a designation by the trust is not necessary — the house is already deemed by subsection 40(4) to have been the trust's principal residence for those years, in accordance with the rule described in ¶2.70(b) above, because Mr. X could have designated the house as his principal residence for those years. Also, in accordance with the rule described in ¶2.70(c) above, the trust is deemed to have been resident in Canada for the years 1995 to 2004 because Mr. X was resident in Canada during those years. Therefore, the trust is able to include all of the years from 1995 to 2011 inclusive in variable B in the formula in ¶2.17 - 2.26. In other words, the trust is able to use the principal residence exemption to completely eliminate the gain otherwise determined on its disposition of the house in 2011.

Example 10

Assume all the same facts as in Example 1, except the following: Mr. X could not have designated the house as his principal residence for the years 1995 to 1998 inclusive because he had already designated his cottage as his principal residence for those years. Under these circumstances, the house that was transferred to the spousal trust for Mrs. X cannot be deemed to have been the principal residence of the trust for the years 1995 to 1998 inclusive. Therefore, the trust can only partially eliminate the gain otherwise determined on its disposition of the house in 2011 by means of the principal residence exemption formula.

2.72 In the case of an inter vivos transfer of property under subsection 73(1), the following should be noted for purposes of any subsequent disposition of the property by the transferee:

- A designation of the property as the principal residence of the transferor — for one or more years prior to the transfer — may be needed in order for the property to be deemed to have been the principal residence of the transferee for those years by means of subsection 40(4) (see ¶2.70(b)). Note that as explained in ¶ 2.13 - 2.14, the transferor will not be able to designate the property as a principal residence for any particular year if another property is designated as a principal residence for that year by the transferor (or, if the year is after the 1981 tax year, by the transferor or any of the other members of the transferor's family unit). If the transferor is able to, and does in fact, designate the property as his or her principal residence for one or more years prior to the transfer, this does not necessarily mean that the transferor must actually file the designation form with the return for the year of the transfer (although the transferor may do so) — for further comments on the necessity to file a designation form, see ¶ 2.15 - 2.16. The transferor should, in any event, complete the designation form and, if it is not filed by the transferor, **it should be retained by the transferee**. Subsequently, if the transferee disposes of the property (or grants an option to another person to acquire the property) and wishes to use the principal residence exemption, the transferee would need to file the designation forms — thatis, the transferee's designation form for any years for which the transferee is designating the property as a principal residence and the transferor's designation form for any years for which his or her designation of the property causes the property to be deemed to have been the principal residence of the transferee
    - if the transferee is the transferor's spouse or common-law partner — only when the situation described in ¶2.15(a) or (b) exists in connection with the transferee's disposition of the property; or
    - if the transferee is a personal trust — in every case (see ¶2.65(a)).
- Any taxable capital gain of the transferee (excluding an alter ego trust) from the disposition of the property or substituted property (which might occur, for example, because the transferee was not able to completely eliminate the gain otherwise determined by means of the principal residence exemption)

could be deemed to be the taxable capital gain of the transferor by virtue of the attribution rules in section 74.2. For a discussion of these rules, see the current version of Interpretation Bulletin IT-511R, Interspousal and Certain Other Transfers and Loans of Property.

Partnership property

2.73 Although a housing unit, a leasehold interest therein, or a share of the capital stock of a co—operative housing corporation can be a partnership asset, a partnership is not a taxpayer and it cannot use the principal residence exemption on the disposition of any such property. However, an individual who is a member of the partnership could use the principal residence exemption to reduce or eliminate the portion of any gain on the disposition of the property which is allocated to that partner pursuant to the partnership agreement, provided that the other requirements of the section 54 definition of **principal residence** are met (for example, if the partner resides in the partnership's housing unit, this would satisfy the *ordinarily inhabited* requirement discussed in ¶ 2.10 - 2.12).

A principal residence outside Canada

2.74 A property that is located outside Canada can, depending on the facts of the case, qualify as a taxpayer's principal residence (see the requirements discussed in ¶ 2.2 - 2.16). A taxpayer who is resident in Canada and owns such a qualifying property outside Canada during a particular tax year can designate the property as a principal residence for that year in order to use the principal residence exemption (see ¶ 2.17 - 2.26 for the meanings of **resident in Canada** and **during**). Should a non-resident of Canada who owns a property outside Canada become a resident of Canada at any particular time, the provisions of the Act normally apply to deem that person to acquire the property at that time at fair market value, thereby ensuring that any unrealized gain on the property accruing to that time will not be taxable in Canada. Thereafter, the comments in the first two sentences of this paragraph may apply.

Non-resident owner of a principal residence in Canada

2.75 It may be possible for a property in Canada that is owned in a particular tax year by a non-resident of Canada to qualify as the non-resident's principal residence (that is, satisfy all the requirements of the section 54 definition of **principal residence** for the non-resident) for that year. The non-resident's spouse could be the one, for example, who satisfies the **ordinarily inhabited** rule — see ¶2.10 - 2.12 (or, alternatively, a subsection 45(2) or (3) election could make the designation of the property as the non-resident's principal residence possible —

see ¶2.50 - 2.51 and ¶2.56). However, the use of the principal residence exemption by a taxpayer is limited by reference to the number of tax years ending after the acquisition date during which the taxpayer was resident in Canada — see ¶2.17 - 2.26 and ¶2.43 - 2.45 (as indicated in ¶2.17 - 2.26, during a year means at any time in the year). Thus, even if a property in Canada owned by a non-resident qualifies as the non-resident's principal residence, the above—mentioned residence in Canada requirement typically prevents the non-resident from using the principal residence exemption to eliminate a gain on the disposition of the property.

2.76 In spite of the limitation mentioned in ¶2.75 in connection with the principal residence exemption, an election under subsection 45(2) or (3) could allow a non-resident owning a property in Canada to defer a taxable capital gain which would otherwise result from a deemed disposition of a property on a change in its use (see ¶2.48 - 2.49 and ¶2.54 - 2.55).

2.77 Where a non-resident owner of a property in Canada has rented out the property in a particular tax year and has filed a subsection 45(2) or (3) election in respect of the property, see ¶ 2.48 - 2.49 and ¶ 2.54 - 2.55 regarding the restrictions on claiming CCA. These restrictions apply where the non-resident elects to report the rental income under section 216. (That election is discussed in Interpretation Bulletin IT-393R2, Election re: Tax on Rents and Timber Royalties — Non-Residents.)

Section 116 certificate for a disposition of a principal residence in Canada by a non-resident owner

2.78 Where a non-resident wishes to obtain a certificate under section 116 for a property in Canada which the non-resident proposes to dispose of or has disposed of within the last 10 days, a prepayment on account of tax must be made or security acceptable to the CRA must be given before the certificate will be issued. Form T2062, Request by a Non-Resident of Canada for a Certificate of Compliance Related to the Disposition of Taxable Canadian Property, or a similar notification, must be filed in connection with a request for a section 116 certificate. Further particulars regarding the above are contained in the current version of Information Circular IC72-17R6, Procedures Concerning the Disposition of Taxable Canadian Property by Non-Residents of Canada — Section 116. Where part or all of any gain otherwise determined on the disposition of the property by the non-resident is or will be eliminated by the principal residence exemption, the amount of prepayment on account of tax to be made or security to be given may be reduced accordingly. An application for such a reduction should be made by means of a letter signed by the taxpayer and attached to the completed Form T2062 or similar notification. Such letter should contain a calculation of the portion of the gain otherwise determined that is or will be so eliminated by the principal residence exemption.

Beneficial ownership

2.79 In the common law jurisdictions, two forms of property ownership are recognized — legal and beneficial. Normally **legal ownership** exists when title is transferred to, recorded in, registered in or otherwise carried in the name of a person. Legal owners are generally entitled to enforce their ownership rights against all other persons. The distinction between legal and beneficial ownership does not exist in civil law; ownership is a unitary concept.

2.80 In the common law jurisdictions, one person's legal ownership of a property may be subject to another person's beneficial ownership of that property. The term **beneficial ownership** is used to describe the type of ownership of a person who is entitled to the use and benefit of the property whether or not that person has concurrent legal ownership. A person who has beneficial ownership rights but not legal ownership can enforce those rights against the holder of the legal title. For example, beneficial ownership frequently arises when property is held in trust for a person in circumstances where, according to the terms of the trust, that person has authority to instruct the trustee to deal with the property as requested. (Where a personal trust, including a spousal trust, is involved, see also the rules mentioned in ¶2.65 - 2.68.)

2.81 Beneficial ownership must be distinguished, however, from the other types of physical possession of property which a person may enjoy. For example, a tenant of a property, or a person who is allowed to occupy it only because the true owner has no objection, is not the beneficial owner of the property. In determining whether a person has beneficial ownership, one should consider such factors as the right to possession, the right to collect rents, the right to call for the mortgaging of the property, the right to transfer title by sale or by will, the obligation to repair, the obligation to pay property taxes and other relevant rights and obligations. Not all of these incidents of ownership need occur concurrently before it is concluded that the person has beneficial ownership of the property, which is a question of fact in each particular case (subject to any determination under the law regarding beneficial ownership such as, for example, in the manner described in ¶2.83 - 2.87).

2.82 Since in most cases the same person has both legal and beneficial ownership, determining ownership on the basis of beneficial ownership alone is not often required. The comments below deal with some situations where a taxpayer is considered to own, and other situations where a taxpayer is considered not to own, a property for purposes of the principal residence exemption.

Ownership issues in the province of Quebec

2.83 Because the province of Quebec is a civil law jurisdiction, not a common law jurisdiction, subsection 248(3) provides a special set of rules for income tax purposes in relation to property subject to certain institutions or arrangements governed by the laws of that province. Subsection 248(3) deems each of the following to be a trust:

a) a usufruct;
b) a right of use or habitation; or
c) substitution.

The trust is deemed to be created by will where (a), (b) or (c) was established by will. The property subject to (a), (b) or (c) is deemed to have been transferred to, and to be held in trust by, the trust. The transfer is deemed to have occurred on, and as a consequence of, the death of the testator where (a), (b) or (c) arises on the death of that person. If the property is the type of property that can otherwise qualify as a principal residence, the deemed trust may be able to use the rules referred to in ¶2.65 - 2.68 to claim the principal residence exemption to reduce or eliminate any gain that would otherwise occur (for tax purposes) as a result of a disposition of the property.

2.84 Subsection 248(3) also deems any person who has a right (whether immediate or future and whether absolute or contingent) to receive all or any part of the income or the capital in respect of property subject to (a), (b) or (c) to be a person who is beneficially interested in the deemed trust. Finally, subsection 248(3) deems property in relation to which any person has, at any time:

d) the right of ownership;
e) a right as a lessee in an emphyteusis; or
f) a right as a beneficiary in a trust (including a right as a deemed beneficiary of a deemed trust described above);

to be beneficially owned by that person, whether or not the property is subject to a servitude.

2.85 Thus, if a person sells his or her rights with respect to property which is subject to (a), (b), (c), (d) or (e) above and the property itself is a property that can otherwise qualify as a principal residence (that is, a housing unit, leasehold interest or co-operative housing corporation shares), that person might be able to use the principal residence exemption to reduce or eliminate any gain that would otherwise occur (for tax purposes) as a result of that disposition of rights. In order for this to occur, of course, all the other requirements of the section 54 definition of principal residence, as described in this Chapter, would have to have been met. For example, the ordinarily inhabited requirement could have been satisfied by the person who sold the rights with respect to the property having inhabited the property during the relevant years.

Sole or joint ownership

2.86 For purposes of claiming the principal residence exemption for a property, the section 54 definition of principal residence requires that the taxpayer own the property **jointly with another person or otherwise**. These words include sole ownership, joint tenancy, tenancy-in-common and co-ownership. Provincial laws are therefore often relevant in determining the ownership of property (including, for example, provincial laws relating to marital property) and should, therefore, be considered along with the comments in this Chapter.

Ownership in dispute

2.87 When a taxpayer's ownership of property is in dispute or in doubt, he or she may resort to the courts for a resolution of the question. In a situation involving a marriage dissolution, for example, one spouse may request the courts to resolve the ownership of property considered to be owned by the other spouse. In such a case, where the first-mentioned spouse acquires ownership pursuant to a court order, such ownership will generally be considered to have been acquired on the effective date specified in the court order regardless of the legal basis or reasons for the order, or on such other date as is considered reasonable if no effective date is specified in the order.

Share in the capital stock of a co-operative housing corporation

2.88 A share in the capital stock of a co-operative housing corporation can qualify as a principal residence property provided that the share was acquired for the sole purpose of obtaining the right to inhabit a housing unit owned by the corporation and the other requirements of the section 54 definition of principal residence, as indicated above, are met. In any event, where a corporation or an association formed solely to hold residential property is really a bare trustee of the property and the terms of the trust arrangement give the beneficiary, that is, shareholder of the corporation or member of the association:

a) the same rights of possession and use of a particular housing unit as the beneficial owner of any housing unit would normally enjoy, and

b) the right to require the corporation or association to deal with the housing unit (for example, sell or mortgage it) as instructed by the shareholder or member, the shareholder or member is considered to be the beneficial owner of the housing unit. These comments do not apply to ownership of a condominium unit that usually vests in the person acquiring it. However, see ¶2.90 concerning the time of acquisition of ownership of a condominium unit.

Interest in a property under an enforceable agreement for sale

2.89 A purchaser's interest or, for civil law, a right in property under an enforceable agreement for sale will, subject to ¶2.90, be considered to constitute ownership of the property. A purchaser's interest in a house bought under the Veterans' Land Act will also be considered to be ownership of property. In these instances, the taxpayer has made a down payment and entered into an obligation to make monthly payments. When the total purchase price is paid, the taxpayer is entitled to acquire title in his or her name.

Ownership issues with condominium units

2.90 When acquiring a residential condominium unit, it is not unusual for a taxpayer to make a down payment, to enter into an agreement of purchase and sale, to enter into an occupancy agreement and to take possession prior to the registration of the condominium. The occupancy agreement may provide for payments which reflect the carrying costs of the condominium until the purchase transaction can be completed. Normally in such a situation, the taxpayer does not own the condominium unit until the condominium is registered under the relevant provincial legislation and the purchase transaction has closed.

Property on leased land

2.91 A taxpayer may in some cases be considered to own, for purposes of the principal residence exemption, a housing unit situated on land not owned by the taxpayer in circumstances where, by reason of the law or according to the terms of the lease, he or she has a leasehold interest in the land. This can occur, for example, in any of the following circumstances:

a) the taxpayer is assigned the leasehold interest in government-owned land and pays a builder to construct a house on the land,
b) the taxpayer builds a house on leased land, or
c) the taxpayer "purchases" (that is, pays what amounts to a purchase price for) a house on leased land.

Acquisition of a property by way of gift or inheritance

2.92 A taxpayer acquires ownership of property by way of gift or inheritance on the date he or she obtains a right to possess the property for his or her enjoyment.

Appendix A

Illustration of the rule in subsection 40(6)

If a taxpayer disposes (or is deemed to dispose) of a property which the taxpayer has owned (whether jointly with another person or otherwise) continuously since before 1982, the rule in subsection 40(6) (see ¶2.30) provides that the gain calculated under the usual method, using the principal residence exemption formula in ¶ 2.17-2.26, cannot be greater than the maximum total net gain determined under an alternative method. Under the alternative method, there is a hypothetical disposition on December 31, 1981 and reacquisition on January 1, 1982 of the property at fair market value.

The maximum total net gain determined under the alternative method is then calculated as follows:

maximum total net gain = pre-1982 gain + post-1981 gain — post-1981 loss where:

- the **pre-1982 gain** is the gain (if any), as reduced by the principal residence exemption formula in ¶2.17-2.26, that would result from the hypothetical disposition at fair market value on December 31, 1981;
- the **post-1981** gain is the gain (if any), as reduced by the principal residence exemption formula in ¶2.17-2.26 without the 1 + in variable B in that formula, that would result from the hypothetical acquisition at fair market value on January 1, 1982 and the subsequent actual (or deemed) disposition; and
- the **post-1981 loss** is the amount of any loss that has accrued from December 31, 1981 to the date of the subsequent actual (or deemed) disposition, that is, the excess (if any) of the fair market value on December 31, 1981 over the proceeds (or deemed proceeds) from the subsequent actual (or deemed) disposition.

The examples which follow illustrate the rule in subsection 40(6). It has been assumed in these examples that, on each actual disposition, no costs were incurred in connection with that disposition.

Example 1

Mrs. X acquired a house in 1975 for $50,000. She and her husband lived in it until February 1996, when she sold it for $115,000, resulting in an actual gain of $65,000 ($115,000 - $50,000). Ever since the sale of the house in 1996, Mr. and Mrs. X have been living in rented premises. In filing her 1996 income tax return, Mrs. X designated the house as her principal residence for 1975 to 1995 inclusive, and thus her gain otherwise determined was completely eliminated by the principal residence exemption formula in ¶2.17-2.26:

Gain otherwise determined is $65,000 (that is, $115,000 — $50,000).

Reduce by the principal residence exemption based on the formula **A** × (**B** ÷ **C**), where:

A is $65,000

B is 1 + 21 (being tax years 1975 to 1995)

C is 22 (being tax years 1975 to 1996)

= $65,000 x (22 ÷ 22)

= $65,000

Gain is therefore $NIL.

Mr. X acquired a lot in 1975 for $7,000 and built a cottage on it in 1979 for $13,000. Mr. and Mrs. X used the cottage as a seasonal residence from 1979 to 2001 inclusive. In the fall of 2001 Mr. X sold the cottage for $65,000, resulting in an actual gain of $45,000 ($65,000 — ($7,000 + $13,000)). In filing his 2001 income tax return, Mr. X designated the cottage property as his principal residence for 1979 to 1981 inclusive, as well as for 1996 to 2001 inclusive. He could not designate the property as his principal residence for 1975 to 1978 inclusive because it was only a vacant lot and thus no one ordinarily inhabited it in those years (see ¶2.29); nor could he designate the property as his principal residence for 1982 to 1995 inclusive because of his wife's designation of the house as her principal residence for those years (see ¶ 2.13-2.14). As a result, not all of his $45,000 gain otherwise determined was eliminated by the principal residence exemption formula in ¶2.17-2.26. However, because the property had been owned by Mr. X continuously since before 1982, subsection 40(6) applied for purposes of computing his gain. The fair market value of the cottage on December 31, 1981 was $30,000.

In addition to the above facts, assume also that Mr. X did not make a subsection 110.6(19) capital gains election with respect to the cottage (see the discussion of this election in ¶2.17-2.26) because he had already used up his $100,000 lifetime capital gains exemption before 1994. Therefore, he had no capital gains election reduction amount (as described in ¶2.17-2.26) with respect to the cottage.

The calculations under subsection 40(6) in connection with Mr. X's 2001 gain on the cottage are as follows:

Usual method for calculating gain:

Gain otherwise determined is $45,000 (that is, $65,000 - $20,000)

Reduce by the principal residence exemption based on the formula **A** × **(B ÷ C)**, where:

A is $45,000

B is 1 + 9 (being tax years 1979 to 1981 and 1996 to 2001)

C is 27 (being tax years 1975 to 2001)

= $45,000 x (10 ÷ 27)

= $16,667

Gain is therefore $28,333.

Alternative method — calculation of maximum total net gain:

Maximum total net gain = pre-1982 gain + post-1981 gain - post-1981 loss

Pre-1982 gain:

Gain otherwise determined is $10,000 (that is, $30,000 - $20,000)

Reduce by the principal residence exemption based on the formula **A** × **(B ÷ C)**, where:

A is $10,000

B is 1 + 3 (being tax years 1979 to 1981)

C is 7 (being tax years 1975 to 1981)

= $10,000 x (4 ÷ 7)

= $5,714

Gain is therefore $4,286

Post-1981 gain:

Gain otherwise determined is $35,000 (that is, $65,000 - $30,000)

Reduce by the principal residence exemption based on the formula A × (B ÷ C), where:

A is $35,000

B is 6 (being tax years 1996 to 2001)

C is 20 (being tax years 1982 to 2001)

= $35,000 x (6 ÷ 20)

= $10,500

Gain is therefore $24,500

Post-1981 loss: Not applicable

Maximum total net gain = pre-1982 gain + post-1981 gain - post-1981 loss

= $4,286 + $24,500 - $Nil

= $28,786.

Result: Mr. X's gain remained at the $28,333 calculated under the usual method since that amount did not exceed the maximum total net gain of $28,786 calculated under the alternative method.

Example 2

Assume the same facts in Example 1 except that the couple is in a common-law relationship rather than a married couple.

In filing his 2001 income tax return, Mr. X designated the cottage property as his principal residence for 1979 to 1992 inclusive, as well as for 1996 to 2001 inclusive. He could not designate the property as his principal residence for 1975 to 1978 inclusive because it was only a vacant lot and thus no one ordinarily inhabited it in those years (see ¶2.29); nor could he designate the property as his principal residence for 1993 to 1995 inclusive because of his common-law partner's designation of the house as her principal residence for those years (see ¶2.13-2.14). As a result, not all of his $45,000 gain otherwise determined was eliminated by the principal residence exemption formula in ¶2.17-2.26.

The calculations under subsection 40(6) in connection with Mr. X's 2001 gain on the cottage are as follows:

Usual method for calculating gain:

Gain otherwise determined is $45,000 (that is, $65,000 - $20,000)

Reduce by the principal residence exemption based on the formula $A \times (B \div C)$, where:

A is $45,000

B is $1 + 20$ (being tax years 1979 to 1992 and 1996 to 2001)

C is 27 (being tax years 1975 to 2001)

$= \$45,000 \times (21 \div 27)$

$= \$35,000$

Gain is therefore $10,000

Alternative method - calculation of maximum total net gain:

Maximum total net gain $=$ pre-1982 gain $+$ post-1981 gain - post-1981 loss

Pre-1982 gain:

Gain otherwise determined is $10,000 (that is, $30,000 - $20,000)

Reduce by principal residence exemption based on the formula $A \times (B \div C)$, where:

A is $10,000

B is $1 + 3$ (being tax years 1979 to 1981)

C is 7 (being tax years 1975 to 1981)

$= \$10,000 \times (4 \div 7)$

$= \$5,714$

Gain is therefore $4,286

Post-1981 gain:

Gain otherwise determined is $35,000 (that is, $65,000 - $30,000)

Reduce by principal residence exemption based on the formula $A \times (B \div C)$, where:

A is $35,000

B is 17 (being tax years 1982 to 1992 and 1996 to 2001)

C is 20 (being tax years 1982 to 2001)

$= \$35,000 \times (17 \div 20)$

$= \$29,750$

Gain is therefore $5,250

Post-1981 loss: not applicable

Maximum total net gain = pre-1982 gain + post-1981 gain - post-1981 loss

$= \$4,286 + \$5,250 - \$Nil$

$= \$9,536$

Result: Although Mr. X's gain calculated under the usual method was $10,000, such gain could not exceed the maximum total net gain of $9,536 calculated under the alternative method. Therefore, the gain was reduced to $9,536.

Appendix B

Illustration of calculation of gain on disposition of a farm property

Assume that a taxpayer resident in Canada sold a 50 hectare farm. The taxpayer owned the farm and occupied the house on it from July 30, 1993 to June 15, 2001. The house and one—half hectare of the land have been designated as the taxpayer's principal residence for the 1993 to 2001 tax years inclusive. The taxpayer's calculations of the gain on the disposition of the farm property, using the two methods permitted by paragraph 40(2)(c), are as follows:

First method (see ¶2.40-2.42)

Allocate proceeds of disposition:

Proceeds of disposition	Principal Residence	Farm	Total Property
Land	$ 10,000*	$ 90,000	$ 100,000
House	$ 50,000	—	$ 50,000
Barn	—	$ 35,000	$ 35,000
Silo	—	$ 15,000	$ 15,000
Total Proceeds of disposition	**$ 60,000**	**$ 140,000**	**$ 200,000**

Allocate adjusted cost base:

Adjusted cost base	Principal Residence	Farm	Total Property
Land	$ 2,000*	$ 58,000	$ 60,000
House	20,000	—	$ 20,000
Barn	—	11,000	$ 11,000
Silo	—	4,000	$ 4,000
Total adjusted cost base	**$ 22,000**	**$ 73,000**	**$ 95,000**

Calculate gain otherwise determined:

Description	Principal Residence	Farm	Total Property
Total proceeds of disposition	$ 60,000	$ 140,000	$ 200,000
Less: Total adjusted cost base	$ 22,000	$ 73,000	$ 95,000
Gain otherwise determined	$ 38,000	$ 67,000	$ 105,000
Less: Principal residence exemption	38,000	—	38,000
Gain	$ NIL	$ 67,000	$ 67,000

* Since the principal residence portion of the land is 1/100 of the total land (that is, one—half hectare divided by 50 hectares), one way (as described in ¶2.40(a)) of assigning values to the principal residence portion of the land would be to simply use $1,000 (that is, 1/100 of $100,000) for the proceeds for such portion of the land and $600 (that is, 1/100 of $60,000) for the adjusted cost base of such portion. Assume, however, that a typical residential lot in the area, although less than one—half hectare in this example, had a fair market value of $10,000 as of the date of sale and $2,000 as of the date of acquisition. As indicated in ¶2.40(b), we would accept the taxpayer's use of the latter amounts, which in this case would result in a greater portion of the gain otherwise determined being eliminated by the principal residence exemption.

Second method (see ¶2.43-2.45)

Calculate gain otherwise determined:

Description	Amount
Proceeds of disposition for total farm property	$ 200,000
Less: Adjusted cost base for total farm property	$ 95,000
Gain otherwise determined	$ 105,000
Less: Principal residence exemption using subparagraph 40(2)(c)(ii) election: $1,000 + (9 × $1,000)	$ 10,000
Gain	$ 95,000

Result: In this example, the first method results in a lower gain to the taxpayer.

Application

This Chapter, which may be referenced as S1-F3-C2, is effective November 24, 2015 and consolidates, replaces and cancels Interpretation Bulletin IT-120R6, *Principal Residence* and Interpretation Bulletin IT-437R, *Ownership of Property (Principal Residence)*.

The history of updates to this Chapter as well as any technical updates from the cancelled interpretation bulletins can be viewed in the Chapter History page.

Except as otherwise noted, all statutory references herein are references to the provisions of the *Income Tax Act*, R.S.C., 1985, c.1 (5th Supp.), as amended and all references to a Regulation are to the *Income Tax Regulations*, C.R.C., c. 945, as amended.

Links to jurisprudence are provided through CanLII.

Income tax folios are available in electronic format only.

Reference

The definition of principal residence in section 54, and paragraphs 40(2)(*b*) and 40(2)(*c*) (also sections 54.1 and 110.6; subsections 13(7), 40(4), 40(6), 40(7), 40(7.1), 45(1), 45(2), 45(3), 45(4), 107(2), 107(2.01), 107(4), 110.6(19) and 220(3.2); paragraph 104(4)(*a*); and subparagraph 40(2)(*g*)(iii) of the Act; and Part XXIII of the Regulations.)

S5-F1-C1: Determining an Individual's Residence Status

Date: November 26, 2015

Series 5: International and Residency

Folio 1: Residency

Chapter 1: Determining an Individual's Residence Status

Summary

The purpose of this Chapter is to explain the position of the CRA concerning the determination of an individual's residence status for income tax purposes and the factors to be taken into account in making that determination.

Under the Canadian income tax system, an individual's liability for income tax is based on his or her status as a resident or a **non-resident** of Canada. An individual who is **resident** in Canada during a tax year is subject to Canadian income tax on his or her worldwide income from all sources. Generally, a **non-resident** individual is only subject to Canadian income tax on income from sources inside Canada.

An individual who is resident in Canada can be characterized as ordinarily resident or deemed resident. An individual who is ordinarily resident in Canada will be subject to Canadian tax on his or her worldwide income during the part of the year in which he or she is resident in Canada; during the other part of the year, the individual will be taxed as a non-resident. An individual who is deemed resident in Canada in a particular year will be subject to Canadian income tax on his or her worldwide income throughout that year. In certain situations, an individual who would otherwise be ordinarily resident or deemed resident in Canada may be deemed not to be resident in Canada pursuant to subsection 250(5) and the tie-breaker rules of an income tax treaty.

The factors to be considered in the determination of an individual's residence status are discussed throughout this Chapter. Many of the comments in this Chapter apply to determinations of residence status for provincial, as well as federal, tax purposes. Taxpayers seeking a less technical overview of these matters may prefer to first review Residency — Individuals on the CRA Web site.

Table of contents

o   General Overview
o   Factual residence — leaving Canada
o   Factual residence — entering Canada
o   Deemed residents of Canada-subsection 250(1)
o   Deemed non-residents — subsection 250(5)
o   How to obtain a determination of residence status

- Application
- Reference

Discussion and interpretation

General Overview

1.1 Under the Canadian income tax system, an individual's liability for income tax is based on his or her status as a **resident** or a **non-resident** of Canada. An individual who is **resident** in Canada during a tax year is subject to Canadian income tax on his or her worldwide income from all sources. Generally, a **non-resident** individual is only subject to Canadian income tax on income from sources inside Canada. An individual may be resident in Canada for only part of a year, in which case the individual will only be subject to Canadian tax on his or her worldwide income during the part of the year in which he or she is resident; during the other part of the year, the individual will be taxed as a non-resident.

Provincial residence

1.2 Many of the comments in this Chapter apply to determinations of residence status for provincial, as well as federal, tax purposes. Generally, an individual is subject to provincial tax on his or her worldwide income from all sources if the individual is **resident** in a particular province **on December 31** of the particular tax year. An individual is considered to be resident in the province where he or she has significant residential ties.

1.3 In some cases, an individual will be considered to be resident in more than one province on December 31 of a particular tax year. This situation usually arises where an individual is physically residing in a province other than the province in which the individual ordinarily resides, on December 31 of the particular tax year. For example, an individual might be away from his or her usual home for a considerable length of time on a temporary job posting or in the course of obtaining a post-secondary education. An individual who is resident in more than one province on December 31 of a particular tax year will be considered to be resident **only** in the province in which the individual has the **most** significant residential ties, for purposes of computing his or her provincial tax payable.

1.4 Taxpayers who live in Canada throughout the year requiring assistance in determining their province of residence for provincial tax purposes should contact their local Tax Services Office. Taxpayers who live outside Canada for all or part of the year who require assistance in making this determination should contact International tax and non-resident enquiries. See also Tax Alert: Working away from home? and Tax Alert: Where you live matters!

Meaning of resident

1.5 The term **resident** is not defined in the Act, however, its meaning has been considered by the Courts. The leading decision on the meaning of **resident** is Thomson v Minister of National Revenue, [1946] SCR 209, 2 DTC 812. In this decision, Rand J. of Supreme Court of Canada held **residence** to be "a matter of the degree to which a person in mind and fact settles into or maintains or centralizes his ordinary mode of living with its accessories in social relations, interests and conveniences at or in the place in question."

Meaning of ordinarily resident

1.6 In determining the residence status of an individual for purposes of the Act, it is also necessary to consider subsection 250(3), which provides that, in the Act, a reference to a person **resident** in Canada includes a person who is **ordinarily resident** in Canada. In Thomson, Estey J. held that, "one is "ordinarily resident" in the place where in the settled routine of his life he regularly, normally or customarily lives".

1.7 In the same decision, Rand J. stated that the expression **ordinarily resident** means, "residence in the course of the customary mode of life of the person concerned, and it is contrasted with special or occasional or casual residence. The general mode of life is, therefore, relevant to a question of its application." Justice Rand also went on to say that, "ordinary residence can best be appreciated by considering its antithesis, occasional or casual or deviatory residence. The latter would seem clearly to be not only temporary in time and exceptional in circumstances, but also accompanied by a sense of transitoriness and of return." The meaning given to the expressions **resident** and **ordinarily resident** as stated by the Supreme Court of Canada in Thomson, have generally been accepted by the Courts.

1.8 To determine residence status, all of the relevant facts in each case must be considered, including residential ties with Canada and length of time, object, intention and continuity with respect to stays in Canada and abroad.

1.9 An individual who is **ordinarily** resident in Canada as described in ¶1.6 - 1.7 is considered to be **factually** resident in Canada. Where an individual is determined not to be factually resident in Canada, the individual may still be **deemed** to be resident in Canada for tax purposes by virtue of subsection 250(1) (see ¶ 1.30 - 1.36). In certain situations, an individual who would otherwise be factually or deemed resident in Canada may be deemed not to be resident in Canada, pursuant to subsection 250(5) (see ¶1.37-1.39).

Factual residence — leaving Canada

Residential ties in Canada

1.10 The most important factor to be considered in determining whether an individual leaving Canada remains resident in Canada for tax purposes is whether the individual maintains residential ties with Canada while abroad. While the residence status of an individual can only be determined on a case by case basis after taking into consideration all of the relevant facts, generally, unless an individual severs all significant residential ties with Canada upon leaving Canada, the individual will continue to be a factual resident of Canada and subject to Canadian tax on his or her worldwide income.

Significant residential ties

1.11 The residential ties of an individual that will almost always be significant residential ties for the purpose of determining residence status are the individual's:

- dwelling place (or places);
- spouse or common-law partner; and
- dependants.

1.12 Where an individual who leaves Canada keeps a dwelling place in Canada (whether owned or leased), available for his or her occupation, that dwelling place will be considered to be a significant residential tie with Canada during the individual's stay abroad. However, if an individual leases a dwelling place located in Canada to a third party on arm's-length terms and conditions, the CRA will take into account all of the circumstances of the situation (including the relationship between the individual and the third party, the real estate market at the time of the individual's departure from Canada, and the purpose of the stay abroad), and may consider the dwelling place not to be a significant residential tie with Canada except when taken together with other residential ties (see ¶ 1.26 for an example of this situation and see ¶ 1.15 for a discussion of the significance of secondary residential ties).

1.13 If an individual who is married or cohabiting with a common-law partner leaves Canada, but his or her spouse or common-law partner remains in Canada, then that spouse or common-law partner will usually be a significant residential tie with Canada during the individual's absence from Canada. Similarly, if an individual with dependants leaves Canada, but his or her dependants remain behind, then those dependants will usually be considered to be a significant residential tie with Canada while the individual is abroad. Where an individual was living separate and apart from his or her spouse or common-law partner prior to leaving Canada, by reason of a breakdown of their marriage or common-law partnership, that spouse or common-law partner will not be considered to be a significant tie with Canada.

Secondary residential ties

1.14 Generally, secondary residential ties must be looked at collectively in order to evaluate the significance of any one such tie. For this reason, it would be unusual for a single secondary residential tie with Canada to be sufficient on its own to lead to a determination that an individual is factually resident in Canada while abroad. Secondary residential ties that will be taken into account in determining the residence status of an individual while outside Canada are:

- personal property in Canada (such as furniture, clothing, automobiles, and recreational vehicles);
- social ties with Canada (such as memberships in Canadian recreational or religious organizations);
- economic ties with Canada (such as employment with a Canadian employer and active involvement in a Canadian business, and Canadian bank accounts, retirement savings plans, credit cards, and securities accounts);
- landed immigrant status or appropriate work permits in Canada;
- hospitalization and medical insurance coverage from a province or territory of Canada;
- a driver's licence from a province or territory of Canada;
- a vehicle registered in a province or territory of Canada;
- a seasonal dwelling place in Canada or a leased dwelling place referred to in ¶1.12;
- a Canadian passport; and
- memberships in Canadian unions or professional organizations.

Other residential ties

1.15 Other residential ties that the Courts have considered in determining the residence status of an individual while outside Canada, and which may be taken into account by the CRA, include the retention of a Canadian mailing address, post office box, or safety deposit box, personal stationery (including business cards) showing a Canadian address, telephone listings in Canada, and local (Canadian) newspaper and magazine subscriptions. These residential ties are generally of limited importance except when taken together with other residential ties, or with other factors such as those described in ¶1.16.

Application of term ordinarily resident

1.16 Where an individual has not severed all of his or her residential ties with Canada, but is physically absent from Canada for a considerable period of time (that is, for a period of time extending over several months or years), the Courts have generally focused on the term **ordinarily resident** in determining the individual's residence status while abroad. The strong trend in decisions of the Courts on this issue is to regard temporary absence from Canada, even on an extended basis, as insufficient to avoid Canadian residence for tax purposes. Accordingly, where an individual maintains residential ties with Canada while abroad, the following factors will be taken into account in evaluating the significance of those ties:

- evidence of intention to permanently sever residential ties with Canada;
- regularity and length of visits to Canada; and
- residential ties outside Canada.

For greater certainty, the CRA does not consider that intention to return to Canada, in and of itself and in the absence of any residential ties, is a factor whose presence is sufficient to lead to a determination that an individual is resident in Canada while abroad.

Evidence of intention to permanently sever residential ties

1.17 Whether an individual intended to permanently sever residential ties with Canada at the time of his or her departure from Canada is a question of fact to be determined with regard to all of the circumstances of each case. Although length of stay abroad is one factor to be considered in making this determination (that is, as evidence of the individual's intentions upon leaving Canada), the Courts have indicated that there is no particular length of stay abroad that necessarily results in an individual becoming a non-resident. Generally, if there is evidence that an individual's return to Canada was foreseen at the time of his or her departure, the CRA will attach more significance to the individual's remaining residential ties with Canada (see ¶ 1.11 - 1.15), in determining whether the individual continued to be a factual resident of Canada subsequent to his or her departure. For example, where, at the time of an individual's departure from Canada, there exists a contract for employment in Canada if and when the individual returns to Canada, the CRA will consider this to be evidence that the individual's return to Canada was foreseen at the time of departure. However, the CRA would have to review each individual's situation on a case-by-case basis to determine whether the individual's remaining residential ties with Canada, including the contract of employment, are sufficient to conclude that the individual continues to be resident in Canada.

Steps taken to comply with the Act

1.18 Another factor that the CRA will consider in determining whether an individual intended to permanently sever all residential ties with Canada at the time of his or her departure from Canada, is whether the individual took into account and complied with the provisions of the Act dealing with the taxation of:

- individuals ceasing to be resident in Canada; and
- individuals who are not resident in Canada.

For example, upon ceasing to be resident in Canada, an individual is required to either pay, or post acceptable security for, the Canadian tax payable with respect to capital gains arising from the deemed disposition of all of the individual's property (with the exception of certain types of property that are listed in subsection 128.1(4)(*b*)). Where applicable, the CRA will look at whether this requirement has been met as an indication of the individual's intention to permanently sever his or her residential ties with Canada at the time the individual left Canada.

1.19 Similarly, the CRA will take into account whether the individual informed any Canadian residents making payments to the individual that the individual intended to become a non-resident upon leaving Canada, with the result that certain payments (including interest, dividend, rent and pension payments) made to the individual after that time might be subject to withholding tax under Part XIII. See ¶ 1.24 for more information relevant to individuals ceasing to be resident in Canada.

Regularity and length of visits to Canada

1.20 Where an individual leaves Canada and permanently severs all of his or her residential ties with Canada, the individual's residence status for tax purposes will not be affected by occasional return visits to Canada, whether for personal or business reasons. However, where such visits are more than occasional (particularly where the visits occur on a regular basis), and the individual has maintained some secondary residential ties with Canada, this factor will be taken into account in evaluating the significance of those remaining ties.

Residential ties elsewhere

1.21 Where an individual leaves Canada and purports to become a non-resident, but does not establish significant residential ties outside Canada, the individual's remaining residential ties with Canada, if any, may take on greater significance and the individual may continue to be resident in Canada. However, because the Courts have held that it is possible for an individual to be resident in more than one place at the same time for tax purposes (see ¶ 1.40 — 1.52), the fact that an individual establishes significant residential ties abroad will not, on its own, mean that the individual is no longer resident in Canada.

Date non-resident status acquired

1.22 The date upon which a Canadian resident individual leaving Canada will become a non-resident for tax purposes is a question of fact that can only be determined after reviewing all of the relevant facts and circumstances of a particular case. Generally, the CRA will consider the appropriate date to be the date on which the individual severs all residential ties with Canada, which will usually coincide with the latest of the dates on which:

- the individual leaves Canada;
- the individual's spouse or common law partner and/or dependants leave Canada (if applicable); or
- the individual becomes a resident of the country to which he or she is immigrating.

1.23 An exception to this will occur where the individual was resident in another country prior to entering Canada and is leaving to re-establish his or her residence in that country. In this case, the individual will generally become a non-resident on the date he or she leaves Canada, even if, for example, the individual's spouse or common law partner remains temporarily behind in Canada to dispose of their dwelling place in Canada or so that their dependants may complete a school year already in progress.

More information

1.24 For general tax information as well as access to useful pamphlets and guides designed specifically for individuals emigrating from Canada, see Leaving Canada (emigrants) and Guide T4058, Non-Residents and Income Tax. If you are an individual leaving Canada to travel or live abroad you may also wish to refer to Individuals - Leaving or entering Canada and non-residents. If you are a federal or provincial government employee who is posted abroad, see Government employees outside Canada.

Factual residence — entering Canada

Establishing residential ties in Canada

1.25 The residence status of an individual is always a question of fact to be determined by taking into account all of the circumstances of the individual. The most important factor in determining whether an individual entering Canada becomes resident in Canada for tax purposes is whether the individual establishes residential ties with Canada. Generally, the comments found in ¶ 1.11 - 1.15 with respect to the residential ties of individuals leaving Canada are equally applicable to individuals entering Canada. As discussed in ¶1.11, an individual's spouse or common-law partner, dependants, and dwelling place, if located in Canada, will almost always constitute significant ties with Canada. In addition, the CRA considers that where an individual entering Canada applies for and obtains landed immigrant status and provincial health coverage, these ties will usually constitute significant residential ties with Canada. Thus, except in exceptional circumstances, where landed immigrant status and provincial health coverage have been acquired, the individual will be determined to be resident in Canada.

Dwelling leased to a third party

1.26 Although a dwelling place in Canada will usually be a significant residential tie with Canada, where an individual leases such a dwelling place to a third party, the dwelling place may be considered not to be a significant residential tie with Canada except when taken together with other residential ties (see ¶ 1.14). For example, a non-resident individual might acquire a dwelling place in Canada for the purpose of residing in that dwelling place upon his or her retirement at some point in the future. If the individual were to lease the dwelling place to a third party during the period of time between acquiring the dwelling place and residing there, then, unless the individual had other residential ties to Canada, the dwelling place would not be a significant residential tie with Canada during that period of time.

1.27 Generally, a lease to a third party would have to be on arm's length terms and conditions for a dwelling place located in Canada not to be considered a significant residential tie with Canada, as discussed in ¶ 1.12. However, in certain situations, particularly where the non-resident individual acquiring the dwelling place has never previously been resident in Canada, a dwelling place that is leased on non-arm's length terms and conditions to a third party (other than the individual's spouse, common-law partner, or dependant), may be considered not to be a significant residential tie with Canada. For example, where a non-resident individual with no existing residential ties with Canada acquires a dwelling place in Canada and leases that dwelling place to his or her sibling (or to some other relative other than a spouse, common-law partner, or dependant) for a rent that is substantially lower than the fair market rental value of the property, that dwelling place will usually not be a significant residential tie to Canada for that individual.

Date resident status acquired

1.28 Where an individual enters Canada and establishes residential ties with Canada as described in ¶1.25 and 1.26, the individual will generally be considered to have become a resident of Canada for tax purposes on the date the individual entered Canada (but see ¶1.32 for comments on sojourners).

More information

1.29 For general tax information as well as access to useful pamphlets and guides designed specifically for individuals immigrating to Canada, see Newcomers to Canada (immigrants) and Pamphlet T4055, Newcomers to Canada.

Deemed residents of Canada—subsection 250(1)

Subsection 250(1)—overview

1.30 An individual who is resident in Canada on the basis of the factors discussed in ¶1.10 - 1.15 or ¶1.25 - 1.27 - that is, a factual resident of Canada — cannot be a deemed resident of Canada under subsection 250(1). Thus, subsection 250(1) does not have any application until it has been determined that the individual is not factually resident in Canada. The distinction between factual resident status and deemed resident status carries with it varying, but significant, tax consequences, due to the importance of residence status for provincial tax purposes and the possible impact of section 114 (see ¶1.32 and Interpretation Bulletin IT-262R2, Losses of Non-Residents and Part-Year Residents). Among other things, because an individual who is deemed to be resident in Canada under subsection 250(1) is not factually resident in Canada, he or she will not be resident in a particular province for provincial tax purposes (but see the discussion in ¶1.31 regarding the situation of deemed residents of Quebec).

This means that:

- the individual will be required to pay the federal surtax in accordance with subsection 120(1), which may be higher or lower than what the individual would pay as provincial tax if he or she were resident in a particular province;
- the individual will not be entitled to any provincial tax credits (refundable or otherwise) that might otherwise be available to the individual (for example, some provinces provide tax credits with respect to property taxes or rental costs associated with an individual's primary dwelling place); and
- the individual will not be entitled to any direct, tax-based, provincial benefits (for example, provincial payments in respect of dependent children or infirm family members).

1.31 An individual who resides in the province of Quebec immediately prior to leaving Canada, and who is deemed to be resident in Canada under subsection 250(1), may be deemed to be a resident of Quebec while abroad under the laws of that province. An individual who is required to pay both the Quebec provincial tax and the federal surtax may apply to the CRA for relief from the federal surtax at the time of filing his or her return.

Sojourners as deemed residents

1.32 An individual who has not established sufficient residential ties with Canada to be considered factually resident in Canada, but who sojourns (that is, is temporarily present) in Canada for a total of 183 days or more in any calendar year, is deemed to be resident in Canada for the entire year, under paragraph 250(1)(*a*). As a result, an individual who sojourns in Canada for a total of 183 days (or more) is taxed differently under the Act than an individual who is factually resident in Canada throughout the same period of time and has subsequently become a non-resident. In particular, an individual who is factually resident in Canada for part of a year is only taxed on his or her worldwide income for that part of the year, in accordance with the rules under section 114. An individual who is deemed to be resident in Canada pursuant to paragraph 250(1)(*a*) is liable for tax on his or her worldwide income throughout the year.

1.33 The CRA considers any part of a day to be a **day** for the purpose of determining the number of days that an individual has sojourned in Canada in a calendar year. However, it is a question of fact whether an individual who is not resident in Canada is **sojourning** in Canada. An individual is not automatically considered to be sojourning in Canada for every day (or part day) that the individual is present in Canada; the nature of each particular stay must be determined separately. To sojourn means to make a temporary stay in the sense of establishing a temporary residence, although the stay may be of very short duration. For example, if an individual is commuting to Canada for his or her employment and returning each night to his or her normal place of residence outside of Canada, the individual is not sojourning in Canada. On the other hand, if the same individual were to vacation in Canada, then he or she would be sojourning in Canada and each day (or part day) of that particular time period (the length of the vacation) would be counted in determining the application of paragraph 250(1)(*a*). In distinguishing a **commuter** from a **sojourner**, relevance should be placed on the country in which an individual spends his or her time away from work. In other words, an individual who comes to Canada for work purposes may nevertheless be considered sojourning in Canada if that individual does not leave the country to spend his or her time away from work.

Other deemed residents

1.34 In addition to individuals sojourning in Canada for a total of 183 days (or more) in any calendar year (see ¶1.32 and 1.33), subsection 250(1) ensures that any individual (other than a factual resident of Canada) who is included in any one of the following categories, is deemed to be a resident of Canada:

a) individuals who were members of the Canadian Forces at any time in the year;

b) individuals who were officers or servants of Canada or a province, at any time in the year, who received representation allowances or who were factually or deemed resident in Canada **immediately prior to appointment or employment** (see ¶1.35) by Canada or the province;

c) individuals who performed services, at any time in the year, outside Canada under an international development assistance program of the Canadian International Development Agency described in section 3400 of the Regulations, provided they were either factually or deemed resident in Canada at any time in the three month period prior to the day the services commenced;

d) individuals who were, at any time in the year, members of the overseas Canadian Forces school staff who have filed their returns for the year on the basis that they were resident in Canada throughout the period during which they were such members;

e) individuals who were at any time in the year a child of, and dependent for support on, an individual described in (a) to (d), and whose income for the year did not exceed the basic personal amount for the year; and

f) individuals who at any time in the year were, under an agreement or a convention (including a tax treaty) between Canada and another country, entitled to an exemption from an income tax that would otherwise be payable in that other country in respect of income from any source, and:

    i) the exemption under the agreement or convention applies to all or substantially all of their income from all sources (that is, they are subject to tax in the other country on less than 10% of their income as a result of the exemption); and

    ii) the individuals were entitled to the exemption because they were related to, or a member of the family of, an individual (other than a trust) who was resident (including deemed resident) in Canada at the particular time.

1.35 For purposes of (b) above, it is the CRA's position that the phrase **immediately prior to appointment or employment** refers to the time immediately prior to the time at which the individual is hired. For greater certainty, it does not refer to the time immediately prior to the time the individual starts work.

1.36 An individual who is not factually resident in Canada, but who is referred to in (a) to (f) of ¶1.34, is deemed to be resident in Canada regardless of where that individual lives or performs services. An individual who ceases to be described in (a) to (e) of ¶1.34 at a particular date in the year will be deemed to be resident in Canada only to that date, pursuant to subsection 250(2). Thereafter, residence will depend on the factors outlined in ¶ 1.10 - 1.21.

Deemed non-residents — subsection 250(5)

Application of subsection 250(5)

1.37 Pursuant to subsection 250(5), an individual will be deemed to be a non-resident of Canada at a particular time if, at that time, although otherwise resident in Canada (either factual or deemed), the individual is considered to be resident in another country under an income tax treaty between Canada and that other country. In other words, subsection 250(5) will apply if the tie-breaker rules in a tax treaty between Canada and another country result in a determination that the individual is resident in the other country.

1.38 Where subsection 250(5) applies, an individual will be deemed to be a non-resident of Canada for all purposes of the Act (that is, the individual will cease to be a resident of Canada from that time). The rules applicable to individuals ceasing to be resident in Canada, including the provisions deeming an individual to dispose of certain property and the Part XIII withholding tax provisions, will apply from that date (see ¶1.39 for further information). Prior to a legislative amendment effective as of February 24, 1998, subsection 250(5) applied only to corporations. Accordingly, subsection 250(5) does not apply to an individual who was resident in another country for treaty purposes, but otherwise resident in Canada, on February 24, 1998, as long as the individual has maintained this **dual** residence status continuously since that time.

More information

1.39 For general tax information relevant to non-residents and deemed non-residents of Canada, see Guide T4058, Non-Residents and Income Tax. For information concerning the tax implications for individuals ceasing to be resident in Canada, refer to Leaving Canada (emigrants).

The tie-breaker rules in tax treaties

1.40 An individual who is a resident of Canada for purposes of the Act is also considered a resident of Canada for purposes of paragraph 1 of the **Residence article** of an income tax treaty between Canada and another country. In some treaties, it is referred to as the Resident, Fiscal Domicile or Fiscal Residence article. Such an individual may also be a resident of the other country for purposes of the same paragraph in the same treaty (a **dual** resident). Whether an individual is considered resident in a country for purposes of paragraph 1 of the Residence article of a particular tax treaty between Canada and another country generally depends on whether the individual is **liable to tax** in that country within the meaning of the particular treaty.

Meaning of liable to tax

1.41 It has been the long-standing position of the CRA that, to be considered **liable to tax** for the purposes of the Residence article of Canada's tax treaties, an individual must be subject to the most comprehensive form of taxation as exists in the relevant country. For Canada, this generally means full tax liability on worldwide income. This is supported by the comments of the Supreme Court of Canada in *The Queen v Crown Forest Industries Limited*, [1995] 2 SCR 802, 95 DTC 5389, wherein the court stated:

> "the criteria for determining residence in Article IV, paragraph 1 involve more than simply being liable to taxation on some portion of income (source liability); they entail being subject to as comprehensive a tax liability as is imposed by a state. In the United States and Canada, such comprehensive taxation is taxation on world-wide income."

1.42 An individual does not necessarily have to pay tax to another country in order to be considered **liable to tax** in that country under paragraph 1 of the Residence article of the tax treaty with Canada. There may be situations where an individual's worldwide income is subject to another country's full taxing jurisdiction, however, the country's domestic laws do not levy tax on an individual's taxable income or taxes it at low rates. In these cases, the CRA will generally accept that an individual is a resident of the other country unless the arrangement is abusive (for example, treaty shopping where the individual is in fact only a **resident of convenience**). Such could be the case, for example, where an individual is placed within the taxing jurisdiction of a particular country in order to gain treaty benefits in a manner that does not create any material economic nexus to that country.

1.43 For purposes of paragraph 1 of the Residence article of a particular tax treaty, the onus rests on an individual to demonstrate that he or she is liable to tax in the other country. The CRA is entitled to rely on the assumption that an individual is not resident in the other country for purposes of the treaty unless the individual can establish otherwise. This position is based on the Supreme Court of Canada's decision in *Johnston v MNR*, [1948] SCR 486, 3 DTC 1182. It is also supported by *McFadyen v The Queen*, [2000] TCJ No. 589, 2000 DTC 2473, which was heard at the Tax Court of Canada and later affirmed by the Federal Court of Appeal (2002 FCA 496, 2003 DTC 5015).

1.44 The Courts have stated that holders of a United States Permanent Residence Card (otherwise referred to as a **Green Card**) are considered to be resident in the United States for purposes of paragraph 1 of the Residence article of the Canada-U.S. Tax Convention. For further information, see the Federal Court of Appeal's comments in *Allchin v R*, 2004 FCA 206, 2004 DTC 6468.

1.45 Where an individual is determined to be a dual resident, the Residence article in the tax treaty will provide **tie-breaker rules** to determine in which country the individual will be resident for purposes of the other provisions of the treaty. If such tie-breaker rules apply and it is determined that an individual is a resident of another country for purposes of a tax treaty between Canada and that country, then subsection 250(5) will deem the individual to be a non-resident of Canada for purposes of the Act (see ¶ 1.37 - 1.39).

Permanent home test

1.46 Tie-breaker rules are found in paragraph 2 of the Residence article of most of Canada's income tax treaties. Usually, these rules rely first on a **permanent home** test to resolve the residence issue. Generally, the **permanent home** test provides that an individual is resident for purposes of the treaty in the country in which the individual has a permanent home available to him or her. A **permanent home** (as that term is used in income tax treaties) may be any kind of dwelling place that the individual retains for his or her permanent (as opposed to occasional) use, whether that dwelling place is rented (including a rented furnished room) or purchased or otherwise occupied on a permanent basis. It is the permanence of the home, rather than its size or the nature of ownership or tenancy, that is of relevance.

1.47 For further guidance on the application of the **permanent home test**, the Courts have referred to the commentary to paragraph 2 of the Residence article of the Organization for Economic Cooperation and Development Model Tax Convention on Income and on Capital, July 2010. The OECD Model Tax Convention states in part, as follows:

> ". . .the permanence of the home is essential; this means that the individual has arranged to have the dwelling available to him at all times continuously, and not occasionally for the purpose of a stay which, owing to the reasons for it, is necessarily of short duration (travel for pleasure, business travel, educational travel, attending a course at a school, etc)."

1.48 In applying the **tie-breaker rules** (see ¶ 1.40 - 1.45), a dual resident individual who is determined to have a permanent home available to him or her in only one country, will be deemed to be a resident of that country for purposes of the treaty. In such cases, it is not necessary to apply the centre of vital interests test outlined in ¶1.50 - 1.51.

1.49 Where an individual has two permanent homes while living outside Canada (for example, a dwelling place rented by the individual abroad and a property owned by the individual in Canada that continues to be available for his or her use, such as a home that is not leased to a third party on arm's length terms and conditions as described in ¶1.12) the permanent home test will not result in a residency determination. Where this is the case, the tie-breaker rules of most treaties then refer to a centre of vital interests test.

Centre of vital interests test

1.50 The **centre of vital interests** test requires a close examination of the individual's personal and economic ties with each country in question, in order to determine with which country those ties are closer. The personal and economic ties to be examined are similar to those used in determining factual residence for purposes of Canadian income tax (see especially ¶ 1.10 - 1.15). For further guidance on the application of the **centre of vital interests** test, the Courts have referred to the commentary to paragraph 2 of the Residence article of the OECD Model Tax Convention, which states in part, as follows:

> "If the individual has a permanent home in both Contracting States, it is necessary to look at the facts in order to ascertain with which of the two States his personal and economic relations are closer. Thus, regard will be had to his family and social relations, his occupations, his political, cultural or other activities, his place of business, the place from which he administers his property, etc. The circumstances must be examined as a whole, but it is nevertheless obvious that considerations based on the personal acts of the individual must receive special attention. If a person who has a home in one State sets up a second in the other State while retaining the first, the fact that he retains the first in the environment where he has always lived, where he has worked, and where he has his family and possessions, can, together with other elements, go to demonstrate that he has retained his centre of vital interests in the first State."

There are other tests that will apply if the **centre of vital interests** test is inconclusive and these will generally be outlined in the Residence article of the applicable tax treaty.

1.51 As confirmed by the Supreme Court of Canada in Crown Forest Industries, reviewing the intention of the parties to a tax treaty is a very important element in delineating the scope of the application of the treaty. Accordingly, the determination of residency for the purposes of a tax treaty remains a question of fact, and each case should be decided on its own facts with an eye to the intention of the parties of the particular convention and the purpose of international tax treaties.

More information

1.52 For more information concerning Canada's tax treaties with other countries, see the Tax Treaties page of the CRA Web site.

How to obtain a determination of residence status

International Tax Services Office

1.53 Taxpayers requiring further general information about how residence status is determined for purposes of Canadian income tax should contact International tax and non-resident enquiries at 1-855-284-5942 (toll free in Canada and the United States), or 613-940-8495 (for service in English), or 613-940-8496 (for service in French). Written enquiries should be addressed to:

> International Tax Services Office
> Post Office Box 9769, Station T
> Ottawa ON K1G 3Y4
> CANADA

1.54 Taxpayers who plan to leave or have left Canada, either permanently or temporarily, should consider completing Form NR73, Determination of Residency Status (Leaving Canada) and reviewing the information referred to in ¶ 1.24. Taxpayers who have entered or sojourned in Canada during the year should consider completing Form NR74, Determination of Residency Status (Entering Canada) and reviewing the information referred to in ¶ 1.29.

1.55 Once completed, Form NR73 or NR74, as applicable, should be mailed to the address given above or faxed to 613-941-2505. In most cases, the CRA will be able to provide an opinion regarding a taxpayer's residence status from the information recorded on the completed form. This opinion is based entirely on the facts provided by the taxpayer to the CRA in Form NR73 or NR74, as applicable. Therefore, it is critical that the taxpayer provide all of the details concerning his or her residential ties with Canada and abroad. This opinion is not binding on the CRA and may be subject to a more detailed review at a later date and supporting documentation may be required at that time.

Income Tax Rulings Directorate

1.56 Where certainty is required in respect of the tax consequences of the proposed departure from or arrival in Canada of a particular individual taxpayer, the Income Tax Rulings Directorate may, in appropriate circumstances, be prepared to issue a binding advance income tax ruling with respect to the residency status of that taxpayer. Generally, such a ruling will only be available where all of the facts of the situation can be ascertained in advance of the proposed departure from or arrival in Canada of the taxpayer. For detailed information regarding applying for an advance income tax ruling, please see the current version of Information Circular IC 70-6R5, Advance Income Tax Rulings or see Income tax rulings and interpretations.

Competent Authority Services

1.57 In limited situations it may be necessary for an individual to request the assistance of Competent Authority Services in order to resolve residency issues with treaty countries. To obtain more information, please refer to the current version of Information Circular IC 71-17R5, Guidance on Competent Authority Assistance Under Canada's Tax Conventions.

Application

This Chapter, which may be referenced as S5-F1-C1, is effective November 26, 2015 and replaces and cancels Interpretation Bulletin IT-221R3, *Determination of an Individual's Residence Status.*

The history of updates to this Chapter as well as any technical updates from the cancelled interpretation bulletin can be viewed in the Chapter History page.

Except as otherwise noted, all statutory references herein are references to the provisions of the *Income Tax Act* R.S.C., 1985, c.1 (5th Supp.), as amended and all references to a Regulation are to the *Income Tax Regulations*, C.R.C., c. 945, as amended.

Links to jurisprudence are provided through CanLII.

Income tax folios are available in electronic format only.

Reference

Sections 2 and 250 (also sections 114, 115, 128.1 and 212 of the Act and section 2607 of the Regulations).

S5-F2-C1: Foreign Tax Credit

Date: December 1, 2015

Series 5: International and Residency

Folio 2: Foreign Tax Credits and Deductions

Chapter 1: Foreign Tax Credit

Summary

Section 126 of the Act makes a foreign tax credit available to a taxpayer who at any time in a year is a resident of Canada, or in certain limited circumstances is a former resident of Canada. References in this chapter to a **year** include a **taxation year** as defined by section 249. A foreign tax credit is a deduction from the taxpayer's Canadian tax otherwise payable that may be claimed in respect of foreign **income or profits tax** paid by the taxpayer for the year. A foreign tax credit can provide a taxpayer with relief from double taxation on certain income, that is, relief from having to otherwise pay full tax to both Canada and another country on that income. In calculating the amount of a foreign tax credit, the taxpayer must determine the particular countries to which their income, gains, and losses should be allocated.

The taxpayer must make separate foreign tax credit calculations for:

- foreign non-business-income tax; and
- foreign business-income tax.

Furthermore, within each of these categories, a separate foreign tax credit calculation is required for each foreign country a taxpayer has paid an **income or profits tax**.

The maximum amount of each foreign tax credit that the taxpayer may claim with respect to either foreign non-business-income tax or business-income tax is essentially equal to the lesser of two amounts:

- the applicable foreign income or profits tax paid for the year; and
- the amount of Canadian tax otherwise payable for the year that pertains to the applicable foreign income.

A further limitation, which occurs only in the calculation of a foreign tax credit for foreign business-income tax, ensures that the taxpayer's foreign tax credit claims for the year concerning foreign non-business-income taxes are deducted first. This ordering rule is designed to allow the taxpayer to maximize foreign tax credit claims over the years, taking into account a rule that only the portion of foreign business-income taxes that is not deductible as a foreign tax credit for the year can be carried over for purposes of a foreign tax credit in other years.

This chapter does not describe the complete details of the foreign tax credit provisions, as the main purpose of the chapter is to give interpretations with respect to some of the most commonly encountered requirements contained in these provisions. For the full details of the provisions referred to in this chapter, please refer to the Act.

This chapter also briefly refers to the following:

- the special foreign tax credit that can apply if the taxpayer is subject to the minimum tax;
- a provision which, if needed, can enable a corporation to maximize its foreign tax credits for the year by means of an elected addition to taxable income for the year, with a corresponding amount of non-capital loss being created for use in other years;
- the deferral of taxation in Canada, in certain situations, in order to provide relief from double taxation that could otherwise occur if Canada taxed the income resulting from a particular transaction in the year it occurs while another country defers its taxation with respect to that transaction; and
- the no economic profit and short-term security acquisitions rules in the foreign tax credit provisions.

It should be noted that the primary subject of this chapter is the foreign tax credit provisions in Canada's domestic income tax law. Although it contains comments regarding certain provisions in tax treaties between Canada and other countries, this chapter does not purport to deal with all treaty provisions that could apply.

The following topics are also outside the scope of this chapter:

- modifications to the foreign tax credit rules that apply to authorized foreign banks
- modifications to the foreign tax credit rules that apply to resource companies

Table of contents

- Discussion and interpretation
  - o General overview
  - o Abbreviations and definitions used
  - o Foreign income or profits tax
  - o Business-income tax
  - o Non-business-income tax

- o No economic profit and short-term securities acquisitions
- o Amount paid by the taxpayer for the year
- o Foreign business income
- o Foreign non-business income
- o Determination of the location of a source of income
- o Tax-exempt income
- o TFSAs and RRSPs
- o Minimum tax
- o Tax sparing
- o The foreign tax credit formula
- o Calculation of the amount of net income from sources in a foreign country
- o Addition to taxable income to prevent reduction to foreign tax credit
- o Relief from double tax by taxing on a deferred basis
- o Carryforward and carryback

- • Application
- • Reference

Discussion and interpretation

General overview

1.1 Residents of Canada are generally taxed on their worldwide income. For many, this includes income earned from business, property, or employment in another country. In most cases, income earned abroad will be subject to taxes in the jurisdiction where it is earned. To ensure that foreign income is not subject to double taxation, the foreign tax credit provisions found in section 126 of the Act provide for a method whereby the income taxes paid to a foreign jurisdiction offset Canadian income tax otherwise payable.

1.2 The foreign tax credit available under section 126 of the Act can operate either in conjunction with or independently of tax treaties, which also reduce double taxation. Where foreign taxes have been paid to a jurisdiction that has a tax treaty with Canada, special attention must be paid to that treaty as it may affect how section 126 applies.

1.3 Before determining the amount of foreign tax credit available to a taxpayer, consideration must be given to the type of income earned. This is because there are two types of foreign tax credit available under section 126: a foreign tax credit for foreign **business-income** taxes and a foreign tax credit for foreign **non-business income** taxes. Additionally, the foreign tax credit is calculated on a country-by-country basis which requires taxpayers to categorize their income based on where the income was earned as well as how it was earned. Another consideration that must be taken into account before calculating the amount of the foreign tax credit available is the nature of the foreign taxes paid. Once a taxpayer's income for a year has been properly categorized, calculated, attributed to the relevant countries where it was earned, and the foreign taxes examined for eligibility, this information may be used to apply for a foreign tax credit when filing a tax return for the year.

Abbreviations and definitions used

1.4 The following abbreviations and definitions are used in this Chapter:

BIT — **Business-income tax** as defined in subsection 126(7).

CTOP(a) — Canadian tax otherwise payable as calculated under paragraph (*a*) of the subsection 126(7) definition of the term **tax for the year otherwise payable under this Part**.

CTOP(b) — Canadian tax otherwise payable as calculated under paragraph (*b*) of the subsection 126(7) definition of the term **tax for the year otherwise payable under this Part**.

CTOP(c) — Canadian tax otherwise payable as calculated under paragraph (*c*) of the subsection 126(7) definition of the term **tax for the year otherwise payable under this Part**.

CTOP(FBI) — Canadian tax otherwise payable that pertains to the foreign business income from a particular foreign business country.

CTOP(FNBI) — Canadian tax otherwise payable that pertains to the foreign non-business income from a particular country

FBI — Foreign business income. This is the taxpayer's total income for the year from **businesses carried on in** the foreign business country by the taxpayer as calculated in accordance with subparagraph 126(2.1)(*a*)(i).

FNBI — Foreign non-business income. This is the total of the taxpayer's foreign non-business income for the year from sources in a particular foreign country as determined by the amount by which their qualifying income exceeds their qualifying losses as outlined in subsection 126(9) and adjusted in accordance with subparagraph 126(1)(*b*)(i).

FTP — Foreign tax paid.

FTP(BIT) — Foreign tax paid for the year but restricted to business-income tax as defined in subsection 126(7). More specifically, it is such part as the taxpayer may claim of the total business-income tax paid by the taxpayer for the year in respect of businesses carried on by the taxpayer in the particular foreign business country, plus the taxpayer's eligible unused foreign tax credits in respect of the particular foreign business country.

FTP(NBIT) — Foreign tax paid, but restricted to non-business-income tax as defined in subsection 126(7). More specifically, it is such part as the taxpayer may claim of any non-business-income tax paid by the taxpayer for the year to the particular foreign country excluding any tax that may be reasonably regarded as having been paid by a corporate taxpayer in respect of income from the share of capital stock of a foreign affiliate of the taxpayer.

Foreign business country — Any particular country other than Canada in which the taxpayer carries on business.

NBIT — Non-business-income tax as defined in subsection 126(7).

SFTC — Special foreign tax credit as defined in subsection 127.54(2). This is a deduction available to individuals subject to minimum tax under section 127.5 and who may not claim a foreign tax credit under section 126.

UFTC — Unused foreign tax credit as defined in subsection 126(7).

WI — Worldwide income for the year.

WI(1) — Worldwide income for the year as adjusted by subparagraph 126(1)(*b*) (ii).

WI(2) — Worldwide income for the year as adjusted by subparagraph 126(2.1)(*a*) (ii).

Foreign income or profits tax

1.5 In order to qualify for the purposes of a foreign tax credit, an amount paid to a foreign jurisdiction must be a tax, not any other type of payment that might be made to the foreign jurisdiction. In general terms, a **tax** is a levy of general application for public purposes enforceable by a governmental authority. A levy imposed by a governmental authority will not be considered a tax if it is a charge meant to recoup the costs for services directly rendered or to finance a specific regulatory scheme. Examples of payments to governmental authorities that do not qualify as payments of a tax include the following:

- user fees
- regulatory charges payments made to acquire a specific right or privilege
- voluntary contributions to governmental authorities

1.6 To qualify for foreign tax credit purposes, a payment of tax:

- must be made to the government of a foreign country or to the government of a state, province or other political subdivision of a foreign country;
- cannot be conditional on the availability of a foreign tax credit in Canada, or a deduction in respect of a dividend received from a foreign affiliate under section 113; and
- must be an **income or profits tax**.

1.7 In determining whether a particular foreign tax qualifies as an **income or profits tax**, the name given to the tax by the foreign jurisdiction is not the deciding factor. Rather, the basic scheme of application of the foreign tax is compared with the scheme of application of the income and profits taxes imposed under the Act. Generally, if the basis of taxation is substantially similar, the foreign tax is accepted as an income or profits tax. To be substantially similar, the foreign tax must be levied on net income or profits (but not necessarily as would be computed for Canadian tax purposes) unless it is a tax similar to that imposed under Part XIII of the Act. Since taxable capital gains are included in a taxpayer's income for Canadian income tax purposes, a foreign tax on what would be considered a capital gain under the Act is also considered to be an income or profits tax for the purposes of section 126.

1.8 If a particular tax imposed by a foreign country is specifically identified, in an elimination of double tax article of an income tax treaty between Canada and that country, as a tax for which Canada must grant a deduction from Canadian taxes on profits, income or gains which arose in that other country and which gave rise to the foreign tax in question, the foreign tax will qualify as an income or profits tax when applying section 126 in conjunction with that treaty article. (See, for example, the United States taxes referred to in paragraph 2(*a*) of Article XXIV of the Canada-United States Income Tax Convention, as amended by the protocols to that convention.)

1.9 Examples of taxes that are **not** levied on net income or profits, and therefore generally will **not** qualify for a foreign tax credit under section 126 include the following:

- resource royalties
- sales, commodity, consumption, or turnover taxes
- succession duties or inheritance taxes
- property or real estate taxes
- customs or import duties
- excise taxes or duties
- gift taxes
- capital or wealth taxes
- documentary or stamp taxes

Despite not qualifying as income or profits taxes, some treaties may specifically provide for a deduction in respect of such foreign taxes paid from Canadian taxes otherwise payable independently of section 126. (See, for example, paragraph 6 of Article XXIX B of the Canada-United States Income Tax Convention, which addresses certain taxes imposed by reason of death.)

1.10 A unitary tax of a state of the United States cannot be regarded as an income or profits tax if it is not computed on the basis of net business income. The following are instances where a unitary tax does not qualify as an income or profits tax:

- The tax represents an annual minimum franchise tax.
- The tax is applicable even when there is no income.
- The calculation of the tax does not attempt to allocate income to the particular state.
- The tax is in the nature of a capital tax.

1.11 A decision as to whether a particular state's unitary tax can be regarded as an income or profits tax for purposes of claiming a foreign tax credit can be made only after a review of the applicable state legislation. (See also the comments regarding a unitary tax in ¶1.18 and 1.38.) A unitary tax that does not qualify as an income or profits tax for purposes of claiming a foreign tax credit would likely be deductible in computing the taxpayer's income pursuant to subsection 9(1) as an expense for the purpose of earning income.

1.12 Where it is clear that an amount of tax has been paid to a foreign governmental authority, a foreign tax levy based on net income as calculated under a prescribed formula is considered to be an income or profits tax if the following conditions are met:

- it can be considered that the formula produces a reasonable approximation of actual net income in typical situations; and
- an attempt to compute actual net income would be significantly affected by arbitrary or estimated expense allocations.

1.12.1 In addition, a foreign tax levied on gross revenue is considered to be an income or profits tax if, after a review of the applicable legislation, it is determined that the tax on gross revenue is part of a comprehensive income tax regime and is tightly linked and subordinate to what would otherwise be accepted as an income or profits tax.

The following factors would be considered when determining whether a particular foreign tax on gross revenue is part of a comprehensive income tax regime and is tightly linked and subordinate to what would otherwise be accepted as an income or profits tax:

- The contextual relationship of the taxes. For example, a single statute containing an option between a tax on gross revenue and a tax on net income may demonstrate that such a tax on gross revenue is part of a comprehensive income tax regime. Furthermore, the ability to elect annually, under a single statute, between a tax on gross revenue and a tax on net income may demonstrate that such a tax on gross revenue is tightly linked to what would otherwise be accepted as an income or profits tax.
- The interaction of their provisions. For example, the elective nature of an annual choice between a tax on gross revenue and a tax on net income, which effectively results in the tax on gross revenue option being capped at what would otherwise be the amount of tax had the taxpayer's tax liability been computed under the tax on net income option, may demonstrate that such a tax on gross revenue is subordinate to what would otherwise be accepted as an income or profits tax. However, if the rate of tax on the tax on net income option is so unreasonably high that it effectively removes the elective nature of a taxpayer's choice to be taxed on gross revenue, such a tax on gross revenue would not be considered to be subordinate to what would otherwise be accepted as an income or profits tax. Moreover, if the ability to elect out of a tax on gross revenue option is irrevocable, such a tax on gross revenue would not be considered to be subordinate to what would otherwise be accepted as an income or profits tax.

When, based on the factors noted above, a particular foreign tax levied on gross revenue is determined to be part of a comprehensive income tax regime and is tightly linked and subordinate to what would otherwise be accepted as an income or profits tax, it is the CRA's view that such a tax on gross revenue would be indirectly determined by reference to a taxpayer's income or profits and, therefore, qualifies as an income or profits tax for the purposes of the Act.

1.13 It should also be noted that an amount which by nature is not an income or profits tax can nevertheless be deemed to have been paid as an income or profits tax to a foreign jurisdiction. For example, see subsection 126(5), which (in conjunction with related definitions and provisions in the Act), deems certain foreign oil and gas levies to have been paid as an income or profits tax to a foreign jurisdiction.

1.14 Once it is established that the amount paid to the foreign jurisdiction is an income or profits tax, the next step is to determine if the tax paid was in regard to business income or non-business income.

Business-income tax

1.15 An income or profits tax paid by the taxpayer to a foreign jurisdiction will generally (subject to the no economic profit and short-term security acquisitions rules discussed at ¶1.29) qualify as business-income tax with respect to the foreign business country to the extent that it is a tax:

- that can reasonably be regarded as being in respect of income from any business carried on by the taxpayer in that country; and
- paid to any foreign jurisdiction.

1.16 Note from the above that the foreign country containing the jurisdiction to which the tax is paid and the foreign business country (that is, the country in respect of which the foreign tax credit is claimed) do not have to be the same country. For example, a Canadian corporation that carries on business in a second country through a permanent establishment from which it earns income from the rental of industrial equipment to a business in a third country and the third country imposes a tax on the rental income.

1.17 A foreign income or profits tax is recognized as BIT **only** to the extent that it pertains to income from a business carried on outside Canada. Whether (or the extent to which) the taxpayer is carrying on a business in or outside Canada is essentially a question of fact to be determined in each particular case. For purposes of deciding this question, consideration should be given to any relevant case law. For the purposes of determining where a business is carried on, see the guidelines starting at ¶ 1.53.

1.18 It may be possible for a unitary tax of a state of the United States to qualify as BIT if it is an income or profits tax (see ¶ 1.5—1.13) that is computed on a Canadian corporation's net business income from carrying on a business in that state. However, in a case where the Canadian corporation would not be liable for the unitary tax on its sales in the particular state if it were not for the activities of its U.S. affiliate or affiliates in that state, it would be arguable that the tax is in respect of the Canadian corporation's investment in its U.S. affiliates rather than in respect of income from any business carried on by the Canadian corporation in the United States, in such a case the tax would not qualify as BIT. See also the comments regarding a unitary tax starting at ¶ 1.10 and also at ¶ 1.38.

1.19 Some taxes that would otherwise qualify as BIT are specifically excluded from the definition. One of these exclusions is any tax that may reasonably be regarded as relating to an amount received or receivable by any other person or partnership from the foreign jurisdiction to which the tax is paid. This excluded tax may qualify, however, as non-business-income tax for the purpose of a subsection 20(12) deduction (but not a NBIT for foreign tax credit purposes) — for further comments, see ¶ 1.25.

Non-business-income tax

1.20 For the purpose of claiming a foreign tax credit, any amount of income or profits tax (subject to the exclusions discussed in ¶ 1.29) paid by a taxpayer to a foreign jurisdiction is included in the taxpayer's non-business-income tax, as defined in subsection 126(7), with respect to the country in which that jurisdiction is located, as long as the amount is not specifically excluded from the definition. The following paragraphs discuss some of these exclusions.

1.21 Any tax (or portion of the tax) that qualifies under subsection 126(7) as business-income tax is not considered to be a NBIT (see ¶ 1.15-1.19). On the other hand, a foreign income or profits tax (or portion of the tax) that might otherwise be considered to be business-related but that does not qualify as BIT is not excluded from the definition, and may therefore be considered a NBIT. Examples of the latter are given in ¶ 1.27.

1.22 NBIT cannot include any portion of a foreign income or profits tax that is deductible under subsection 20(11). This exclusion, which is provided for in paragraph (*b*) of the NBIT definition, applies regardless of whether or not the amount qualifying for deduction under subsection 20(11) is actually deducted by the taxpayer when reporting income (for detailed information on subsection 20(11) deductions see Interpretation Bulletin IT-506, Foreign income taxes as a deduction from income). It should be noted that only foreign income or profits tax paid by an individual (which includes a trust) in respect of foreign-source income from a property, other than real or immovable property, which is in excess of 15% of such income as calculated under the Act (that is, the gross income under the Act, not the income net of foreign taxes), is deductible under subsection 20(11). This means that for the purposes of claiming a foreign tax credit, NBIT can include (subject to the other applicable rules in section 126) the following:

- in the case of an individual (which includes a trust):
  - o foreign income or profits tax in respect of foreign-source income from property, other than real or immovable property, up to an amount which does not exceed 15% of such income as calculated under the Act (that is, the gross income under the Act, not the income net of foreign taxes); and
  - o all foreign income or profits tax in respect of foreign-source income from the disposition or rental of real or immovable property; and
- in the case of any other taxpayer, all foreign income or profits tax in respect of foreign-source income from any property (only individuals, which includes trusts, are subject to the above-mentioned 15% limitation).

1.23 For purposes of claiming a foreign tax credit, NBIT cannot include any amount that is deducted under subsection 20(12). This exclusion is provided for in paragraph (*c*) of the definition of NBIT and reflects the fact that an amount that qualifies as NBIT can be used either for purposes of a subsection 126(1) foreign tax credit or for the purposes of claiming a deduction from income under subsection 20(12). The following should be noted:

- The taxpayer must first calculate income, taking into account any amounts **deducted** under subsection 20(11) (see ¶1.22) and subsection 20(12). These deductions may in fact result in nil income.
- If an amount of income does exist, the taxpayer then determines whether there is any taxable income. (See the comments at ¶ 1.93 regarding the addition of an amount in computing taxable income as permitted by section 110.5.)
- If there is an amount of taxable income, the taxpayer then determines CTOP(a), which will be used in the calculation of CTOP(FNBI) (see ¶ 1.74).
- Finally, the taxpayer determines the amount of foreign tax credits to be claimed. For this purpose, paragraph (*c*) of its definition requires that any amount deducted under subsection 20(12) be excluded from NBIT. Thus, for the purpose of calculating the amount of a foreign tax credit under section 126(1), any amount deducted under subsection 20(12) is excluded from FTP(NBIT). Also, the amounts, if any, deducted under subsections 20(11) and 20(12):
  o reduce the amount calculated for FNBI in the foreign tax credit formula (for further particulars, see ¶ 1.80-1.82); and
  o have an effect on other variables in ¶1.74-1.77.

1.24 If CTOP(FNBI) is less than FTP(NBIT), it is not possible to claim the full amount of FTP(NBIT) as a subsection 126(1) foreign tax credit. This could occur because either CTOP(a) or FNBI is too low. (A situation where FNBI could be nil—even though foreign tax has been paid—is described in ¶ 1.48.) Furthermore, any portion of FTP(NBIT) for a particular tax year that cannot be, or is not, claimed as a subsection 126(1) foreign tax credit for the tax year, cannot be carried over and claimed as a foreign tax credit for another year. If an amount of what would otherwise qualify as NBIT for purposes of a foreign tax credit cannot be claimed as such, and dollar-for-dollar tax relief through a reduction to Canadian tax otherwise payable is not obtained, subsection 20(12) provides relief through a deduction in computing income.

1.25 NBIT for foreign tax credit purposes cannot include any foreign income or profits tax (or portion of the tax) paid by the taxpayer that may reasonably be regarded as relating to an amount that any other person or partnership has received, or is entitled to receive, from the foreign jurisdiction to which the tax was paid. For example, if a foreign country's tax is withheld on income from property paid to a taxpayer resident in Canada, but a portion of the tax is refunded or refundable to the foreign payer of the income, such portion of the tax is excluded from the taxpayer's FTP(NBIT) when calculating the amount of foreign tax credit available (see ¶1.74). However, such portion of the tax may qualify for inclusion in the taxpayer's NBIT for the purpose of a subsection 20(12) deduction.

1.26 If an individual claims an overseas employment tax credit under subsection 122.3(1), the individual's NBIT cannot include any foreign income tax (or portion of the tax) that may reasonably be regarded as attributable to the taxpayer's income from employment to the extent of the lesser of the amounts determined under paragraphs 122.3(1)(*c*) and (*d*) in respect of that income for the year. If the individual is entitled to, but does not claim the overseas employment tax credit, the full amount of foreign income tax on the relevant overseas employment income can be included in the calculation of the individual's NBIT (subject, of course, to the other exclusion rules in the definition of NBIT). This means, for example, that the individual typically can choose to include foreign income tax on this type of income in the calculation of NBIT where the overseas employment tax credit would be rendered ineffective because of the application of the minimum tax under section 127.5 (a special foreign tax credit can be claimed against the minimum tax—see ¶ 1.70). Note that amendments to section 122.3 effective for 2013 and future years phase out the availability of the overseas employment tax credit in most situations causing it to be unavailable for 2016 and subsequent tax years.

1.27 The following are examples of foreign taxes that cannot qualify as a BIT because they are not taxes paid by the taxpayer on income from the taxpayer carrying on a business in a country other than Canada (as discussed in ¶ 1.5—1.13 above), however, they may qualify as NBIT (see ¶ 1.21):

- United States tax on income from a business carried on by a U.S. subchapter S corporation (also known as an S Corp. which is taxed as a flow-through entity (that is, similar to a partnership) for US tax purposes) but paid by its principal shareholder, a U.S. citizen resident in Canada, because the business was not carried on by the person who paid the tax
- foreign tax paid in respect of a capital gain on the sale of a property used by the taxpayer in carrying on a business in a foreign country, because a capital gain is not income from carrying on a business
- foreign tax paid to the extent that it is in respect of a business (or a part of a business) that is carried on in Canada (see, however, ¶ 1.48)

1.28 A foreign income or profits tax which meets the subsection 126(7) definition of NBIT will nevertheless fail to qualify for purposes of a subsection 126(1) foreign tax credit to the extent that the tax may reasonably be regarded as having been paid by a corporation in respect of its income from shares of the capital stock in its foreign affiliates, as indicated in the description of FTP(NBIT). (See, however, the relief from double taxation provided for in section 113, subsections 91(4) and 91(5).) If an amount representing a return of capital on a Canadian corporation's shares in the capital stock of a foreign affiliate is considered to be a dividend under the United States *Internal Revenue Code* earnings and profits rules, U.S. taxes paid by the Canadian corporation on that amount are considered to be in respect of its income from such shares and thus these taxes do not qualify for inclusion in FTP (NBIT).

No economic profit and short-term securities acquisitions

1.29 Subsection 126(4.1) limits the availability of a foreign tax credit for taxes in respect of property (other than capital property) in cases where it is not reasonable to expect that the taxpayer will realize an **economic profit** as defined in subsection 126(7). The evaluation of expected profitability is made as of the time the property is acquired. Profitability is estimated over the entire period for which it is expected that the property will be continuously held. If it is reasonably expected that there will be no economic profit, the foreign tax paid in respect of the property and related transactions is not included in the taxpayer's BIT or NBIT for any tax year. Where subsection 126(4.1) denies the credit, a deduction from income may still be available under subsection 20(12.1) for the foreign tax paid. If a related transaction involves the acquisition of another property, subsection 126(4.1) is not applied independently in respect of the other property.

1.30 If a taxpayer disposes of a share or debt obligation which was held for less than one year, the BIT or NBIT that the taxpayer may claim is limited to the amount of Canadian tax that would be payable at a notional rate on the gross income from the security for the period which it was held. The formula to calculate the maximum BIT or NBIT and the properties to which the formula does not apply are found in subsections 126(4.2) and (4.3), respectively.

1.31 Subsection 126(4.4) provides that certain dispositions and acquisitions of property that are either deemed to be made by certain provisions of the Act or made in the course of certain rollover transactions are not dispositions or acquisitions for the purposes of subsections 126(4.1) and (4.2).

Amount paid by the taxpayer for the year

1.32 Before an amount of foreign tax can be used in the calculation of a foreign tax credit (as either FTP (NBIT) or FTP (BIT)), it must be **paid...for the year**, whether paid before, during or after the year in question. The words, **for the year** relate to the year for which the taxpayer is liable to pay tax (that is, when it is exigible) to the foreign jurisdiction for the income which is considered to have been earned under the foreign jurisdiction's tax law, even though the income may not be realized in Canada during the same tax year. Where a foreign country uses a tax year different than the tax year used in Canada, the foreign taxes actually paid must be prorated to match the Canadian tax year. For example, in the case of individuals, where a foreign country uses a tax year other than a calendar year, the tax paid by the taxpayer for the year in the foreign jurisdiction is the taxes actually paid prorated on a calendar year basis.

1.33 Once paid, the Canadian dollar equivalent of the foreign tax (converted into Canadian currency in accordance with whichever method and rate of exchange described in ¶1.42-1.44 may be appropriate in the circumstances) may be taken into account in computing a foreign tax credit for the tax year to which the foreign tax relates. Any portion of a taxpayer's foreign tax which is paid but which will be, or is, refunded to the taxpayer is not considered to be tax paid for the year. In other words, the foreign tax paid for the year for purposes of claiming a foreign tax credit cannot be more than the applicable finally-determined foreign tax liability (that is, the Canadian dollar equivalent of that amount).

1.34 As discussed in ¶1.5, voluntary contributions to governmental authorities are not considered a tax and therefore cannot contribute to the amount of foreign tax paid. If a resident of Canada voluntarily pays to a foreign jurisdiction an amount that, according to the domestic law of that country can be levied as tax but according to the terms of a treaty between Canada and that country cannot be so levied, the amount is considered to have been paid voluntarily and cannot be considered to be foreign tax paid for the year for purposes of a foreign tax credit. Any refund of such voluntary payment in a subsequent year would not reduce any amount of foreign tax paid for that subsequent year.

1.35 If, for example, a resident of Canada receives income from sources in another country which has been subject to withholding tax at a rate in excess of the rate specified in a treaty between Canada and that country, such excess is not considered to be foreign tax paid for the year for purposes of the foreign tax credit. The maximum credit allowed will be determined on the basis of the treaty rate and the taxpayer should seek a refund of the excess withholding tax from the foreign revenue authorities.

1.36 An initial allowance of, or an adjustment to, a foreign tax credit in respect of foreign taxes paid for the year may be included in an assessment, reassessment or additional assessment of tax for the year, or in a notification that no tax is payable for the year. See section 152 for the time frames and conditions under which an assessment, reassessment or additional assessment of tax, or a notification that no tax is payable can be issued.

1.37 A taxpayer's foreign tax credit calculation can include only a foreign income or profits tax that is paid by the taxpayer. Subject to ¶1.32-1.35 above, the recipient of foreign-source income is considered to have paid any amount withheld and remitted by the payer of the income on account of, or in settlement of, the recipient's foreign tax liability. Payment is considered to have been made at the time the amount was withheld.

1.38 A tax is not considered to be paid by the taxpayer for foreign tax credit purposes if the actual liability for the tax lies with another person. For example, a unitary tax of a state of the United States does not qualify as being paid by a Canadian corporation, for purposes of that corporation's claiming a foreign tax credit, if the actual liability for the tax lies with one or more of its U.S. affiliates (see also the comments regarding a unitary tax starting at ¶ 1.10 and at ¶ 1.18).

1.39 The appropriate share of the foreign taxes paid by a partnership of which the taxpayer is a member is considered to be tax paid by the taxpayer. For the purposes of claiming a foreign tax credit, the amount of the foreign income must be calculated in accordance with section 96 and all other applicable provisions of the Act. The taxpayer's appropriate share of the foreign taxes paid is generally the same proportion of the total foreign taxes paid by a partnership as the taxpayer's share of income is to the total income of the partnership. These amounts may not necessarily match the amounts calculated under the tax laws of the foreign jurisdiction.

1.39.1 Where a taxpayer's direct or indirect share of a partnership's income, as calculated under the relevant foreign tax law, is less than their direct or indirect share as calculated under the Act, any income or profit taxes paid to a foreign jurisdiction in respect of the income of the partnership cannot be taken into account in computing the taxpayer's BIT, NBIT, FTP(BIT) or FTP(NBIT), except where any exception listed under subsection 126(4.12) is applicable. A foreign tax credit is generally denied where an investment in a partnership is characterized as an equity investment under the Act but is considered a debt instrument under the relevant foreign tax law.

Proposed legislative change

On August 27, 2010, the Department of Finance released a package of proposed legislative changes. Included in the proposals is a provision to add new subsections (4.11)-(4.13) to section 126, applicable to tax years ending after March 4, 2010. If enacted as proposed, new subsections (4.11)-(4.13) will operate to restrict the foreign tax credits available in certain situations involving partnerships. New subsection 126(4.11) denies the availability of a foreign tax credit where a member's direct or indirect share of the partnership's income, as calculated under the relevant foreign tax law, is less than the taxpayer's direct or indirect share as calculated under the Act. Exceptions to this new rule will be included in subsection 126(4.12). Combined, these provisions will generally deny a foreign tax credit where an investment in a partnership is characterized as an equity investment under the Act but is considered a debt instrument under the relevant foreign tax law. New subsection 126(4.13) ensures that, for the purposes of these new rules, members of an upper-tier partnership will also be considered to be members of any partnership of which the upper-tier partnership is a direct or indirect member.

1.40 The payment of an amount of foreign tax by an agent on behalf of a Canadian resident taxpayer is equivalent to a payment by the taxpayer. Whether a principal/agent relationship exists is a question of fact based on Canadian law and is not affected by the treatment of the relationship by foreign tax authorities. Thus, foreign tax paid by an agent of a resident of Canada can qualify for the foreign tax credit of the principal even though the agent was assessed the foreign tax on the basis that the activities were for the agent's own account, provided that the tax can in fact be considered to be that of the principal. The following are examples of situations where the tax typically can be considered to be that of the principal:

- The agent can recover the tax paid from the principal.
- The tax is paid by the agent from sales made by the agent on behalf of the principal and the amount of the tax paid is included in the gross amount of the sales income of the principal.

1.41 If two individuals, one or both of which is resident in Canada, have paid a foreign income tax on a community income basis (for example, spouses filing a joint return in the United States), an appropriate share of the foreign tax paid may be included in the foreign tax credit calculation of each individual resident in Canada. The amount paid is generally allocated to each such individual in the proportion that such individual's respective foreign income is of all the income that gave rise to the foreign tax, rather than the amounts actually paid by each individual.

1.42 For the purpose of claiming a foreign tax credit, the income taxes payable to a foreign government in a foreign currency should be converted to Canadian dollars at the same rate at which the income itself was converted. For business income, this conversion could be done monthly, quarterly, semi-annually or annually, using the average rate for the period, depending on the taxpayer's normal method of reporting income. For investment income which was subject only to a tax similar to that imposed by Part XIII of the Act, the conversion rate should be the rate applicable on the date of receipt of the income, although use of the average rate for the month or the mid-month rate would usually be acceptable. For other types of income, such as salaries and wages, the average rate for the months in which they are earned is the most appropriate rate. For capital gains, the rate should approximate the rate applicable at the time the gain was realized. Taxpayers may also choose to use the relevant spot rates for the days on which the particular amounts of foreign income and foreign tax arose in accordance with paragraph 261(2)(*b*). Whichever method the taxpayer chooses, it should be consistently applied from one year to all others.

1.43 The rules in subsection 39(2) will apply to gains or losses arising from the currency conversion of the amounts of foreign income and the foreign taxes (just as in the case of a foreign exchange gain or loss on the payment of any other debt denominated in a foreign currency) due to a fluctuation in the exchange rates causing a difference between:

- the Canadian dollar equivalent of the amount of the foreign tax liability used for purposes of the foreign tax credit, as determined in accordance with ¶1.42 above; and
- the Canadian dollar equivalent of the amount (or amounts) paid in settlement of the foreign tax liability determined as of the date (or dates) of payment.

1.44 If the taxpayer has overpaid the tax, the overpayment is not allowable as a foreign tax credit (see ¶ 1.32-1.35). The overpayment should be converted to Canadian dollars under the rules discussed in ¶1.42, and any difference between this figure and the Canadian dollar value of a refund of the overpayment, computed as of the day of its receipt, will be a gain or loss on exchange to which the rules in subsections 39(1) to (2.1) will apply.

Proposed legislative change

On October 24, 2012, the Department of Finance released a package of proposed legislative changes. Included in the proposals is a replacement of subsection 39(2) with a new subsections 39(1.1), 39(2), and 39(2.1). If enacted as proposed, gains or losses from the disposition of foreign currency by an individual (other than a trust) will be addressed under new subsection 39(1.1). Foreign exchange gains and losses in respect of asset dispositions, other than those addressed by new subsection 39(1.1), will now be addressed by subsection 39(1). New subsection 39(2) will apply to gains or losses from the fluctuation of foreign currency not addressed by subsections 39(1) or 39(1.1), and not in respect of a transaction or event in respect of shares of the capital stock of the taxpayer. New subsection 39(2.1) will address certain taxpayers repaying indebtedness to their foreign affiliates. Tax debt denominated in foreign currency will be addressed under new subsection 39(2). Under new subsection 39(2) foreign currency gains or losses will no longer be pooled together, instead each gain or loss will be treated as a separate gain or loss. In addition, the existing $200 carve-out rule will be moved to section 39(1.1) and will no longer apply to the gains or losses related to tax debt denominated in a foreign currency.

New subsections 39(1.1) and 39(2) will apply to gains made and losses sustained in tax years beginning after August 19, 2011, except where the gain or loss applies to a foreign affiliate of a taxpayer. New subsections 39(1.1) and 39(2) will apply to the foreign affiliate tax years that end after August 19, 2011 except that, if the taxpayer makes certain elections, new subsections 39(1.1) and (2) will apply in respect of tax years of all foreign affiliates of the taxpayer that end after June 2011. New subsection 39(2.1) will apply in respect of the portions of loans received and indebtedness incurred on or before August 19, 2011 that remain outstanding on that date and that are repaid, in whole or in part, on or before August 19, 2016.

1.45 Evidence of the payment of foreign tax is to accompany each return in which a foreign tax credit is claimed. If a taxpayer's foreign tax liability is settled by an amount withheld by the payer of the related income (that is, in a way which is analogous to tax under Part XIII of the Act), a copy of the foreign tax information slip is usually satisfactory. In most other cases, a copy of the tax return filed with the foreign government is required together with copies of receipts or documents establishing payment. The CRA should be notified of any increase or decrease in the amount of foreign tax paid as a result of a subsequent assessment or reassessment by the foreign tax authority, and the rules discussed in ¶ 1.32 - 1.35, and ¶1.42-1.44 should be followed to the extent they are applicable. If the foreign assessment or reassessment results in additional foreign tax paid, proof of payment should be provided.

Foreign business income

1.46 The total amount of a taxpayer's income from businesses carried on by the taxpayer in a particular foreign country is included in the calculation of FBI, in the foreign tax credit formula with respect to that country. Amounts that could otherwise be regarded as income from property are included in FBI as business income if such income amounts pertain to or are incident to the foreign business activities of the taxpayer. FBI cannot include income from carrying on a business in Canada (see the comments in ¶1.15-1.19, and ¶ 1.53-1.56 with regard to the question of whether a business is carried on in Canada or in a foreign country).

1.47 Tax-exempt income cannot qualify for inclusion in FBI, in the foreign tax credit formula. See the comments in ¶ 1.66-1.68 for more information regarding tax-exempt income and foreign tax credits.

Foreign non-business income

1.48 The FNBI, in the foreign tax credit formula represents the taxpayer's income from sources in a particular foreign country, as calculated in accordance with subparagraph 126(1)(*b*)(i). The calculation made in subparagraph 126(1)(*b*)(i) is subject to certain assumptions and adjustments. One of these assumptions is that "**no businesses** were carried on by the taxpayer **in that country**." Although income from carrying on a business in Canada is not explicitly excluded from FNBI by that assumption, such income generally cannot be included in FNBI because such income is not income from a source in a foreign country as required by subparagraph 126(1)(*b*)(i). Sections 3 and 4 reflect, among other things, that a business is a source of income for purposes of Part I of the Act. It follows that, for purposes of subparagraph 126(1)(*b*)(i), the location or locations where a business exists as a source of income is the location or locations where the business is carried on. Therefore, to the extent that income is derived from carrying on a business in Canada, it is considered to be income from a source in Canada, not income from a source in a foreign country, and thus it cannot be included in FNBI.

1.48.1 However, where in computing a taxpayer's income from a business carried on in Canada, an amount is included in respect of interest paid or payable after February 27, 2004 to the taxpayer by a person resident in a country other than Canada, and the taxpayer has paid to the government of that other country NBIT for the year with respect to the amount, this amount is deemed to be income from a source in that other country under paragraph 126(6)(*d*), such that the income can be included in FNBI.

Proposed legislative change

On July 16, 2010, the Department of Finance released a package of proposed legislative changes. Included in the proposals is a provision to add a paragraph (*d*) to subsection 126(6). Where income derived from carrying on a business in Canada is interest paid to the business by a person resident in a country other than Canada, and the business has paid NBIT to that other country on the income, proposed paragraph 126(6)(*d*) will, if enacted as proposed, deem the income to be income from a source in that other country such that the income can be included in FNBI.

1.49 Also, for purposes of granting a foreign tax credit for foreign income taxes paid, as referred to in an elimination of double tax article of an income tax treaty between Canada and a foreign country, what would otherwise be income from a source in Canada but which is deemed to be income from a source in that foreign country (see, for example, paragraph 3 of Article 21 of the Canada-United Kingdom Income Tax Convention) is income included in FNBI for that country. For example, the net income derived from a loan made to a non-resident by a lending institution that is resident in Canada in the course of its business carried on in Canada can be included in FNBI if such income is:

- subject to income tax in the foreign country in which that non-resident resides; and
- deemed, in the manner and for the purposes described above, by the income tax treaty between Canada and that country to be income from a source in that country.

1.50 By virtue of subparagraph 126(1)(*b*)(i), a corporation's foreign non-business income (that is, the **corporation's** FNBI, in the foreign tax credit formula) does not include income of the corporation from shares of the capital stock of a foreign affiliate of the corporation. This is consistent with the fact that a corporation's foreign non-business-income tax in respect of such income does not qualify for purposes of a subsection 126(1) foreign tax credit—see FTP(NBIT) in the definitions, and also ¶ 1.28.

1.51 Unlike a corporation, an **individual's** foreign non-business income (that is, the individual's FNBI, in the foreign tax credit formula) does include the individual's income from a share of the capital stock of a foreign affiliate (and the individual's NBIT in respect of that income is not excluded from FTP(NBIT)). Note that subparagraph 126(1)(*b*)(i) provides that a subsection 91(5) deduction in respect of dividends received will not be taken into account when calculating the foreign non-business income, that is, it will not reduce the FNBI in the foreign tax credit formula.

Determination of the location of a source of income

1.52 If there is an applicable tax treaty between Canada and a country in which the taxpayer has a source of income, the treaty may deem the income to arise in one of either Canada or the foreign country for the purposes of eliminating double taxation under that treaty. An example of such a treaty-based sourcing rule is discussed in ¶1.49 above. Such sourcing rules are specific to the treaty in which they are found and do not alter the determination of the location of a source of income for purposes beyond that treaty's scope.

Business income

1.53 While a determination of the place where a particular business (or a part of the business) is carried on (that is, the location of the source of the business income—see the comments starting at ¶1.48) necessarily depends upon all the relevant facts, such place is generally the place where the operations in substance, or profit generating activities, take place. For the following particular types of business, the following factors (among others) should be given consideration:

- development and sale of real or immovable property — the place where the property is situated;

- merchandise trading — the place where the sales are habitually completed, but other factors, such as the location of the stock, the place of payment or the place of manufacture, are considered relevant in particular situations;
- transportation or shipping — the place of completion of the contract for carriage, and the places of shipment, transit and receipt;
- trading in intangible property, or for civil law incorporeal property (for example, stocks and bonds) — the place where the purchase or sale decisions are normally made;
- money lending — the place where the loan arrangement is in substance completed;
- personal or movable property rentals — the place where the property available for rental is normally located;
- real or immovable property rentals — the place where the property is situated; and
- service — the place where the services are performed.

1.54 Other factors which are also relevant, but generally given less weight than the factors listed above include, but are not limited to:

- the place where the contract for the sale of property or the provision of services is formed or entered into;
- the place where payment is received;
- the place where assets of the business are located; and
- the intent of the taxpayer to do business in the particular jurisdiction.

1.55 In the case of a single business comprised of more than one of the above-mentioned activities, each activity is considered separately for purposes of determining in which country or countries the business is carried on (this situation should not be confused with the situation in which the taxpayer has separate businesses—see Interpretation Bulletin IT-206R, Separate businesses). If, however, one activity of a business is clearly incidental to a predominant one, the incidental activity is not considered when determining in which country or countries the business is carried on. For example, if a vendor of machinery provides customers with an engineer to supervise the installation of the machinery, this service would generally be considered to be incidental to the activity of selling the machinery; however, this type of service could in some cases be considered to be a significant activity on its own, depending on the machinery being sold, the nature of the installation service, and the terms of the contract with the customer.

1.56 If a business is carried on in more than one country, a reasonable proportion of the net income from the business must be allocated to each country. For this purpose, see the comments in ¶ 1.80—1.88 regarding the determination of net income from a source or sources in a particular foreign country.

Employment income

1.57 The location of the source of an individual's office or employment is considered to be the physical place where he or she normally performs the related duties. If those duties require the individual to spend a significant part of the time in a country other than Canada, the individual may be subject to tax in that foreign country on a portion of his or her remuneration. In such cases, an apportionment of the individual's regular salary or wages based on the number of working days spent in Canada, and in that other country, is usually considered appropriate in determining the foreign-source income from the employment for the purpose of the foreign tax credit calculation. Director fees are generally considered to be earned where the director meetings are held, and commission income is earned in the country in which the effort was expended for the purpose of gaining such remuneration.

Income from property

1.58 If interest is earned and the interest is income from property rather than income from business as described in ¶ 1.46, the residence of the debtor ordinarily determines the location of the source of the income. Other factors that may help determine the location of the source of interest income include: where the contract giving rise to the interest income was formed, where payments are made, where any loaned funds are put to use or where any property securing a loan is located. In most situations these additional factors will have less weight than the residence of the debtor.

1.59 If a resident of Canada receives a dividend on shares of a corporation which is resident in a foreign country and not resident in Canada, the dividend will normally be recognized as being from a source in that foreign country. In determining a dividend-paying corporation's country of residence for purposes of a foreign tax credit, the possible impact of the following should be considered:

- the provisions in an income tax treaty (if any) between Canada and the particular foreign country in question, that can determine the corporation's residence for the purposes of the treaty; and
- subsection 250(5), which (in conjunction with such a treaty) may deem the corporation to be not resident in Canada.

1.60 If income is derived from the rental of tangible property, or for civil law corporeal property, and the income is income from property rather than income from business as in ¶1.46 and ¶ 1.53—1.54, the location of the source of the income is considered to be:

- in the case of income from the rental of real or immovable property, the country where the property is located; and

- in the case of income from the rental of other tangible or corporeal property, the country where the property is used.

1.61 The location of the source of a royalty payment is the country in which the related right is used or exploited. For example, a royalty payment received by a resident of Canada on the amount of ore extracted from a mine situated in a foreign country is income from a source in that foreign country. As a further example, a royalty payment received by a resident of Canada from a resident of a foreign country, on a written work created in Canada and copyright-protected in that foreign country under its copyright laws, is income from a source in that foreign country.

Capital gains

1.62 In determining the country to which a taxpayer's capital gain or capital loss on a disposition of real or immovable property (land and buildings) should be allocated, the major factor to be considered is the geographic location of the property. In the case of capital property other than real or immovable property, the country to which the capital gain or capital loss should be allocated is usually based on the geographic location at which the sale or disposition took place and title was transferred. However, in certain situations, the nature of the property sold and the factors discussed in ¶ 1.53—1.54 may also be informative. (See ¶1.65 for example, in the case of stocks or bonds).

1.63 If there has been a deemed disposition of property under the Act, any resulting capital gain or capital loss is allocated to Canada rather than to a foreign country, regardless of the geographic location of the property at the time of the deemed disposition. For example, where a taxpayer has ceased to be resident in Canada, a taxable capital gain resulting from a deemed disposition of property under paragraph 128.1(4)(*b*) is considered to be Canadian-source income, which therefore cannot be included in the FNBI in the foreign tax credit formula for purposes of claiming a foreign tax credit under subsection 126(1). (The resulting pre-departure Canadian taxes may, however, be reduced by a foreign tax credit, under subsection 126(2.21), for a portion of any post-departure foreign taxes resulting from a subsequent actual disposition of the property.)

1.64 A different result for a deemed disposition can sometimes occur by means of a tax treaty:

Example

Ms. X emigrated on January 31, 2012, from Canada to the United States. Because of the operation of paragraph 128.1(4)(*b*) of the Act, Ms. X had a capital gain from a deemed disposition of land she owned in the United States, at fair market value on January 31, 2012. Using paragraph 7 (in conjunction with paragraph 1) of Article XIII of the Canada-United States Income Tax Convention, Ms. X elected to be taxed in 2012 by the United States (in accordance with the U.S. *Internal Revenue Code*) on the capital gain accruing on the land up to January 31, 2012. Under subparagraph 3(*a*) of Article XXIV of the Convention, the capital gain so taxed by the United States became a U.S.-source capital gain for purposes of clause 2(*a*)(i) of Article XXIV. As a result, Ms. X included the taxable capital gain that occurred under the Canadian Act in the FNBI for 2012. This allowed Ms. X to claim a subsection 126(1) foreign tax credit against her Canadian tax otherwise payable for the 2012 tax year. (On December 15, 2013, Ms. X, at that time a non-resident of Canada, sold the land and paid tax to the United States as a result of the capital gain accruing from February 1, 2012, to December 15, 2013. This post-departure foreign tax did not qualify for a foreign tax credit under subsection 126(2.21) of the Act as no part of the gain accrued while she was resident in Canada.)

1.65 Generally, the place where a stock or bond is sold is the securities or stock exchange in which it is sold, regardless of the location of the security issuer's transfer office. Where a sale is not made through a securities or stock exchange, a number of factors (weighted in favour of those factors less susceptible to manipulation) must be considered in establishing where the sale is made. These include:

- the location, residence, or place of business of:
  o   the issuer;
  o   the issuer's transfer office;
  o   the owner of the security; or
  o   the owner's selling agent;
  o   where the title is transferred;
- where the contract is negotiated, signed, and executed;
- where the shares are located;
- where payment is made; and
- any relevant provisions in the governing corporate statutes.

Tax-exempt income

1.66 Income that is tax-exempt income is not counted for the purposes of a foreign tax credit since it is income already protected from double taxation by a tax treaty. Therefore, any income that is tax-exempt income cannot be included in the foreign tax credit formula variables, FNBI or FBI. **Tax-exempt income** is defined in subsection 126(7) as income from a source in a country where the following two conditions are met in respect of that income:

- First, the taxpayer is entitled to an exemption, because of a tax treaty between Canada and the other country, from all income or profits taxes, imposed in that country, to which the treaty applies; and
- Second, no income or profits tax to which the treaty does not apply is imposed in any country other than Canada.

1.67 In the case of a disposition resulting in a foreign-source allowable capital loss which would otherwise have resulted in a foreign-source capital gain that was tax-exempt income, the allowable capital loss is not subtracted when calculating FNBI.

Example

Mr. A, who is a resident of Canada, has a taxable capital gain from the sale of shares. The sale occurred on a stock exchange in a foreign country and the taxable capital gain is considered to have its source in that foreign country. However, under the terms of the tax treaty between the foreign country and Canada, the gain is exempt from income or profits taxes imposed by the foreign country (for example, Article 13 of the treaty states that the gain is taxable only where the alienator is resident and the alienator, Mr. A, is resident in Canada and is not resident in the foreign country for the purposes of the treaty). Furthermore, the gain is not subject to an income or profits tax by a political subdivision of that foreign country or by any other foreign jurisdiction. Therefore, Mr. A's taxable capital gain is tax-exempt income and he cannot include it in the FNBI for that country when calculating the amount of a foreign tax credit.

1.68 If, for example, a taxpayer resident in Canada is exempt from income or profits taxes levied by a foreign country because of a tax treaty but pays an income or profits tax to a political subdivision of that country (income tax treaties typically do not cover taxes levied by a political subdivisions, for example, states, provinces, cities, and counties), the second condition above would not be fulfilled. As a result, the income on which the political subdivision's tax is paid would not be tax-exempt income and such income would qualify for inclusion in the FNBI in the foreign tax credit formula.

TFSAs and RRSPs

1.69 Income earned in a tax free savings account or in a registered retirement savings plan is not counted for the purposes of a foreign tax credit. Likewise, any foreign taxes paid on foreign income earned on qualifying investments held in a RRSP or through a TFSA arrangement is not counted for the purposes of a foreign tax credit. When determining the amount of an available foreign tax credit, a taxpayer should exclude the foreign taxes paid in respect of his or her TFSA and RRSP holdings from the calculation of FTP(NBIT) and any foreign income earned in his or her **RRSP** or **TFSA** arrangement should be excluded from the calculation of WI(1) and FNBI.

Minimum tax

1.70 If an individual who is subject to minimum tax under section 127.5 pays income or profits taxes to a foreign jurisdiction during a particular tax year, that individual may not claim a foreign tax credit under section 126 as a deduction from the federal minimum tax payable for that year. However, section 127.5 provides for the deduction of a special foreign tax credit in computing the federal minimum tax payable in this situation. The SFTC may be claimed using Form T691, Alternative Minimum Tax. The SFTC can be equal to, or in certain circumstances be greater than, the foreign tax credit to which the individual would normally be entitled under section 126. The SFTC, which is defined in subsection 127.54(2), is calculated as being the greater of:

a) the total of all amounts deductible under section 126 from the individual's tax for the year, and
b) the lesser of:
   • the individual's foreign taxes for the year; and
   • the individual's foreign income for the year multiplied by the appropriate percentage for the tax year.

1.71 For the purpose of the SFTC, **foreign taxes** and **foreign income** for a tax year are defined in subsection 127.54(1). Foreign taxes may be described as the BITs (see ¶1.15—1.19) paid by the individual for the year in respect of businesses carried on in foreign countries plus two-thirds of the NBITs (see ¶1.20—1.28) paid by the individual for the year to foreign jurisdictions. The two-thirds amount takes into account the fact that the provinces provide a foreign tax credit in respect of foreign taxes on foreign non-business income. Foreign income is the total of the individual's income for the year from his or her carrying on businesses in countries other than Canada and all income from countries other than Canada for which he or she has paid NBIT to foreign jurisdictions. The appropriate percentage for a tax year is the lowest percentage referred to in subsection 117(2) that is applicable in determining tax payable under Part I for the year.

1.72 For more information on the minimum tax see Guide 5000-G, General Income Tax and Benefit Guide, for the year and Form T691.

Tax sparing

1.73 A tax treaty between Canada and a foreign country typically contains a provision (referred to here as the double tax relief provision) under which

Canada is required to give a resident of Canada (the taxpayer) relief from double taxation by allowing a deduction, from the taxpayer's Canadian tax, in respect of an income or profits tax payable by the taxpayer to the foreign country. The double tax relief provision typically is made subject to the laws of Canada regarding such a deduction from Canadian tax, which are chiefly, the foreign tax credit rules in the Act. Such a double tax relief provision is contained, for example, in paragraph 2(*a*) of Article 23 of the Canada-India Income Tax Agreement (the Canada-India treaty). The treaty may also contain a tax sparing provision under which, for purposes of the double tax relief provision, income or profits tax payable to the foreign country by the taxpayer is deemed or considered to include any such taxes (the spared taxes) that would have been so payable if it had not been for an exemption from, or reduction of, tax having been granted by the foreign country (as specified in the tax sparing provision—see, for example, paragraph 4 of Article 23 of the Canada-India treaty). Such a tax sparing provision in a treaty generally causes the spared taxes to be taken into account—as if they had been paid to the foreign country—for purposes of calculating a foreign tax credit. (It may be possible in some cases for greater tax relief to be obtained in respect of the spared taxes—see Interpretation Bulletin IT-506, for further comments.)

The foreign tax credit formula

Full-year residents of Canada

Non-business income

1.74 For each foreign jurisdiction to which a taxpayer pays a NBIT, a separate foreign tax credit is calculated under subsection 126(1). Foreign NBIT includes any foreign taxes paid on foreign-source capital gains since capital gains are not considered to be business income for Canadian taxation purposes. The amount of foreign tax credit that is available under subsection 126(1), for NBIT paid by a Canadian resident taxpayer throughout the tax year to a particular country other than Canada, is equal to the lesser of the two amounts FTP (NBIT) and CTOP (FNBI). The second amount, CTOP(FNBI) is determined using the formula:

CTOP(FNBI) = FNBI ÷ WI(1) x CTOP(a)

Example

A resident of Canada has worldwide income, WI(1), for the year of $50,000. Of that total, $30,000 is the foreign non-business income, FNBI, for a particular foreign country and the taxpayer's foreign tax paid on the non-business-income, FTP(NBIT), to that country is $6,500. The taxpayer's Canadian tax otherwise payable, CTOP(a), of $10,000 (in the calculation of which the full $50,000 of world income is taken into account) is reduced to $4,000 by a foreign tax credit of $6,000, this amount being the lesser of the $6,500 FTP(NBIT) and the Canadian tax otherwise payable that pertains to the foreign non-business income from that particular country, CTOP(FNBI).

Applying the formula, FNBI ÷ WI(1) x CTOP(a):

= $30,000 ÷ $50,000 x $10,000

= $6,000

Business-income

1.75 For each foreign jurisdiction to which a taxpayer pays a BIT a separate foreign tax credit is calculated. The amount of foreign tax credit that is available under subsection 126(2), for BIT paid by a Canadian resident taxpayer throughout the year in respect of businesses carried on in a particular foreign business country, is least of the three amounts FTP(BIT), CTOP(FBI), and X (described in ¶1.77).

1.76 The second amount, CTOP(FBI), is determined using the formula:

CTOP(FBI) = (FBI ÷ WI(2) x CTOP(c)) + Y

Where Y is the portion (as determined under paragraph 126(2.1)(*b*)) of any subsection 120(1) tax for the tax year (on income that is income not earned in a province) that pertains to the income from businesses carried on in the particular foreign business country.

1.77 The third amount, X, takes into account a rule that, if the taxpayer's FTP(NBIT) **cannot** be fully claimed as a foreign tax credit for the year (because the CTOP(FNBI) in ¶1.74 is a lower amount), the unused portion of the FTP(NBIT) cannot be carried over and used in another year while any portion of FTP(BIT) that cannot be deducted as a foreign tax credit may qualify as an UFTC and be applied to other tax years. The amount, X, ensures that the taxpayer's subsection 126(1) NBIT foreign tax credit claims are deducted before any subsection 126(2) BIT foreign tax credits. This ordering rule is designed to allow the taxpayer to maximize both the foreign tax credits deducted for the tax year and the amount of UFTC for the year that can be applied to other years. Amount X is determined using the formula:

X = CTOP(b) — Z

Where Z is the total of all subsection 126(1) NBIT foreign tax credits claimed for the year.

1.78 Corporations claiming a foreign tax credit pursuant to section 126 should use the Form T2 Schedule 21, Federal and Provincial or Territorial Foreign Income Tax Credits and Federal Logging Tax Credit. Other taxpayers claiming a foreign tax credit should use Form T2209, Federal Foreign Tax Credits.

Part-year residents

1.79 If an individual (which includes a trust) is resident in Canada throughout part of the year and non-resident throughout another part of the year, section 114 applies. If section 114 applies, WI(1) in ¶1.74 and WI(2) in ¶1.76 will be modified pursuant to subparagraphs 126(1)(*b*)(ii) and 126(2.1)(*a*)(ii), respectively. WI(1) will be calculated in a manner which reflects the taxpayer's non-Canadian income only while he or she was a resident of Canada. WI(2) will be calculated in a manner which reflects the taxpayer's non-Canadian income only while he or she was resident in Canada and will also alter the availability of certain deductions applicable to his or her Canadian-source income, for the purposes of calculating the foreign tax credit.

Calculation of the amount of net income from sources in a foreign country

General

1.80 The income amounts that are used for FNBI and FBI in the foreign tax credit formula are **net income** amounts determined in accordance with the provisions of the Act, not under the laws of the foreign jurisdiction (see ¶1.83-1.86). Thus, both mandatory and permissive deductions (where taken) must be included when calculating FNBI and FBI. Common deductions applicable in most cases will include direct costs as well as reasonable allocations of overhead expenses.

1.81 For example, when determining the amount of a foreign tax credit for NBIT, if an amount of foreign income or profits tax is deducted under subsection 20(11) or 20(12) and if the income (from the same source as the source of the income to which that tax pertains) is included in the foreign tax credit formula variable, FNBI, with respect to the foreign country in question, the amount of that tax must also be deducted when calculating the FNBI. In other words, any amount of foreign tax deducted under subsections 20(11) or 20(12) cannot be represented in the claim for a foreign tax credit. This arises from the operation of subsections 20(11) or 20(12), as the case may be, in conjunction with subsection 4(3) (see ¶1.85, and Interpretation Bulletin IT-506, for a discussion of subsections 20(11) and 20(12)) and is consistent with the following rules:

- The amount deducted under subsection 20(11) or 20(12) is also deducted when calculating the foreign tax credit formula variable, WI(1). This is because a subsection 20(11) or 20(12) deduction is a deduction for purposes of calculating section 3 income.
- The amount deductible under subsection 20(11) or the amount deducted under subsection 20(12) is excluded from FTP(NBIT) in the foreign tax credit formula (see ¶ 1.22—1.24) with respect to the particular foreign country in question.

1.82 For purposes of calculating the net income amount to be used for FNBI or FBI in the foreign tax credit formulas, the possible impact of an income tax treaty between Canada and the foreign country should also be considered. For example, see paragraph 3 of Article XXIV of the Canada-United States Income Tax Convention.

1.83 Income from sources in a foreign country is computed under the rules given in sections 3 and 4 of the Act, subject to the additional rules contained in subparagraphs 126(1)(*b*)(i) or 126(2.1)(*a*)(i), as the case may be. Where profits or losses arise from multiple jurisdictions they should be allocated between jurisdictions in a manner that reflects the contribution of the activities in each jurisdiction that gave rise to those profits or losses, which may not necessarily be the way tax legislation of the foreign jurisdiction allocates the income. For purposes of calculating FNBI or FBI for a particular foreign country, amounts of net income or net loss from each applicable source in that country are added together or netted, as the case may be. Also, certain amounts in respect of taxable capital gains and allowable capital losses from sources in that country are taken into account when calculating FNBI.

1.84 The rules provided by section 4 apply to the calculation of the net income (or loss) from a particular source of income, or from sources of income in a particular place, for the purpose of (among other things) calculating a foreign tax credit under section 126. Subject to the specific rules contained in subsection 4(3) (see ¶1.85), each type of allowable deduction (including an outlay or expense) in arriving at a taxpayer's total income under section 3 is, theoretically, allocable in whole or in part to a source of income in a particular country. Ordinarily such an allocation can be made on the basis of a factual relationship between the particular deduction and the gross income arising from a source in a particular country. This is not always the case, however, and some types of deductions that frequently present apportionment problems are discussed in ¶1.87-1.88.

1.85 For purposes of a foreign tax credit under section 126, subsection 4(3) generally provides that all deductions permitted in computing a taxpayer's income for the year under Part I of the Act apply, either wholly or in part, to a particular source of income or to sources in a particular place. The reference to a

particular place would, of course, include a place in a foreign country. However, subsection 4(3) contains some exceptions to this general rule. Each deduction applied in calculating the taxpayer's total income under section 3 that is not specifically referred to in the exceptions in subsection 4(3) must be allocated on a **reasonable** basis among all sources of income to which they can reasonably be applied, including those in foreign countries. The deduction amounts allocated in this manner to income from a particular source in a particular foreign country must be deducted when calculating either FNBI or FBI in the foreign tax credit formulas, as the case may be, for that country.

1.86 An allocation of expenses to a source of gross income in a particular foreign country for financial statement purposes is normally accepted for the purpose of computing a foreign tax credit for that country, provided that the rules of subsection 4(3), as discussed above, are satisfied. Once a basis for allocation has been established, future allocations are expected to be made on a consistent basis.

1.87 Various methods of allocating interest expenses to sources of income are accepted in particular situations. For example, a specific tracing method is appropriate when funds are borrowed and used for an identifiable purpose related to the earning of income in a particular country. For interest on general purpose borrowing, an allocation based on relative net asset values in different countries may be appropriate in some cases. An allocation of interest expenses based on the relationship of gross incomes in different countries is accepted only when a less arbitrary method is not readily evident. The location of property assigned as security for an amount borrowed is not necessarily an indication that the funds obtained were for the purpose of earning income from a source in the same country in which the property is located.

1.88 The total amount of capital cost allowance claimed by a taxpayer for a tax year must be allocated among the countries to which it relates. The allocation cannot exceed the allowable maximums under Part XI of the Regulations in respect of property situated in a particular country. In particular, the limitation in the case of rental properties must be respected on a country-by-country basis. Subject to these conditions, capital cost allowance deductions may be arbitrarily allocated to income sources in various countries.

Capital gains and losses

1.89 Subject to the exceptions for tax-exempt income, the taxpayer should include all foreign-source taxable capital gains arising in the particular country in the foreign tax credit formula variable, FNBI, and his or her worldwide taxable capital gains in the variable WI(1). In calculating these variables, the taxpayer should subtract any applicable foreign-source allowable capital losses to the extent that such losses are deductible in calculating the taxpayer's income under section 3 of the Act. The taxpayer should also deduct any capital gains deduction claimed under section 110.6 from both FNBI and WI(1), and any foreign taxes paid in respect of such a deducted amount should not be included in the taxpayer's FTP (NBIT). This Canadian tax treatment would not be affected by a different treatment under the tax law of the particular foreign jurisdiction to which the capital gain or loss is allocated by the taxpayer. For example, the capital gain or loss so allocated might be considered by the foreign jurisdiction to be a gain or loss of a business nature, whether or not the capital property disposed of was used in the business of the taxpayer at the time of its disposition. Any tax in the nature of an income, gains, or profits tax that is paid for the year to a foreign jurisdiction in respect of a capital gain should be included in the non-business-income tax paid to that jurisdiction.

1.90 Net capital losses from other tax years claimed under paragraph 111(1)(*b*) when computing the taxpayer's taxable income do not reduce the foreign tax credit formula variable FNBI, but are deducted in calculating the variable WI(1).

1.91 Separate foreign tax credit calculations under subsection 126(1) must be made for each country to which NBIT is paid. Accordingly, in a situation where a taxpayer has a taxable capital gain allocated to one foreign country and an allowable capital loss allocated to another foreign country, the taxable capital gain is included in computing the foreign tax credit formula variable FNBI for the first country and the allowable capital loss is subtracted in computing FNBI for the second country to the extent that such allowable capital loss is deductible in computing the taxpayer's income for the year under section 3.

Example:

Assume the following income details for Taxpayer A:

Description	Canada ($)	Country X ($)	Country Y ($)	Total ($)
Taxable capital gains	2,000	10,000	NIL	12,000
Allowable capital losses	NIL	NIL	(15,000)	(15,000)
Other non-business income	NIL	28,000	21,500	49,500
Business income	23,000	21,000	22,000	66,000

The calculation of Taxpayer A's FNBI for each foreign country is as follows:

Description	Country X ($)	Country Y ($)

Taxable capital gains	10,000	NIL
Allowable capital losses	N/A	(12,000)*
Other non-business income	28,000	21,500
FNBI	38,000	9,500

The calculation of Taxpayer A's WI(1) (which is used in his or her foreign tax credit calculations for both foreign countries) is as follows:

Description	$
Taxable capital gains	12,000
Allowable capital losses	(12,000)*
Other non-business income	49,500
Business income	66,000
WI(1)	115,500

* The amount of allowable capital losses that is subtracted in calculating the above variables under subsection 126(1) is limited to $12,000. This is because only $12,000 of the $15,000 allowable capital losses incurred in the year is deductible in computing Taxpayer A's income for the year under section 3 of the Act. That is, the amount of the taxpayer's allowable capital losses for the year deductible under subparagraph 3(b)(ii) cannot exceed the taxpayer's $12,000 taxable capital gains for the year included under subparagraph 3(b)(i), because the net amount calculated under paragraph 3(b) cannot be less than nil.

1.92 The taxpayer may have allowable capital losses for more than one foreign country. In such a situation, where the total allowable capital losses for all countries (including Canada) exceeds the amount of such losses that is deductible in computing the taxpayer's income under section 3, the taxpayer may allocate the foreign-source portion of the deductible losses among the foreign countries, for purposes of calculating FNBI for each respective country, in such a way that:

• the amount of allowable capital losses allocated to any particular foreign country does not exceed the allowable capital losses actually incurred in that country; and
• the aggregate of the Canadian portion (if any) of the allowable capital losses and the various amounts allocated to the foreign countries is equal to the total amount of allowable capital losses that is deductible in calculating the taxpayer's income under section 3 of the Act.

Example:

Assume the following income details for Taxpayer B:

Description	Country X $	Country Y $	Country Z $	Foreign Total $	Canada $	Total $
Taxable capital gains	3,000	1,000	2,000	6,000	3,500	9,500
Allowable capital losses	(5,000)	(1,500)	(1,000)	(7,500)	(7,000)	(14,500)
Other non-business income	3,500	NIL	4,200	7,700	NIL	7,700
Business income	1,200	2,400	1,600	5,200	1,800	7,000

Taxpayer B calculates FNBI for each foreign country as follows:

Description	Country X $	Country Y $	Country Z $
Taxable capital gains	$ 3,000	$ 1,000	$ 2,000
Allowable capital losses, as allocated by the taxpayer*	(4,000)*	(1,000)*	(1,000)*
Other non-business income	3,500	NIL	4,200
FNBI	2,500	NIL	5,200

The calculation of Taxpayer B's WI(1) (which is used in Taxpayer B's foreign tax credit calculations for all foreign countries) is as follows:

Description	$
Taxable Capital Gains	9,500
Allowable capital losses	(9,500)*
Other non-business income	7,700
Business income	7,000
WI(1)	14,700

* Of the \$14,500 allowable capital losses incurred by Taxpayer B for the year, only \$9,500 is deductible under subparagraph 3(*b*)(ii) for purposes of computing income for the year under section 3 of the Act, because taxable capital gains included under subparagraph 3(*b*)(i) are only \$9,500. For purposes of subsection 126(1), the \$9,500 deductible allowable capital losses are deducted in calculating Taxpayer B's WI(1). The Canadian-source portion of the \$9,500 deductible losses is \$3,500 (even though the actual Canadian-source allowable capital losses are \$7,000), because the Canadian-source taxable capital gains included under subparagraph 3(*b*)(i) are only \$3,500. Therefore, the foreign-source portion of the \$9,500 deductible allowable capital losses is \$6,000, which is allocated among the three foreign countries. The amount allocated to each country is subtracted in calculating Taxpayer B's FNBI for that country. Taxpayer B can allocate the \$6,000 among the three foreign countries in any manner, as long as the rules given in ¶1.92 are met.

The comments in this example are subject to the rules concerning tax-exempt income as discussed under the heading Tax-exempt income above.

Addition to taxable income to prevent reduction to foreign tax credit

1.93 For the purpose of claiming a foreign tax credit for a particular year, in certain situations where a corporation would not otherwise be able to fully utilize the foreign income or profits taxes that it has paid, section 110.5 may make it possible to do so. An example where such a situation would occur is if a loss for the year reduced the corporation's total income to an amount less than its foreign source income and the resulting CTOP(FNBI) was less than FTP(NBIT) in the foreign tax credit formula for foreign non-business-income taxes, or the resulting CTOP(FBI) was less than FTP(BIT) in the foreign tax credit formula for foreign business-income taxes.

1.94 Section 110.5 allows a corporation to add any extra amount in computing its taxable income, to the extent that this causes an increase to any amount deductible by the corporation as a foreign tax credit under subsection 126(1) or (2) but does not cause any increase to an amount deductible by the corporation in a provision set out in paragraph 110.5(*b*). The corporation may add an amount of extra income which increases an amount deductible under subsection 126(1) or (2) as well an amount deductible under a provision listed in paragraph 110.5(*b*) as long as the deduction under an increased 110.5(*b*) provision is not claimed. The amount added under section 110.5 in computing taxable income is added in the calculation of WI(1) or WI(2) in the foreign tax credit formulas, as the case may be. (This is provided for in the adjustments in subparagraphs 126(1)(*b*)(ii) and 126(2.1)(*a*)(ii), respectively).

1.95 Effective use of section 110.5 occurs when:

- the additional amount added in computing taxable income causes CTOP(a) or CTOP(c), as the case may be, in the foreign tax credit formula to increase;
- this in turn causes CTOP(FNBI) or CTOP(FBI) to increase; and

- this in turn allows more, or all, of the FTP(NBIT) or the FTP(BIT) to be deducted as a foreign tax credit under subsection 126(1) or (2).

1.96 The amount added under section 110.5 in computing the corporation's taxable income is also added in calculating its non-capital loss for the year, which may be carried over to and used in other tax years (see Interpretation Bulletin IT-232R3, Losses — Their Deductibility in the Loss Year or in Other Years). In other words, the additional foreign taxes that are used in the year (in the form of an increase to the foreign tax credit for the year by means of section 110.5) are effectively converted into the potential for tax savings for other years by the creation of a non-capital loss (or increase to an existing non-capital loss) for the year that can be used in those other years.

Relief from double tax by taxing on a deferred basis

1.97 Double taxation may occur if Canada and another country levy tax in different tax years with respect to a particular transaction and the taxpayer thus cannot make proper use of the foreign tax credit provisions. (A foreign tax credit under section 126 must be in respect of foreign taxes paid for the year—see ¶ 1.32.) However, relief from such double taxation may be possible in some cases by means of a provision in a reciprocal tax treaty between Canada and the other country (see, for example, paragraph 8 of Article XIII of the Canada-United States Income Tax Convention) in conjunction with section 115.1 of the Act. Further particulars on this topic may be found in the current versions of the following:

- Interpretation Bulletin IT-173R2, Capital Gains Derived in Canada by Residents of the United States, and Interpretation Bulletin IT-173R2SR, Capital Gains Derived in Canada by Residents of the United States (special release revision)
- Interpretation Bulletin IT-420R3, Non-Residents — Income Earned in Canada, and Interpretation Bulletin IT-420R3SR, Non-Residents-Income Earned in Canada (special release revision)
- Information Circular 71-17R5, Guidance on Competent Authority Assistance Under Canada's Tax Conventions

Carryforward and carryback

General

1.98 Some taxpayers who earned foreign business income may not be able to claim all of their FTP(BIT) for a particular foreign business country in a particular tax year as a foreign tax credit in that same year. Paragraph 126(2)(*a*) permits a taxpayer resident in Canada at any time in the year who carried on a business in a foreign country in a particular tax year, to include in the amount available as a foreign tax credit for that year all or a portion of the **unused foreign tax credit** (UFTC) associated with that country from other years. The amount of UFTC that may be claimed in the current year must come from the ten immediately preceding tax years or the next three immediately following tax years (see ¶1.102). Note that for tax years that ended on or before March 22, 2004, the carryforward period is only seven tax years.

1.99 The definition of UFTC in subsection 126(7) provides that UFTC is to be calculated separately for each foreign country in which business is carried on and for each tax year (that is, calculated on a country-by-country and year-by-year basis). The UFTC of a taxpayer for a tax year is the amount by which the BIT exceeds the amount of such BIT that is deductible as a foreign tax credit for the year in respect of that country.

1.100 The effect of the word **deductible** in the definition of UFTC means that where the business-income tax is not deducted to the full extent possible as a foreign tax credit in the year to which it relates, any deductible portion not so claimed will not be available for carryover but will be lost.

1.101 If a taxpayer deducts, from their tax otherwise payable for a particular year, an amount as a foreign tax credit for the year which is less than the least of the three amounts discussed in ¶1.75, the portion of the BIT paid equal to the difference between the amount deducted and the least of the three amounts will be lost by virtue of paragraph (*b*) of the definition of UFTC in subsection 126(7) of the Act and cannot form part of the UFTC for the particular year.

1.102 The effect of the inclusion of UFTC in paragraph 126(2)(*a*) is that a Canadian resident taxpayer may carry UFTC from the current year back into the three immediately preceding tax years or forward into the next ten immediately following tax years, subject to the rules in subsection 126(2.3). These rules provide that:

- the amount of foreign tax credit claimed under paragraph 126(2)(*a*) for a tax year is considered first to be in respect of BIT for that year with any remainder considered to be a deduction in respect of UFTC;
- UFTCs must be utilized against Part I tax in the order in which they arose (for example, UFTC in respect of a particular country for the 2009 tax year must be applied before UFTC for 2010 in respect of that country); and
- an amount of UFTC for a year deducted against Part I tax in one year may not be deducted again in a subsequent year.

Prescribed form

1.103 If a taxpayer wishes to claim UFTC of the current year in one of the preceding tax years, paragraph 152(6)(*f*.1) requires that the taxpayer elect to do so in prescribed form. For corporate taxpayers, this election is made on Part 4 (Request for a federal foreign business income tax credit carryback) of T2 Schedule 21, Federal and Provincial or Territorial Foreign Income Tax Credits and Federal Logging Tax Credit. Individual taxpayers wishing to apply UFTCs in one of the preceding tax years should use Form T1-ADJ, T1 Adjustment Request, and trusts should use Form T3-ADJ, T3 Adjustment Request. The election to claim an amount of UFTC must be filed with the CRA no later than the day on which the taxpayer's income tax return for the current year is due. Without the filing of a timely election, the benefits of the UFTC carryback provisions are unavailable. For corporate taxpayers, Part 3 (Continuity of unused federal foreign business income tax credits) of Schedule 21 of the T2 return provides a schedule in which to calculate unused federal foreign business income tax credits to be carried forward to future years.

Ceasing or commencing business

1.104 Paragraph 126(2)(*a*) permits a taxpayer to make a claim for UFTC carryforward or carryback in any year during which that taxpayer carried on business in the foreign country (subject to the ten year carryforward limit and the three year carryback limit). Thus, if a taxpayer does not carry on a business in a foreign country during a tax year, that taxpayer may not claim UFTC carryforward or UFTC carryback in that particular tax year.

Amalgamation

1.105 When an amalgamation of two or more taxable Canadian corporations qualifies under section 87 and one or more of the predecessor corporations to the amalgamation had UFTC available at the time of the amalgamation, paragraph 87(2)(*z*) contains rules for calculating the following:

- the UFTC of the amalgamated corporation (Amalco); and
- any reduction in the amount that may be claimed under paragraph 126(2) (*a*) by Amalco as a foreign tax credit by virtue of subsection 126(2.3).

1.106 The rules deem Amalco to be the same corporation as, and a continuation of, each relevant predecessor corporation to enable any UFTC of that predecessor corporation to be carried forward by Amalco. Thus, if one of the predecessor corporations had UFTC to carry forward for its tax year ending immediately before the amalgamation, this amount could be carried forward into Amalco's first ten tax years subject to the restrictions contained in paragraph 126(2)(*a*) and subsection 126(2.3). Paragraph 87(2)(*z*) also provides that the above rules shall in no respect affect:

- the fiscal period of Amalco or any of its predecessor corporations; or

- the tax payable under the Act by any predecessor corporation. Thus UFTC of Amalco may not be carried back and applied as a credit against tax otherwise payable by a predecessor corporation.

Winding-up

1.107 Where subsection 88(1) applies on a winding-up, paragraph 88(1)(*e*.7) permits the parent corporation to claim the UFTC of its subsidiary following the winding-up. To the extent that a subsidiary's UFTC for a year has not been deducted, it will be considered to be the parent's UFTC for the parent's tax year in which the subsidiary's tax year ended. This rule ensures that on a winding-up, the carryforward period for the subsidiary's unused foreign tax credit for any particular tax year will be maintained in the parent corporation.

Application

This Chapter, which may be referenced as S5-F2-C1 is effective December 1, 2015 and replaces and cancels Interpretation Bulletin IT-270R3, *Foreign Tax Credit*, Interpretation Bulletin IT-395R2, *Foreign Tax Credit — Foreign-Source Capital Gains and Losses* and Interpretation Bulletin IT-520(consolidated), *Unused Foreign Tax Credits — Carryforward and Carryback*.

The history of updates to this Chapter as well as any technical updates from the cancelled interpretation bulletins can be viewed in the Chapter History page.

Except as otherwise noted, all statutory references herein are references to the provisions of the *Income Tax Act*, R.S.C., 1985, c.1 (5th Supp.), as amended and all references to a Regulation are to the *Income Tax Regulations*, C.R.C., c. 945, as amended.

Links to jurisprudence are provided through CanLII.

Income tax folios are available in electronic format only.

Reference

Sections 126 (Also sections 3, 4, 110.5, 115.1, 122.3, 127.5, 127.54, subsections 39(2), 20(11), 20(12), and paragraphs 87(2)(*z*), 88(1)(*e*.7), 111(1)(*b*), 128.1(4)(*b*), 152(6)(*f*.1)), and 249.

S6-F1-C1, Residence of a Trust or Estate

Date: November 25, 2015

Series 6: Trusts

Folio 1: Trusts and Residency Issues

Chapter 1: Residence of a Trust or Estate

Summary

The purpose of this Chapter is to provide the Canada Revenue Agency's (CRA) views concerning the determination of the residence status of a trust (as that term is defined in subsection 248(1)) for Canadian income tax purposes. It also discusses the factors to be taken into account in making this residency determination. The comments in this Chapter dealing with factual residence will apply to determinations of residence status for federal, as well as provincial tax purposes.

For greater certainty, the term **trust** includes an estate (unless the context otherwise requires) and the term **estate**, for civil law purposes, includes a succession.

The CRA issues income tax folios to provide technical interpretations and positions regarding certain provisions contained in income tax law. Due to their technical nature, folios are used primarily by tax specialists and other individuals who have an interest in tax matters. While the comments in a particular paragraph in a folio may relate to provisions of the law in force at the time they were made, such comments are not a substitute for the law. The reader should, therefore, consider such comments in light of the relevant provisions of the law in force for the particular tax year being considered.

Discussion and interpretation

Factual residence

1.1 The residence of a trust in Canada, or in a particular province or territory within Canada, is a question of fact to be determined according to the circumstances in each case.

1.2 The Supreme Court of Canada (Fundy Settlement v. Canada, 2012 DTC 5063, 2012 SCC 14) has clarified that residence of a trust will be determined by the principle that for purposes of the *Income Tax Act* a trust resides where its real business is carried on, which is where the central management and control of the trust actually takes place.

1.3 Usually the management and control of the trust rests with, and is exercised by, the trustee, executor, liquidator, administrator, heir or other legal representative of the trust. In this Chapter the word **trustee** is used to refer to any such person in relation to a trust. In its decision in *Fundy Settlement*, the Supreme Court of Canada affirmed the view that the residence of the trustee does not always determine the residence of a trust.

1.4 It is not uncommon for more than one trustee to be involved in exercising the central management and control over a trust. The trust will reside in the jurisdiction in which the more substantial central management and control actually takes place.

1.5 In some situations, the facts may indicate that a substantial portion of the central management and control of the trust rests with someone other than the trustee, such as the settlor or the beneficiaries of the trust. Regardless of any contrary provisions in the trust agreement, the actions of these other persons in respect of the trust must be considered. It is the jurisdiction in which the central management and control is factually exercised that will be considered in determining the residence of the trust.

1.6 For example, when making a determination as to the jurisdiction in which the central management and control of a trust is exercised, the CRA will consider any relevant factor, which may include:

- the factual role of a trustee and other persons with respect to the trust property, including any decision-making limitations imposed thereon, either directly or indirectly, by any beneficiary, settlor or other relevant person; and
- the ability of a trustee and other persons to select and instruct trust advisors with respect to the overall management of the trust.

For this purpose, the CRA will look to any evidentiary support that demonstrates the exercise of decision-making powers and responsibilities over the trust.

1.7 After an examination of all factors, it may be determined that a trust is resident in Canada even if another country considers the trust to be resident in that other country.

Deemed residence

1.8 Trusts that are not factually resident in Canada may be deemed to be resident in Canada for a tax year under the non-resident trust rules in section 94 for certain purposes, including computing the income of the trust and determining its liability for Part I tax. These rules are applicable to a factually non-resident trust (other than an exempt foreign trust) if there is a resident contributor to the trust or a resident beneficiary under the trust. Note however that paragraph 94(4)(*h*) ensures that a deemed resident trust is not considered resident for purposes of applying the attribution rule in subsection 75(2), as discussed in 1.11. A detailed description of those provisions would be beyond the scope of this Chapter.

1.9 Generally, each of the resident contributors to a deemed resident trust (except for any electing contributors in respect of it), and the resident beneficiaries under the trust, are jointly and severally, or solidarily, liable with the trust for many of its obligations, including its Part I tax liability.

1.10 The *Income Tax Conventions Interpretation Act* contains rules that govern the interpretation of certain provisions of the tax treaties negotiated by Canada. Section 4.3 of this act came into force on March 5, 2010 to clarify that under Canadian law, a trust that is deemed to be resident in Canada by subsection 94(3) will be deemed to be a resident of Canada and not a resident of the other contracting state for the purposes of applying a particular tax convention. This will be the case notwithstanding the provisions of the particular convention or of the act giving the convention the force of law in Canada.

Other considerations

1.11 Subsection 75(2) is an attribution rule applicable in respect of trusts factually resident in Canada and created after 1934. The rule generally applies where property is held by such a trust on condition that:

- the property, or property substituted for it, may revert to the person from whom it was directly or indirectly received, or pass to persons determined by that person subsequent to the creation of the trust or

- during the existence of the person, the property may be disposed of only with the concurrence of that person.

When either of these conditions is met, any income or loss from or taxable capital gain or allowable capital loss in respect of the property, or property substituted for it, is attributable to that person while resident in Canada.

1.12 Subsection 250(6.1) operates to avoid unintended tax consequences that may arise under a number of provisions of the *Income Tax Act* that require a trust to be resident in Canada throughout a tax year. Specifically, subsection 250(6.1) deems a trust that ceases to exist at any time in a tax year to be resident in Canada during the remaining period in the year if it was resident in Canada immediately before it ceased to exist.

1.13 Taxpayers requiring further general information about how the residence status of a trust is determined for purposes of Canadian income tax should contact the CRA at 1-800-959-8281 or in French at 1-800-959-7383 (toll free in Canada and the United States). Written enquiries should be addressed to:

International and Ottawa Tax Services Office
Post Office Box 9769, Station T
Ottawa ON K1G 3Y4
CANADA

Application

This updated Chapter, which may be referenced as S6-F1-C1, is effective November 25, 2015.

When it was first published on September 19, 2014, this Chapter replaced and cancelled Interpretation Bulletin IT-447, *Residence of a Trust or Estate.*

The history of updates to this Chapter as well as any technical updates from the cancelled interpretation bulletin can be viewed in the Chapter History page.

Except as otherwise noted, all statutory references herein are references to the provisions of the *Income Tax Act*, R.S.C. 1985, c.1 (5th Supp.), as amended and all references to a Regulation are to the *Income Tax Regulations*, C.R.C., c. 945, as amended.

Links to jurisprudence are provided through CanLII.

Income tax folios are available in electronic format only.

Reference

Subsection 2(1) (also subsection 75(2), section 94, subsections 104(1) and (2), and 250(6.1)).

Subject: *Income Tax Act*
             Election re Tax on Rents and Timber Royalties —
             Non-Residents

Date: February 21, 1994

Reference: Section 216 (also sections 3, 115, 118 to 118.9 and 219, subsections
             2(3), 104(7), 107(2), 120(1), 124(1), 126(1) and 215(3), and
             paragraphs 13(21)(d.1), 111(1)(a), 111(8)(c), 212(1)(d) and 212(1)
             (e) of the Income Tax Act and section 400 and subsection 2602(1)
             of the Income Tax Regulations)

Application

This bulletin replaces and cancels Interpretation Bulletin IT-393R dated August
12, 1983.

Summary

Certain rent and timber royalty payments from sources in Canada that are made
to a non-resident person are subject to non-resident withholding tax at a rate of
25% (unless reduced by a reciprocal tax treaty) of the gross amount of the
payments. However, the non-resident may be able to save tax by subsequently
electing to file a Canadian income tax return and instead be taxed on the net
income derived from these payments in a manner similar to that in which a
resident of Canada would be taxed.

This bulletin discusses the types of income that qualify for the election, the
required separate return, the unavailability of certain deductions and of the non-
refundable tax credits, and certain provincial income tax implications. Also
discussed are the provisions for the recapture of capital cost allowance and the
non-deductibility of a loss reported under the election against income for the
year reported on any other return or against income of other years. The
Canadian resident payer or an agent must still withhold and remit the non-
resident tax in the first place on the gross rents or royalties, but the tax return
subsequently filed by the non-resident can result in some or all of the tax so
remitted being refunded. Also, there is an election available which allows an
agent receiving the rents or royalties to withhold and remit tax on the net
amount available from those rents or royalties.

Discussion and Interpretation

1. Non-resident corporations and individuals (including estates and trusts) that receive rent from real property situated in Canada, or that receive a timber royalty on a timber resource property or a timber limit in Canada, are generally subject to Part XIII tax under paragraphs 212(1)(d) and (e), respectively, on the gross amount received. Subject to any relevant tax treaty, the rate of withholding tax is 25%. Alternatively, an election may be made under subsection 216(1) to file an income tax return and pay tax under Part I on that income as though the taxpayer were resident in Canada. This alternative is also available to a non-resident member of a partnership which receives such Income.

2. Where the renting of real property by a non-resident is a business carried on in Canada by the taxpayer, the provisions of Part XIII and the alternative treatment under section 216 are not applicable. Income from a business carried on in Canada is taxed pursuant to Part I of the Act and is also subject to the relevant income taxes of any province or territory in which such business is carried on. In this situation, the taxpayer is required to file a return reporting the taxable income earned in Canada as determined under section 115. For more details on this subject, see the current version of IT-420, Non Residents Income Earned in Canada, and of IT-171, Non-Resident Individuals — Computation of Taxable Income Earned in Canada and Non-Refundable Tax Credits.

3. A person who elects under subsection 216(1) to report Canadian source real property rent or timber royalty income as though resident in Canada must file the appropriate income tax return within two years (within six months, in the situation described in 9 below) from the end of the taxation year in which the income was received. It is not necessary for the person to have been a non-resident throughout the year. Thus, for example, an individual who immigrated to or emigrated from Canada during the year may elect under subsection 216(1) to report such income received during the part of the year in which he or she was a nonresident. A subsection 216(1) return must include all Canadian source real property rent and timber royalty income that would otherwise be taxable under Part XIII for the taxation year (or part of the year in which the person was a non-resident).

Furthermore, the subsection 216(1) return must be filed

    a) as though the non-resident had no income other than the above-mentioned rent and timber royalty income, and

    b) without affecting the liability of the non-resident person for tax otherwise payable under Part 1.

As a result, the subsection 216(1) return is separate from any other return required for the year. For example, a non-resident would report section 115 taxable income earned in Canada from a business or employment in Canada on a Part I return separate from the return for subsection 216(1) income. If the non-resident had a loss from sources described in section 115, that loss could not be applied against income reported on the subsection 216(1) return.

4. Except as noted in 5 below, an election under subsection 216(1) permits a non-resident to claim those Part I deductions available to a resident in computing income under section 3. Thus, the non-resident can deduct those expenses (including capital cost allowance) incurred in earning the subsection 216(1) income, as well as any applicable amounts in subdivision e of Division B. For example, although the income reported on a subsection 216(1) return does not qualify as "earned income" for purposes of claiming a registered retirement savings plan premium, the nonresident might nevertheless, in limited circumstances, be able to claim such a premium on a subsection 216(1) return, such as in a situation where the non-resident was a resident in the immediately preceding year and had "earned income" for that year. A "subdivision e" deduction cannot, of course, be claimed twice (e.g. once on a section 115 return and again on a subsection 216(1) return). By virtue of paragraph 216(1)(c), no deductions are allowable in computing taxable income on a non-resident's subsection 216(1) return. Thus, Division C amounts such as noncapital losses are not deductible. Also, by virtue of paragraph 216(1)(d), the nonrefundable tax credits described in sections 118 to 118.9 (such as the basic personal credit or the medical expense credit) are not deductible in computing the tax payable on a subsection 216(1) return.

5. Subsection 216(8) provides that, for greater certainty, no deduction is allowed in computing the income or the tax payable of a person who elects under subsection 216(1) if that deduction is not permitted under Part 1 for a non-resident. For example, a nonresident would be denied a foreign tax credit under subsection 126(1) and a non-resident trust would be denied a deduction by virtue of subsection 104(7) for distributions to a nonresident beneficiary, since those provisions are specifically dependent upon actual or deemed residency in Canada.

6. A non-resident's rent from real property in Canada can be reported under section 216 only if it is not income from carrying on a business in Canada (see 2 above). As a result, rent that can be reported under section 216 does not represent "income earned in the year in a province" by a non-resident individual or "taxable income earned in the year in a province" by a corporation, since these terms as defined in subsection 2602(1) and section 400 of the Income Tax Regulations, respectively, include only the income from a business. Rent reported under section 216 by an individual is therefore subject to the additional tax under subsection 120(1) and is not subject to tax by any province or territory whose individual income taxes are collected by the Government of Canada.

Similarly, rent reported under section 216 by a corporation is not eligible for the deduction from tax provided by subsection 124(1) and is not subject to tax by any province or territory whose corporate income taxes are collected by the Government of Canada. Income reported under section 216 by a corporation is also not subject to "branch tax" under section 219 (the branch tax is discussed in the current version of IT-137, Additional Tax on Certain Corporations Carrying on Business in Canada).

7. Where capital cost allowance has been claimed (or deemed by subsection 107(2) to have been claimed) by a taxpayer on a particular property situated in Canada for purposes of calculating the rent or timber royalty income from that property under section 216, any recapture of that capital cost allowance arising on the disposition of the property (or an interest in the property) in a subsequent taxation year will be taxable under subsection 216(5). Similar to a subsection 216(1) return, a subsection 216(5) return is separate from any other return filed for the year such as a return to report section 115 taxable income earned in Canada. In addition to the capital cost allowance recapture (or the non-resident's share of the recapture), the subsection 216(5) return must also include all Canadian source real property rent and timber royalty income that occurs in the year of the recapture (or in such part of the year in which the taxpayer is a nonresident) and that would otherwise be taxable under Part XIII. The other rules that apply for purposes of filing a return under subsection 216(1), as described above, generally also apply for purposes of filing a return under subsection 216(5). However, a subsection 216(5) return is filed because it is required when that provision applies, rather than because the non-resident elects to do so. Also, the two year filing period mentioned in 3 above does not apply, i.e. a subsection 216(5) return must be filed by the deadline that would apply if the non-resident were a resident.

8. In certain cases, it may be that what is reported on a section 216 return is a loss from rents or from timber royalties. In such a case,the taxpayer may not set off such a loss against income for the same taxation year reported on any other return required under Part I, since to do so would conflict with the rule in 3(b) above. Of course, if a taxpayer has a loss for the year from one section 216 property and income for the same year from another section 216 property, the loss would be set off against the income. For example, if the loss from the one property was $5,000 and the income from the other property $2,000, the net income reported on the section 216 return would be nil. However, a section 216 loss may not be deducted in other years under paragraph 111(1)(a) because, by virtue of paragraph 111(8)(c), such a loss does not qualify as a non-capital loss.

9. Even though the non-resident payee may elect to file a section 216 return (which, as indicated in 3 above, can be done within two years from the end of the year in which the income is received), the Canadian resident payer or an agent,

as the case may be, is nevertheless required by section 215 to withhold at the appropriate rate (see 1 above) and remit an amount to the Receiver General in payment of Part XIII tax on the gross amount of the non-resident's real property rents or timber royalties. In most cases, the difference between the Part XIII tax so remitted and the Part I tax liability resulting from the section 216 return will result in a subsequent refund to the non-resident. Where certain conditions are met, an election under subsection 216(4) may be made by an agent or other person acting on behalf of the non-resident who would otherwise be required by subsection 215(3) to remit the Part XIII tax on the gross rents or royalties. This election is available where the non-resident (or each non-resident who is a member of a partnership) has filed with the Minister an undertaking in prescribed form (Form NR6) to file a return of income under Part I for a taxation year as permitted by subsection 216(1), but within six months (rather than the two years described in 3 above) from the end of the relevant taxation year. The subsection 216(4) election allows the agent or other person to withhold and remit at the applicable rate on "any amount available" out of the rents or royalties received for remittance to the non-resident. The expression "any amount available" describes the excess of rents or royalties collected over any disbursements deductible in computing income by virtue of the election under subsection 216(1). Such disbursements would include non-capital outlays relating to repairs and maintenance, property taxes, property management fees and interest and service charges relating to the financing of the property in question. Non-cash items, such as capital cost allowance, are not deductible for this purpose. Further particulars on the subsection 216(4) election may be found in the current version of Information Circular 77-16, Non-Resident Income Tax.

If you have any comments regarding the matters discussed in this bulletin, please send them to:

Director, Technical Publications Division
Legislative and Intergovernmental Affairs Branch
Revenue Canada — Customs, Excise and Taxation
875 Heron Road
Ottawa, Ontario
K1A 018

Explanation of Changes for Interpretation Bulletin IT-393R2 Election re Tax on Rents and Timber Royalties — Non-Residents

Introduction

The purpose of the Explanation of Changes is to give the reasons for the revisions to an interpretation bulletin. It outlines revisions that we have made as a result of changes to the law, as well as changes reflecting new or revised departmental interpretations.

Overview

This bulletin discusses the section 216 election that is available to a non-resident to pay Part I tax on Canadian source rents from real property and timber royalties. We have revised the bulletin primarily as a result of changes to the law under Bill C-139 and to expand the bulletin to include a discussion on the subsection 216(4) election available to an agent receiving section 216 rents or royalties.

The comments in the bulletin are not affected by proposed amendments to the Income Tax Act contained in Bill C-9, which received first reading in the House of Commons on February 4, 1994, or in the draft legislation released on August 30, 1993 (a Bill for this legislation will likely be introduced in the House in the current session of Parliament).

Legislative and Other Changes

Clarification changes: Throughout the new bulletin, there are some additions and changes to the text which we have made solely to clarify or elaborate on the information given, without changing the substance of what was said in the old bulletin. Also, the order of some paragraphs has been changed.

Old ¶ 4: This has been discontinued for the reason stated below under "New ¶ 5".

New ¶ 4 (replaces old ¶ 5): The words in parentheses in the first sentence of old ¶ 5 are discontinued in new ¶ 4 for the reason stated below under "New ¶ 5". The example regarding a deduction for an RRSP premium has been modified to reflect the amendments to the RRSP rules which became law in 1988 by the enactment of Bill C-52. The last sentence of new ¶ 4 indicates that the non-refundable tax credits cannot be claimed by the non-resident (on a return filed under subsection 216(1)). This restriction is contained in paragraph 216(1)(d), which was added to the law under Bill C-139 (as a result of the introduction of the non-refundable tax credits under the same Bill C-139).

New ¶ 5: This paragraph describes the "for greater certainty" provision, subsection 216(8), which was added under Bill C-139, preventing a non-resident who files a return under section 216 from claiming any deduction that is not permitted to a non-resident under Part I of the Act. Because of this "for greater certainty" provision, old ¶ 4 and the words in parentheses in the first sentence of old ¶ 5 are no longer necessary and have been discontinued in the new bulletin.

Old ¶ 7: This paragraph is not continued in the new bulletin. As the paragraph indicates, the general averaging provisions were repealed for years subsequent to 1981. Forward averaging is being phased out and cannot be used for income reported after 1987 by virtue of amendments to sections 110.4 and 120.1 under Bill C-139.

New ¶ 7 (replaces old ¶ 8): New ¶ 7 is similar to old ¶ 8, but has been modified to restrict the discussion on CCA recapture to that reported on a subsection 216(5) return in respect of CCA originally claimed on a section 216 return. (The discussion on recapturing CCA claimed on a section 150 return is outside the scope of this bulletin.) The last sentence of old ¶ 8 is discontinued in new ¶ 7 because the current tax treaty between Canada and the United States does not contain a relieving provision like Article XIIIA(2) of the old treaty.

New ¶ 8 (replaces old ¶ 9): The last sentence in old ¶ 9 indicates that a loss reported by a non-resident under section 216 cannot be deducted under paragraph 111(1)(a) in the previous or a subsequent year in which the taxpayer was a resident. In *Pandju Merali v. The Queen*, 88 DTC 6173, [1988] 1 C.T.C. 320, the Federal Court of Appeal found that there was nothing in the Act to prevent such a loss application in the 1981 taxation year. However, the law was then amended to nullify the application of this decision after the 1982 year: the last sentence of new ¶ 8 discusses paragraph 111(8)(c) the effect of which, as amended under Bill C-2, is that a loss reported under section 216 cannot qualify as a non-capital loss for the 1983 and subsequent taxation years.

New ¶ 9: We have added this paragraph to the bulletin to provide additional information to non-residents filing under section 216, regarding:

- the requirement that the Canadian resident payer or agent withhold and remit Part XIII tax on the gross rents or timber royalties; and
- the subsection 216(4) election that permits the agent or other person acting on behalf of the nonresident to withhold and remit on the net amount available out of the rents or royalties.

Global Affairs Canada

Contact Us [http://www.international.gc.ca/department-ministere/contact_us-contactez_nous.aspx]

Your comments are important to us. We will address your concerns as quickly as possible, but the fastest way for us to do so is to help you find the information already available online. Please use our accessibility section for help with documents you cannot open properly.

Interested in reaching a Global Affairs Canada employee? Search the Government of Canada Employee Directory.

Enquiries on services and programs

Note: Global Affairs Canada does not deal with immigration issues. Please go to Citizenship and Immigration Canada.

If you have questions about a specific service, please use the following links to direct you to the right contacts. If you can not find the service or program you are looking for, our General Enquiries group can assist you.

Authentication of documents	Trade
• Information about how to have Canadian documents authenticated	• Doing business abroad • Doing business with Canada • Information about Canadian foreign policy or international trade

Travel enquiries	Education and youth
• Passport • Canadian visa, citizenship or immigration • Travel Reports & Warnings • Emergency assistance abroad • Travel publications (Bon Voyage But...) • Information on travelling abroad • Contact or locate a Canadian embassy, consulate or high commission	• Order a publication • Jules Léger Library • Youth and education programs • International Scholarships

Careers	General
• Employment • Students	• Spokepersons • General questions about Canada • Technicial difficulties • Other

Telephone:

1-800-267-8376 (toll-free in Canada)

613-944-4000 (in the National Capital Region and outside Canada)

Facsimile:

613-996-9709

Email:

If your browser cannot support forms, please e-mail our Enquiries Service

Write to:

Enquiries Service (LOS)
Global Affairs Canada
125 Sussex Drive
Ottawa, ON, Canada
K1A 0G2

If you wish to receive documents by mail, do not forget to include your full postal address.

If you are deaf, hard of hearing, or you have a speech impediment and use a text telephone, you can access the TTY service from 9 a.m. to 5 p.m. your local time by calling 613-944-9136 (in Canada only).

List Of Canadian Government Offices Abroad

Afghanistan — KABUL
Embassy of Canada
Address: Street No. 15, House No.
256, Wazir Akbar Khan, Kabul
Tel.: 93 (0) 701 108 800
Fax: 93 (0) 701 108 805
E-Mail: kabul@international.gc.ca
Internet: http://www.afghanis-tan.gc.ca

Albania — TIRANA
Consulate of Canada
Address: Rr: Deshmoret e 4 Shkur-tit Pallati i Ri mbrapa Akademise se Arteve Kati II, Tirana, Albania
Tel.: 355 (4) 225 7274 or 225 7275
Fax: 355 (4) 225 7273
E-Mail: canadalb@canada.gov.al
See also: Italy, Rome

Algeria — ALGIERS
Embassy of Canada
Address: 18 Mustapha Khalef St.,
Ben Aknoun, Algiers, Algeria
Postal Address: P.O. Box 48,
Alger-Gare 16306, Algeria
Tel.: 213 (0) 770-083-000
Fax: 213 (0) 770-083-070
E-Mail: alger@international.gc.ca
Internet: http://www.algeria.gc.ca

American Samoa — APIA
Australian High Commission
Address: Beach Road, Apia, Samoa
Postal Address: P.O. Box 704, Apia, Samoa
Tel.: 68 (5) 23 411
Fax: 68 (5) 23 159
E-Mail: ahc.apia@dfat.gov.au
Internet: www.samoa.embassy.go-v.au/apia/home.html

Andorra
See: Spain, Madrid

Angola — LUANDA
Consulate of Canada
Address: Rua Rei Katyavala 113,
Luanda, Angola
Postal Address: P.O. Box 3360,
Luanda, Angola
Tel.: 244 222 448-371, 448-377, or 448-366
Fax: 244 222 449-494
E-Mail: consul.can@angonet.org
See also: Zimbabwe, Harare

Anguilla
See: Barbados

Antigua and Barbuda
See: Barbados

Argentina — BUENOS AIRES
Embassy of Canada
Address: Tagle 2828, C1425EEH
Buenos Aires, Argentina
Tel.: 54 (11) 4808-1000
Fax: 54 (11) 4808-1111
E-Mail: bairs-cs@international.gc.-ca
Internet: http://www.argentina.gc.-ca

Armenia — YEREVAN
Consulate of Canada
Address: 10 Vazgen Sargsian Street,
103-4, Yerevan, 0010, Armenia
Tel.: 374 (10) 56-79-90 or 374 (99) 40-12-38 (cell)
Fax: 374 (10) 56-79-90
E-Mail: concda@gmail.com
See also: Russia, Moscow

Aruba
See: Venezuela, Caracas

Australia — CANBERRA
High Commission of Canada

Address: Commonwealth Avenue, Canberra ACT, Australia 2600
Tel.: 61 (2) 6270-4000
Fax: 61 (2) 6270-4060
E-Mail: cnbra@international.gc.ca
Internet: http://www.australia.gc.ca

Australia — PERTH
Consulate of Canada
Tel.: 61 (8) 9322-7930
Internet: http://www.australia.gc.ca

Australia — SYDNEY
Consulate General of Canada
Address: Level 5, Quay West Building, 111 Harrington Street, Sydney, NSW 2000, Australia
Tel.: 61 (2) 9364-3000
Fax: 61 (2) 9364-3098
E-Mail: sydny@international.gc.ca
Internet: http://www.australia.gc.ca

Austria — VIENNA
Embassy of Canada
Address: Laurenzenberg 2, A-1010, Vienna, Austria
Tel.: 43 (1) 531-38-3000
Fax: 43 (1) 531-38-3910
E-Mail: vienn-cs@international.gc.ca
Internet: http://www.austria.gc.ca

Azerbaijan
See: Turkey, Ankara

Azores
See: Portugal, Ponta Delgada; Portugal, Lisbon

Bahamas — NASSAU
Consulate of Canada
Address: Shirley Street Plaza, Nassau, Bahamas
Postal Address: P.O. Box SS-6371, Nassau, Bahamas
Tel.: (242) 393-2123 or 393-2124
Fax: (242) 393-1305

E-Mail: info@cdnbahamas.com

Bahamas — KINGSTON
High Commission of Canada
Address: 3 West Kings House Road, Kingston 10, Jamaica
Postal Address: P.O. Box 1500, Kingston, Jamaica
Tel.: (876) 926-1500
Fax: 1-876-733-3493
E-Mail: kngtn-cs@international.gc.ca
Internet: www.jamaica.gc.ca

Bahrain — MANAMA
Consulate of Canada
Address: Al Jasrah Tower, 12th Floor, Building No. 95, Road 1702, Block 317, Diplomatic Area, Manama, Bahrain
Postal Address: P.O. Box 2397, Manama, Bahrain
Tel.: 973 (17) 536270
Fax: 973 (17) 532520
E-Mail: canadabh@qayszubilaw.com
See also: Saudi Arabia, Riyadh

Bangladesh — DHAKA
High Commission of Canada
Address: United Nations Road, Baridhara, Bangladesh
Postal Address: P.O. Box 569, Dhaka, Bangladesh
Tel.: 880 (2) 885-1111
Fax: 880 (2) 885-1138
E-Mail: dhaka.consular@international.gc.ca
Internet: http://www.bangladesh.gc.ca

Barbados — BRIDGETOWN
High Commission of Canada
Address: Bishop's Court Hill, St. Michael, P.O. Box 404, Bridgetown, Barbados BB11113
Tel.: (246) 629-3550

Fax: (246) 437-7436
E-Mail: bdgtn-cs@international.gc.ca
Internet: http://www.barbados.gc.ca

Belarus
See: Poland, Warsaw

Belgium — BRUSSELS
Embassy of Canada
Address: Avenue de Tervuren 2, 1040, Brussels, Belgium
Tel.: 32 (2) 741-0611
Fax: 32 (2) 741-0619
E-Mail: bru@international.gc.ca
Internet: http://www.belgium.gc.ca

Belize — BELIZE CITY
Consulate of Canada
Address: 80 Princess Margaret Drive, Belize City, Belize
Postal Address: P.O. Box 610, Belize City, Belize
Tel.: (501) 223-1060
Fax: (501) 223-0060
E-Mail: cdncon.bze@btl.net

Belize — GUATEMALA CITY
Embassy of Canada
Address: Edyma Plaza Building, 8th Floor, 13 Calle 8-44, Zona 10, Guatemala City, Guatemala
Postal Address: P.O. Box 400, Guatemala City, Guatemala
Tel.: (502) 2363-4348
Fax: (502) 2365-1216
E-Mail: gtmla-cs@international.gc.ca
Internet: www.guatemala.gc.ca

Benin — COTONOU
Consulate of Canada
Address: Haie Vive, behind Tripostal and Cotonou airport, Benin

Postal Address: P.O. Box 1124, Tripostal 04, (Cadjehoun), Cotonou, Benin
Tel.: (229) 21 30 50 79 or (229) 95 95 11 80
E-Mail: jhounton@yahoo.fr
See also: Burkina Faso, Ouagadougou

Bermuda — HAMILTON
Consulate of Canada
Address: 73 Front Street, 4th Floor, Hamilton HM 12, Bermuda
Tel.: (441) 292-2917
Fax: (441) 292-9307
See also: United States, New York

Bhutan
See: India, New Delhi

Bolivia — LA PAZ
Embassy of Canada (Program Office)
Address: 2678, Calle Victor Sanjinez, Edificio Barcelona, 2nd Floor, Plaza España (Sopocachi), La Paz, Bolivia
Tel.: 591 (2) 241-5141
Fax: 591 (2) 241-4453
E-Mail: lapaz@international.gc.ca
See also: Peru, Lima

Bonaire
See: Venezuela, Caracas

Bosnia and Herzegovina
See: Austria, Vienna

Botswana — GABORONE
Consulate of Canada
Address: Mokolwane House, Fairgrounds, Gaborone, Botswana
Postal Address: P.O. Box 2111, Gaborone, Botswana
Tel.: (267) 3904411
Fax: (267) 3904411
E-Mail: canada.consul@info.bw

See also: Zimbabwe, Harare

Brazil — BRASILIA
Embassy of Canada
Address: Setor de Embaixadas Sul, Avenida das Nações, Quadra 803, Lote 16, 70410-900 Brasília, D.F., Brazil
Tel.: 55 (61) 3424-5400
Fax: 55 (61) 3424-5490
Email: brsla-cs@international.gc.ca
Internet: www.brazil.gc.ca

Brazil — BELO HORIZONTE
Consulate of Canada
Address: Edifício Lumiere: Hospital de Olhos Dr. Ricardo Guimarães, Rua da Paisagem 220, 3rd Floor, Vila da Serra, 30161-970, Belo Horizonte-MG, Brazil
Tel.: 55 (31) 3047-1225
Fax: 55 (31) 3289-2150
E-Mail: belohorizonte@international.gc.ca
Internet: http://www.brazil.gc.ca

Brazil — RIO DE JANEIRO
Consulate General of Canada
Address: Avenida Atlântica 1130, 13th Floor, Copacabana, 22021-000 Rio de Janeiro, Brazil
Tel.: 55 (21) 2543-3004
Fax: 55 (21) 2275-2195
E-Mail: rio-cs@international.gc.ca
Internet: http://www.brazil.gc.ca

Brazil — SÃO PAULO
Consulate General of Canada
Address: Centro Empresarial Nações Unidas — Torre Norte, Avenida das Nações Unidas, 12901, 16th Floor, 04578-000 São Paulo-SP,
Tel.: 55 (11) 5509-4321
Fax: 55 (11) 5509-4260
E-Mail: spalo-cs@international.gc.ca

Internet: http://www.brazil.gc.ca

British Virgin Islands
See: Barbados, Bridgetown

Brunei Darussalam — BANDAR SERI BEGAWAN
High Commission of Canada
Address: 5th Floor, Jalan McArthur Building, No. 1, Jalan McArthur, Bandar Seri Begawan, Brunei Darussalam
Postal Address: P.O. Box 2808, Bandar Seri Begawan, BS8675, Brunei Darussalam
Tel.: 673 (2) 22-00-43
Fax: 673 (2) 22-00-40
E-Mail: bsbgn@international.gc.ca
Internet: http://www.brunei.gc.ca

Bulgaria — SOFIA
Consulate of Canada
Address: 7 Pozitano Street, Block #3, 1st Floor, Office #4, 1000 Sofia, Bulgaria
Tel.: 359-2-969-9710
Fax: 359-2-981-6081
E-Mail: consular@canada-bg.org
See also: Romania, Bucharest

Burkina Faso — OUAGADOUGOU
Embassy of Canada
Address: 316 Professeur Ki-Zerbo Street, Ouagadougou, Burkina Faso
Postal Address: P.O. Box 548, Ouagadougou, 01, Kadiogo Province, Burkina Faso
Tel.: 226 25 49 08 00 or 226 25 31 18 94
Fax: 226 25 49 08 10 or 226 25 31 19 00
E-Mail: ouaga@international.gc.ca
Internet: http://www.burkinafaso.gc.ca

Burma (Myanmar) — YANGON
Embassy of Canada
Address: 9th Floor, Centrepoint Towers, 65 Sule Pagoda Road, Yangon, Burma
Tel.: 95 1 384 805
Fax: 95 1 384 806
E-Mail: YNGON@international.gc.ca
Internet: www.canadainternational.gc.ca/burma-birmanie/
See also: Thailand, Bangkok

Burundi — BUJUMBURA
Consulate of Canada
Address: Hôtel Club du Lac Tanganyika, Chaussée d'Uvira, Bujumbura, Burundi
Postal Address: P.O. Box 7112, Bujumbura, Burundi
Tel.: 257 22 24-58-98
Fax: 257 22 24-58-99
E-Mail: bujumbura@canadaconsulate.ca
See also: Kenya, Nairobi

Cabo Verde
See: Senegal, Dakar

Cambodia — PHNOM PENH
Embassy of Australia
Address: 27-29 Street 75, Sangkat Srah Chak, Khan Daun Penh, Phnom Penh, Cambodia
Tel.: 855 023 430 811
Fax: 855 023 430 812
E-Mail: PNPEN@international.gc.ca
See also: Thailand, Bangkok

Cameroon — YAOUNDÉ
High Commission of Canada
Address: Les Colonnades building, Bastos, Yaoundé, Cameroon
Postal Address: P.O. Box 572, Yaoundé, Cameroon
Tel.: 237 222-50-39-00

Fax: 237 222-50-39-04
E-Mail: yunde@international.gc.ca
Internet: http://www.canadainternational.gc.ca/cameroon-cameroun

Canary Islands
See: Spain, Madrid

Cayman Islands — SEVEN MILE BEACH
Consulate of Canada
Address: 1st Floor Landmark Square, 64 Earth Close, Seven Mile Beach, Cayman Islands
Postal Address: P.O. Box 30086, Grand Cayman, KY1-1201
Tel.: (345) 949-9400
E-Mail: cdncon.cayman@candw.ky
See also: Jamaica, Kingston

Central African Republic — BANGUI
Consulate of Canada
Address: Cabinet ARC, Bangui, Central African Republic
Postal Address: P.O. Box 514, Bangui, Central African Republic
Tel.: 236 70 50 22 39 or 236 75 50 22 39
Fax: 236 21 61 18 39
E-Mail: consulatbangui@yahoo.fr
See also: Cameroon, Yaoundé

Chad — N'DJAMENA
Consulate of Canada
Address: Rue 1190, Quartier Moursal, Côté Dembé, N'Djamena, Chad
Postal Address: P.O. Box 6013, N'Djamena, Chad
Tel.: 235 631 95680
E-Mail: honcon@honconca-chad.org
Internet: www.canadainternational.gc.ca/sudan-soudan/
See also: Sudan, Khartoum

Chile — ANTOFAGASTA
Tel.: 56 (9) 4269-2636
E-Mail: honcon.canada.antofagasta@gmail.com

Chile — SANTIAGO
Embassy of Canada
Address: Nueva Tajamar 481, Torre Norte, 12th Floor, Las Condes, Santiago, Chile
Postal Address: P.O. Box Casilla 139, Correo 10, Santiago, Chile
Tel.: 56 (2) 2652-3800
Fax: 56 (2) 2652-3916
E-Mail: stago-consular@international.gc.ca
Internet: http://www.chile.gc.ca

China — BEIJING
Embassy of Canada
Address: Consular Section, 19 Dongzhimenwai Dajie, Chao Yang District, Beijing 100600, China
Tel.: 86 (10) 5139-4000
Fax: 86 (10) 5139-4448
E-Mail: beijing.consular@international.gc.ca
Internet: http://www.china.gc.ca

Consular district:
Beijing, Tianjin, Gansu, Liaoning, Jilin, Heilongjiang, Shandong, Shanxi, Inner Mongolia, Ningxia, Shaanxi, Qinghai, Xinjiang, Xizang (Tibet), Henan and Hebei.

China — CHONGQING
Consulate General of Canada
Address: Room 1705, Metropolitan Tower, Wu Yi Lu, Yu Zhong District, Chongqing 400010, China
Tel.: 86 (23) 6373-8007
Fax: 86 (23) 6373-8026
E-Mail: chonq@international.gc.ca
Internet: http://www.chongqing.gc.ca

Consular district:
Chongqing, Sichauan, Yunnan and Guizhou.

China — GUANGZHOU
Consulate General of Canada
Address: China Hotel Office Tower, Suite 801, Liu Hua Lu, Guangzhou, Guangdong 510015, China
Tel.: 86 (20) 8611-6100
Fax: 86 (20) 8611-6196
E-Mail: guangzhou.consular@international.gc.ca
Internet: http://www.guangzhou.gc.ca

Consular district:
Guangdong, Guangxi, Fujian, Jiangxi, Hunan and Hainan.

China — HONG KONG
Consulate General of Canada
Address: 8th and 9th Floors, 25 Westlands Road, Quarry Bay, Hong Kong SAR, China
Postal Address: 8th Floor, 25 Westlands Road, Quarry Bay, Hong Kong SAR, China
Tel.: 85 (2) 3719 4700
Fax: 85 (2) 2847 7561
E-Mail: hkong-cs@international.gc.ca
Internet: http://www.hongkong.gc.ca

Consular district:
Hong Kong and Macao

China — SHANGHAI
Consulate General of Canada
Address: ECO City Building, 8th floor, 1788 Nanjing Xi Lu-Jing An District, Shanghai, 200040, China
Tel.: 86 (21) 3279-2800
Fax: 86 (21) 3279-2801
E-Mail: shanghai.consular@international.gc.ca

Internet: http://www.shanghai.gc.ca

Consular district:
Jiangsu, Anhui, Zhejiang, Hubei and the city of Shanghai.

Colombia — BOGOTÁ
Embassy of Canada
Address: Cra. 7, No. 114-33, Piso 14, Bogotá Colombia
Postal Address: P.O. Box 110067, Bogotá Colombia
Tel.: 57 (1) 657-9800
Fax: 57 (1) 657-9912
E-Mail: bgota@international.gc.ca
Internet: http://www.colombia.gc.ca

Colombia — CARTAGENA
Consulate of Canada
Address: Edificio Centro Ejecutivo Bocagrande, Carrera 3, No. 8-129, Oficina No. 1103, Cartagena, Colombia
Tel.: 57 (5) 665-5838
Fax: 57 (5) 665-5837
E-Mail: cartagena@international.gc.ca

Comoros
See: Tanzania, Dar es Salaam

Cook Islands
See: New Zealand, Wellington

Costa Rica — SAN JOSÉ
Embassy of Canada
Address: La Sabana Executive Business Centre, Building No. 5, 3rd Floor, behind the Contraloría General de la República, San José Costa Rica
Postal Address: P.O. Box 351-1007, San José, Costa Rica
Tel.: 506 2242-4400
Fax: 506 2242-4410
E-Mail: sjcra@international.gc.ca
Internet: http://www.costarica.gc.ca

Côte d'Ivoire (Ivory Coast) — ABIDJAN
Embassy of Canada
Address: Immeuble Trade Centre, 23 avenue Noguès, Le Plateau, Abidjan, Côte d'Ivoire
Postal Address: P.O. Box 4104, Abidjan, 01, Côte d'Ivoire
Tel.: 225 20 30 07 00
Fax: 225 20 30 07 20
E-Mail: abdjn@international.gc.ca
Internet: http://www.canadainternational. gc.ca/cotedivoire

Croatia — ZAGREB
Embassy of Canada
Address: Prilaz Gjure Dezelica 4, 10000 Zagreb, Croatia
Tel.: 385 (1) 488-1200 or 488-1238
Fax: 385 (1) 488-1230
E-Mail: zagrb@international.gc.ca
Internet: http://www.croatia.gc.ca

Cuba — GUARDALAVACA
Consulate of Canada
Address: Hotel Atlantico, Suite 1, Guardalavaca, Holguín, Cuba
Tel.: (53-24) 430-320
Fax: (53-24) 430-321
E-Mail: guardalavaca@international.gc.ca

Cuba — HAVANA
Embassy of Canada
Address: Calle 30, No. 518 esquina a 7 ma, Miramar, Havana, Cuba
Tel.: (53-7) 204-2516
Fax: (53-7) 204-2044
E-Mail: varadero@international.gc.ca
Internet: http://www.cuba.gc.ca

Cuba — VARADERO
Consulate of Canada
Address: Calle 13 e/Avenida Primera y Camino del Mar, Varadero, Matanzas, Cuba

Tel.: 53 (45) 61-2078
Fax: 53 (45) 66-7395
E-Mail: varadero@international.gc.ca

Curaçao
See: Venezuela, Caracas

Cyprus — ATHENS
Embassy of Canada
Street Address: 48 Ethnikis Antistaseos Street, Chalandri, 152 31, Athens, Greece
Tel.: 30 (210) 727-3400
Fax: 30 (210) 727-3480
E-Mail: athns-cs@international.gc.ca
Internet: www.greece.gc.ca

Cyprus — NICOSIA
Consulate of Canada
Address: 15 Themistocles Dervis Street, 066 Nicosia, Cyprus
Postal Address: P.O. Box 22125-1517, Nicosia, Cyprus
Tel.: 357 (2) 2775-508
Fax: 357 (2) 2779-905
E-Mail: info@consulcanada.com.cy

Czech Republic — PRAGUE
Embassy of Canada
Address: Ve Struhach 95/2, 160 00 Prague 6, Czech Republic
Tel.: 420 272 101 800
Fax: 420 272 101 890
E-Mail: prgue-cs@international.gc.ca
Internet: http://www.czechrepublic.gc.ca

Democratic Republic of Congo (Kinshasa) — KINSHASA
Embassy of Canada
Address: 17, avenue Pumbu, Commune de Gombe, Kinshasa, Congo (Kinshasa)

Postal Address: P.O. Box 8341, Kinshasa, 1, Congo (Kinshasa)
Tel.: 243 996 021 500
Fax: 243 996 021 510 or 243 996 021 511
E-Mail: kinshasa@international.gc.ca
Internet: http://www.canadainternational.gc.ca/congo/

Denmark — COPENHAGEN
Embassy of Canada
Address: Kristen Bernikowsgade 1, Copenhagen K., DK-1105, Denmark
Tel.: 45 33-48-32-00
Fax: 45 33-48-32-20
E-Mail: copen@international.gc.ca
Internet: http://www.denmark.gc.ca

Djibouti — DJIBOUTI
Consulate of Canada
Address: Place Lagarde, Djibouti
Postal Address: P.O. Box 1188, Djibouti
Tel.: 25 (3) 2135-38-59 or 2135-59-50
Fax: 25 (3) 2135-00-14
E-Mail: georgalis@intnet.dj
See also: Ethiopia, Addis Ababa

Dominica
See: Barbados, Bridgetown

Dominican Republic — PUNTA CANA
Office of the Embassy of Canada
Address: Carretera Veron — Bavaro Km. 2 1/2, Amstar Business Center, Building 4, Office 404, Punta Cana, Dominican Republic
Tel.: (809) 455-1730
Fax: 809-455-1734

Dominican Republic — PUERTO PLATA
Consulate of Canada

Address: Calle Villanueva No 8, Edificio Abraxas, Puerto Plata, Dominican Republic
Tel.: (809) 586-5761
Fax: (809) 586-5762
E-Mail: canada.pop@gmail.com

Dominican Republic — SANTO DOMINGO
Embassy of Canada
Address: Av. Winston Churchill 1099 Torre Citigroup en Acrópolis Center, 18th Floor Ensanche Piantini, Santo Domingo, Dominican Republic
Postal Address: P.O. 2054, Santo Domingo 1, Dominican Republic
Tel.: (809) 262-3100
Fax: (809) 262-3108
E-Mail: sdmgo@international.gc.ca
Internet: http://www.dominicanrepublic.gc.ca

Ecuador — GUAYAQUIL
Consulate of Canada
Address: Avenida Francisco de Orellana, Number 234, Blue Towers Building, 6th Floor, Office 604, Guayaquil, Ecuador
Tel.: (593-4) 263-1109 Ext.: 101
E-Mail: cancongye@gmail.com
Internet: http://www.ecuador.gc.ca

Ecuador — QUITO
Embassy of Canada
Address: Av. Amazonas N37-29 and Union Nacional de Periodistas, Eurocenter Building, 3rd Floor (one block north of the Supreme Court Building, near Amazonas and United Nations), Quito, Ecuador
Postal Address: P.O. Box 17-11-6512, Quito, Ecuador
Tel.: 593 (2) 245-5499
Fax: 593 (2) 227-7672
E-Mail: quito@international.gc.ca

Internet: http://www.ecuador.gc.ca

Egypt — CAIRO
Embassy of Canada
Postal Address: Nile City Towers, 2005 (A) Corniche El Nile, South Tower, 18th floor, Cairo, Egypt
Tel.: 202 2461 2200
Fax: 202 2461 2201
E-Mail: cairo-cs@international.gc.ca
Internet: http://www.egypt.gc.ca

El Salvador — SAN SALVADOR
Embassy of Canada
Address: Gigante Financial Centre, Tower A, Lobby 2, Alameda Roosevelt and 63 Avenue S, Colonia Escalón, San Salvador, El Salvador
Tel.: (503) 2279-4655/ 4657/ 4659
Fax: (503) 2279-0765
E-Mail: ssal@international.gc.ca
Internet: http://www.elsalvador.gc.ca

Equatorial Guinea
See: Nigeria, Abuja

Eritrea — ASMARA
Address: Abeneh Street 745, House No. 152/154, Tiravolo, Asmara, Eritrea
Postal Address: P.O. Box 3962, Asmara, Eritrea
Tel.: 291 (1) 18 18 55 or 291 (1) 18 64 90
Fax: 291 (1) 18 64 88
E-Mail: mkcca1@yahoo.com

Eritrea — KHARTOUM
Embassy of Canada
Address: 29 Africa Road, Block 56, Khartoum 1, Sudan
Postal Address: P.O. Box 10503, Khartoum, 1, Sudan
Tel.: 249 156 550 500
Fax: 249 156 550 501

E-Mail: khrtm@international.gc.ca
Internet: www.canadainternatio-
nal.gc.ca/sudan-soudan/

Estonia — TALLINN
Office of the Embassy of Canada
Address: Toom Kooli 13, 2nd
Floor, 15186 Tallinn, Estonia
Tel.: 372 627-3311/10
Fax: 372 627-3312
E-Mail: tallinn@canada.ee
Internet: http://www.estonia.gc.ca
See also: Sweden, Stockholm

Ethiopia — ADDIS ABABA
Embassy of Canada
Address: Old Airport Area, Nefas
Silk Lafto Sub City, Kebele 04,
House No.122, Addis Ababa,
Ethiopia
Postal Address: P.O. Box 1130,
Addis Ababa, Ethiopia
Tel.: 251 (0) 11 371 0000
Fax: 251 (0) 11 371 0040
E-Mail: addis-cs@international.gc.-
ca
Internet: http://www.canadainter-
national.gc.ca/ethiopia-ethiopie/

Falkland Islands
See: United Kingdom, London

Fiji — NADI
Consulate of Canada
Address: 6 Cawa Road, Martintar,
Nadi, Fiji
Postal Address: P.O. Box 10690,
Nadi, Fiji
Tel.: 679 9924 999 (mobile)
Fax: 679 672 1936 or 679 672 4489
E-Mail: vyases@connect.com.fj
See also: New Zealand, Wellington

Finland — HELSINKI
Embassy of Canada
Address: Pohjoisesplanadi 27C,
00100 Helsinki, Finland

Postal Address: P.O. Box 779,
Helsinki, 00101
Tel.: 358 (9) 228-530
Fax: 358 (9) 601-060
E-Mail: hsnki@international.gc.ca
Internet: http://www.finland.gc.ca

France — LYON
Consulate of Canada
Address: 18, Avenue du Marechal
de Saxe 69006 Lyon, France
Tel.: 33 (0)4 72 37 86 67
Fax: 33 (0)4 72 83 53 57
E-Mail: lyon@international.gc.ca

France — NICE
Consulate of Canada
Address: 10, rue Lamartine, 06000
Nice, France
Tel.: 33 (0)4 93-92-93-22
Fax: 33 (0)4 93-92-55-51
E-Mail: nice@international.gc.ca

France — PARIS
Embassy of Canada
Address: 35, avenue Montaigne,
75008 Paris, France
Tel.: 33 (0)1 44 43 29 00 / Consular
services: 33 (0)1 44 43 29 02
Fax: 33 (0)1 44 43 29 86
E-Mail: paris-consulaire@interna-
tional.gc.ca
Internet: http://www.france.gc.ca

France — TOULOUSE
Consulate of Canada
Address: 10, rue Jules-de-Rességui-
er, 31000 Toulouse, France
Tel.: 33 (0)5 61-52-19-06
Fax: 33 (0)5 61-55-40-32
E-Mail: toulouse@internatio-
nal.gc.ca

French Guiana — GEORGETOWN
See: Guyana, Georgetown

French Polynesia

See: New Zealand, Wellington

Gabon — LIBREVILLE
Consulate of Canada
Address: Quartier Batterie IV, Pont de Gué-Gué 1st street behind the European Union, Libreville, Gabon
Tel.: 241 01 44 29 65
E-Mail: conhongab@gmail.com
See also: Cameroon, Yaoundé

Gambia, The — BANJUL
British High Commission
Address: 48 Atlantic Road, Fajara, Banjul, The Gambia
Postal Address: P.O. Box 507, Banjul, The Gambia
Tel.: 220 4495133
Fax: 220 4496134
E-Mail: bhcbanjul@gamtel.gm
See also: Senegal, Dakar

Georgia — TBILISI
Consulate of Canada
Address: 34 Rustaveli Avenue, Third Floor, Tbilisi, Georgia, 0108
Tel.: 995 (32) 298-2072
Fax: 995 (32) 218-2052
E-Mail: ccogeorgia@gmail.com
See also: Turkey, Ankara

Germany — BERLIN
Embassy of Canada
Address: Leipziger Platz 17, 10117 Berlin, Germany
Tel.: 49 (30) 20312 470; 49 (30) 20312 0
Fax: 49 (30) 20 31 24 57
E-Mail: brlin-cs@international.gc.ca
Internet: http://www.germany.gc.ca

Germany — DÜSSELDORF
Consulate of Canada
Address: Benrather Strasse 8, 40213 Düsseldorf, Germany

Tel.: 49 (211) 17 21 70
Fax: 49 (211) 35 91 65
E-Mail: ddorf@international.gc.ca
Internet: http://www.germany.gc.ca

Germany — MUNICH
Consulate of Canada
Address: Tal 29, 80331 Munich, Germany
Tel.: 49 (89) 21 99 57 0
Fax: 49 (89) 21 99 57 57
E-Mail: munic@international.gc.ca
Internet: http://www.germany.gc.ca

Germany — STUTTGART
Consulate of Canada
Address: Leitzstrasse 45, 70469 Stuttgart, Germany
Tel.: 49 (711) 22 39 67 8
Fax: 49 (711) 22 39 67 9
E-Mail: stuttgart@canada.de
Internet: http://www.germany.gc.ca

Ghana — ACCRA
High Commission of Canada
Address: 42 Independence Avenue, Accra, Ghana
Postal Address: P.O. Box 1639, Accra, Ghana
Tel.: 233 (302) 21 15 21 or 22 85 55
Fax: 233 (302) 21 15 23 or 77 37 92
E-Mail: accra@international.gc.ca
Internet: http://www.canadainternational.gc.ca/ghana/

Gibraltar
See: United Kingdom, London

Greece — ATHENS
Embassy of Canada
Address: 48 Ethnikis Antistaseos Street, Chalandri, 152 31, Athens, Greece
Tel.: 30 (210) 727-3400
Fax: 30 (210) 727-3480
E-Mail: athns-cs@international.gc.ca

Internet: http://www.greece.gc.ca

Greece — THESSALONIKI
Consulate of Canada
Address: 19, N. Kountouriotou
Street, 546 24, Thessaloniki, Greece
Tel.: 30 (2310) 256350
Fax: 30 (2310) 256351
E-Mail: petmezas_canada@thessa-
law.gr
Internet: http://www.greece.gc.ca

Greenland — NUUK
Consulate of Canada
Address: Tuapannguit 48, 3900
Nuuk, Greenland
Postal Address: P.O. Box 1012, 3900
Nuuk, Greenland
Tel.: (299) 31-1647 or (299) 55-3289
E-Mail: lpdaniel@greennet.gl
See also: Denmark, Copenhagen

Grenada
See: Barbados, Bridgetown

Guadeloupe
See: France, Paris

Guam — POHNPEI, Micronesia
See: Micronesia, Pohnpei

Guatemala — GUATEMALA CITY
Embassy of Canada
Address: Edyma Plaza Building, 8th
Floor, 13 Calle 8-44, Zona 10,
Guatemala City, Guatemala
Postal Address: P.O. Box 400, Gua-
temala City, Guatemala
Tel.: (502) 2363-4348
Fax: (502) 2365-1216
E-Mail: gtmla-cs@internatio-
nal.gc.ca
Internet: http://www.guatemala.gc.-
ca

Guinea

See: Senegal, Dakar

Guinea — BISSAU
See: Senegal, Dakar

Guyana — GEORGETOWN
High Commission of Canada
Address: High and Young Streets,
Georgetown, Guyana
Postal Address: P.O. Box 10880,
Georgetown, Guyana
Tel.: (592) 227-2081; 227-2082; 227-
2083; 227-2084 or 227-2085
Fax: (592) 225-8380
E-Mail: grgtn@international.gc.ca
Internet: http://www.guyana.gc.ca

Haiti — PORT-AU-PRINCE
Embassy of Canada
Address: Delmas Road, between
Delmas 75 and 71, Port-au-Prince
Tel.: 011 (509) 2-812-9000, 3-702-
9996
E-Mail: prnce@international.gc.ca
Internet: http://www.haiti.gc.ca

Honduras — TEGUCIGALPA
Office of the Embassy of Canada
Address: Centro Financiero CITI,
3rd Floor, Boulevard San Juan
Bosco, Colonia Payaquí Tegucigal-
pa, Honduras
Tel.: (504) 2232-4551
Fax: (504) 2239-7767
E-Mail: tglpa@international.gc.ca
See also: Costa Rica, San José

Hong Kong
See: China, Hong Kong

Hungary — BUDAPEST
Embassy of Canada
Address: Ganz utca 12-14, 1027
Budapest, Hungary
Tel.: 36 (1) 392-3360
Fax: 36 (1) 392-3390
E-Mail: bpest@international.gc.ca

Internet: http://www.hungary.gc.ca

Iceland — REYKJAVIK
Embassy of Canada
Address: 14 Tungata, 101 Reykjavik, Iceland
Postal Address: P.O. Box 1510, Reykjavik, Iceland, 121
Tel.: (354) 575-6500
Fax: (354) 575-6501
E-Mail: rkjvk@international.gc.ca
Internet: http://www.iceland.gc.ca

India — CHANDIGARH
Consulate General of Canada
Address: SCO #54-56, Sector 17-A, Chandigarh 160 017, India
Tel.: 91 (172) 505-0300
Fax: 91 (172) 505-0341
E-Mail: chadg-cs@international.gc.ca
Internet: http://www.india.gc.ca

India — KOLKATA (formerly Calcutta)
Consulate of Canada
Address: Duncan House, 31 Netaji Subhas Road, Kolkata 700 001, India
Tel.: 91 (33) 2242-6820
Fax: 91 (33) 2242-6828
E-Mail: ccklkta@rp-sg.in
Internet: http://www.india.gc.ca

India — MUMBAI (formerly Bombay)
Consulate General of Canada
Address: Tower 2, 21st Floor, Indiabulls Financial Centre, Senapati Bapat Marg, Elphinstone Road West, Mumbai 400 013, India
Tel.: 91 (22) 6749-4444
Fax: 91 (22) 6749-4454
E-Mail: mmbai@international.gc.ca
Internet: http://www.india.gc.ca

India — NEW DELHI
High Commission of Canada
Address: 7/8 Shantipath, Chanakyapuri, New Delhi 110 021, India
Postal Address: P.O. Box 5207, New Delhi 110 021, India
Tel.: 91 (11) 4178-2000
Fax: 011-4178-2023
E-Mail: delhi.consular@international.gc.ca
Internet: http://www.india.gc.ca

Indonesia — BALI
Consulate General of Australia
Address: Jalan Tantular No. 32, Renon, Denpasar, Bali, Indonesia.
Postal Address: P.O. Box 3243, Renon, Denpasar, Bali, Indonesia
Tel.: 62 (361) 241-118
Fax: 62 (361) 221-195 or 62 (361) 241-120 (Visa enquiries only)
E-Mail: bali.congen@dfat.gov.au

Indonesia — JAKARTA
Embassy of Canada
Address: World Trade Centre, 6th Floor, Jl. Jend Sudirman, Kav. 29, Jakarta 12920, Indonesia.
Postal Address: P.O. Box 8324/JKS.MP, Jakarta, 12084 Indonesia
Tel.: 62 (21) 2550-7800
Fax: 62 (21) 2550-7811
E-Mail: jkrta@international.gc.ca
Internet: http://www.indonesia.gc.ca

Iran
See: Turkey, Ankara

Iraq
See: Jordan, Amman

Ireland — DUBLIN
Embassy of Canada
Address: 7-8 Wilton Terrace, Dublin 2, Ireland

Tel.: 353 (1) 234-4000
Fax: 353 (1) 234-4001
E-Mail: consul.dublin@internatio-nal.gc.ca
Internet: http://www.ireland.gc.ca

Israel, the West Bank and the Gaza Strip — RAMALLAH
Representative Office of Canada
Address: 12 Elias Odeh Street, Ra-mallah, West Bank
Postal Address: P.O. Box 18604, Jerusalem 91184, or P.O. Box 2286, Ramallah, West Bank
Tel.: 972 (2) 297-8430
Fax: 972 (2) 297-8446
E-Mail: rmlah@international.gc.ca
Internet: http://www.westbankand-gaza.gc.ca

Israel, the West Bank and the Gaza Strip — TEL AVIV
Embassy of Canada
Address: Canada House, 3/5 Nirim Street, 4th Floor, Tel Aviv 67060, Israel
Postal Address: P.O. Box 9442, Tel Aviv, 61093, Israel
Tel.: 972 (3) 636-3300
Fax: 972 (3) 636-3383
E-Mail: taviv@international.gc.ca
Internet: http://www.israel.gc.ca

Italy — ROME
Embassy of Canada
Address: Via Zara 30, Rome 00198, Italy
Tel.: 39 06-85444-2911
Fax: 39 06-85444-2912
E-Mail: consul.rome@internatio-nal.gc.ca
Internet: http://www.Italy.gc.ca

Italy — UDINE
Consulate of Canada
Address: 4, Via Elio Morpurgo, 33100 Udine, Italy

Tel.: 39 0432-229709
E-Mail: consul.canada.udine@g-mail.com

Italy — MILAN
Consulate of Canada
Address: 3, Piazza Cavour, 6th floor, 20121 Milan, Italy
Tel.: 39 02 6269-4238
Fax: 39 2901-3600
E-Mail: consul.canada.milan@g-mail.com

Jamaica — KINGSTON
High Commission of Canada
Address: 3 West Kings House Road, Kingston, Jamaica
Postal Address: P.O. Box 1500, Kingston, Jamaica
Tel.: (876) 926-1500
Fax: (876) 733-3493
E-Mail: kngtn-cs@internatio-nal.gc.ca
Internet: http://www.jamaica.gc.ca

Jamaica — MONTEGO BAY
Consulate of Canada
Address: 29 Gloucester Street, Montego Bay
Tel.: (876) 632-0371
Fax: (876) 632-3690
E-Mail: cancon@flowja.com

Japan — FUKUOKA
Address: c/o Kyshu Electric Power Co., Inc. 1-82 Watanabe-dori 2-chome, Chuo-ku, Fukuoka, Japan, 810-8720
Tel.: 81 (92) 726-6348
Fax: 81 (92) 726-6348
E-Mail: info@canadian-consulate-ukuoka.jp
Internet: http://www.japan.gc.ca

Japan — HIROSHIMA
Consulate of Canada

Address: c/o Chugoku Electric Power- er Co. Inc., 4-33 Komachi, Naka- ku, Hiroshima-shi, Hiroshima-ken, Japan, 730-8701
Tel.: 81 (82) 246-0057
Fax: 81 (82) 504-7006
Internet: http://www.japan.gc.ca

Japan — NAGOYA
Consulate of Canada
Address: Nakato Marunouchi Building, 6F, 3-17-6 Marunouchi, Naka-ku, Nagoya-shi, Aichi-ken, Japan, 460-0002
Tel.: 81 (52) 972-0450
Fax: 81 (52) 972-0453
E-Mail: ngoya@international.gc.ca
Internet: http://www.japan.gc.ca

Japan — OSAKA
Consulate of Canada
c/o Tsuda Sangyo Co. Ltd., 1-8-19 Hirabayashi Minami, Suminoe-ku Japan, 559-8550
Tel.: 81 (6) 6681-0250
E-Mail: canadianconsulate@tsu- da.co.jp
Internet: japan.gc.ca

Japan — SAPPORO
Consulate of Canada
Address: Canada Place, Poseidon Maruyama 2F, 26-1-3 Odori Nishi, Chuo-ku, Sapporo, Japan 064-0820
Tel.: 81 (11) 643-2520
Fax: 81 (11) 643-2520
E-Mail: ryojikan@yamani.com
Internet: http://www.japan.gc.ca

Japan — TOKYO
Embassy of Canada
Address: 3-38 Akasaka 7-chome, Minato-ku, Tokyo, Japan, 107- 8503
Tel.: 81 (3) 5412-6200
Fax: 81 (3) 5412-6289

E-Mail: tokyo-consul@internatio- nal.gc.ca
Internet: http://www.japan.gc.ca

Jordan — AMMAN
Embassy of Canada
Address: 133 Zahran Street, Am- man, Jordan
Postal Address: P.O. Box 815403, Amman, 11180, Jordan
Tel.: 962 (6) 590 1500
Fax: 962 (6) 590 1501
E-Mail: amman@international.gc.- ca
Internet: http://www.jordan.gc.ca

Kazakhstan — ASTANA
Embassy of Canada
Address: Kabanbay Batyr Street 13/1, Astana, 010000, Kazakhstan
Tel.: 7 (7172) 475 577
Fax: 7 (7172) 475 587
E-Mail: astnacs2@internatio- nal.gc.ca
Internet: www.kazakhstan.gc.ca

Kenya — NAIROBI
High Commission of Canada
Address: Limuru Road, Gigiri, Nairobi, Kenya
Postal Address: P.O. Box 1013, Nairobi, 00621, Kenya
Tel.: 254 (20) 366-3000
Fax: 254 (20) 366-3900
E-Mail: nrobi@international.gc.ca
Internet: http://www.canadainter- national.gc.ca/kenya/

Kiribati — TARAWA
High Commission of Australia
Address: Bairiki, Tarawa, Kiribati
Tel.: 686 21-184 or 90-184
Fax: 686 21-904
E-Mail: ahc_tarawa@dfat.gov.au
See also: New Zealand, Wellington

Korea, North (DPRK) — PYON-GYANG
Swedish Embassy
Address: Munsudong, Daehak Street, Taedonggang District, Pyongyang, Democratic People's Republic of North Korea
Tel.: 850 (2) 381-7908, 381-7904, or 381-7485
Fax: 850 (2) 381-7663
E-Mail: ambassaden.pyongyang@-foreign.ministry.se
Internet: http://www.swedenabroad.com/en-GB/Embassies/Pyongyang

Korea, South — BUSAN
Consulate of Canada
Address: c/o Dongsung Chemical Corporation, 99 Sinsan-ro (472 Shinpyung-dong), Saha-gu, Busan 604-721, Republic of Korea
Tel.: 82 (51) 204-5581
Fax: 82 (51) 204-5580

Korea, South — SEOUL
Embassy of Canada
Address: 21 Jeongdong-gil (Jeongdong), Jung-gu, Seoul (100-120), Republic of Korea
Tel.: 82-2-3783-6000
Fax: 82-2-3783-6112
E-Mail: seoul@international.gc.ca
Internet: http://www.korea.gc.ca

Kosovo — ZAGREB
Embassy of Canada
Address: Prilaz Gjure Dezelica 4, 10000 Zagreb, Croatia
Tel.: 385 (1) 488-1200 or 488-1238
Fax: 385 (1) 488-1230
E-Mail: zagrb@international.gc.ca
Internet: www.croatia.gc.ca

Kuwait — KUWAIT CITY
Embassy of Canada

Address: Villa 24, Block 4, 24 Al-Mutawakkal Street, Da'aiyah, Kuwait City, Kuwait
Postal Address: P.O. Box 25281, Kuwait City, Safat 13113, Kuwait
Tel.: 965 2256-3025
Fax: 965 2256-0173
E-Mail: kwait@international.gc.ca
Internet: http://www.kuwait.gc.ca

Kyrgyz Republic — BISHKEK
Consulate of Canada
Address: 189 Moskovskaya Avenue, Bishkek, 720010, Kyrgyz Republic
Tel.: 996 (312) 65-01-01 or 65-05-06
Fax: 996 (312) 65-01-01
E-Mail: canada_honcon@akipress.org
See also: Kazakhstan, Astana

Laos — VIENTIANE
Embassy of Australia
Address: KM4, Thadeua Road, Watnak Village, Sisattanak District, Vientiane, Laos
Tel.: 856 (0) 21 35 38 34
Fax: 856 (21) 353-801
E-Mail: VNTNE@international.gc.ca
See also: Thailand, Bangkok

Latvia — RIGA
Embassy of Canada
Address: 20/22 Baznicas Street, 6th Floor, Riga LV-1010, Latvia
Tel.: 371 6781-3945
Fax: 371 6781-3960
E-Mail: riga@international.gc.ca
Internet: http://www.latvia.gc.ca
See also: Sweden, Stockholm

Lebanon — BEIRUT
Embassy of Canada
Address: First Floor, Coolrite Building, 43 Jal El Dib Highway (seaside), Beirut, Lebanon

Postal Address: P.O. Box 60163, Jal El Dib, Beirut, Lebanon
Tel.: 961 (4) 726-700
Fax: 961 (4) 726-702
E-Mail: berut-cs@international.gc.ca
Internet: http://www.lebanon.gc.ca

Lesotho
See also: South Africa, Pretoria

Liberia
See: Côte d'Ivoire, Abidjan

Libya
See: Tunisia, Tunis

Liechtenstein
See: Switzerland, Berne

Lithuania — VILNIUS
Office of the Canadian Embassy
Address: Business Centre 2000, Jogailos St. 4, 7th Floor, Vilnius 01116, Lithuania
Tel.: 370 (5) 249-0950
Fax: 370 (5) 249-7865
E-Mail: vilnius@canada.lt
Internet: http://www.balticstates.gc.ca
See also: Sweden, Stockholm

Luxembourg — LUXEMBOURG
Consulate of Canada
Address: 15, rue Guillaume Schneider, L-2522 Luxembourg, Luxembourg
Tel.: 35 (2) 262-70-570
Fax: 35 (2) 262-70-670
E-Mail: canada@pt.lu
Internet: http://www.luxembourg.gc.ca
See also: Belgium, Brussels

Macao

See: China, Hong Kong

Macedonia[1] **— SKOPJE**
Consulate of Canada
Address: Blagoj Davkov No. 2/1, 1000 Skopje, Macedonia
Tel.: 389 (2) 3225-630
Fax: 389 (2) 3220-596
E-Mail: honcon@unet.com.mk
See also: Serbia, Belgrade

Madagascar
See: South Africa, Pretoria

Malawi
See: Mozambique, Maputo

Malaysia — KUALA LUMPUR
High Commission of Canada
Address: 17th Floor, Menara Tan & Tan, 207 Jalan Tun Razak, 50400 Kuala Lumpur, Malaysia
Postal Address: P.O. Box 10990, 50732 Kuala Lumpur, Malaysia
Tel.: 6 (03) 2718-3333
Fax: 6 (03) 2718-3399
E-Mail: klmpr-cs@international.gc.ca
Internet: http://www.malaysia.gc.ca

Malaysia — PENANG
Consulate of Canada
Address: 3007, Tingkat Perusahaan 5, Prai Industrial Park, 13600 Prai, Penang, Malaysia
Tel.: 6 (04) 389-3300
Fax: 6 (04) 389-2300
E-Mail: tyt@lbsb.com
Internet: http://www.malaysia.gc.ca

Maldives
See: Sri Lanka, Colombo

Mali — BAMAKO
Embassy of Canada

---

[1] Known as Former Yugoslav Republic of Macedonia in UN and other international bodies.

Address: Immeuble Séméga, Route de Koulikoro, Commune II, Bamako, Mali
Postal Address: P.O. Box 198, Bamako, Mali
Tel.: 223 44 98 04 50
Fax: 223 44 98 04 55
E-Mail: bmakog@international.gc.ca
Internet: http://www.mali.gc.ca

Malta — VALLETTA
Consulate of Canada
Address: Demajo House, 103 Archbishop Street (Triq L-Arcisqof), Valletta VLT 09, Malta
Tel.: 356 2552-3233
Fax: 356 2552-3232
E-Mail: canhcon@demajo.com
See also: Italy, Rome

Marshall Islands
See: Micronesia, Pohnpei

Martinique
See: France, Paris

Mauritania — NOUAKCHOTT
Consulate of Canada
Address: Al Khayma city center, 10 Mamadou Konaté Street, 3rd floor, Nouakchott, Mauritania
Postal Address: P.O. Box 428, Nouakchott, Mauritania
Tel.: 222 45-29-26-97 or 222 46-76-63-67 (emergency only)
Fax: 222 45-29-26-98 or 222 45-25-64-21
See also: Morocco, Rabat-Souissi

Mauritius — PORT LOUIS
Consulate of Canada
Address: 18 Jules Koenig Street, c/o Blanche Birger Co. Ltd., Port Louis
Postal Address: P.O. Box 209, Port Louis
Tel.: (230) 212-5500

Fax: (230) 208-3391
E-Mail: canada@intnet.mu
See also: South Africa, Pretoria

Mayotte
See: Tanzania, Dar es Salaam

Mexico — ACAPULCO
Consular Agency of Canada
Address: Pasaje Diana, Avenida Costera Miguel AlemU 121, L-16, Fracc. Magallanes, 39670 Acapulco, Guerrero, México
Tel.: 52 (744) 484-1305, 481-1349
Fax: 52 (744) 484-1306
E-Mail: aplco@international.gc.ca

Mexico — CABO SAN LUCAS
Consular Agency of Canada
Address: Carretera Transpeninsular Km. 0.5, Local 82, Col. El Tezal, 23454 Cabo San Lucas, Baja California Sur, México
Tel.: 52 (624) 142-4333
Fax: 52 (624) 142-4262
E-Mail: lcabo@international.gc.ca

Mexico — CANCÚN
Consulate of Canada
Address: Centro Empresarial, Oficina E7, Blvd. Kukulcan Km. 12, Zona Hotelera, 77599 Cancún, Quintana Roo, México
Tel.: 52 (998) 883-3360/883-3361
Fax: 52 (998) 883-3232
E-Mail: cncun@international.gc.ca

Mexico — GUADALAJARA
Consulate of Canada
Address: World Trade Center, Av. Mariano Otero 1249, Torre Pacifico Piso 8, Col. Rinconada del Bosque, 44530 Guadalajara, Jalisco, México
Tel.: 52 (33) 1818 4200
Fax: 52 (33) 1818 4210
E-Mail: gjara@international.gc.ca

Mexico — MAZATLÁN
Consular Agency of Canada
Address: Centro Comercial La Marina Business and Life, Blvd. Marina Mazatlán 2302, Office 41, Col. Marina Mazatlán, 82103 Mazatlán, Sinaloa, Mexico
Tel.: 52 (669) 913-7320
Fax: 52 (669) 914-6655
E-Mail: mztln@international.gc.ca

Mexico — MEXICO CITY
Embassy of Canada
Address: Calle Schiller No. 529, Colonia Polanco, 11580 México, D.F., México
Postal Address: P.O. Box 40-045, 06141 México, D.F., México
Tel.: 52 (55) 5724-7900
Fax: 52 (55) 5724-7943
E-Mail: mxico@international.gc.ca
Internet: http://www.mexico.gc.ca

Mexico — MONTERREY
Consulate General of Canada
Address: Torre Gomez Morin 955, Ave. Gomez Morin No. 955, Suite 404, Col. Montebello, 66279 San Pedro Garza Garcia, Nuevo Léon, México
Tel.: 52 (81) 2088 3200
Fax: 52 (81) 2088 3230
E-Mail: monterrey@international.gc.ca

Mexico — OAXACA
Consular Agency of Canada
Address: Multiplaza Brena, Pino Suárez 700, Local 11 B, Col. Centro, 68000 Oaxaca, México
Tel.: 52 (951) 513-3777 / 503-0722
Fax: 52 (951) 515-2147
E-Mail: oxaca@international.gc.ca

Mexico — PLAYA DEL CARMEN
Consular Agency of Canada

Address: Plaza Paraíso Caribe, Modulo C, Planta 2, Oficina C21 - 24, Av. 10 Sur entre Calle 3 y 5 Sur, M-35, Lote 1, Colonia Centro, 77710 Playa del Carmen, Quintana Roo, México
Tel.: 52 (984) 803-2411
Fax: 52 (984) 803-2665
E-Mail: crmen@international.gc.ca

Mexico — PUERTO VALLARTA
Consular Agency of Canada
Address: Plaza Peninsula, Local Sub F, Boulevard Francisco Medina Ascencio 2485, Zona Hotelera Norte, 48300 Puerto Vallarta, Jalisco, México
Tel.: 52 (322) 293-0098/293-0099
Fax: 52 (322) 293-2894
E-Mail: pvrta@international.gc.ca

Mexico — TIJUANA
Consulate of Canada
Address: Germán Gedovius No.10411-101, Condominio del Parque, Zona Río, 22320 Tijuana, Baja California Norte, México
Tel.: 52 (664) 684-0461
Fax: 52 (664) 684-0301
E-Mail: tjuna@international.gc.ca

Micronesia (FSM) — POHNPEI
Embassy of Australia
Address: H & E Enterprises Building, Kolonia, Pohnpei, Micronesia
Postal Address: P.O. Box S, Kolonia, Pohnpei
Tel.: 691 320-5448
Fax: 691 320-5449
See also: Australia, Canberra

Moldova
See: Romania, Bucharest

Monaco — MONACO
Consulate of Canada

Address: 23, rue Emile de Loth, MC 98000, Monaco
Tel.: 377 97 70 62 42
Fax: 377 97 70 62 52
E-Mail: consulat.canada-mona-co@amb-canada.fr
See also: France, Paris

Mongolia — ULAANBAATAR
Embassy of Canada
Address: Sukhbaatar Square 2, Central Tower, Suite 608, Sukhbaatar District, Horoo 8, Ulaanbaatar, Mongolia
Postal Address: P.O. Box 1028, Ulaanbaarar, 14200
Tel.: (976-11) 332-500
Fax: (976-11) 332-515
E-Mail: ulaan@international.gc.ca
Internet: www.mongolia.gc.ca

Montenegro
See: Serbia, Belgrade

Montserrat
See: Barbados, Bridgetown

Morocco — RABAT-SOUISSI
Embassy of Canada
Address: 66 Mehdi Ben Barka Avenue, Rabat-Souissi, Morocco
Postal Address: P.O. 2040 Rabat-Ryad, Morrocco, 10 000
Tel.: 212 (0) 537 54 49 49
Fax: 212 (0) 537 54 48 53
E-Mail: rabat@international.gc.ca
Internet: http://www.morocco.gc.ca

Mozambique — MAPUTO
High Commission of Canada
Address: Kenneth Kaunda Avenue, Maputo 1138, Mozambique
Tel.: 258 (21) 492-623
Fax: 258 (21) 492-667
E-Mail: mputo@international.gc.ca

Internet: http://www.canadainternational.gc.ca/mozambique/

Namibia — WINDHOEK
Consulate of Canada
Address: Suite 403, First Floor, Office Tower, Maerua Mall, Jan Jonker Street, Windhoek, Namibia
Tel.: 264 (61) 251 254
Fax: 264 (61) 251 686
E-Mail: canada@africaonline.com.-na
See also: South Africa, Pretoria

Nauru
High Commission of Australia
Address: MQ45 NPC OE, Aiwo District, Nauru
Tel.: 674 444 3380
Fax: 674 444 3382
E-Mail: david.costa@dfat.gov.au
See also: Australia, Canberra

Nepal — KATHMANDU
Consulate of Canada
Address: 47 Lal Darbar Marg, Kathmandu, Nepal
Postal Address: P.O. Box 3596
Tel.: 977 (1) 444-1976
Fax: 977 (1) 443-4713
Internet: http://www.canadaconsul@mail.com.np
See also: India, New Delhi

Netherlands — THE HAGUE
Embassy of Canada
Address: Sophialaan 7, 2514 JP The Hague, The Netherlands
Tel.: 31 (70) 311-1600
Fax: 31 (70) 311-1620
E-Mail: hague@international.gc.ca
Internet: http://www.netherlands.gc.ca

New Caledonia — NOUMÉA
Consulate General of Australia

Address: Immeuble Norwich, Level 2, 11 Georges Baudoux Street, Artillerie, Noumea, New Caledonia
Tel.: 687 272 414
E-Mail: Consular.Noumea@dfat.-gov.au
See also: Australia, Canberra

New Zealand — WELLINGTON
High Commission of Canada
Address: Level 11, 125 The Terrace, Wellington 6011, New Zealand
Postal Address: P.O. Box 8047, Wellington 6143, New Zealand
Tel.: 64 (4) 473-9577
Fax: 64 (4) 471-2082
E-Mail: wlgtn@international.gc.ca
Internet: http://www.newzealand.gc.ca

Nicaragua — MANAGUA
Embassy of Canada (Program Office)
Address: De Los Pipitos, 2 Blocks West, El Nogal Street No. 25, Bolonia, Managua, Nicaragua
Postal Address: P.O. Box 25, Managua, Nicaragua
Tel.: 505-2268-0433,-3323
Fax: 505-2268-0437
E-Mail: mngua@international.gc.-ca
See also: Costa Rica, San José

Niger — NIAMEY
See: Mali, Bamako

Nigeria — ABUJA
High Commission of Canada
Address: 13010G, Palm close, Diplomatic drive, Central Business District, Abuja, Nigeria
Tel.: 234 (9) 461-2900
Fax: 234 (9) 461-2902
E-Mail: abuja@international.gc.ca
Internet: http://www.canadainternational.gc.ca/nigeria/

Nigeria — LAGOS
Deputy High Commission of Canada
Address: 4 Anifowoshe Street, Victoria Island, Lagos, Nigeria
Tel.: 234 (1) 271-5650
Fax: 234 (1) 271-5651
E-Mail: lagos@international.gc.ca
Internet: http://www.canadainternational.gc.ca/nigeria/

Niue
See: New Zealand, Wellington

Northern Marianas
See: Micronesia, Pohnpei

Norway — OSLO
Embassy of Canada
Address: Wergelandsveien 7, 0244 Oslo, Norway
Tel.: 47 22-99-53-00
Fax: 47 22-99-53-01
E-Mail: oslo@international.gc.ca
Internet: http://www.norway.gc.ca

Oman — MUSCAT
Address: 7th Floor, Getco Tower, Muscat, Oman
Postal Address: P.O. Box 84, Muscat, 100, Oman
Tel.: (968) 2479 4928
Fax: (968) 2470 382
See also: Riyadh, Saudi Arabia

Pakistan — ISLAMABAD
High Commission of Canada
Address: Diplomatic Enclave, Sector G-5, Islamabad, Pakistan
Postal Address: P.O. Box 1042, Islamabad, Pakistan
Tel.: 92 (51) 208-6000
Fax: 92 (51) 208-0902
E-Mail: isbadcs@international.gc.-ca
Internet: http://www.pakistan.gc.ca

Pakistan — KARACHI
Consulate of Canada
Address: c/o Beach Luxury Hotel,
3rd floor, Moulvi Tamiz Khan
Road, Karachi 74000, Pakistan
Tel.: 92 (21) 561-0685
Fax: 92 (21) 561-0674
E-Mail: honcon@avari.com
Internet: http://www.pakistan.gc.ca

Pakistan — LAHORE
Consulate of Canada
Address: 102-A, First Floor, Siddiq
Trade Centre, 72 Main Boulevard,
Gulberg, Lahore, Pakistan
Tel.: 92 (42) 578-1763
Fax: 92 (42) 578-1967
E-Mail: info@canconlhr.org.pk
Internet: http://www.pakistan.gc.ca

Palau
See: Micronesia, Pohnpei

Panama — PANAMA
Embassy of Canada
Address: Torres de Las Americas,
Tower A, 11th Floor, Punta
Pacifica, Panama City, Panama
Postal Address: P.O. Box Apartado
0832-2446, Panama City, Panama
Tel.: (507) 294-2500
Fax: (507) 294-2514
E-Mail: panam@international.gc.-
ca
Internet: http://www.panama.gc.ca

**Papua New Guinea — PORT
MORESBY**
High Commission of Australia
Address: Godwit Road, Waigani,
NCD, Port Moresby, Papua New
Guinea
Tel.: 675 325-9333
Fax: 675 325-9239
E-Mail: ahcpmsb_consular@dfat.-
gov.au

Internet: http://www.png.embassy.-
gov.au//pmsb/home.html
See also: Australia, Canberra

Paraguay — ASUNCIÓN
Consulate of Canada
Address: 3 Profesor Ramirez at
Juan de Salazar (between Perú and
Padre Pucheu), Asunción
Tel.: 595 (21) 227-207
Fax: 595 (21) 227-208
E-Mail: honconpy@tigo.com.py
See also: Argentina, Buenos Aires

Peru — LIMA
Embassy of Canada
Address: Calle Bolognesi 228,
Miraflores, Lima 18, Peru
Postal Address: P.O. Box 18-1126,
Correo Miraflores, Lima, 18, Peru
Tel.: 51 (1) 319-3200
Fax: 51 (1) 446-4912
E-Mail: lima@international.gc.ca
Internet: http://www.peru.gc.ca

Philippines — CEBU
Address: RD Corporate Center, 96
Gov. M.C. Cuenco Avenue, Cebu
City 6000, Philippines
Tel.: 63 32 256 3320
Fax: 63 32 238 3421
E-Mail: canada.cebu@gmail.com
Internet: www.philippines.gc.ca

Philippines — MANILA
Embassy of Canada
Address: Floors 6-8, RCBC Plaza
Tower 2, 6819 Ayala Avenue,
Makati City, Manila, Philippines
Postal Address: P.O. Box 2168,
Makati City 1220, 1261 Makati,
Philippines
Tel.: 63 (2) 857-9000, 857-9001
Fax: 63 (2) 843-1082
E-Mail: manil@international.gc.ca
Internet: http://www.philippi-
nes.gc.ca

Poland — WARSAW
Embassy of Canada
Address: ul. Jana Matejki 1/5, 00-481, Warsaw, Poland
Tel.: 48 (22) 584-3100
Fax: 48 (22) 584-3101 or 48 (22) 584-3192
E-Mail: wsaw@international.gc.ca
Internet: http://www.poland.gc.ca

Portugal — FARO
Consulate of Canada
Address: Rua Frei Lourenço de Santa Maria No. 1, 1st Floor, Apartado 79,
8000-352 Faro, Portugal
Tel.: 351 289-80-3757
Fax: 351 289-88-0888
E-Mail: canada.faro@sapo.pt

Portugal — LISBON
Embassy of Canada
Address: Avenida da Liberdade 196-200, 3rd Floor, 1269-121 Lisbon, Portugal
Tel.: (351) 213 164 600
Fax: (351) 213 164 693
E-Mail: lsbon.consular@international.gc.ca
Internet: http://www.portugal.gc.ca

Puerto Rico — SAN JUAN
Consulate of Canada
Address: Hato Rey Center, 268 Ponce de Leon, Suite 1111, San Juan (Hato Rey), Puerto Rico, U.S.A., 00918
Tel.: (787) 759-6629
Fax: (787) 294-1205

Qatar — DOHA
Embassy of Canada
Address: Tornado Tower, 30th Floor, Majlis Al Taawon Street, Doha, Qatar
Postal Address: P.O. Box 24876 Doha, Qatar

Tel.: (974) 4419-9000
Fax: (974) 4419-9035
E-Mail: dohag@international.gc.ca
Internet: http://www.canadainternational.gc.ca/qatar/

Republic of Congo (Brazzaville)
See: Democratic Republic of Congo (Kinshasa)

Romania — BUCHAREST
Embassy of Canada
Address: 1-3 Tuberozelor Street, 011411 Bucharest, Sector 1, Romania
Tel.: (4) 021-307-5000
Fax: (4) 021-307-5010
E-Mail: bucst@international.gc.ca
Internet: http://www.romania.gc.ca

Russia — MOSCOW
Embassy of Canada
Address: 23 Starokonyushenny Pereulok, Moscow, 119002, Russia
Tel.: 7 (495) 925-6000
Fax: 7 (495) 925-6004 or 7 (495) 925-6025
E-Mail: mosco@international.gc.ca
Internet: http://www.russia.gc.ca

Russia — VLADIVOSTOK
Consulate of Canada
Address: 707-59 Kragnogo Znameni prospekt, Vladivostok 690002, Russia
Tel.: 7 (4232) 49-11-88
Fax: 7 (4232) 49-11-88
E-Mail: can.consulate.vl@gmail.com
Internet: http://www.russia.gc.ca

Rwanda — KIGALI
Office of the High Commission for Canada
Address: 1534 Akagera Street, Kigali, Rwanda

Postal Address: P.O. Box 1177, Kigali, Rwanda
Tel.: 250 252 573 210 or 252 573 278
Fax: 250 252 572 719
E-Mail: kgali@international.gc.ca

Saint-Barthélemy
See: France, Paris

Saint Kitts and Nevis
See: Barbados, Bridgetown

Saint Lucia
See: Barbados, Bridgetown

Saint Martin
See: Barbados, Bridgetown

Saint-Pierre-et-Miquelon —
SAINT-PIERRE
Consulate of Canada
Address: 16, rue Jacques Debon, 97500, Saint-Pierre, Saint-Pierre et Miquelon
Postal Address: P.O. Box 4370, Saint-Pierre, Saint-Pierre et Miquelon
Tel.: 508 41-55-10
Fax: 508 41-55-10
E-Mail: consul.canada.stpierreetmiquelon@amb-canada.fr
Internet: www.france.gc.ca
See also: France, Paris

Saint Vincent & the Grenadines
See: Barbados, Bridgetown

Samoa — APIA
High Commission of Australia
Address: Beach Road, Apia, Samoa
Postal Address: P.O. Box 704, Apia
Tel.: 68 (5) 23 411
Fax: 68 (5) 23 159
Internet: http://www.samoa.embassy.gov.au/apia/home/html
See also: New Zealand, Wellington

San Marino
See: Italy, Rome

São Tomé and Principe
See: Nigeria, Lagos

Saudi Arabia — JEDDAH
Consulate of Canada
Address: Ali Reza Tower, 11th Floor, Medinah Road, Jeddah, Saudi Arabia
Postal Address: P.O. Box 9484, Jeddah, 21413, Saudi Arabia, Saudi Arabia
Tel.: 966 (12) 653-0597, 653-0434
Fax: 966 (12) 653-0538
E-Mail: canada.consulate.jeddah@mattarest.com
Internet: http://www.saudiarabia.gc.ca

Saudi Arabia — RIYADH
Embassy of Canada
Address: Diplomatic Quarter, Riyadh, Saudi Arabia
Postal Address: P.O. Box 94321, Riyadh, 11693, Saudi Arabia, Saudi Arabia
Tel.: 966 (11) 488-2288
Fax: 966 (11) 488-1997
E-Mail: ryadh@international.gc.ca
Internet: http://www.saudiarabia.gc.ca

Senegal — DAKAR
Embassy of Canada
Address: corner of Galliéni and Amadou Cissé Dia Streets, Dakar, Senegal
Postal Address: P.O. Box 3373, Dakar, Senegal
Tel.: 221 33 889 4700
Fax: 221 33 889 4720
E-Mail: dakar@international.gc.ca
Internet: http://www.senegal.gc.ca

Serbia — BELGRADE

Embassy of Canada
Address: Kneza Milosa 75, 111711 Belgrade, Serbia
Tel.: 381 (11) 306-3000
Fax: 381 (11) 306-3042
E-Mail: bgrad.consular-consulaire@international.gc.ca
Internet: http://www.serbia.gc.ca

Seychelles
See: Tanzania, Dar es Salaam

Sierra Leone
See: Ghana, Accra

Singapore — SINGAPORE
High Commission of Canada
Address: One George Street, #11-01 Singapore 049145
Postal Address: P.O. Box 845, Singapore, 901645
Tel.: 65 6854-5900
Fax: 65 6854-5913
E-Mail: spore@international.gc.ca
Internet: http://www.singapore.gc.ca

Sint Maarten
Consulate of Canada
Address: Dawn Beach Estate, Sint Maarten
Postal Address: P.O. Box Green Starshell Rd #18, Dawn Beach Estate, Sint Maarten
Tel.: (721) 543-6261,
(561) 304-8862 or (721) 587-1364
Fax: (721) 543-6291
E-Mail: CanadaConsulsxm@Gmail.com
See also: Barbados, Bridgetown

Slovakia — BRATISLAVA
Office of the Embassy of Canada
Address: Carlton Savoy Building, Mostova 2,
811 02 Bratislava, Slovakia
Tel.: 421 (2) 5920-4031

Fax: 421 (2) 5443-4227
E-Mail: brtsv@international.gc.ca

Slovenia — LJUBLJANA
Consulate of Canada
Address: Linhartova cesta 49a., 1000 Ljubljana, Slovenia
Tel.: 386 (1) 252-4444
Fax: 386 (1) 252-3333
E-Mail: canada.consul.ljubljana@siol.net
See also: Hungary, Budapest

Solomon Islands — HONIARA
Australian High Commission
Address: Corner Hibiscus Avenue and Mud Alley, Honiara, Solomon Islands
Tel.: 677 21 561
Fax: 677 23 691
Internet: http://www.solomonislands.embassy.gov.au/honi/home.html
See also: Australia, Canberra

Somalia
See: Kenya, Nairobi

South Africa — CAPE TOWN
Consulate of Canada
Address: 1502 Metlife Centre, Walter Sisulu Avenue, Foreshore, Cape Town 8001, South Africa
Postal Address: P.o. Box 7202, Roggebaai, 8012, Western Cape, South Africa
Tel.: 27 21 421 1818
Fax: 27 21 421 4342
E-Mail: canada.capetown@law-shields.co.za
Internet: http://www.southafrica.gc.ca

South Africa — DURBAN
Consulate of Canada
Address: Unit 2, Richefond Circle, Ridgeside Office Park, Umhlanga,

4319, Durban, Kwa-Zulu Natal, South Africa
Postal Address: P.O. Box 1558, Umhlanga, 4320, Durban, Kwa-Zulu Natal, South Africa
Tel.: 27 31 536 8214
Fax: 27 31 536 8187
E-Mail: rmcelligott@telkomsa.net

South Africa — JOHANNES-BURG
High Commission of Canada Trade Office
Address: Cradock Place, 1st Floor, 10 Arnold Road, off Cradock Avenue, Rosebank, Johannesburg 2196, South Africa
Postal Address: P.O. Box 1394, Parklands 2121, Johannesburg, South Africa
Tel.: 27 (11) 442-3130
Fax: 27 (11) 442-3325
E-Mail: jobrg@international.gc.ca
Internet: http://www.canadainternational.gc.ca/southafrica-afrique-dusud/

South Africa — PRETORIA
High Commission of Canada
Address: 1103 Arcadia Street, Hatfield, Pretoria, 0083, South Africa
Postal Address: Private Bag X13, Hatfield, Pretoria, 0028, South Africa
Tel.: 27 (12) 422-3000
Fax: 27 (12) 422-3052
E-Mail: pret@international.gc.ca
Internet: http://www.canadainternational.gc.ca/southafrica-afrique-dusud/

South Sudan
See: Kenya, Nairobi

Spain — BARCELONA
Consulate of Canada

Address: Plaça de Catalunya, 9, 1°, 2ª - 08002, Barcelona, Spain
Tel.: 34 93 270 3614
Fax: 34 933 170 541
E-Mail: bclna@international.gc.ca

Spain — MADRID
Embassy of Canada
Address: Torre Espacio, Paseo de la Castellana 259D, 28046 Madrid, Spain
Tel.: (34) 91 382 8400
Fax: (34) 91 382-8490
E-Mail: espana.consulaire/consular@international.gc.ca
Internet: http://www.spain.gc.ca

Spain — MÁLAGA
Consulate of Canada
Address: Horizonte Building, Plaza de la Malagueta 2, 1st Floor, 29016 Málaga, Spain
Tel.: 34 95 222-3346
Fax: 34 95 222-9533
E-Mail: cancon@microcad.es

Sri Lanka — COLOMBO
High Commission of Canada
Address: 33-A 5th Lane, Colombo 03, Sri Lanka
Postal Address: P.O. Box 1006, Colombo, Sri Lanka
Tel.: 94 (11) 532-6232 or 522-6232
Fax: 94 (11) 532-6299 or 522-6299
E-Mail: clmbo-cs@international.gc.ca
Internet: http://www.srilanka.gc.ca

Sudan — KHARTOUM
Embassy of Canada
Address: 29 Africa Road, Block 56, Khartoum 1, Sudan
Postal Address: P.O. Box 10503, Khartoum, 1, Sudan
Tel.: 249 156 550 500
Fax: 249 156 550 501
E-Mail: khrtm@international.gc.ca

Internet: http://www.canadainter-
national.gc.ca/sudan-soudan/

Suriname — PARAMARIBO
Address: Assuria Verzekeringen,
Grote Combeweg 37
Postal Address: Assuria Verzekerin-
gen, Grote Combeweg 37, Paramar-
ibo, Suriname
Tel.: 597 424575 / 597 424527
Fax: 597 425962
E-Mail: lconsulatecanada-
prmbo@sr.net
See also: Guyana, Georgetown

Swaziland
See: Mozambique, Maputo

Sweden — GOTHENBURG
Consulate of Canada
Address: Mässans gata 18, Gothen-
burg, Sweden
Tel.: 46 (0) 31 707 4288
Fax: 46 (0) 31 154 099
E-Mail: per@jessing.nu

Sweden — STOCKHOLM
Embassy of Canada
Address: 23 Klarabergsgatan,
Stockholm, Sweden
Postal Address: P.O. Box 16129,
Stockholm, 10323 Sweden
Tel.: 46 (0) 8 453-3000
Fax: 46 (0) 8 453-3016
E-Mail: stkhm-cs@internatio-
nal.gc.ca
Internet: http://www.sweden.gc.ca

Switzerland — BERNE
Embassy of Canada
Address: Kirchenfeldstrasse 88,
CH-3000 Berne, Switzerland
Postal Address: P.O. Box 234,
CH-3000, Berne, Switzerland
Tel.: 41 (31) 357 3200
Fax: 41 (31) 357 3210
E-Mail: bern@international.gc.ca

Internet: http://www.switzer-
land.gc.ca

Switzerland — GENEVA
Permanent Mission of Canada to
the Office of the United Nations
Address: 5, avenue de l'Ariana,
CH-1202 Geneva, Switzerland
Tel.: 41 (22) 919-92-00
Fax: 41 (22) 919-92-33
E-Mail: genev@international.gc.ca
Internet: www.international.gc.ca/
genev/

Syria
See: Lebanon, Beirut

Taiwan — TAIPEI
Trade Office of Canada
Address: 6F, Hua-Hsin (Citibank
building), No. 1 SongZhi Road,
Xinyi District, Taipei, 11047,
Taiwan
Tel.: 886 (2) 8723-3000
Fax: 886 (2) 8723-3590
E-Mail: tapei-cs@international.gc.-
ca
Internet: http://www.canada.org.tw

Tajikistan
See: Kazakhstan, Astana

Tanzania — DAR ES SALAAM
High Commission of Canada
Address: 38 Mirambo Street,
Corner Garden Avenue, Dar es
Salaam, Tanzania
Postal Address: P.O. Box 1022, Dar
es Salaam, Tanzania
Tel.: 255 (22) 216-3300
Fax: 255 (22) 211-6897
E-Mail: dslam@international.gc.ca
Internet: http://www.tanzania.gc.ca

Thailand — BANGKOK
Embassy of Canada

Address: 15th Floor, Abdulrahim Place, 990 Rama IV, Bangrak, Bangkok, 10500, Thailand
Postal Address: P.O. Box 2090, Bangkok, 10501, Thailand
Tel.: 66 (0) 2646-4300
Fax: 66 (0) 2646-4345
E-Mail: bangkok-consul@international.gc.ca
Internet: http://www.thailand.gc.ca

Thailand — CHIANG MAI
Consulate of Canada
Address: 151 Super Highway, Tambon Tahsala, Amphur Muang, Chiang Mai, 50000, Thailand
Tel.: 66 (0) 5385-0147 or 5324-2292
Fax: 66 (0) 5385-0147
E-Mail: cancon@loxinfo.co.th
Internet: http://www.thailand.gc.ca

Timor-Leste (East Timor) — DILI
Embassy of Australia
Address: Avenida dos Mártires da Pátria, Dili, Timor-Leste
Tel.: 670 332-2111
Fax: 670 332-2247
E-Mail: austemb_dili@dfat.gov.au
Internet: http://www.easttimor.embassy.gov.au/dili/home.html
See also: Indonesia, Jakarta

Togo — Lomé
See: Ghana, Accra

Tokelau
See: New Zealand, Wellington

Tonga — NUKU'ALOFA
High Commission of Australia
Address: Salote Road, Nuku'alofa, Tonga
Tel.: 676 23-244
Fax: 676 23-243
Internet: http://www.tonga.embassy.gov.au/ntfa/home.html
See also: New Zealand, Wellington

Trinidad and Tobago — PORT OF SPAIN
High Commission of Canada
Address: 3-3A Sweet Briar Road, Maple House, St. Clair, Port of Spain
Postal Address: P.O. Box 1246, Port of Spain
Tel.: 1 (868) 622-6232 (6-CANADA)
Fax: 1 (868) 628-2581
E-Mail: pspan@international.gc.ca
Internet: http://www.trinidadandtobago.gc.ca

Tunisia — TUNIS
Embassy of Canada
Address: Lot 24, rue de la Feuille d'Érable, Cité des Pins, Tunis, Tunisia
Postal Address: P.O. Box 48, 1053 Les Berges du Lac II, Tunis, Tunisia
Tel.: 216-70-010-200
Fax: 216-70-010-393
E-Mail: tunis-cs@international.gc.ca
Internet: www.tunis.gc.ca

Turkey — ANKARA
Embassy of Canada
Address: Cinnah Caddesi No. 58, Çankaya 06690, Ankara, Turkey
Tel.: 90 (312) 409-2700
Fax: 90 (212) 357-1000
E-Mail: ankra@international.gc.ca
Internet: http://www.turkey.gc.ca

Turkey — ISTANBUL
Consulate of Canada
Address: 209 Buyukdre Caddesi, Tekfen Tower - 16th Floor, Levent 4, Istanbul, Turkey
Tel.: 90 (212) 385-9700
Fax: 90 (212) 357-1000

E-Mail: ISTBLCS@internatio-
nal.gc.ca
Internet: http://www.turkey.gc.ca

Turkmenistan
See: Turkey, Ankara

Turks and Caicos Islands
See: Jamaica, Kingston

Tuvalu
See: New Zealand, Wellington

Uganda — KAMPALA
Consulate of Canada
Address: Jubilee Insurance Centre,
14 Parliament Avenue, Kampala,
Uganda
Postal Address: P.O. Box 37434,
Kampala, Uganda
Tel.: 256 (414) 258-141 and 348-141
or 256 (312) 260-511
Fax: 256 (414) 349-484
E-Mail: Kampala@canadaconsula-
te.ca
See also: Kenya, Nairobi

Ukraine — KYIV
Embassy of Canada
Address: 13A Kostelna Street,
Kyiv 01901, Ukraine
Tel.: 380 (44) 590-3100
Fax: 380 (44) 590-3134
E-Mail: kyiv@international.gc.ca
Internet: http://www.ukraine.gc.ca

Ukraine — LVIV
Consulate of Canada
Address: 2 / 4 Academika
Bohomoltsia Street, Lviv 79005,
Ukraine
Tel.: 380 32 2601572
Fax: 380 32 2601154
E-Mail: oksmyr@mail.lviv.ua
Internet: http://www.ukraine.gc.ca

**United Arab Emirates — ABU
DHABI**
Embassy of Canada
Address: Abu Dhabi Trade Towers
(Abu Dhabi Mall), West Tower,
9th Floor
Postal Address: P.O. Box 6970,
Abu Dhabi, United Arab Emirates
Tel.: 971 (2) 694-0300
Fax: 971 (2) 694-0399
E-Mail: abdbi@international.gc.ca
Internet: http://www.canadainter-
national.gc.ca/uae-eau/

United Arab Emirates — DUBAI
Consulate of Canada
Address: 19th Floor, Jumeriah Emi-
rates Towers, Sheikh Zayed Road,
Dubai, United Arab Emirates
Postal Address: P.O. Box 52472,
Dubai, United Arab Emirates
Tel.: 971 (4) 404-8444
Fax: 971 (4) 314-5556/5557
E-Mail: dubai@international.gc.ca
Internet: http://www.canadainter-
national.gc.ca/uae-eau

United Kingdom — BELFAST
Consulate of Canada
Tel.: 44 (0) 2897-542405
E-Mail: Canada.consul.bel@aol.-
co.uk

United Kingdom — EDINBURGH
Consulate of Canada
Tel.: 44 (0) 7702 359-916
E-Mail: canada.consul.edi@gmail.-
com

United Kingdom — LONDON
High Commission of Canada
Address: Canada House,
Trafalgar Square, London,
SW1Y 5BJ, England,
United Kingdom
Tel.: 44 (0) 207 004 6000
Fax: 44 (0) 207 004 6053

E-Mail: ldn.consular@international.gc.ca
Internet: http://www.unitedkingdom.gc.ca

United Kingdom — WALES
Consulate of Canada
Tel.: 44 (0)165 6662 413
E-Mail: canadaconsul.wales@merthyrmawr.com

United States — ATLANTA
Consulate General of Canada
Address: 1175 Peachtree Street N.E., 100 Colony Square,
Suite 1700, Atlanta, Georgia, U.S.A., 30361-6205
Tel.: (404) 532-2000
Fax: (404) 532-2050
E-Mail: atnta@international.gc.ca
Internet: http://www.atlanta.gc.ca

United States — BOSTON
Consulate General of Canada
Address: 3 Copley Place, Suite 400, Boston, Massachusetts, U.S.A., 02116
Tel.: (617) 247-5100
Fax: (617) 247-5190
E-Mail: bostn@international.gc.ca
Internet: http://www.boston.gc.ca

United States — CHICAGO
Consulate General of Canada
Address: Two Prudential Plaza, 180 North Stetson Avenue, Suite 2400, Chicago, Illinois, U.S.A., 60601
Tel.: (312) 616-1860
Fax: (312) 616-1877
E-Mail: chcgo@international.gc.ca
Internet: http://www.chicago.gc.ca

United States — DALLAS
Consulate General of Canada
Address: 500 N. Akard Street, Suite 2900, Dallas, Texas, U.S.A., 75201

Tel.: (214) 922-9806
Fax: (214) 922-9815
E-Mail: dalas@international.gc.ca
Internet: http://www.dallas.gc.ca

United States — DENVER
Consulate General of Canada
Address: 1625 Broadway, Suite 2600, Denver, Colorado, U.S.A., 80202
Tel.: (303) 626-0640
Fax: (303) 572-1158
E-Mail: denvr-g@international.gc.ca
Internet: http://www.denver.gc.ca

United States — DETROIT
Consulate General of Canada
Address: 600 Renaissance Center, Suite 1100, Detroit, Michigan, U.S.A., 48243-1798
Tel.: (313) 446-4747
Fax: (313) 567-2164
E-Mail: dtrot@international.gc.ca
Internet: http://www.detroit.gc.ca

United States — HONOLULU
Consulate General of Australia
Address: Penthouse Suite, 1000 Bishop Street, Honolulu, Hawaii, U.S.A., 96813-4299
Tel.: (808) 529-8100
Fax: (808) 529-8142

United States — LOS ANGELES
Consulate General of Canada
Address: 550 South Hope Street, 9th Floor, Los Angeles, California, U.S.A., 90071-2327
Tel.: (213) 346-2700
Fax: (213) 620-8827
E-Mail: lngls@international.gc.ca
Internet: http://www.losangeles.gc.ca

United States — MIAMI
Consulate General of Canada

Address: 200 South Biscayne Boulevard, Suite 1600, Miami, Florida, U.S.A., 33131
Tel.: (305) 579-1600
Fax: (305) 374-6774
E-Mail: miami@international.gc.ca
Internet: http://www.miami.gc.ca

United States — MINNEAPOLIS
Consulate General of Canada
Address: 701 Fourth Avenue South, Suite 900, Minneapolis, Minnesota, U.S.A., 55415-1899
Tel.: (612) 333-4641
Fax: (612) 332-4061
E-Mail: mnpls@international.gc.ca
Internet: http://www.minneapolis.gc.ca

United States — NEW YORK
Consulate General of Canada
Address: 1251 Avenue of the Americas, Concourse Level, New York, New York, U.S.A., 10020-1175
Tel.: (212) 596-1759
Fax: (212) 596-1666/1790
E-Mail: cngny@international.gc.ca
Internet: http://www.newyork.gc.ca

United States — SAN FRANCISCO
Consulate General of Canada
Address: 580 California Street, 14th Floor, San Francisco, California, U.S.A., 94104
Tel.: (415) 834-3180
Fax: (415) 834-3189
E-Mail: sfran@international.gc.ca
Internet: http://www.sanfrancisco.gc.ca

United States — SEATTLE
Consulate General of Canada
Address: 1501 4th Ave, Suite 600, Seattle, Washington, U.S.A., 98101
Tel.: (206) 443-1777
Fax: (206) 443-9662

E-Mail: seatl@international.gc.ca
Internet: http://www.seattle.gc.ca

United States — WASHINGTON
Embassy of Canada
Address: 501 Pennsylvania Avenue, N.W., Washington, D.C., U.S.A., 20001
Tel.: (202) 682-1740
Fax: (202) 682-7738
E-Mail: wshdc.consul@international.gc.ca
Internet: http://www.washington.gc.ca

Uruguay — MONTEVIDEO
Embassy of Canada
Address: Plaza Independencia 749, oficina 102, 11100, Montevideo, Uruguay
Tel.: 598 (2) 902-2030
Fax: 598 (2) 902-2029
E-Mail: mvdeo@international.gc.ca
Internet: http://www.uruguay.gc.ca

Uzbekistan
See: Russia, Moscow

Vanuatu — PORT VILA
High Commission of Australia
Address: Winston Churchill Avenue, Port Vila
Postal Address: P.O. Box 111, Port Vila
Tel.: 678 22777 (24 hours)
Fax: 678 23948
Internet: http://www.vanuatu.highcommission.gov.au/pvla/home.html
See also: Australia, Canberra

Venezuela — CARACAS
Embassy of Canada
Address: Avenida Francisco de Miranda con Avenida Altamira Sur, Altamira, Caracas 1060, Venezuela

Postal Address: P.O. Box 62302, Embassy of Canada, Caracas 1060A, Venezuela
Tel.: 58 (212) 600-3000/264-0833
Fax: 58 (212) 261-8741
E-Mail: crcas@international.gc.ca
Internet: http://www.venezuela.gc.-ca

Vietnam — HANOI
Embassy of Canada
Address: 31 Hung Vuong Street, Hanoi, Vietnam
Tel.: 84 (4) 3734-5000
Fax: 84 (4) 3734-5049
E-Mail: hanoi@international.gc.ca
Internet: http://www.vietnam.gc.ca

Vietnam — HO CHI MINH CITY
Consulate General of Canada
Address: 9th Floor, The Metropolitan, 235 Dong Khoi Street, District 1, Ho Chi Minh City, Vietnam
Tel.: 84 (8) 3827-9899
Fax: 84 (8) 3827-9936
E-Mail: hochi@international.gc.ca
Internet: http://www.vietnam.gc.ca

Virgin Islands (U.S.)
See: United States, Miami

Yemen — SANA'A
See: Saudi Arabia, Riyadh

Zambia — LUSAKA
High Commission of Canada
Address: 5199 United Nations Avenue, Lusaka, Zambia
Postal Address: P.O. Box 31313, Lusaka, Zambia
Tel.: 260 (211) 25-08-33
Fax: 260 (211) 25-41-76
E-Mail: lusaka@international.gc.ca
Internet: http://www.tanzania.gc.ca

Zimbabwe — HARARE
Embassy of Canada
Address: 45 Baines Avenue, Harare, Zimbabwe
Postal Address: P.O. Box 1430, Harare, Zimbabwe
Tel.: 263 (4) 252-181, 252-182, 252-183, 252-184, or 252-185
Fax: 263 (4) 252-186 or 252-187
E-Mail: Hrare-cs@international.gc.ca
Internet: http://www.zimbabwe.gc.-ca

Index

Permanent establishment, 24, 52, 74, 92, 109

Personal effects. *See* Customs and excise

Personal services. *See* Tax treaties

Pets, 144

Planning. *See* Tax planning

Powers of attorney, 179

Prescribed international organization, 126-127

Principal residence
    capital gain, calculation of, 56-58
    capital loss, 36, 65
    change of use, 36, 64-65
        election, 37, 65
    death of non-resident, 177-178
    deemed disposition, 36-37, 39
    designation, 36, 62
    establishing non-resident status, 3
    exemption, 62-63
    lease of, 4, 15, 35
    non-arm's length lease/rental, 4, 15, 18
    questions and answers. *See* Questions and answers
    rental of, 15, 18
    sale of, 17, 63-64

Private health plans, 139-140
    Canada, 140-141
    employer-paid premiums, 132

Professional membership dues, 134

Property
    capital, 107-108
    foreign, 116
    gains arising from disposition, 42, 50
    income. *See* Income
    non-resident transfer of, 55-56
    taxable Canadian. *See* Taxable Canadian property

Protocol. *See* Tax treaties

Provincial health insurance. *See* Health insurance

Questions and answers
    183-day rule, 16

Directory

Canada Revenue Agency

2204 Walkley Road, Ottawa, Ontario
K1A 1A8 CANADA

Phone: 613-940-8495/1-855-284-5942
(collect calls are accepted)
Fax: 613-941-2505
www.cra-arc.gc.ca

Department of Finance
www.fin.gc.ca/treaties-convention/
treatystatus_-eng.asp

Canada Border Services
www.cbsa.asfc.gc.ca

Global Affairs Canada

125 Sussex Drive, Ottawa, Ontario
K1A 0G2 CANADA

Phone: 613-944-4000/1-800-267-8376
www.international.gc.ca

Garry R. Duncan FCPA, FCA, CFP
14 Yorkwood Trail
Brampton, ON
Canada
L6R 3J3
Phone: 905-455-6802
Cell: 416-277-6506
garryduncan@rogers.com

TIME ZONES

WORLD MAP OF TIME ZONES[*]

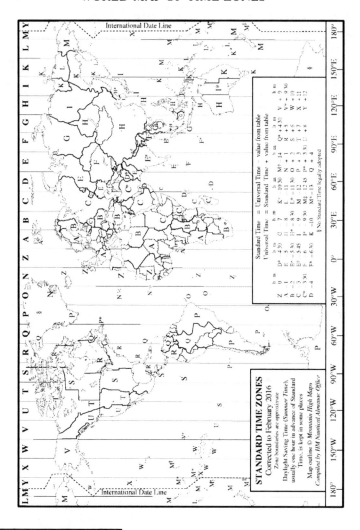

FOREIGN CURRENCY

COUNTRY	MONETARY UNIT
Argentina	peso
Australia	dollar
Austria	euro
Bahamas	dollar
Belgium & Luxembourg	euro
Brazil	new real
Burma (Myanmar)	kyat
Chile	peso
China	renminbi
Columbia	peso
Czech Republic	koruna
Denmark	krone
East Caribbean	E.C. dollar
European Monetary Unit	EURO
Fiji	dollar
Finland	euro
France, Monaco, North Africa	euro
Communauté Financière Africaine	franc C.F.A.
Comptoirs Français du Pacifique	franc C.F.P.
Germany	euro
Ghana	cedi
Greece	euro
Honduras	lempira
Hong Kong	dollar
Hungary	forint

COUNTRY	MONETARY UNIT
Iceland	krona
India	rupee
Indonesia	rupiah
Ireland	euro
Israel	shekel
Italy	euro
Japan	yen
Malaysia	ringgit
Mexico	nuevo peso
Morocco	dirham
Netherlands	euro
Neth. Antilles	florin
New Zealand	dollar
Norway	krone
Pakistan	rupee
Panama	balboa
Peru	nuevo sol
Phillippines	peso
Poland	zloty
Portugal	euro
Russia	rouble
Singapore	dollar
South Africa	rand
South Korea	won
Spain	euro
Sri-Lanka	rupee
Sweden	krona

COUNTRY	MONETARY UNIT
Switzerland	franc
Taiwan	new dollar
Thailand	baht
Trinidad & Tobago	dollar
Tunisia	dinar
Turkey	lira
United Kingdom	pound
United States	dollar
Venezuela	bolivar

METRIC / U.S. & IMPERIAL CONVERSION

VOLUME MEASURE CONVERSION—IMPERIAL

1	litre	=	1.761 pints	=	0.881 quarts	=	0.220 gallons
1	pint	=	0.568 litres	=	1/2 quart	=	1/8 gallon
1	quart	=	1.136 litres	=	2 pints	=	1/4 gallon
1	gallon	=	4.544 litres	=	8 pints	=	4 quarts

VOLUME MEASURE CONVERSION — U.S.

1	litre	=	2.113 pints	=	1.057 quarts	=	0.264 gallons
1	pint	=	0.473 litres	=	1/2 quart	=	1/8 gallon
1	quart	=	0.946 litres	=	2 pints	=	1/4 gallon
1	gallon	=	3.785 litres	=	8 pints	=	4 quarts

LINEAR MEASURE CONVERSION

1	metre	=	1.093 yards	=	39.37 inches
1	yard	=	0.914 metres	=	36 inches
1	centimetre	=	0.394 inches	=	0.0328 feet
1	inch	=	2.54 centimetres	=	1/12 foot
1	foot	=	30.48 centimetres	=	12 inches
1	kilometre	=	0.621 miles		
1	mile	=	1.609 kilometres		

MASS MEASURE CONVERSION

1	gram	=	0.035 ounces	=	0.002 pounds
1	ounce	=	28.35 grams	=	1/16 pound
1	pound	=	453.59 grams	=	16 ounces
1	kilogram	=	35.274 ounces	=	2.205 pounds
1	ounce	=	0.028 kilograms	=	1/16 pound
1	pound	=	0.454 kilograms	=	16 ounces

IMPORTANT CONTACTS

Name	Address	Phone/Fax/e-mail

IMPORTANT CONTACTS

Name	Address	Phone/Fax/e-mail

NOTES

NOTES